Understanding
CAREERS

To all my mentors over the years: Dennis Pym,
Derek Pugh, Philip Rossell, Roy McLennan, Brian Henshall, and Michael Arthur

Understanding
CAREERS
The Metaphors of Working Lives

KERR INKSON
University of Otago, New Zealand

SAGE Publications
Thousand Oaks ▪ London ▪ New Delhi

For information:

Sage Publications, Inc.
2455 Teller Road
Thousand Oaks, California 91320
E-mail: order@sagepub.com

Sage Publications Ltd.
1 Oliver's Yard
55 City Road
London EC1Y 1SP
United Kingdom

Sage Publications India Pvt. Ltd.
B-42, Panchsheel Enclave
Post Box 4109
New Delhi 110 017 India

Printed in the United States of America

Library of Congress Cataloging-in-Publication Data

Inkson, Kerr.
Understanding careers: The metaphors of working lives/Kerr Inkson.
    p. cm.
Includes bibliographical references and index.
ISBN 978-1-4129-4007-8 (cloth)—ISBN 978-0-7619-2950-5 (pbk.)
   1. Career development. 2. Vocational guidance. 3. Occupations. 4. Professions.
5. Quality of work life. I. Title.
HF5381.I54 2007
306.3′6—dc22   2006001826

This book is printed on acid-free paper.

10   11   12   13   14   8   7   6   5   4   3   2

Acquisitions Editor:	Al Bruckner
Editorial Assistant:	MaryAnn Vail
Production Editor:	Denise Santoyo
Typesetter:	C&M Digitals (P) Ltd.
Cover Designer:	Ravi Balasuriya

Contents

List of Cases

Acknowledgments

This book has been assisted in its development by a huge number of people—mentors, colleagues, students, friends, acquaintances, publishing people, helpers with much better computer skills than mine, and of course academics and writers whom I have never met but whose work has nevertheless informed and in some cases inspired me. In the space available to me, I am able to thank only a few.

The inspiration for the book came from Gareth Morgan's wonderful text *Images of Organization,* which was first published by Sage in 1986. *Images* was, and is, a masterful exposition of organization theory in terms of multiple metaphoric images, which served as a template for considering careers in metaphorical terms. I am eternally grateful for Gareth's example and particularly gratified that 20 years after *Images* the same publisher, Sage, has chosen to publish this book.

I was first introduced to the study of careers in 1991 by Canadian academic Tupper Cawsey, who persuaded me to assist him in a study, in New Zealand, of the turbulence of managerial careers. I immediately found the phenomenon we were looking at interesting beyond measure, and career studies has been my major area of research ever since. This was one of those fortunate chances that characterize many careers, and I thank Tupper most sincerely for the start he gave me. Thereafter, my main mentor and buddy in career studies has been Michael Arthur, my coauthor on a wonderful project called *The New Careers,* also published by Sage. Michael is a hugely creative and energetic thinker about careers who has constantly stimulated my own ideas, shared opportunities with me, opened doors for me, and served as a tremendous supporter of and advisor about this book.

In my ongoing research on careers, my New Zealand friends have worked with me as partners, each one focusing his or her own "take" on the subject and each one giving me something new to think about and to learn. You will find their experience as well as mine throughout these pages. I am especially indebted to Judith Pringle for educating me about gender differences in careers and for her great contribution to *The New Careers,* to Barbara Myers for her part in our exciting work on international careers, and to Polly Parker for her constant support of, not to mention her excellent guidance about, my own career, including this book. Maree

Kinloch was an enthusiastic and skilled research assistant on the middle chapters. Bronwyn Boon offered valuable advice concerning Chapter 2. Thank you, too, Tricia Alach, Heather Carpenter, Stuart Carr, Anne de Bruin, Ann Dupuis, Sheena Hudson, Maria Humphries, Eva McLaren, Mary Mallon, Simon Peel, Lynette Reid, Paul Spoonley, Kaye Thorn, and Nithiya Tharmaseelan for helping me to think more clearly about careers through your own research. And my thanks to John Monin of the Department of Management and International Business, Massey University; to Graham Elkin of the Department of Management, University of Otago; and to their departmental colleagues for understanding the needs of this book and writer and for providing conditions, space, facilities, time, and encouragement for me to do the work. Thanks, too, to Sue McSkimming for her sterling work on the diagrams reproduced in the book.

Among my overseas colleagues I owe a special debt of gratitude to Norm Amundson for his ongoing interest in, and collaboration with me on, research on career metaphors and particularly their use in counseling. Philip Dewe, a New Zealander, provided me with a base at Birkbeck College in London to do my initial work on this book in 2002. Lotte Bailyn, Laurie Cohen, Audrey Collin, Bob DeFillippi, Monica Higgins, Jenny Kidd, Judi Marshall, and Ed Schein shared their thoughts on career metaphors usefully with me in early deliberations. Zella King stretched my thinking on career self-management. Peter Heriot provided early encouragement and Mark Savickas gave wonderful feedback on an initial proposal for the book. Dave Thomas has been a good friend and has helped me to extend my ideas about international and cross-cultural aspects of career. My buddies in the Careers Division of the Academy of Management have also been very supportive, particularly Yehuda Baruch, Jon Briscoe, Hugh Gunz, Tim Hall, Maury Peiperl, and Sherry Sullivan. The established careers textbooks first authored by John Arnold, Yehuda Baruch, Jeff Greenhaus, and Bob Reardon provided excellent role models and standards for this one.

I also want to thank my Australian collaborator, Mary McMahon, for the wonderful chapter on metaphor and counseling, which she wrote on short notice and which I believe provides a great climax to the book. And we are both grateful to Mary's friend and colleague Liz Bamford for reading and providing feedback on this chapter.

Sage Publications has been supportive throughout the project, and I want to thank Al Bruckner in particular for his enthusiastic adoption of my book proposal, his ongoing encouragement and feedback, his constant willingness to answer every question I asked, his coordination of reviews, and his flexibility with deadlines when I fell behind schedule. MaryAnn Vail has also been very helpful, and I owe a special debt to the various anonymous reviewers who on three separate occasions (initial proposal, halfway through, and final draft) provided an enormous amount of useful feedback and encouragement: I believe the book is much improved as a result of their feedback. Thanks to Cheryl Duksta, copyeditor, and Denise Santoyo, Project Editor, for their professionalism, patience, and courtesy, and for the great design of the book.

Last, I thank my wonderful wife, Nan Inkson, for her patience and understanding throughout the process and her excellent editorial assistance, particularly with referencing and permissions, in the latter stages. I owe you, Nan. May the next book be yours.

Introduction

Four Career Problems

Steve, 16 years of age, has to decide which program to specialize in at school. He wants to focus on English and social studies, which he loves, but his parents want him to stick to math and science, which he is good at but dislikes. "You'll have better career prospects," says Steve's father. Is he right? What should Steve do?

∿∿∿∿∿∿∿

Marquita, 28 years old, is a Black American from a poor background. She has three children whom she supports as best she can by taking odd jobs, mainly cleaning offices and factories. She has a friend who has a college degree and has decided she wants to better herself. She thinks she might like to be a teacher. But she has no college degree, no qualifications, and no relevant experience. Is her dream realistic? How can she find out? What can she do?

∿∿∿∿∿∿∿

Stacey, 33 years of age, is a successful corporate manager and is married to Dave, a 35-year-old high school music teacher. They want to start a family. But they both love their work and don't want to give it up. Both are anxious to "get to the top." Stacey earns a higher salary than Dave, and they have developed a lifestyle that depends on her high income and bonuses. How can they meet both their family objectives and their work objectives?

∿∿∿∿∿∿∿

Ramon, 48 years of age, is a mechanical engineer. For 25 years he worked as an engineer and later as a manager for the same company. Not long ago the company was taken over, and Ramon was laid off. He realizes that his fortunes were very much tied to his company and that his engineering know-how is out of date. He feels he is "on the scrap heap" and wonders how to make a fresh start.

The previous vignettes are oversimplified but real. In all of them, there is a fundamental problem to solve. The problems are all related to employment and work. The people have to make decisions that are likely to have major long-term repercussions. In short, the decisions are all about careers.

For most of us, our careers are at the forefront of our attention. They provide our daily bread, our sense of identity, our means of achievement. Along with religious observance and family relations, they are what we judge our lives by. They determine our happiness, self-esteem, self-fulfillment, and mental health.

Many people work directly or indirectly in the area of careers. Teachers and educators prepare students for their careers. Career advisors and counselors provide information and guidance aimed at helping clients to have successful careers. Organizational managers look for positive partnerships between employees' careers and successful business. Most important, ordinary people struggle to develop their own careers to satisfy their diverse needs for financial, social, and psychological benefits. All these people can therefore benefit from understanding careers.

The aim of this book is to provide a framework of ideas to assist you to understand how careers work. No doubt you are reading the book in connection with an academic program you are completing related to careers. It is hoped that you will also be able to apply at least some of the content of this book to understand more, not only about careers in general, but also about your own career and the careers of people you know. Perhaps this book will even enable you to improve your decision making about your career and thereby enhance your career satisfaction and success.

The topic of careers can be looked at in many different ways, each having its own special view to offer. In this book, these different views are represented as metaphors—for example, the career as a journey, the career as a resource, the career as a story. Each view has something to contribute to your overall understanding of careers.

The structure of this book is simple. In Chapter 1, I introduce career studies and show how metaphors can be used to understand careers. In Chapters 2 through 10, I take nine metaphors, one for each chapter, and show how each can add to the picture. These chapters cover a wide range of theory and information about careers, including material from sociology, psychology, social psychology, education, and management studies. In Chapter 11, I draw some lessons of the new understanding of careers for planning and developing one's career. In the final chapter, my colleague Mary McMahon, an experienced career counselor, discusses the field of career counseling and the specific impact of metaphor on it.

How to Use This Book

In writing this book, I assumed that most readers are in a course of study, and this book will support the efforts of readers' instructors. (If this is not the case, don't worry. The book will still work for you!) Therefore I provide some features that will help to integrate the book into your other learning.

Case Studies

A feature of the book is the case study careers. You will find several of these per chapter—more than 50 cases in all—each providing specific information about real careers as a means of illustrating the theoretical content. This reinforces my view that to understand how careers work, you need constantly to think about real careers.

End-of-Chapter Questions

Study questions at the end of each chapter ask you to try to use the content to explain things about your career or others' careers. Your instructor may prescribe some of these questions in assignments, but if not, it would be a good idea to have a stab at them on paper on your own. If you don't have a career yet, consider your experiences as a student as part of your career. Learning happens when you try to apply it.

"Live" Career Case Studies

The best career to think about is of course your own—you know more about your career than anyone. However, if you are still young, you may feel that you haven't yet had time for enough career experience to provide good data.

I therefore recommend that you also look to other people—relatives and friends—to provide you with case material from their experiences. In particular, to apply theory on a chapter-by-chapter basis to a single case, consider commencing now the case study exercise in the following section and continue with it on a week-by-week basis as you read the book or as your course proceeds. Being able to understand even one career in depth is more worthwhile than remembering all the theoretical material in the book.

Case Study Exercise

Find a friend or relative (parents are ideal) at least 30 years old who would be willing to talk with you, in confidence and at length, from time to time about his or her career. Then write about the person's career as a kind of case study or mini-biography. As you read the chapters of this book, seek to apply the end-of-chapter questions to this case.

The first thing to do is to get your case person's trust and ensure the person is willing to give you information, not just information about the various jobs the person held in his or her career (the "objective" career) but also the person's thoughts and feelings about it—for example, the person's reasons for changing jobs and his or her aspirations at different times (the "subjective" career).

This is not an exercise you need to fear. Hundreds of my students have done this, usually with a parent, and universally they report that people like talking about their careers and that both parties enjoy the experience. If you are like some of my students, you may even come to experience a new and more positive understanding of—and a closer relationship with—the person.

When you interview the person, keep records of the person's answers and write these up as a case, checking with your case participant for accuracy. Start by writing a basic outline of the person's career, chronologically, with dates. (You can use the case of Aston in Chapter 1 as a model.) As you read the various chapters, consider the case study questions at the end of each chapter and reinterview the person as you need to; often, a brief 5-minute question-and-answer session covering the topics in a chapter is enough. If you are conscientious about this, by the time you finish the book, you will have a fine understanding of at least one career.

Good luck!

Career and Metaphor

Contrasting Experiences of Career

Elaine, analyst-programmer: What a great career I have chosen! I love what I do. Every weekday, I wake up and think, "Great, I have to go to work today!" And when I get there, it's so cool! The work is interesting, the people are fun, and there are no real rules and restrictions. We just get on with it. And the learning is phenomenal. There's always something new to pick up. I can see the road ahead, more programming, better programming, and then maybe a move into project management. Programming plus! If they had told me at university that my working life could be this good, I would never have believed them.

〜〜〜〜〜〜〜

Darren, social worker: What a terrible career I've gotten into! When I started, I was idealistic, but after 10 years of dealing with the very bottom rung of society all day, every day, it's getting me down. The drug addicts, the alcoholics, the child abusers, the people who simply can't run their lives, and a society and a system that just doesn't care about them—that's all I ever see. My caseload has doubled over the years, and I'm accountable if anything goes wrong—I can't begin to provide decent service for all of them. The pay is lousy, and the promotion prospects are zilch. Nowadays, I frankly wish I'd never got into this, but my family relies on the income, and I don't seem to be qualified for anything else.

These stories are not meant to imply that a career as a programmer is better than a career as a social worker. Some social workers are as happy and fulfilled as Elaine, and some programmers are as miserable as Darren. Rather, the two stories illustrate the extremes of career satisfaction and dissatisfaction.

Somehow Elaine has been able to stay in control of her career, whereas Darren has lost control of his. Not only is Darren dissatisfied, but also his mental health may be at risk. Moreover, with such a poor attitude to his work, he is unlikely to be providing good service to his clients.

How did Darren make a choice to which he seems so unsuited? Could he have avoided the fix he finds himself in by taking action at an earlier stage? It seems clear that he needs to learn to manage his career better. Perhaps he should make a major career change. But how? And to what?

And what about you? Is your career more like Elaine's or more like Darren's? If it is like Elaine's, what can you do to make sure it stays that way? If it is more like Darren's, how can you change it? If your career hasn't started yet, what can you do now to ensure that in 10 years' time you will feel more like Elaine than like Darren? Studying careers and developing good career self-management based on what you learn may provide important practical skills.

Over the past few decades, careers have been the subject of extensive research, particularly regarding some of the issues alluded to in the examples of Elaine and Darren. Here are just some of the ways that your career may also affect your well-being and the kinds of action you can take in response:

- There needs to be a balance between your work career and your family and nonwork pursuits. Imbalance may be damaging to both parts of your life (Greenblatt, 2002). You need to monitor your priorities and your actions and communicate with your family and others about these matters.
- People differ in their personal makeup, such as background and interests (Holland, 1997; Schein, 1993). Your career should ideally be congruent with your makeup. To find congruence, you need to know yourself well, have a good idea of what jobs are available, and be sensitive to changes in either yourself or the environment.
- People mature and age. As you age your energies and priorities will change. At some times in your life, you may be interested in exploring the world, at other times you'll want to make a major change, at others you'll simply want to protect your energy, health, and lifestyle (Scandura & Lankau, 1997). At some stages, there are likely to be significant pressures on your career due to family commitments (Eby, Casper, Lockwood, Bordeaux, & Brinley, 2005). Your career needs to be responsive to these changes.
- Careers involve many decisions and choices. Some options may be blind alleys. You may like your job now but hate it later. You may make a bad choice. You may find yourself employed but unpromotable. You may be laid off. But if you look ahead intelligently before committing yourself, perhaps these scenarios can be avoided. If they can't be avoided, maybe you can prepare yourself to deal with them. Career planning can help you safeguard your future (Reardon, Lenz, Sampson, & Peterson, 2006).

These are the kinds of practical issues that career studies deals with. By understanding how careers work, you can empower yourself to improve your career chances. Academic researchers have expounded relevant knowledge. Educators, counselors, and managers have developed good careers practices. This knowledge and practice is reported in this book.

Defining *Career*

What does the word *career* mean? In times gone by, career was a mark of privilege. Only a few—nearly all males—in professions such as the military, law, or medicine would talk about their career. Others might have a *trade* or an *occupation*, such as carpenter, maid, cook, or accounts clerk. Most people thought in terms of *having a job, making a living*, or *being employed*: They sold their labor and their skills for the best price they could get.

Nowadays, the term *career* is much more common. Almost any occupation one can name can be considered as the basis for, or part of, a career. Web sites listing employment vacancies often advertise not *jobs* but *career opportunities*, apparently promising the chance of changing the rest of one's life for the better.

Here is one definition of *career:* "the evolving sequence of a person's work experiences over time" (Arthur, Hall, & Lawrence, 1989, p. 8). This definition has important implications:

- Based on this definition, each person has only one career. If someone says, "Oh, I've had three different careers," they probably mean they have worked in three different occupations or industries. But their experiences in these different situations are all part of the same career. The Arthur et al. definition encourages people to look for ways in which different experiences are related to each other within the same career.

- The phrase *evolving sequence* denotes that a career is not a momentary thing. It involves continuity and change. To understand a career, we need to look at what came before each experience and how the past relates to the present. We may even want to try to project our understanding into the future, for example, in career planning.

- The phrase *work experiences* focuses on employment but does not confine careers to paid work. Activities outside employment involve experiences that are relevant to one's career. For example, parenting at home may provide important career skills. A hobby such as woodcarving or mountaineering may become the basis of a full-time career.

- The term *experiences* also brings up the question "what kind of experiences?" Objective experiences that are apparent to everyone, such as having a particular job or working regular office hours? Or subjective experiences, apparent internally to the person in the career, such as career ambitions, job satisfaction, and emotional feelings about career progress? The answer is both. Career studies looks at both the objective career and the subjective career.

- The term *over time* implies longevity. A career potentially lasts a lifetime.

The Context of Careers

One problem in career studies is a tendency to think of careers as being about people's experiences in their occupations and jobs and to not look beyond that. Unfortunately, this way of thinking is an oversimplification because careers are affected by major influences beyond the job itself—for example, by wider economic and social systems, by the organization worked in, and by the family. To understand careers, therefore, we need to consider the wider contexts in which people and their jobs are embedded. If you want to plan your career and make important career decisions, understanding the surrounding context, and likely future developments in that context, will give you major benefits.

Consider the case of Darren, the dissatisfied social worker described at the beginning of this chapter. What is his problem? He has a bad relationship with his job. How can he resolve that problem? Most would say—and a career counselor might well agree—that Darren should change his job and possibly his occupation. The counselor might investigate Darren's abilities and interests, suggest alternatives, and try to assist Darren to find work in which he felt happier.

There are two problems with this. First, it considers the problem purely from Darren's perspective. The problem is seen as his problem, and the solution is seen to lie in his hands. But suppose Darren's problem is caused in part by the context within which he is employed. The wider problem of the malfunctioning agency may perhaps be solved not by Darren's action to escape the situation but by collaborative action between him, his colleagues, and his bosses to change the agency. If that were done, Darren's career might come right without him leaving. To understand the career we need to understand its context. Solving career problems may be done in a variety of ways.

Second, the solution of having Darren move to another job depends on the existence of suitable alternatives. Suppose, for example, that Darren likes painting with oils and is good at it. A good career move for him might be to take up oil painting for satisfaction and money. But the viability of this solution depends on the existence of a market for Darren's paintings. His paintings may sell, but they may not. It is no good making career decisions on the basis of personal preference alone. Again the context—this time the labor market in which Darren must find a new career—is critical. The tendency to consider careers only from the standpoint of the individual, and to try to resolve career problems only through individual action, is understandable but flawed. Only by taking a wider perspective on our careers can we fully understand them.

Careers therefore depend not only on individual preferences and choices but also on the opportunity structures that provide the work that people do. The labor market—the supply of, and demand for, work of various sorts—is of critical importance and is affected by a wider range of factors:

- Demographic factors include the makeup of, and changes in, the population, particularly the population seeking employment, including numbers, age, gender, ethnic origin, education, skills, and experience.

- Economic factors include the growth or decline in the economy, business confidence, international trade conditions, interest rates, and other factors influencing business startups and current wage rates.
- Labor market factors affect the opportunities available to people. Some industries and occupations decline, whereas others grow dramatically. In recent years, for example, manufacturing has offered fewer jobs, whereas information systems and personal services have offered many more.
- Social factors, which affect people's lifestyle choices both as consumers and as producers, include the demand for traditional and new products and services and the desire to enter the workforce, have a career, have more than one job, protect one's financial security, or seek affluence.
- Organizational factors include business or occupational bureaucracies, the prevalence of large versus small organizations, the conditions for self-employment, organizational structures and restructuring, and the trends of permanent versus temporary employment and full-time versus part-time work.
- Technological factors include substitution of machines for manual labor and skills and computerization of clerical and coordination activities. Changes in jobs and occupations can be caused by technological advancement.

Careers and Countries

The previous list takes a relatively narrow view of career contexts because it was created with the United States, the United Kingdom, and other developed and industrialized nations in mind. In Third World countries, we might want to add, for example, political factors such as authoritarian governments. Looking at careers in other countries and cultures is important because it gives us a sense of humility and appreciation for the special, and mainly benign, conditions in which we in the industrialized world develop our careers and because, as will be demonstrated in Chapter 6, careers are increasingly international: We never know when our career will take us abroad into unfamiliar contexts.

Skorikov and Vondracek (1993), for example, noted the effects of the dissolution of the old communist-controlled USSR on careers. Under communism, work was considered important, not in terms of individual achievement or self-fulfillment but only insofar as work performance assisted the collective good. Systems of advancement were hierarchy based, "political," nepotistic, and corrupt, and people advancing in their careers were objects of contempt. Career decisions were not chosen by individuals but allocated by central authorities and organizations. About 1990, when the authorities attempted to encourage Western-style individualism and proactive career behavior, they found that individuals were unable or unwilling to change their entrenched negative attitudes to career.

Although some of these phenomena sometimes occur in the West, the previous account from Russia defines a context that is very different from that predominating in most Western nations. In many countries, poverty and lack of economic opportunity might mean that contextual concepts that provide the backdrop assumed for career studies—for example, freedom of choice, free enterprise, open labor market, peace, occupation, profession, occupational choice, hierarchy, progress, personal development, full employment, and work ethic—might make Western concepts of career quite alien.

The very idea of *career* as defined and explicated in this book takes a view of life based on the value of individualism, in which it is assumed that one's identity is defined according to individual characteristics, rather than by the characteristics of the groups to which one belongs, and that individual interests, rather than group, family, or community interests, dominate one's decision making. The United States and many European countries are high on individualism (Hofstede, 2003). Theories of career therefore characterize the career as a long-term individual project through which each person seeks individual "career success," which is judged purely by individual achievement, rewards, and satisfaction. The notions of collective experience of careers, or collective criteria for career success, appear little in the literature. But many societies are explicitly collectivist in their worldview and behavior (Hofstede, 2003). In some of these societies, the notion of an individual career might not have much meaning.

I therefore signal here that to include cross-cultural aspects of career in this book is too big a stretch. This book discusses careers in the context of developed democratic economies, though even within and between these countries career behavior may be affected by cross-cultural and other contextual differences to which all careers research and practice need to be sensitive (Blustein & Ellis, 2004). Readers seeking to extend their view to other countries are referred, as a starting point, to Thomas and Inkson (in press).

A Brief History of Careers

The context within which careers take place is in constant change, and that means that the nature of careers also changes over time. When considering the advice your parents give you—based on their experience—about how to start your career, remember that they started their careers perhaps 30 years ago, and the principles that worked for them may not work for you. Understanding how the careers environment has changed over time is a considerable advantage.

In the early 20th century, technological advancement replaced many jobs, and trades such as barrel making, riveting, and bricklaying declined and in some cases virtually disappeared. So, too, did domestic service. A cult of efficiency squeezed inefficiently organized jobs out of existence. Substantial gender segregation occurred, with men occupying the more responsible jobs and those requiring physical strength, and women being mainly confined to light factory work, such as sewing, and retail and domestic service. Once married, women engaged in unpaid work in the home.

The post–World War II years brought huge changes in the contextual factors affecting careers and in careers themselves. Some of the major changes are shown in Table 1.1.

Table 1.1   Late 20th-Century Trends and Their Effects on Careers

Nature of Change	Effect on Careers
"Welfare state," protectionist, and full employment policies of many countries, 1940–1980	Considerable career security for many people
Larger and more complex organizations (up to 1980)	Availability of loyalty-based organizational careers providing steady advancement in large organizations
Market-oriented economic policies of many countries from 1980	Higher unemployment, exposure of careers to economic cycles
Restructuring of organizations for lower costs and greater efficiencies	Layoffs, unanticipated transfers, career destabilization, McJobs
Mechanization—less manual work, more service and managerial work	Changed occupational structures—move from physical jobs to knowledge jobs
Aging society—greater longevity	Careers stretched beyond age 65 years
Emancipation of women, two-income households	Enlarged labor pool, changes in traditional male occupations, dual-career couples
Greater affluence, more discretionary spending	Growth of industries such as luxury goods and hospitality, with new career opportunities
Professionalization of specialist occupations	Structuring and protection of professional career paths through required qualifications
Growth of information technology	New occupations, organizations, and careers in information technology, major changes in the work in other jobs
Globalization—multinational organizations relocating business for lowest cost	Displacement of manufacturing and some service jobs to Third-World countries, beginning of global careers

The top four rows of Table 1.1 detail major economic organizational effects on careers. The mid-20th-century fashion for full employment provided working people with some protection against the economic cycle, and universal education created greater opportunities for them to become upwardly mobile. In this benign environment, organizations also changed, becoming larger and more complex. Smart companies cultivated loyal long-term workforces by offering organizational careers, with inducements such as guaranteed promotions, sophisticated training and development programs, and company pensions.

However, this changed in many countries in the 1980s, when the fashion grew for market-based economic policies and for less government protection for business. Businesses found that in a world of rapid change, cutthroat competition, and little protection, they could best protect themselves by minimizing their long-term labor costs and maximizing their labor flexibility.

This led, in the 1980s and 1990s, to what seemed to many employees to be an orgy of restructuring. Some organizations downsized and laid off many staff members. Others delayered, removing the hierarchical ladders up which staff members advanced in their careers. Others replaced long-term employees with contractors, who had no assurance of continuing employment. Some industries, such as the film industry, increasingly organized around temporary projects rather than permanent jobs. Many careers were destabilized, and the individuals concerned had to start over, developing new career skills and attitudes. Also, reorganization of the service sector for greater efficiency created more relatively unskilled "McJobs," where the employee is easily replaceable.

All of these devices increased companies' numerical flexibility, enabling them to reduce the core of permanent employees, while increasing the number of contingent workers whose employment depended on fluctuations in business. To improve their functional flexibility, that is, their ability to redeploy people from jobs that were no longer needed into jobs that were, companies used techniques such as multiskilling and teamwork, again affecting individuals' range of skills and thereby their careers.

In the meantime, other changes were taking place. Many manual jobs were mechanized, reducing the number of jobs available. In contrast, the demand for services grew—for example, in sales, secretarial, administrative, financial, and hospitality work—creating many new career opportunities. Careers became both more skilled and more secure, and improved health and longevity lengthened them into a retirement phase. More spending was discretionary, and industries such as luxury goods and leisure grew, creating further diversity in career opportunities.

In a changing social climate, newly emancipated women returned to the work-force in increasing numbers, though usually in the traditional bastions of female employment, such as retail, secretarial, nursing, and teaching work. Professional bodies and trade unions developed sophisticated means of controlling entry to occupations and progression within them and of ensuring good conditions for their members.

Another major change was the information technology revolution symbolized by the invention of the minicomputer in the 1970s that transformed organizations and careers. Today's organizations do not just have information systems; they *are* information systems (Senge, 1990). The jobs and career opportunities of their employees are increasingly defined by information systems expertise and skills.

Last, globalization—the establishment of businesses on a global rather than a local basis—makes careers ever more independent of geographical location. Globalization enables business activities to be dispersed round the world to wherever they can be done most profitably. This changes the long-term opportunity structures of careers in all countries involved—meaning all of the countries in the world—and causes sudden disruptions to local careers as opportunities shift. When you telephone your local company with an order, comment, or complaint, the chances are increasing that the person who answers the phone, speaking politely in perfect English, will actually be located in the Indian subcontinent, where his or her labor costs only a fraction of the price it would be in the United States or United Kingdom. More people travel or migrate internationally as part of their work. Careers have gone global (Inkson, Lazarova, & Thomas, 2005).

How have these changes affected the nature of careers? Theorists interested in careers have introduced a range of career-related concepts and have suggested various new forms of career to help us understand:

- Some suggest that a career is, in essence, a series of *psychological contracts* between employer and employee, in which each has implicit expectations of, and obligations to, the other (Herriot & Pemberton, 1996). Rousseau (1995) and others suggested that these contracts have moved from being relational to being transactional—that is, specifying a short-term exchange of benefits rather than a long-term relationship with expectations of mutual loyalty. As a result, members of the workforce, scarred by their experiences of restructuring, have become increasingly disloyal and selfish—or, to put a more positive spin on it, independent and assertive—in their career behavior.
- Books with titles such as *The Career Is Dead—Long Live the Career* (Hall & Associates, 1996) argue that traditional, hierarchical organizational careers have all but disappeared. The effect of restructuring has been to make organizations increasingly boundaryless—both internally and externally—and to make boundaryless careers (Arthur & Rousseau, 1996), in which individuals move between organizations with increasing frequency, more common. Boundaryless careerists must base their careers increasingly on portable career competencies, such as up-to-date expertise, contacts, and reputation.
- The growth of options other than full-time permanent employment—for example, temporary work; part-time work; contract work; self-employment, work for cash payments in the black economy; and service work in the evenings, at night, and on weekends—has led many workers to develop what Charles Handy called portfolio careers (Handy, 1989; Templer & Cawsey, 1999). In a portfolio career, the individual, rather than pursuing a single, full-time job, balances a portfolio of different and changing opportunities.
- The focus of many people's career objectives has moved from employment to employability (Fugate, Kinicki, & Ashforth, 2004). As skill requirements change, so too must prospective employees change: They must develop new skills. Education and apprenticeship, once thought of as a once-and-for-all career preparation, must now be considered a process of lifelong learning to meet ever-changing demands and to retain employability.

Are these moves toward transactional contracts and protean, boundaryless, portfolio careers, and a focus on employability and lifelong learning, good for those pursuing careers and good for society? It is hard to say. Enterprising types of careerists probably welcome the proliferation of new opportunities, whereas those oriented to security and stability may feel threatened (Holland, 1997; see Chapter 5). Proponents of the new environment argue that the new career forms contribute to a more efficient, flexible, and dynamic economy; reduce people's dependence on their employers; and provide new opportunities for talented people from any background to reap the benefits of their expertise and adaptability (Arthur & Rousseau, 1996). Opponents deplore the new insecurity of employment and worry that for many employees boundarylessness means unemployment and marginalization (Pringle & Mallon, 2003), and for employing organizations it means loss of their heart and soul (Cappelli, 1999). The desirability of what has been termed the *new careers* (Arthur, Inkson, & Pringle, 1999) will be returned to from time to time in subsequent chapters.

A Brief History of Career Studies

The history of careers is paralleled by a history of career studies. Savickas and Baker (2005) trace the antecedents of vocational psychology back to 19th-century events such as the founding of the YMCA (Young Men's Christian Association) in Boston in 1851. In 1909, Frank Parsons published the first systematic book in the area, *Choosing a Vocation*. Parsons advocated that people should understand themselves, understand the requirements and other conditions of different lines of work, and use true reasoning to find a match between the two. This philosophy has been the basis of the fit-the-person-to-the-job, or trait-and-factor, approach to careers, which remains critical to the careers guidance field. Over the years, psychologists have made great strides in the measurement of career-relevant human characteristics, such as abilities, aptitudes, personality, values, and interests.

After the Second World War, theory and research about careers blossomed. The trait-and-factor approach continued to focus on initial choice of occupation. For example, Anne Roe (1956) theorized that motivational and personality factors developed in childhood predisposed the choice of particular occupations, and John Holland (1959, 1997) published an influential theory of occupational choice based on vocational interests. Academics such as Donald Super (1953, 1980) and Eli Ginzberg (Ginzberg, Ginsburg, Axelrad, & Herma, 1951) took a wider view, developing theories based on the view that there was more to careers than initial choices—careers were lifelong developmental processes.

Another tack was taken by theorists who emphasized that careers result from individual action, particularly the processes of decision making and adjustment through which individuals plan and implement their careers. Key theories were those of Lofquist and Dawis (1969) on work adjustment; Krumboltz (1979) on career as a form of social learning; Peterson, Sampson, and Reardon (1991) on cognitive information-processing theory; and Lent, Brown, and Hackett (1994) on the social cognitive theory of career decision making. Hansen's (1997) integrative life planning theory is a good example of a theory that attempts to translate itself into action available to individuals to enhance their careers.

Such theories, together with the trait-and-factor and developmental approaches to career, form the basis of individually oriented career development theory and—along with theories of counseling—of modern career counseling practice. An excellent compendium of career development theory is provided by Brown and Associates (2002).

These career development theories have tended, however, to take a psychological view of careers and, with some exceptions (Gottfredson, 2002; Vondracek, Lerner, & Schulenberg, 1986; Vondracek & Porfeli, 2002), have perhaps paid insufficient attention to their social, organizational, and societal contexts. Sociologists have also been interested in careers, and indeed the Chicago School of Sociology long viewed the analysis of careers as a means of studying the wider society (Hughes, 1958). Studies of variables such as social class, gender, ethnicity, and education suggested that careers are highly constrained by wider factors and may be a representation of social structure rather than of individual makeup, development, and action (e.g., Blau & Duncan, 1967; Johnson & Mortimer, 2002; Mayrhofer, Meyer, Iellatchitch, & Schiffinger, 2004). Social psychological theories relevant to careers include theories of social capital, which stress that careers develop as representations of interpersonal relationships and social networks (Granovetter, 1974), and role theory, in which a career is seen as a sequence of roles expected of the individual by the individual, employers, family, and others (Biddle & Thomas, 1966) and in which role (job-to-job) transitions take on special importance (Nicholson, 1984).

In the 1970s, business school academics began to study careers, perceiving them as being at an intersection of interest for the career aspirant and his or her employing organization (e.g., Hall, 1976). Although the restructuring phenomena previously described removed some of the apparent commonality of interest between individual and organization, a strong tradition of research has since considered career management by organizations and the benefits that it can entail for both parties (Cascio, 2003; Herriot, 1992). This approach also focuses on what might be called the geography of careers, that is, career journeys—the directions, routes, and pathways that careers typically follow (Kanter, 1989).

Brown (2002) notes that all of these theories are based on the philosophical position of logical positivism—that is, they are based on notions of empirical evidence, testability, and logical proof. An alternative, which since about 1990 has gained a strong following in career studies, is the notion of *constructivism* or *social constructionism,* which holds that people construct their own realities. If that is correct, then individuals construct their own realities of their careers, and the conduct of career studies and indeed career counseling is about understanding individuals' understanding of their own careers (Young & Collin, 2004).

Career Studies: Separate Realities

Some of these different perspectives of career have proceeded relatively independently. In particular, the career development view of the career guidance movement, the social structure view of the sociologists, and the career management view of employers and business school people have to some extent ignored each other.

- The career development movement tends to view the career as a set of personal, psychologically based issues. Indeed, vocational psychology has developed as an important specialty within applied psychology (Savickas, 2004; Savickas & Baker, 2005). The career development movement tends to understand well the processes of career decision making, such as in initial educational and occupational choices made by high school students and college graduates. But it does not consider so extensively the context of careers—for example, institutional discrimination, the labor market, and formal organizations—or the long-term patterns that careers typically follow. Also, it is better at considering career behavior and decision making between jobs than the equally important topic of career development within jobs. In terms of practice, it recommends interventions involving individuals' problem solving related to their own careers, feedback and guidance by skilled counselors, and the empowerment of clients for their own career actions.

- The sociological view is strongly influenced by evidence of the way in which careers are determined by social structural variables, such as social class, education, and gender, but pays less attention to individual differences and individual action in pursuit of careers. In terms of practice, it recommends policy and legislative interventions designed to reduce inequalities and improve the career opportunities of minorities or radical action toward the same ends, or both.

- The career management view emphasizes the role of organizations in career behavior through the organizational contexts they provide for individuals to pursue their careers and the organization's management of human resources. But it underestimates both the limiting effects of the wider context and the extent of individuals' responsibility for, and control over, their own careers. In terms of practice, it favors direct interventions by management to offer employees career pathways and career development opportunities to mutual benefit.

The result of these differences of emphasis is that there are seemingly three separate research literatures on the topic. For example, when I compared two recent edited "state of the art" volumes, one from the career development movement (Brown & Associates, 2002) and one from career management (Peiperl, Arthur, Goffee, & Morris, 2000), I found they had less than 5% of their references in common. This book takes a more eclectic view. For a full understanding of careers, these different "worldviews" of the topic have much to offer each other, and they all have much to offer the student of careers. In the belief that students, whether of sociology, psychology, education, counseling, or business, deserve a broader view of the topic, all of the viewpoints discussed previously are included in this book. Recently, there are new conceptualizations of careers as part of much wider social systems, in a systems theory approach (Patton & McMahon, 1999). Also, attempts have been made to develop more all-embracing integrated contextualist theories of career (Young, Valach, & Collin, 2002), though so far these theories have been hard to translate into action by either career practitioners or people pursuing careers.

The Use of Metaphor

For those with good powers of visualization, each of the worldviews discussed previously generates its own images of the individual career protagonist. The sociological view elicits pictures of a tiny person overwhelmed by massive forces beyond his or her control. The psychological view, in contrast, invites us to see an autonomous person, perhaps a Dick Whittington type or a superhero, struggling to find satisfaction and success in his or her battles in a difficult environment. The business view is of an employee, a "busy bee," working hard as part of a team and progressing happily along career pathways thoughtfully provided by a supportive employer for mutual benefit.

Such notions, very common in career thinking, are metaphors. They represent a natural human tendency to render complex and abstract phenomena understandable by making them concrete, and as far as possible human, in our minds. Metaphorical thinking is common in all human thinking and all discourse (Ortony, 1993). And, because metaphorical thinking is particularly common in relation to careers and potentially expands our understanding, a series of career metaphors frames this book.

A metaphor is a figure of speech in which a point is made about one thing by substituting something else that demonstrates a particular quality of the first in a dramatic way. Thus, instead of saying, "the soldier was strong and ferocious," we might say, "the soldier was a lion." The term *lion* embodies an extreme form of strength and ferocity and has a dramatic impact that the terms *strong* and *ferocious* lack. The metaphor also enables us to summarize complex qualities using a single word.

Using metaphors has benefits and disadvantages. Metaphor is inevitable and natural in human thought processes (Ortony, 1993). People think in metaphors. Metaphors often provide compelling images that sum up phenomena wonderfully, much as "a single picture is worth a thousand words." Metaphors also encourage creativity and help us see things in new ways.

In addition, metaphors may be used to induce us to see things that aren't there and to force other views into the background. Philosopher John Locke railed against metaphor as "the artificial and figurative application of words . . . for nothing else but to insinuate wrong ideas, move passions, and thereby mislead the judgment" (cited in Chia, 1996, p. 134). To see what he meant, check out some TV commercials next time you are viewing. Watch for metaphors: the house as a lifestyle, the bed as a magic carpet, the product consumer as a superhero, and so on. Advertisers use metaphors to persuade. In considering metaphors, retain some skepticism, seek evidence to support the metaphor, and recognize that every metaphor has its limitations.

In 1986, Gareth Morgan made a landmark contribution to organization studies when he published *Images of Organization,* a wonderful book that used the method of multiple metaphor to analyze organizations in terms of key metaphors, such as "machine," "organism," "culture," "brain," and "political system." We all know organizations that have those characteristics. For example, when an organization is described as a machine, we see it as efficient, rational, rigid, and inflexible.

Morgan argued that the metaphors of machine, organism, culture, brain, and others can be applied to any organization. Each metaphor reveals a special truth about the organization and about organizations in general. Because organizations are complex and multifaceted, no metaphor on its own tells the whole truth. But between them, a range of metaphors can provide a reasonably complete picture.

Career Metaphors

If Morgan is right, then presumably we can use metaphor to illuminate our understanding of careers. What career metaphors can we generate?

The use of metaphor to describe careers is common. Over the past few years, I have explored the use of metaphor in career discourse by academics, counselors, and lay people (Inkson, 2002, 2004; Inkson & Amundson, 2002). I have heard people describe their careers, for example, as "a roller coaster ride," "a car stuck in the sand," "the family's fuel tank," "a house of cards," "a hall of crazy mirrors," "a straight line," and "an LSD trip." These images often go far beyond the most detailed résumé in conveying the overall shape of the career and the person's feelings about the career.

Career metaphors generated by ordinary people, employing organizations, and the mass media also work their way into our consciousness. Consider the commonplace "career path," "career ladder," "career plateau," "fast track," "glass ceiling," "milestones," and "turning point." All represent the commonest career metaphor of all—the career as a journey.

But "journey" is only one of many metaphors commonly used to describe careers. Other frequent metaphors are "playing the game," "office politics," "left on the bench," "open door," "square peg in a round hole," and "story of my life." Academics have added metaphors such as "career anchors" (Schein, 1993), "career tournament" (Rosenbaum & Miller, 1996), "career climbing frame" (Gunz, 1989), and "career craft" (Poehnell & Amundson, 2002) to our understanding. The terms "portfolio career" (Handy, 1989) and "boundaryless career" (Arthur & Rousseau, 1996), introduced earlier, are also metaphors. In a study of graduate employees in a large British company, El-Sawad (2005) categorized the metaphors they used to describe their career experience under eight headings: journeys (e.g., "career ladder"), competition (e.g., "rat race"), horticulture (e.g., "corporate mushroom"), imprisonment (e.g., "life sentence"), military (e.g., "fighting battles"), school-like surveillance (e.g., "someone looking over my shoulder"), Wild West (e.g., "watch your back"), and nautical (e.g., "treading water"). Hall and Chandler (2005) drew attention to the special dynamics that exist when a career is perceived as *a calling*—work one is called to do by some higher force. And Bright and Pryor (2005) focused on the sheer unpredictability of careers to invoke the metaphor of careers as "chaos" and invoke "chaos theory" and its concept of attractors to develop an alternative approach to career counseling. All of these metaphors express their own point of view about careers. All have something to say to us. All have the potential to make us think about things in ways we may not have thought previously.

This book seeks to stimulate your interest by looking at careers through successive metaphorical lenses (e.g., the career as a journey, the career as seasons of the year, the career as a story). In everyday career thinking, it seems that there are a number of key, archetypal metaphors. Most established research and theory about careers can also be grouped and discussed under these metaphorical headings (Inkson, 2004):

- *Inheritances,* or predetermined outcomes passed on from our background and our parents
- *Cycles,* or identifiable stages through which each of us must inevitably progress
- *Actions* of our own, through which we impose our will on the world
- *Fit,* as in "square pegs fitting in square holes"—occupational slots into which each of us must fit

- *Journeys,* as indicated earlier
- *Roles* acted out in a theater of life
- *Relationships* arising from networks of contacts and interactions with others
- *Resources* that organizations use as inputs to their own purposes
- *Stories* about our lives, which we tell to ourselves and to other people

Careers can be any, or all, of these. Each of these metaphors has something to say about careers. Each is true up to a point, but only up to a point. Each represents a particular way of thinking about careers. Taken together, they may provide a wide understanding of careers. In the next nine chapters of this book, each of the nine metaphors is explained and examined in detail. After reading these chapters, you should have a more complete, balanced, and integrated understanding of careers and how they work.

A Case Study

As a starting point, read the following detailed account of a real career. I subsequently analyze this career in terms of the nine metaphors.

Aston, 53 Years of Age, Senior Manager, State Government Department, Australia

Aston was born and brought up in the United Kingdom. His father was a telephone engineer and his mother a teacher; thus, Aston had what the British call a lower middle-class background. He achieved well at primary school and with the encouragement of his parents applied for, and won, a scholarship to a prestigious private school. With further encouragement from his parents and teachers, he performed well in an elite setting. At the age of 18 years, on the advice of his school, he enrolled for a civil engineering degree at a British university—the first member of his family ever to have enrolled in a university. It was a promising start to his career.

However, Aston soon found that he had little aptitude for technical drawing. He dropped out after a term and asked himself, "What do I want to do?" Deciding that he wanted to be a manager, he secured a scholarship from a British manufacturing company to study management sciences at another university. While there, Aston's interest moved from the manufacturing side of business to finance and accounting. This interest was given a practical slant in his first job, as a graduate trainee in a finance company. He got married to his childhood sweetheart, Ashley, whose earnings as an administrator in the court system enabled him to work his way through his degree.

(Continued)

(Continued)

Surveying the scene in Britain, Aston and Ashley decided that they might have better opportunities elsewhere and that they should emigrate. They set off traveling with no clear final destination in mind. As luck would have it, their first port of call, a major Australian city where Ashley had a relative, proved congenial, and both Aston and Ashley secured good employment there almost immediately. They have spent the rest of their careers to date in this city. Aston's job was as a trainee research officer in a government department involved in the design, construction, and maintenance of public buildings. He tackled a number of projects, but one of them, involving job classification, soon stood out. The work involved analyzing and integrating data and presenting it in various verbal or written forms, including meetings. This added advocacy to his range of skills. There was a lot of classification work to be done, and Aston quickly became the recognized expert.

After 2 years, Aston was promoted to head of a newly formed systems development department that also incorporated his previous work. He was beginning to feel that his particular skills and interests were concerned with facilitation—creating and developing systems that made it easier for others to achieve objectives. He felt the broad area of management services was his niche. During this time, Ashley became pregnant, left the workforce, and had their first child. A second followed 4 years later, and Ashley would not return to the workforce for 10 years. As sole breadwinner, Aston focused ever more strongly on his work and career.

A year after the birth of his first child, he was appointed to a government commission to review a major piece of legislation relating to the management of public servants. After 6 months, the commission reported. Due to a change of government, the report was never implemented, but Aston's work on it led directly to his next opportunity: an appointment as a senior management services officer—essentially human resource (HR) manager—of a government department. Aston was still in his 20s, and the opportunity was a good one. Over the next few years, he learned a lot about human resource management, but eventually he began to find the bureaucracy he was working in "suffocating." He decided he should seek a more important role and began to look for senior HR positions. After unsuccessfully applying for several such jobs in the public service, he was appointed as HR manager to a major public sector housing agency.

He held the job for 11 years, from his early 30s to his early 40s. It was a challenging role. The agency had developed a moribund structure based on a seniority system, but recently a new chief executive officer (CEO) had started to modernize it. The CEO also started an HR function and brought in Aston as the first outsider to be appointed to a senior position. Aston implemented new systems, and major progress was made. He found his early years in the role highly fulfilling. He was known in the organization as "Mr. Change." He also gained formal accounting qualifications on a part-time study basis. After about 5 years, he began to feel it was time to move on, but new opportunities for organizational change induced him to stay. Also, one of his children became seriously ill, and he wanted to avoid the additional stress of a job move and devote more time to his family.

Eventually, however, there were other internal pressures to move. His reform-minded CEO left. Aston had begun to see the need to change systems he himself had implemented in his early years in the job— clearly work for someone else. But now he felt tied to the public service, particularly to its pension scheme in which he now had a sizeable investment. So again he began to apply for public service positions that offered a broader scope of work in management services and human resource management. It took some time, but eventually he was appointed administration and HR director of a major teaching hospital. To assist him in his new position, he took two colleagues from the agency with him.

In the first year and a half in his new position, Aston focused on solving industrial relations problems—an area in which he had a good track record from his previous position. Again, he found this initial work fulfilling. However, the election of a new government brought new policies, including competitive tendering for health services. This development used Aston's skills in the HR and financial areas, and he quickly became a kind of in-house project manager for the preparation and evaluation of competitive tendering processes. The solutions that he developed and prototyped were efficient, but unfortunately they also did away with part of his own role. In addition, a new CEO did not share the same objectives. When the organization was restructured, there was no place for Aston, and he was laid off.

This was part of a major hiatus in Aston's life. Now age 44, he was experiencing major undiagnosed health problems that were beginning to affect his performance at work. There were also difficulties in his marriage, one of them being that over many years he had become overinvolved in his career. He had thought that in pursuing his work with energy—for example, attending breakfast meetings and spending long hours at the office and evenings in his study dealing with paperwork and leaving his family to their own devices—he was doing the right thing. He now realized he was wrong and that he had grown away from his wife and children. In the space of 12 months, he lost his job, his health problem was diagnosed as one requiring a major lifestyle change, and he and Ashley decided to separate.

Fortunately, the employment problem resolved itself immediately. The day after he was laid off, an acquaintance called Gemma, the manager of a public service consulting agency, called Aston. She knew of his work and offered him employment as a consultant to assist medical organizations with competitive tendering matters. But because of uncertainties about the future, she was able to offer him only a 6-month contract. Aston threw himself gratefully into his new role. When the 6-month contract was up, he was offered another and then another. As his confidence and competence improved, he was given increased responsibilities.

Then, after 3 years on temporary contracts, his phone rang again. This time Gemma invited him to apply for a vacant position as contract manager to an agency in the area of public transport. The work would be to competitively tender for, and manage, contracts for public transport services. Aston applied and got the job. His 50th birthday passed. The work went well, and his responsibilities expanded to include human resources and finance aspects. At the time of this writing, Aston is 53. He recognizes that this may be his last paid job before he retires, and he is devoting increased time and energy to the unpaid work he does as a sports administrator.

One factor that Aston considers key to his career is networks, which have been important due to his ongoing employment and reputation in one city and his consistency in working for the public service. Through his contacts, he is able to get a lot of information by telephone. However, this networking is becoming weaker as more people enter public service from outside.

Metaphors for Aston's Career

What insights do metaphors give about Aston's career and about careers in general?

Aston's Career as an Inheritance

Inheritances are career resources (and sometimes handicaps) that come into our careers from the past—for example, our innate abilities and personality, gender, social background, and education. We "inherit" these characteristics from our parents and elsewhere. Some we cannot change, and others we can change only with difficulty.

Aston's career uses an inheritance of above-average intelligence and some special aptitudes, such as numeracy and verbal expression. These were partly built into his genetic makeup and may also have been developed through his education. However, he apparently had little aptitude for spatial relations—a key element in technical drawing—and this led to his career having a false start in an engineering program. From his middle-class background and his elite school, Aston gained values such as his strong work ethic. His male gender and White ethnicity probably played a part in the types of jobs he pursued, and was appointed to, throughout his career.

Thus Aston's career, for good or ill, was from the start assisted and also constrained by forces beyond his control. All careers are affected, for good or ill, by such legacies. The inheritance metaphor, dealt with in detail in Chapter 2, involves the things people bring into their careers that cannot easily be changed.

Aston's Career as a Cycle

A cycle is a period of time in which a succession of events or phenomena is completed. The cycle most frequently used as a metaphor for human lives is the seasons—spring, summer, fall, and winter (Levinson et al., 1978). In Aston's career, we can discern classic career seasons, such as growth, exploration, establishment, and maintenance (Super, 1957). There was growth in Aston's childhood and education; exploration in his abortive engineering career and early movements through manufacturing, finance, and management services; establishment in his development of expertise in management services; and maintenance in his continuation in that type of work despite turbulent times. We can also see shorter cycles—for example, cycles, within specific jobs, of novelty, action, progress, and disillusion. At one point, Aston even found himself thinking of reforming the structures that he had built 10 years previously.

Aston's seasons are also affected by his personal development as child and adult and by aging. His family cycles of courtship, marriage, child rearing, and the empty nest create additional rhythms, complicated by his marriage breakup. We sense an eventual depletion of energy when he looks to reduce his commitment to work. Are these rhythms inevitable? By looking at the cycles typically affecting careers (in Chapter 3), we can find out.

Aston's Career as Action

Whereas inheritance and cycle emphasize patterns imposed on Aston's career, action emphasizes his ==personal efforts.== Aston's career is a result of his own actions. He has done much to achieve his goals—earn a living; express his identity, abilities, and personality; and do something useful for others. The metaphor emphasizes that he creates his career through his own actions.

Action is based on planning and decision making. Aston made short-term plans. He adapted his plans to opportunity. He and his wife executed a plan to emigrate and then seized unexpected opportunities when they reached Australia. As Aston's career proceeded, he did not decide exactly what job he would have in 5 years' time, but he gathered information, determined what he enjoyed and was talented in, developed new skills, chose general directions, applied for jobs of the right type, and seized appropriate opportunities. He built on his strengths and extended into new areas. He also made rational decisions (e.g., he stayed in the public sector to safeguard his pension). Thus, Aston constantly thought about, planned, and made decisions about his career, constructing it as he acted it out. Chapter 4 presents more information about action, self-expression, and the way career choices are made.

Aston's Career as Fit

In the common "square peg in a round hole" saying, individuals are pegs who should have a good fit with their holes, or careers.

Aston was constantly aware of the extent of his fit and tried to improve it. For example, his initial rejection of engineering stemmed from a feeling of poor fit, and he moved into an area that seemed a better fit. He developed financial skills and looked for jobs that fit them. Later, he began to feel that management services were his niche. Later still, his unique mix of financial and HR skills made him an ideal fit for work in competitive tendering. If we wish, we can view Aston's career as a continuing search for the perfect fit.

One problem is that neither the peg nor the hole stays the same shape for long. Aston changed, developed new ambitions and skills, and needed new, different work. His jobs were redefined, restructured, and sometimes eliminated. At one point, he found the personnel manager job okay but the surrounding bureaucracy suffocating. In his constant search for fit, Aston continuously assessed himself and compared himself with external opportunities. So must we all. Fortunately, as I show in Chapter 5, the psychology of careers offers a lot of help.

Aston's Career as a Journey

"Journey" is the most common career metaphor of all. Journeys imply mobility, getting to a new place.

Aston's showed mobility when he moved from Britain to Australia, which was distant in geographical terms but quite close in terms of cultural similarity. But physical space and cultural space are not the only dimensions of career journeys.

Aston traveled through a series of different *occupations*. He traveled through a series of different *organizations*. He traveled within these occupations and organizations as well as between them. He crossed *boundaries*, initially including international ones, but stayed within others, such as his city and the public sector. By the end of the journey, he was at a higher status *altitude* than at the beginning.

Aston's journey is unique, but by thinking about it we can develop insights into the mobility aspects of career. Does a career journey have to have a destination? Is getting to where one is headed more or less important than enjoying the experience as we go? If we compare different routes—for example, routes confined to one occupation versus routes that travel between occupations—what are the advantages and disadvantages? What are the implications of the trends for careers to become, like Aston's, *boundary-crossing* and *international* journeys? All these are legitimate issues and will be discussed in Chapter 6.

Aston's Career as Roles

As Aston's interests, skills, and self-image changed over time so did his work roles—engineer, financial expert, management services manager, HR manager, and so on. To a large extent, these roles were defined not by Aston but by his employing organizations, bosses, and work colleagues. But he tried to put his own definition and imprint on them. Also, the roles changed—for example, at one stage he added work for a government commission to his role and then used the momentum to leap into a new role in personnel management. At another time, his whole role was redefined as an advisor about tendering. Every so often, Aston moved to a new work role yet brought aspects of his previous performance into it.

Aston also occupied different roles in his changing home life. Early on he was a son, child, and student. Later, he became a young man, husband, father, and breadwinner. Later still, he was a middle-aged divorcé. Each of his roles was defined by sets of expectations that others—his employers, his family—had of him. In this sense, his career was like a theatrical performance, with others writing the script. But Aston's performance also included his own expression of himself.

As many of us do, Aston was, as it were, rushing between different theaters to play different roles, and sometimes the roles conflicted. The existence of multiple roles and changing expectations within each role sometimes make careers difficult. In Chapter 7 I discuss these and related issues.

Aston's Career as Relationships

We often think of careers as individual, but most are very social. Career behavior can be compared to party behavior—constantly moving around, meeting old friends, and making new ones. Careers are facilitated by social contacts. Careers weave their way through acquaintanceships, friendships, groups, and organizations, and they create further networks as they go. Sometimes these networks provide major career impetus or direction.

Aston's initial career networks were family ones, involving his parents and his wife. The career connection in Australia was found through a relation. As Aston's career progressed, he became involved in a network of contacts in the public service of his city, and these contacts helped his work and career for many years. He found telephone contacts with these people invaluable in enabling him to do his various jobs. And his networks included not only direct contacts but contacts through reputation—at one stage someone who did not know him but knew of his work offered him a job immediately after he was laid off: Aston knew how to work his networks. The network element of careers is discussed in more detail in Chapter 8.

Aston's Career as a Resource

Both Aston and his employers used his career to achieve their objectives. His qualifications, experience, expertise, and work created a resource that his employers could combine with their other resources to create products and services. For example, at one stage he worked with a modernizing boss to reform a moribund agency. His career was a resource for the agency, but his experience at the agency also became a resource for his career.

Over time, Aston added expertise in finance, HR, and information technology to his career resource. He also gained advocacy skills, public sector experience, a reputation in his city, and networks of useful contacts. As Aston changed jobs and as the context changed, parts of the resource lost their value. As they did, Aston constantly sought to develop new competencies, thereby increasing the size and relevance of the resource.

Aston's employers provided him with remuneration and training as an investment in the resource he embodied. But Aston, through his time, expertise, and effort, simultaneously invested in his employers. The resource metaphor focuses on the developing capability that every career has to contribute to a wider cause and the way that employers as well as employees facilitate such development. This metaphor is further explored in Chapter 9.

Aston's Career as a Story

When we talk about our careers, we are telling stories. Aston's career history, outlined earlier, is a faithful reproduction of what Aston told me. But it is not the only story one could tell about Aston's career. Would Aston tell the same story in a job application? Did he tell the same early-career story 20 years ago, and will he tell the same story again in 20 years' time? Would his family members, friends, and employers tell the same story about him? Probably not, because there is no single true story of any career, particularly if the stories include subjective as well as objective elements. There is nothing necessarily dishonest about multiple stories: They simply indicate subjective biases, memory lapses, and the different purposes of the stories.

Careers may be no more or less than the stories we tell about them. And stories have a vital function in society: They help us to understand who we are and what our lives are about. They provide us with the logic to explain the past and give us direction for the future. They provide role models and archetypes that others may imitate. If we know how career stories work, we can tell our own and interpret others'. The shadowy world of career stories is explored in Chapter 10.

Conclusion

I have shown nine totally different views of Aston's career. It is as if each metaphor provided a different lens to view the same phenomenon. Through each lens, we see different things. Each view appears to be valid, and there is some overlap between them. If the explanations seem long and complex, that is because careers are long and complex. But perhaps the illustration also helps us to see that each metaphor generates its own unique insights. The discipline of thinking about careers in terms of each of the nine metaphors is a rigorous one but one that I believe will pay off over time in terms of your general understanding of careers and your specific understanding of your own career and the careers of others. In the nine chapters that follow, I explain what we can learn about careers by using each of the metaphors.

Key Points in This Chapter

- Careers are important sources of human satisfaction and dissatisfaction that people need to manage. Key issues are work–nonwork balance, congruence, maturity and aging, and rational choices.
- A definition of *career* is "the evolving sequence of a person's work experience over time."
- Careers take place in a context and are affected by demographic, economic, social, organizational, and technological factors.
- The context of careers changes over time: Since 1980, careers have been destabilized by economic and organizational restructuring, competition, globalization, the growth of information technology, and other factors. Career effects include a move from relational to transactional psychological contracts, the decline of organizational careers, and the growth of new forms of career.
- The field of career studies has evolved over time from its original, psychological trait-and-factor and human development theories to include a range of approaches from sociology, social psychology, and business studies.
- A metaphor is a figure of speech that substitutes one idea for another to demonstrate features of the first. Careers are often described by metaphors, such as the "pathway" metaphor or the "square peg in a round hole" metaphor. Multiple metaphor is a way of expressing a range of viewpoints about careers.
- The career metaphors considered in this book are "inheritance," "cycle," "action," "fit," "journey," "roles," "relationships," "resource," and "stories."

Questions From This Chapter

General Questions

1. Outline three career decisions or problems that you or the people you know currently face.

2. How would you advise Darren to solve the career problem he currently faces?

3. Which of the various types of theory in career studies seems to you to have the most relevance to your career and today's careers in general? Why?

4. Use metaphor to describe one or more authority figures you know (e.g. managers, tutors, instructors). What is the meaning you are trying to convey with the metaphors? How well do the metaphors fit?

5. List all of the career metaphors you can find in this chapter. Then divide them into categories that seem similar. What are your main categories?

6. Read the story of Aston's career. Outline some principles you think Aston used in managing it. Which of the metaphors do you think best describes his career, and why?

Career Case Study Questions

1. How have the late 20th-century changes in Table 1.1 affected the career of your case person? Which have had the greatest effects?

2. Ask your career case person to provide, and justify, metaphors for his or her career. Do the same for your own career.

3. Think about the nine key metaphors outlined in the chapter in relation to your case career. Which offer the most in terms of understanding the career? Which intuitively interest you in terms of your own career? Why?

References

Arthur, M. B., Hall, D. T., & Lawrence, B. S. (Eds.). (1989). *Handbook of career theory.* Cambridge, UK: Cambridge University Press.

Arthur, M. B., Inkson, K., & Pringle, J. K. (1999). *The new careers: Individual action and economic change.* London: Sage.

Arthur, M. B., & Rousseau, D. (Eds.). (1996). *The boundaryless career: A new employment principle for a new organizational era.* New York: Oxford University Press.

Biddle, B. J., & Thomas, E. J. (Eds.). (1966). *Role theory: Concepts and research.* New York: Wiley.

Blau, P. M., & Duncan, O. D. (1967). *The American occupational structure.* New York: Wiley.

Blustein, D. L., & Ellis, M. V. (2004). The cultural context of career assessment. *Journal of Career Assessment, 8*(4), 379-390.

Bright, J. E. H., & Pryor, R. G. L. (2005). The chaos theory of careers: A user's guide. *Career Development Quarterly, 53*(4), 291-305.

Brown, D. (2002). Introduction to theories of career development and choice: Origins, evolution and current effects. In D. Brown & Associates, *Career choice and development* (4th ed., pp. 3-23). San Francisco: Jossey-Bass.

Brown, D., & Associates. (2002). *Career choice and development* (4th ed.). San Francisco: Jossey-Bass.

Cappelli, P. (1999). *The new deal at work: Managing the market-driven workforce.* Boston: Harvard Business School Press.

Cascio, W. F. (2003). *Managing human resources: Productivity, quality of life, profits* (6th ed.). Boston: McGraw-Hill.

Chia, R. (1996). Metaphors and metaphorization in organizational analysis: Thinking beyond the thinkable. In D. Grant & C. Oswick (Eds.), *Metaphor and organizations* (pp. 127-145). Thousand Oaks, CA: Sage.

Eby, L. T., Casper, W. J., Lockwood, A., Bordeaux, C., & Brinley, A. (2005). Work and family research in IO/OB: Content analysis and review of the literature. *Journal of Vocational Behavior, 66*(1), 124-197.

El-Sawad, A. (2005). "Becoming a lifer": Unlocking career through metaphor. *Journal of Occupational and Organizational Psychology, 78*(1), 23-41.

Fugate, M., Kinicki, A. J., & Ashforth, B. E. (2004). Employability: A psycho-social construct, its dimensions, and applications. *Journal of Vocational Behavior, 65*(1), 14-38.

Ginzberg, E., Ginsburg, S., Axelrad, S., & Herma, J. (1951). *Occupational choice: An approach to a general theory.* New York: Columbia University Press.

Gottfredson, L. S. (2002). Gottfredson's theory of circumscription, compromise and self-creation. In D. Brown & Associates, *Career choice and development* (4th ed., pp. 85-148). San Francisco: Jossey-Bass.

Granovetter, M. (1974). *Getting a job: A study of contacts and careers.* Cambridge, MA: Harvard University Press.

Greenblatt, E. (2002). Work-life balance: Wisdom or whining? *Organizational Dynamics, 32*(2), 177-193.

Gunz, H. (1989). The dual meaning of managerial careers: Organizational and individual levels of analysis. *Journal of Management Studies, 26*(3), 225-250.

Hall, D. T. (1976). *Careers in organizations.* Pacific Palisades, CA: Goodyear.

Hall, D. T., & Associates. (1996). *The career is dead—Long live the career: A relational approach to careers.* San Francisco: Jossey-Bass.

Hall, D. T., & Chandler, D. E. (2005). Psychological success: When the career is a calling. *Journal of Organizational Behavior, 26*(2), 155-176.

Handy, C. (1989). *The age of unreason.* London: Business Books.

Hansen, L. S. (1997). *Integrative life planning—Critical tasks for career development and changing life patterns.* San Francisco: Jossey-Bass.

Herriot, P. (1992). *The career management challenge: Balancing individual and organizational needs.* Newbury Park, CA: Sage.

Herriot, P., & Pemberton, C. (1996). Contracting careers. *Human Relations, 49*(6), 759-790.

Hofstede, G. (2003). *Culture's consequences: Comparing values, behaviors, institutions and organizations across nations.* Thousand Oaks, CA: Sage.

Holland, J. L. (1959). A theory of vocational choice. *Journal of Counseling Psychology, 6,* 35-45.

Holland, J. L. (1997). *Making vocational choices: A theory of vocational personalities and work environments* (2nd ed.). Odessa, FL: Psychological Assessment Resources.

Hughes, E. C. (1958). *Men and their work.* Glencoe, IL: Free Press.

Inkson, K. (2002). Thinking creatively about careers: The use of metaphor. In M. A. Peiperl, M. B. Arthur, & N. Anand (Eds.), *Career creativity: Explorations in the remaking of work* (pp. 15-34). New York: Oxford University Press.

Inkson, K. (2004). Images of career: Nine key metaphors. *Journal of Vocational Behavior, 65*(1), 96-111.

Inkson, K., & Amundson, N. E. (2002). Career metaphors and their application in theory and counseling practice. *Journal of Employment Counseling, 39*(3), 98-108.

Inkson, K., Lazarova, M. B., & Thomas, D. C. (Eds.). (2005). Global careers [Special issue]. *Journal of World Business, 40*(4), 349-440.

Johnson, M. K., & Mortimer, J. T. (2002). Career choice and development from a sociological perspective. In D. Brown & Associates (Eds.), *Career choice and development* (4th ed., pp. 37-81). San Francisco: Jossey Bass.

Kanter, R. M. (1989). Careers and the wealth of nations: A macro-perspective on the structure and implications of career forms. In M. B. Arthur, D. T. Hall, & B. S. Lawrence (Eds.), *Handbook of career theory* (pp. 506-521). Cambridge, UK: Cambridge University Press.

Krumboltz, J. D. (1979). A social learning theory of career decision making. In A. M. Mitchell, G. B. Jones, & J. D. Krumboltz (Eds.), *Social learning and career decision making* (pp. 19-49). Cranston, RI: Carroll.

Lent, R. W., Brown, S. D., & Hackett, G. (1994). Towards a unifying social cognitive theory of career and academic interest, choice and performance. *Journal of Vocational Behavior, 45,* 79-122.

Levinson, D. J., Darrow, C. N., Klein, E. B., Levinson, M. H., & McKee, B. (1978). *The seasons of a man's life.* New York: Knopf.

Lofquist, L., & Dawis, R. V. (1969). *Adjustment to work.* East Norwich, CT: Appleton-Century-Crofts.

Mayrhofer, W., Meyer, M., Iellatchitch, A., & Schiffinger, M. (2004). Careers and human resource management: A European perspective. *Human Resource Management Review, 14*(4), 473-498.

Morgan, G. (1986). *Images of organization.* Beverly Hills, CA: Sage.

Nicholson, N. (1984). A theory of work-role transitions. *Administrative Science Quarterly, 29,* 172-191.

Ortony, A. (1993). *Metaphor and thought* (2nd ed.). Cambridge, UK: Cambridge University Press.

Parsons, F. (1909). *Choosing a vocation.* Boston: Houghton Mifflin.

Patton, W., & McMahon, M. (1999). *Career development and systems theory: A new relationship.* Pacific Grove, CA: Brooks/Cole.

Peiperl, M. A., Arthur, M. B., Goffee, R., & Morris, T. (Eds.). (2000). *Career frontiers: New conceptions of working lives.* Oxford, UK: Oxford University Press.

Peterson, G. W., Sampson, J. P., & Reardon, R. C. (1991). *Career development and services: A cognitive approach.* Pacific Grove, CA: Brooks/Cole.

Poehnell, G., & Amundson, N. (2002). CareerCraft: Engaging with, energizing, and empowering career creativity. In M. A. Peiperl, M. B. Arthur, & N. Anand (Eds.), *Career creativity: Explorations in the re-making of work* (pp. 105-122). New York: Oxford University Press.

Pringle, J. K., & Mallon, M. (2003). Challenges for the boundaryless career odyssey. *International Journal of Human Resource Management, 14*(5), 839-853.

Reardon, R. C., Lenz, J. G., Sampson, J. P. Jr., & Peterson, G. W. (2006). *Career development and planning: A comprehensive approach* (2nd ed.). Mason, OH: Thomson Custom Solutions.

Roe, A. (1956). *The psychology of occupations.* New York: Wiley.

Rosenbaum, J., & Miller, S. R. (1996). Moving in, up, or out: Tournaments and other institutional signals of career attainments. In M. B. Arthur & D. M. Rousseau (Eds.), *The boundaryless career: A new employment principle for a new organizational era* (pp. 350-369). New York: Oxford University Press.

Rousseau, D. M. (1995). *Psychological contracts in organizations: Understanding written and unwritten agreements.* Thousand Oaks, CA: Sage.

Savickas, M. L. (2004). Vocational psychology, overview. In C. Spielberger (Ed.), *Encyclopaedia of applied psychology* (pp. 655-667). Amsterdam: Elsevier.

Savickas, M. L., & Baker, D. B. (2005). The history of vocational psychology: Antecedents, origins and early development. In W. B. Walsh & M. L. Savickas (Eds.), *Handbook of vocational psychology* (3rd ed., pp. 15-49). Mahwah, NJ: Erlbaum.

Scandura, T. A., & Lankau, M. J. (1997). Relationships of gender, family responsibility and flexible work hours to organizational commitment and job satisfaction. *Journal of Organizational Behavior, 18*(4), 977-991.

Schein, E. H. (1993). *Career anchors: Discovering your real values* (Rev. ed.). London: Pfieffer.

Senge, P. (1990). *The fifth discipline: The art and practice of the learning organization.* New York: Doubleday.

Skorikov, V., & Vondracek, F. W. (1993). Career development in the Commonwealth of Independent States. *Career Development Quarterly, 41*(4), 314-329.

Super, D. E. (1953). A theory of vocational development. *American Psychologist, 30,* 88-92.

Super, D. E. (1957). *The psychology of careers.* New York: Harper & Row.

Super, D. E. (1980). A life-span, life-space approach to career development. *Journal of Vocational Behavior, 16,* 282-298.

Templer, A. J., & Cawsey, T. F. (1999). Rethinking career development in an era of portfolio careers. *Career Development International, 4*(2), 70-76.

Thomas, D. C., & Inkson, K. (in press). Careers across cultures. In M. Peiperl & H. Gunz (Eds.), *Handbook of career studies.* Thousand Oaks, CA: Sage.

Vondracek, F. W., Lerner, R. M., & Schulenberg, J. E. (1986). *Career development: A life-span developmental approach.* Mahwah, NJ: Erlbaum.

Vondracek, F. W., & Porfeli, E. (2002). Integrating person- and function-centered approaches in career development theory and research. *Journal of Vocational Behavior, 61*(3), 386-397.

Young, R. A., & Collin, A. (2004). Introduction: Constructivism and social constructionism in the career field. *Journal of Vocational Behavior, 64*(3), 373-389.

Young, R. A., Valach, L., & Collin, A. (2002). A contextualist explanation of career. In D. Brown & Associates (Eds.), *Career choice and development* (4th ed., pp. 205-252). San Francisco: Jossey-Bass.

CHAPTER 2

Careers as Inheritances

A Flying Start

Megan grew up in England. At school, she showed a talent for art and design. At 15 years of age, she was able to find work with a major fashion designer on a couture collection and later spent several years learning about design on London's Savile Row. Eventually, she enrolled at London's St Martin's College of Art & Design to study fashion design. The climax of her education was her graduation show—attended by her parents—at which family friends modeled her designs on the catwalk. Fortunately for Megan, a number of fashion houses attended her show, and eventually a London boutique bought her entire collection. International publicity followed. Megan launched her own label the same year and was appointed chief designer at the French couture house Chloë in March 1997, succeeding Karl Lagerfeld in one of the most high-profile posts in the industry. Her first collection for the house, in Paris in October 1997, suggested to industry experts that she was indeed a real talent. Sensual and romantic, the collection was hailed a triumph. The following season, Chloë's sales figures proved that Megan's efforts had both raised its profile and lifted its profits. Megan was clearly headed for a stellar international career in fashion design.

What do you make of Megan's extraordinarily successful start to her career? Was it really due to talent? Or to hard work? Or to luck? Or perhaps to a combination of all three?

It may cast a new perspective on the case to reveal at this point that the name "Megan" is a pseudonym and that the real occupant of the stellar career was actually named Stella. Readers who are knowledgeable about the fashion industry may already have guessed that Megan is in fact Stella McCartney (see www.vogue.co.uk/whos_who/Stella_McCartney/default.html). Stella's parents who attended her college fashion show were her father, ex-Beatle Sir Paul McCartney, and her late mother, heiress Linda McCartney. The family friends who helped out by modeling included world-famous supermodels Kate Moss and Naomi Campbell. The fashion designer whom Stella worked with in her formative years was the well-known Christian Lacroix. No wonder the media were interested in Stella's show. No wonder Chloë appointed such a famous name, even though it belonged to a young and inexperienced person. Does the story of Megan begin to take on a new light?

None of this denies that Stella McCartney was—and is—a very good designer. Nor is it impossible that even without her famous parents and friends, Stella would still have had the talent to succeed. But perhaps Stella's instant stardom was made a lot more likely by her background. Perhaps she inherited some of her father's creative, artistic genes. Perhaps her relatively privileged upbringing helped her to make the most of what talent she possessed. Undoubtedly, her parents' fame, fortune, and friends created opportunities for her that she would not otherwise have had.

To *inherit* means to "receive (property, rank, title) by legal descent or succession" or to "derive a quality or characteristic genetically from one's ancestors" (Allen, 1990, p. 608). Stella's story emphasizes that, to a large extent, by the time we commence our careers, aspects of them may already have been predetermined.

Structure Versus Individual Action

Some career inheritances, such as our parentage, genetic makeup, sex, and race, we are born with. Others, such as our values, motivation, and education, are developed in childhood largely as a result of family influences and become part of what we bring to a career. We have little if any control of such inheritances. They may—as in Stella's case—be spectacularly helpful, or they may alternatively seem like millstones around our necks. They are often constructed around society's *structures*—for example, rules or hierarchies determining how much wealth or education you need to receive certain opportunities; what social class you need to be in; what gender, age, or ethnicity you need to be; what sexual orientation you need to have; or what contacts you require, to have a real chance.

By considering inheritances, it is therefore possible to predict aspects of our careers in advance, such as whether we will have a professional or a manual occupation. The son of a wealthy, White, Harvard-educated male lawyer is many times more likely to become a lawyer himself than is the daughter of a Black single mother on welfare and with only an elementary school education. By the time we commence our careers, perhaps in our early 20s, we are mostly already predisposed and prepared to conduct them along predictable lines. After we embark on our careers, we face various barriers (and also opportunities) in terms of social structures and the way that they relate to our inheritance. For example, some companies employing graduates may favor male graduates from particular Ivy League schools: If you seek employment with these companies, you may find that you simply have the wrong inheritance.

Sociologists tend to believe that aspects of social structure are major determinants of careers (Johnson & Mortimer, 2002). Social structure includes divisions by social class, gender, and race, as well as institutional structures, such as government rules and regulations, centralized authority, and bureaucratic organization. However talented and motivated you may be, according to this view you may find your career progress barred because you were born "on the wrong side of the tracks" or the occupation you want to enter is an "old boys' club." Entry to a job or occupation may be controlled by strict rules and regulations—for example, the requirement of hard-to-obtain tertiary qualifications. Other prejudices abound—for example, tall people are given greater responsibility than are short people, and as a result height is statistically related to career success (Judge & Cable, 2004). The social structure principle suggests that careers are mostly predetermined by larger forces beyond individual control.

An alternative view is that rather than structures determining individual career outcomes, individuals can transcend social structures through their own energy. Some argue that in the current era social and organizational structures are weakening, providing greater opportunities for individual career action (Weick, 1996). In the past, plenty of individuals determined their own career paths in the face of severe structural constraints—and succeeded. An example is Colin Powell, the West Indian slum child who followed a U.S. Army career and eventually became one of the most powerful men in the world (Persico & Powell, 1995). But is this an exception that proves the rule? Can people empower themselves to achieve their career goals, or are their careers determined in advance by forces beyond their control?

Thus, social structure defines parameters and barriers that limit careers to particular pathways and forms. In contrast, people, as agents of their own destiny, can sometimes take proactive individual career action to create their own careers, perhaps even overcoming some of the barriers of social structure (Peiperl & Arthur, 2000). Consider the battle between individual action and structure in the career of Nita.

Struggling Against Structure

Nita came from a minority immigrant group (Pacific Islanders) that was discriminated against in the labor market and that generally occupied low-level jobs or was unemployed. Despite this, Nita's parents attained good jobs and middle-class status and hoped for the same for Nita. Rejecting their advice to seek formal qualifications, Nita left school at a young age and became a waitress, then a cleaner and a factory worker. While struggling to make a living in unskilled jobs, she had three children. In her late 20s, she decided to study, went to college, and, despite major privations and difficulties as she brought up her children at the same time, eventually trained as a teacher. Her work in middle-class schools enabled her to see how the education system fails people in her ethnic group, and she developed and implemented a personal mission to improve the education of her people in what she saw as a racist system.

Source: Arthur, Inkson, & Pringle (1999).

Nita's career represents a fascinating example of the struggle for personal autonomy in the face of structural constraints. In rejecting the influence of her parents and accepting work and family status stereotypical of her gender and race, she initially allowed prevailing social structures to determine her career. Later, through a remarkable act of willpower and ability against the odds, assisted perhaps by underlying inherited middle-class values, she elevated herself to unanticipated career success. But her ethnic inheritance left its mark indelibly on the way that she conducted her long-term career as a teacher.

In Western democracies, particularly in America, there is a strong popular belief in the career-related values of individualism, achievement, and equality of opportunity (Williams, 1965), leading to the popular view that determined individuals can succeed against all odds, even if they come from the humblest background. The fictional story of the rags-to-riches hero Horatio Alger, popular in the early 20th century, epitomizes this view (Kluegel & Smith, 1986). It has a modern counterpart in the unknown-to-famous scenarios played out on our television screens in programs such as *American Idol*. There is, however, more than a little wishful thinking in these stories. For every rags-to-riches Horatio Alger or idolized pop star, there are many wannabes who are marginalized in labor markets where there are many more aspirants than opportunities. Much as we might like to believe that the careers "game" is played on a level playing field, where everyone has an equal chance to succeed, the truth is that career inequality is structured in our society in many different ways. The belief in equality of career opportunity may be a myth that increases our degree of comfort with the reality of *in*equality of opportunity.

The playing field, then, is not level, but perhaps if we understand what some of the major bumps and biases are, we can at least start to think about how these barriers might limit our careers and whether we can do anything to overcome them.

Field and Habitus

The French sociologist Pierre Bourdieu had a schema for understanding society that shows us the different types of structural constraint that apply to careers (Mayrhoferet et al., 2004; Wacquant, 1998). Bourdieu talked about two critical concepts: field and habitus:

- *Fields* are the social spaces in which people live their lives and are characterized by internal complexity and hierarchy. Fields arise in education, religion, economic life, and other areas in which we face structural constraints, rules, boundaries, and expected practices. Fields contain institutions and individuals who occupy dominant or less dominant positions. They limit us but they simultaneously challenge us to conserve the rules if we are dominant or to subvert or overcome them if we are constrained. Thus, the field has metaphorical characteristics of "battlefield" or even "tournament" (Rosenbaum, 1984). Indeed, a career path tournament game is available, designed to increase players' awareness of sociological barriers to their careers (Scholl, 1999).

For example, in pursuing her career as a fashion designer, Stella entered an industry field that has its own ways of operating, its own rules and norms, and its own hierarchies, criteria, and networks of association. These are strong social structures: Stella and other newcomers need to learn how they work. Although people may have some individual power in this situation—for example, Stella, as we saw, has major network advantages—there are strong structural limitations.

- *Habitus,* according to Bourdieu, is the system of internal, personal, enduring dispositions through which we perceive the world. We acquire habitus through exposure to the social conditions around us, which we typically receive from, and share with, others in our predominant social groups, including family. Thus, we internalize external constraints and opportunities and build and develop our habitus over time from new experiences. We can, for example, expect the habitus of the young Stella to have incorporated a worldview in which being involved in a glamour industry and mixing with the rich and famous were strongly incorporated. We would be surprised if we learned that her background had given her a strong disposition toward a career in the heavy engineering or insurance industries. Habitus is the vehicle in which much of our inheritance of values, interests, ideas, motivations, and social connections are incorporated.

Field and habitus are intimately related to each other. "As the mediation between past influences and present stimuli, habitus is at once *structured,* by the patterned social forces that produced it, and *structuring:* it gives form and coherence to the various activities of an individual across the separate spheres [fields] of life" (Wacquant, 1998, p. 221).

Gender provides an example. As will be shown, gender is the source of many constraints, rules, and norms in different career fields. A woman seeking to become a firefighter or commando, for example, will, in the field, face formal and informal processes and barriers tending to keep her out of these occupations or relegating her to junior positions within them. The barriers may include discouragement from family and others, aptitude or endurance tests oriented to male standards of physical capability, biased interviews, special tests of character, and ridicule and scorn from other firefighters, managers, and others (Burke, 2001; Hicks Stiehm, 1996; Morgan, 2003). At the same time, her habitus, informed by a lifetime of indoctrination from family, school, community, popular media, and the like, may be giving her messages that she should "stay away." The outcome is the product of the two sets of forces. Looked at in that way, it does not appear that the woman has much power of self-determination.

The idea of field and habitus has been specifically applied to careers:

Career fields are the social context within which individual members of the workforce make their moves . . . career habitus is understood as a frame of thinking, perceiving and acting within career fields. It is both the product of a social field's structure and a main force of re-structuring these fields. Career field and career habitus are linked in a circular relationship. [Players'] career habitus . . . disposes [them] towards recognising and playing the rules of the career field. (Mayrhofer et al., 2004)

Note the metaphor of "playing the game within its rules." This view is similar to the classic formula by Parsons (1909) for good career decision making (see Chapter 1). Parsons advocated that people should strive to understand their own abilities and inclination (habitus, but with a special understanding of the way in which abilities and inclinations develop) and the opportunities and difficulties of different occupations (field, with special application to social structures). They should then use logical reasoning to relate these two groups of facts to make good career decisions. The "inheritance" metaphor suggests, however, that for those with a poor inheritance who understand their situation, logical reasoning might well be overwhelmed by despair or anger.

Careers as Prisons

One interesting metaphor raised by the idea of social structure and by the specific concepts of field and habitus is that of the career as a "prison." Does that sound a little negative? Does some people's inheritance condemn them to a life of imprisonment? Surely everyone can build a successful career if they act with determination and work hard to make the most of their talents?

If you think that, consider the plight of American slaves prior to the Civil War. Their careers were totally controlled by the rules and norms of the day—they might as well have been in prison. Even today there are continuing complaints against multinational companies that employ Third-World employees, including children, in paid but slavelike conditions (e.g., Palley, 2002). In India's caste system, the lowest caste, known as the untouchables, can do only the most servile, "unclean" tasks and must live out their entire careers within the caste, with no possibility of upward mobility (Ghurye, 1961).

Imprisonment of these types is an objective, observable condition, created clearly by social structure (field). But it is often supported by people's inherited view of what is appropriate (habitus). Slavery or low-caste membership may be more acceptable to the slaves and low-caste people who have been, as it were, "born into it" and have come to accept it as their unenviable but inevitable lot than it is to those who are suddenly enslaved. Similarly, disability may also limit career opportunities dramatically due to restrictions on what a disabled person can do (field), but it also leads to its own psychology of career aspiration and development (habitus) (Feldman, 2004). Habitus supports field in a subtle prolongation of the status quo.

It may be argued that slavery and caste systems are historical and cultural anomalies and that no one in today's free democracies can be considered to be imprisoned by their career. Perhaps, but it may all be a matter of degree. Why, for example, do we use the metaphor "golden handcuffs" to describe a situation where senior staff are tied to their organizations by luxurious personal benefits that will immediately cease if they leave, leading possibly to commitment without loyalty (Cappelli, 2000)? Is this not a form of imprisonment? Many people describe themselves ruefully as company slaves—desirous of escaping but also frightened of the dangers of freedom.

El-Sawad (2005) strikingly described the career mentality and discourse of young, apparently upwardly mobile British employees in blue-chip companies: Many saw themselves as "lifers" (serving life sentences) in companies and company systems that they neither enjoyed nor respected but that offered them too many tangible benefits for them to voluntarily escape. Perhaps the inheritance of desire for status was too strong for them. Company methods for securing staff loyalty (field) and the materialistic attitudes of the staff (habitus) may combine to secure staff compliance. Another form of imprisonment occurs when workers who have invested heavily in acquiring qualifications in a subject, such as medicine, subsequently realize that they do not enjoy the work they are qualified for and feel trapped in a career that they do not want.

Other employees find themselves trapped on a career plateau (see Chapter 3) from which they feel they cannot escape either upward or outward (Bardsley & Sherstyuk, 2001; Ledwith & Colgan, 1996). Older workers often feel trapped within their current job, not especially liking it but fearful that if they leave no one else will employ them and they will be on the scrap heap. Some live in constant fear that the company will restructure and their job will disappear: Not only are they in prison, but they are on Death Row, not yet finally condemned but ever fearful of the end of their careers.

Imprisonment imagery is not uncommon in career studies, and one aim of this book, regardless of the power of social structure to constrain and even imprison careers, should be to empower you and those you advise to be constantly vigilant of the dangers of career imprisonment and resourceful in avoiding and escaping prisonlike careers.

Inheritance and Social Structure

Inheritance can be mysterious and apparently unstructured: One study, for example, shows that we may even inherit careers from our names—for example, people named Denis or Denise are disproportionately more likely to become dentists, a fact due, according to the authors, to people's implicit egotism (Pelham, Mirenberg, & Jones, 2002).

More generally, however, the rules of career inheritance are more obvious. In the remaining sections of this chapter, we look at some of the main features of social structure—social class, including wealth and occupational structures; education; gender; ethnicity; and family background—to explore their effects on careers.

Social Class

Social class is based on the existence, in every society, of structured inequalities in wealth; earnings; power, prestige; and access to medical care, education, housing, and social welfare—which systematically favor certain individuals. Social class is relevant to a discussion of careers because these differences affect a person's career opportunities.

Henslin (1997) provided an example of a visit to a shelter for the homeless in New Orleans:

> The shelter was the same as those I had visited [elsewhere], only dirtier. The dirt, in fact was the worst I had encountered in my research, and this was the only shelter to insist on payment to sleep in one of its filthy beds. The men looked the same—disheveled and haggard, wearing that unmistakable expression of despair—just like the homeless anywhere. . . . Poverty wears the same tired face.
>
> Next morning, just a block away from the shelter . . . huge posters . . . advertising wares available nearby, glared at me, obscenely out of joint with the reality of despair I had just left. Almost life-sized pictures portrayed finely dressed men and women, proudly strutting in elegant suits, dresses, jewellery, and furs. The prices were astounding—perhaps not just to some, but certainly to the homeless I had just left.
>
> Occasionally the facts of social class hit home with brute force. This was one of those moments. (p. 252)

Many sociologists agree that differences in social class exist and that it is best conceptualized as a set of layers—like geographical strata—which would place Henslin's New Orleans homeless on the lowest stratum and the well-heeled consumers in the posters somewhere near the top. However, there is less agreement as to how social class should be defined and measured. Karl Marx believed that class was determined largely by *wealth*—the ownership of property (Marx & Engels, 1848/1967). Weber (1922/1978) took the more sophisticated view that the possession of particular skills and qualifications might be as important as property wealth in determining the life chances of individuals. A third possibility is that class is based on power, but of course power may simply be a product of wealth or of skills and qualifications. All three variables tend, in fact, to be intercorrelated.

Authorities also differ on how many categories need to be used to provide a good description of class differences. For example one schema, shown in Table 2.1, divides the U.S. population into six classes—a capitalist class, two distinct middle classes, and three working classes.

Notice a few things about this table. First, there are several different criteria of class. Second, the criteria may be related to each other—for example, those in particular jobs will receive higher income, but the relationships will be far from perfect, and this may make individuals hard to classify exactly. Third, occupation is an important criterion of social class. In relation to careers, this is important because it implies that people's career choices, the type of occupation they pursue and the income they are able to earn, help to fix their social class. For example, when a factory worker's daughter becomes a medical doctor, the associated changes in her education and income also tend to redefine her in social class terms.

Sociologists have long used occupation as a proxy for social class (Goldthorpe, Lewellyn, & Payne, 1980; Treiman, 1977). There is wide agreement in society about the relative status of different occupations. Faced with the occupations of secretary, truck driver, judge, high school teacher, and street sweeper, most people would rank them in order of prestige: judge, high school teacher, secretary, truck driver, street sweeper. Such rankings are relatively consistent over time and across different

Table 2.1   The U.S. Social Class System

Social Class	Education	Occupation	Income	% of Population
Capitalist	Prestigious university	Investors, owners, executives	$500K+	1%
Upper middle	College or university, often postgraduate	Professionals, upper managers	$90K+	14%
Lower middle	High school, possibly college	Semiprofessionals, lower managers, craftspeople	About $40K	30%
Working class	High school	Factory and clerical workers, retail salespeople	About $30K	30%
Working poor	Some high school	Laborers, service workers, low-paid workers	About $18K	22%
Underclass	Some high school	Unemployed, on welfare	About $10K	3%

countries. Required education and skill level are associated with occupations. Professional and managerial jobs requiring substantial education and receiving high remuneration are everywhere classified near the top, and unskilled manual jobs toward the bottom.

Observation of others' occupations enables us, if we wish, to gauge roughly the class status or location on society's pecking order of each of our friends, neighbors, and acquaintances. *Status anxiety*—the desire to gain self-esteem, to mark oneself as superior or at least equal to others—affects most of us (De Botton, 2004). The question asked soon after meeting someone for the first time, "And what do you do?", may be an innocent conversational gambit or a means of gaining a quick estimate of the other person's status in society.

Children are assumed to belong to the same social class as their parents. Thus, a judge's child would be viewed as a person from an upper class or upper middle-class home or from a privileged background. Such categorizations were, however, easier to apply 50 years ago, when most families were nuclear and had a sole, or main, breadwinner, the father, whose occupation was treated as a proxy for class or status. How do we classify a family in which the mother is a lawyer and the mother's new partner is a janitor?

In terms of career metaphors, we can treat the social class of people as they prepare for their career and commence it as part of their inheritance. Note that our concept of class includes wealth, income, education, and occupation. Each of these can play a vital part in influencing the career chances of the individual. Parents' money can be used to buy their children a superior education or influential contacts or polished manners or even a business. Parents' education and their practice of superior occupations give them important knowledge, insight, values, contacts, and communication skills, which they can pass on to their children and use themselves to provide opportunities for their children. Moreover, middle-class family backgrounds typically involve and provide higher aspirations, particularly for personal achievement, than do working-class backgrounds. All these mechanisms tend to give the higher classes more of a flying start in their careers.

Social Mobility

All this makes it clear that the (family-determined) social class or status of an individual at the start of his or her career is likely to play a major part in the final level that the person reaches. But everyday observation tells us that it is not an all-powerful determining factor. We all know, or know of, people who have been outstandingly successful despite their underprivileged backgrounds. Bill Clinton, U.S. president from 1993–2001, is an example. And we all know of people who come from family backgrounds of great wealth and privilege but who are relative failures in their careers. People can be *socially mobile*—that is, they can move from one social class or level to another (Blau & Duncan, 1967). Such changes may be due to other aspects of their inheritance, such as the innate abilities, aptitudes, and personality characteristics they inherit genetically, or to ambitions or work habits developed in childhood or to simple good or bad luck.

Of particular importance for career studies in the notion of *intergenerational mobility*—the change of social class made by family members from one generation to the next. If social class were all-powerful, then we would expect it to be frozen across generations. For example, the children of lower middle-class parents would always remain in the lower middle class, generation after generation. The higher the level of intergenerational mobility, the lower the influence of class. A popular view is that as society becomes more egalitarian (i.e., provides chances more equally) or more meritocratic (i.e., provides changes on the basis of merit or ability rather than on the basis of class or status), social class will become less important and intergenerational mobility will increase.

In fact, the position is complicated by the changing occupational patterns and class structures of society. In most developed countries, there have been fundamental changes. Many manual jobs have been automated and restructured out of existence; new skilled occupations, particularly those connected with telecommunications, information technology, and professional services, have grown rapidly; industries such as financial services have dramatically increased the demand for skilled professional staff; larger proportions of the population have undertaken tertiary education; and the average income and level of affluence have increased. This *structural mobility* tends to change the class structure—or at least the proportion of people who belong in each specific class—over time. Thus, upward intergenerational mobility becomes more likely, and downward mobility less likely, as time goes by. Featherman and Hauser (1978), for example, demonstrated that half of all sons eventually moved above their fathers in social status, whereas only a sixth moved below.

Education

In their authoritative review of sociological factors affecting careers, Johnson and Mortimer (2002) paid particular attention to education. They noted, for example, that national education systems differ markedly, for example, in the extent to which they educate by means of generalist versus vocational courses. Because U.S. schools have generalist programs, students tend to move around more in the early stages of their careers than their counterparts in countries such as Germany, whose education is more specialized. Access to good education and attainment within it are influenced by other aspects of inheritance, such as parental wealth. Even in the first grade, children from higher socioeconomic groups perform better (Entwisle & Alexander, 1993), and these early differences may become exaggerated over time as continuing differences in quality of education kick in (Kerckhoff, 1995). Not only one's own socioeconomic status but also that of one's fellow students may affect outcomes (Lee & Bryk, 1989).

Many other factors over which individual students have no control have been shown to affect their educational attainment and thereby their careers (Johnson & Mortimer, 2002). In tertiary education, variations in college resources and reputation, teaching quality, and the presentation of specific disciplines continue to add to, subtract from, or change the inheritance that people bring into their careers.

Race

Another factor, clearly inherited and clearly affecting career opportunities, is race. For example, in the United States more than double the proportion of African Americans are unemployed as Whites, and more than three times as many are below the poverty line. Internationally, there is good evidence that immigrants, even those with good qualifications and career backgrounds, are often employed to fill relatively unskilled and casual positions. Employment discrimination against particular racial groups clearly exists; however, there is debate as to whether the failure of certain racial groups to advance is due mainly to their race or to the commonly associated feature of their typically lower class status, which might apply whatever their race (Wilson, 1981).

To examine the kinds of effects that an adverse inheritance of class, race, and education may have on a person's career, consider Troy's case.

From Job to Job to Job

Troy was from a dark-skinned ethnic minority. His background involved poverty and crime. Living at home with his parents, he felt an obligation to pay for his keep, and he left school as soon as he could. His first job was dirty, unskilled work in a chicken factory. However, after 3 years he showed enough perseverance to be promoted to supervisor. One day, because he was keen on his work, he turned up at the factory early for work: The manager assumed he had come to steal and fired him. Not knowing how to oppose an unfair dismissal, and now with a girlfriend and baby to support, Troy looked for another job, found one as a laborer in a metal processing factory, and stuck to it through 4 years of arduous work in hot, dirty conditions. However, the company relocated, and he was laid off. He was next hired as a garbage collector, employed to collect refuse around the streets, and has been in the job for several years. He enjoys his job and admires his boss, the owner/driver of the garbage truck. At 28 years of age, his aspirations are modest: to be a good "family man," stay together with his girlfriend and son, and keep working. He says the boss has promised to let him drive the garbage truck one day.

Source: Arthur et al. (1999).

On the face of it, Troy has much to commend him as a worker: He is steadily employed, meets family obligations, and shows more loyalty to his employers than they show to him. But his inheritance—his ethnic origins, working-class status, lack of family role models, lack of education—appear to limit his career ambition and development and mark him for a questionable career future.

Gender

Most of us are born unambiguously either male or female. That part of our inheritance remains with us for life and is likely to play a major part in the determination of our career paths. Biology determines that some tasks, such as the bearing and initial feeding of children, can only be performed by women. Differences in physical constitution and instinct encourage the gender segregation of tasks such as hunting and child rearing. From time immemorial, the gender segregation of work means gender inheritance has a major effect on the way people live their lives, including their working lives (Wright, 1997).

The development of industrial societies established patterns of rigid gender segregation. Basically, men engaged in paid work, whereas women supported their families through unpaid domestic labor. Women could be employed as paid workers in certain occupations—for example, low-skilled factory work, retail and domestic service, and, for a small number of better educated women, nursing and teaching. All other work, and particularly all managerial and professional work, was done by men. When women married, they were expected, and often compelled, to devote their working hours to the unpaid work of caring for their husband and family. Therefore, a typical female career might consist of a few years' work in a relatively junior capacity, followed by a lifetime as a "housewife." A few women who never married might pursue lifetime careers in paid work but could expect promotion only in exceptional cases. It is easy to see that if social class may have set major limits on the careers of many men, the combined effects of social class and gender must have seemed like a veritable straitjacket to independent-minded women.

During the 20th century, and particularly in its second half, what has been termed a *genderquake* took place (Wolf, 1993). Manufacturing—traditionally largely staffed by men—declined, and service work—where women arguably have greater interest and skills—increased. Women, including married women, increasingly entered the workforce. From being perhaps 20% of the total U.S. workforce in 1900 and 30% in 1950, by 2000 they had reached an estimated 48% (Henslin, 1997). Dual-career couples and families; working, single mothers; and multiple-career, reconstituted families became common. In that sense, women are no longer as constrained as they once were from following a full career in full-time work.

What has changed a lot less, however, is the practice of segregating jobs, occupations, and therefore careers into men's work and women's work and doing so in such a way that men continue to occupy most of the positions of power and authority in society and enjoy much higher earnings than women (according to one estimate, a third higher on average; U. S. Bureau of the Census, 2000). Some argue that the genderquake is illusory and that attitudes to women at work have changed little (Wilson, 1999).

The gender segregation of the labor market has two dimensions—horizontal and vertical (Hakim, 1979):

- *Horizontal segregation* divides work occupationally into men's jobs and women's jobs. Thus, in any developed society, we may expect more than two thirds of traveling salespeople, computer programmers, warehouse staff, police officers, medical doctors, lawyers, managers, skilled trade workers, and truck drivers to be men. But we can also expect most primary schoolteachers, nurses, midwives, sewing machine operators, checkout operators, secretarial and clerical workers, and retail shop assistants to be women. In some of these occupations, the dominating gender may have more than 90% of the jobs. As an example, Table 2.2 indicates the gendering of various major occupational groups in the United Kingdom in 2001.
- *Vertical segregation* divides work hierarchically, into the more senior, responsible, and better paid jobs and the more junior, less responsible, and worse-paid jobs. Typically, men occupy the former types of jobs, and women occupy the latter. For example, in universities, it is common for women to have equal or greater numbers than men at the research assistant or assistant professor level but for men to dominate full professor, department chair, and dean positions. A prevailing theme in recent commentaries on the contemporary workplace is that of a glass ceiling in organizations: The glass ceiling allows women to see what goes on at the top of the organization that employs them but does not allow them to reach such positions (Cotter, Hermsen, Ovadia, & Vanneman, 2001; Morrison, 1992). For example, in 2005 only 9 out of 500 chief executive officers (CEOs) of the largest companies in the United States were women ("Women CEOs of Fortune 500 Companies," 2005).

The combination of horizontal and vertical segregation gives rise to stereotypical authority relationships: the male manager dictating to the female secretary; the male doctor being assisted by the female nurse; the male lawyer giving instructions to the female legal assistant. RosaBeth Moss Kanter's book *Men and Women of the Corporation* (1977) provides classic evidence of the careers of both managers' secretaries and managers' wives being largely determined by the success of their bosses/husbands. Again, these barriers to occupation, even in today's liberated world, can lead to women consistently underestimating their career potential and men failing to consider particular "female" occupations to which they may be ideally suited.

How does gender segregation arise in occupations? Again it is likely that both field and habitus are involved. In the field, structural differences in terms of gender segregation continue from the past, through inertia, tradition, prejudice, and the conscious or unconscious desire of men to protect their relatively privileged position. From an early age, children's thinking is colored by what they see around them

Table 2.2   Employees of Working Age, by Gender, United Kingdom, 2001

Occupation	Men (%)	Women (%)
Managers and senior officials	18	8
Professional occupations	13	11
Associate professional and technical	13	13
Administrative and secretarial	6	24
Personal service	2	13
Sales and customer service	5	13
Skilled trades	17	2
Machine operatives	13	3
Elementary occupations (unskilled)	13	12
TOTAL	100	100

Source: Fulcher & Scott (2003, p. 627).

and incorporate into their developing habitus: The person who looks after them most at home is a woman; the person who comes home from work is a man; their kindergarten and primary teachers are typically women; the sports stars and senior managers and police officers they see on television are typically men. And so it goes. However much their parents may encourage them to believe that gender doesn't make a difference or that "girls can do anything," the evidence before their eyes tells a different story (e.g., Barak, Feldman, & Noy, 1991).

The effects of gender are combined with those of status in the form of *cognitive maps,* in which the locations of occupations are structured against the dimensions of prestige and masculine/feminine sextype (Gottfredson, 1981). One map is shown in Figure 2.1. According to Gottfredson, such maps are common to people from all walks of life and are gradually assembled by children as they develop. Basically, such maps represent a kind of consensus career habitus.

Gender segregation and stereotyping appear to be declining but to a limited extent. There has, for example, been a huge growth in the number of women moving into management in recent years, yet women appear still to be constrained from reaching the highest levels and are paid less than their male counterparts (McDonald, 2004; Powell & Graves, 2003; Rosener, 1997). Many more women have become entrepreneurs (Weiler & Bernasek, 2001). Smaller numbers of women have colonized male bastions, such as engineering, science, law, the police force, and the armed services. Psychologically, things are changing, too. Young women are more self-confident about their careers and willing to consider a much wider range of options (Burke, 2001). Ultimately, the problem of attracting men to "feminine" careers, such as preschool and primary teaching, may be a bigger problem (Cushman, 2005).

Gender affects careers in additional ways, such as occupational segregation. For example, women differ from men in their patterns of career development and

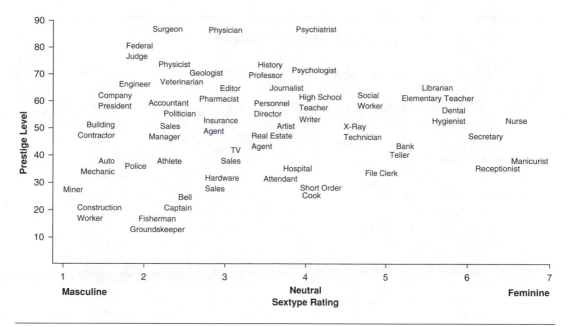

Figure 2.1   Map of Occupations According to Prestige and Sextype Ratings

Source: From Gottfredson (1981). Copyright ©1981 by the American Psychological Association. Adapted with permission.

energy over time (see Chapter 3) and in their patterns of mobility within and between organizations (Valcour & Tolbert, 2003). Such differences are caused in part by women's special responsibility for child rearing and by their tendency to be marginalized in the workforce for long periods of their careers.

Sexual orientation also affects careers. Even though equal opportunities legislation supposedly protects gay and lesbian workers, they often face complex and subtle forms of discrimination and differential treatment in the workplace (Humphrey, 1999) leading to limitations on their career aspirations (Niesche, 2003). However, the relationships here are complex: For example, Peplau and Fingerhut (2004) demonstrate that lesbian women typically have higher earnings than their heterosexual female peers, possibly because of lesbians' greater need to provide for their children.

Careers and Family

Are our careers, literally, inherited from our parents (Goodale & Hall, 1976)? Do they run in families? Do we tend to repeat the occupations followed by our parents? Can you see any such patterns in your own family?

There is substantial evidence that career development commences in childhood (Watson & McMahon, 2005). Specifically, parents intervene actively in their children's career development (Young & Friesen, 1992). Consider the following case.

An Inherited Career

My grandfather, James Inkson, was a retail butcher. In the early 20th century, he owned a shop in Aberdeen, Scotland, where he would receive livestock or carcasses, butcher them on the premises, turn them into steaks or flaps or sausages, and sell them to local customers.

He had two sons, James (Jimmy) and John. Both lived over the shop as they grew up and worked in the shop or delivered meat to customers. The younger son, John (my father), was academically gifted: From an early age, his father earmarked him for a professional occupation. The family scrimped and saved so that he could go to a local private school. He became a schoolteacher.

Jimmy, the elder son, had no such pretensions, and when he was 12 years old, his father apprenticed him to the butcher's trade. Jimmy spent most of his career in the shop. When Jimmy finished his apprenticeship, his father made him a paid employee. After retiring, Jimmy's father made him the manager of the shop. When his father died, Jimmy inherited the shop. Later, business declined and the shop was sold, but Jimmy continued to work as a butcher—his only real skill—for other employers until he retired. He died a few years later of chronic bronchitis, probably contracted over the years in the cold, damp conditions in which he had spent his life's work.

Source: Kerr Inkson, personal reminiscence.

Jimmy Inkson was a classic case of career inheritance from the family. His childhood socialization, preemployment experiences, and male role models were all about the butcher's trade. One wonders whether he ever considered any other kind of career and what his family would have thought if he had suggested it. In turn, he inherited his father's trade, jobs, and business. It was truly a family career.

Such examples are common. Another is the example of well-known media tycoon Rupert Murdoch, whose father was successively a journalist, an editor, an acquisitions manager, and a newspaper owner in Australia. Murdoch received early experience in journalism, editing, and newspaper management, and, in a more lateral leap, broadcasting, from an early age, and subsequently became a dominant force in the media industries of Australia, the United Kingdom, and the United States (Anand, Peiperl, & Arthur, 2002; Shawcross, 1997). In 2005, with Rupert Murdoch still active but in his 70s, his son Lachlan, who appeared to have inherited much of his father's business and position in society, unexpectedly resigned from his father's organization to pursue a different lifestyle (Higgins, 2005)—perhaps a classic example of the reaction of individual action against predetermined structures (see Chapter 4).

From what has already been said, it is apparent that the social class of a family can directly influence the education and types of occupation (e.g., white collar versus blue collar) pursued by its members. Parents, particularly fathers who are psychologically close to their children, inculcate particular values related to career aspirations and occupational choice (Hoffman, Hofacker, & Goldsmith, 1991; Johnson, 2001). The 20th-century loss of employment on farms and indeed the loss of small family farms broke up long intergenerational patterns of the inheritance of farming careers (Elder, Rudkin, & Conger, 1995). There is evidence that the children of self-employed parents also tend to become self-employed (Moore, 2000; Mulholland, 2003). Bear in mind, though, that the correlations between the occupations of parents and those of their children, although positive, tend to be modest: There is still plenty of scope for people to take up careers quite unlike their parents'. The following case is a poignant example of a long-term and wholly positive inheritance of occupation.

Inheriting His Father's Mantle

Donald Poulson (1910–1989) was a geneticist and professor and later emeritus professor of biology at Yale University. His son Chris pursued a variety of nonacademic occupations before entering academia in middle age and becoming a professor of business management. In 2001, Chris recognized his father, the inheritance principle, and the whole human cycle of life and inheritance, in the following poem.

The earnest young man
Holding his pipe
Sitting in front of a wall
   of books
smiling slightly at the camera
becomes
An old man
Peering from unfocused eyes
Over a bushy white beard
Standing in academic robes
In front of the camera
On the day the son
Inherits his father's
   mantle.

The Return
Divesting myself of
boyhood attire
I ventured bare-backed
Into the adult world.
Hatless and coatless
I wandered abroad.
Gathering the unfamiliar attire
I covered myself
Until the child was
Unrecognizable in the man.
As the day wanes and
The chill of evening approaches,
I wrap myself in my father's cloak.

Source: Chris Poulson, by permission.

Perhaps more important than the influence of parents' occupations on their children's occupations is the link between parents' occupations and their children's habitus and thereby their career attitudes. Kohn and Schooler (1983), for example, argued that fathers' occupations critically influence the work values and career ambitions of their children. Parents' supportiveness in parent-child relationships also appears to facilitate self-confidence in children (Mortimer, Lorence, & Kumka, 1986). It may be that the best contribution this book can make to some of its readers is to ask them to research and practice career-enhancing behavior, appropriate to their roles as parents.

Inheritance and Childhood: Gottfredson's Theory

I have argued that your career inheritance is not just what you inherit at birth but what you inherit at birth plus the modifications and additions that have taken place to your initial inheritance by the time you start your career. A 16-year-old boy's burning ambition to be a steeplejack or a doctor may thus result from a complex combination of social structure variables (class, gender, etc.) and childhood reflection. In this case, the inheritance is strong and specific before the career even starts. Linda Gottfredson (1981, 2002) developed the most complete and persuasive theory of how this process operates.

Gottfredson's (2002) theory shows how career decisions and direction have a basis that is in part genetic:

> The genetic propensities with which we are born, including temperament, are the precursors of general personality and ability traits that will soon take form. These propensities act like a compass, inclining us toward, or away from, possible forms of experience . . . (for example, risky versus safe, people-related versus things-related). . . . This compass colors our past experiences and influences our future choices. . . . In other words, nature activates and develops nurture. (p. 117)

According to Gottfredson, as genetic traits combine with ongoing experience, career interests and aspirations, and ultimately adult social niches, including those pertaining to careers, are framed in childhood. Thus, the theory combines three of the metaphors on which this book is based:

- The "inheritance" metaphor outlined in this chapter
- The "fit" metaphor (Chapter 5), which essentially views careers as a process of fitting oneself to congruent work positions
- The "cycle" metaphor (Chapter 3), which describes characteristic cycles of development through which we inevitably pass as our careers progress

Essentially, Gottfredson (2002) stated that as children mature they gradually become more aware of their inheritance of class, gender, and so forth and that affects their interaction with the world of work. To find a good fit between themselves and the environment, children gradually refine their choices to take more account of different aspects of their inheritance. From age 3 years to the late teens, the process plays itself out along a predictable cycle of stages as different aspects of inheritance: For example, children become aware of sex role differentiation early (at age 6 to 8 years) before they pay much attention to social class (age 9 to 13 years).

Gottfredson (2002) showed that occupations can be mapped according to prestige (e.g., the social-class scales mentioned earlier) and masculinity/femininity.

For example, librarian is a high-prestige, feminine job, whereas construction worker is a relatively low-prestige, masculine job. Children then begin to assess the compatibility of jobs with their own self-concept of their social class, gender, and personal characteristics.

Gottfredson (2002) referred to her theory as a "theory of circumscription, compromise, and self-creation." Circumscription involves the progressive development of a zone of acceptable alternatives defined by boundaries relating to the prestige and sextype of the occupation, as shown in Figure 2.2. The upper prestige boundary—the tolerable-effort boundary—is determined by the amount of effort a person is willing to exercise in pursuit of a desired high-prestige occupation, and the lower one—the tolerable-level boundary—is determined by the lowest level of prestige the person is willing to accept. The tolerable-sextype boundary reflects the degree of masculinity or femininity of occupation the person will accept. The theory is thus a theory of acceptable career boundaries.

Circumscription—literally "laying down limits, confining, restricting" (Allen, 1990)—means narrowing the zone from which acceptable occupations can be chosen by eliminating unacceptable alternatives, a characteristic of children ages 3

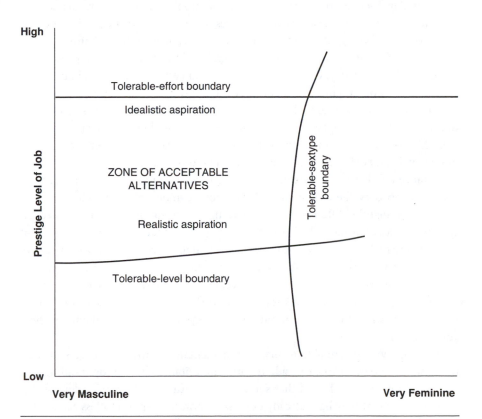

Figure 2.2   Circumscription of Aspirations for a Hypothetical Middle-Class Boy of Average Intelligence

Source: From Gottfredson (1981). Copyright © 1981 by the American Psychological Association. Reproduced with permission.

to 13 years. Compromise, characteristic of adolescents older than 13 years, further reduces the list of alternatives within the zone due to teens' greater realism and enables them to focus instead on less acceptable but more accessible options.

In some respects, particularly in its attention to self-concept, fit, and stages of development in career thinking, Gottfredson's (1981) theory resembles developmental theories, such as that of Super (1957; see Chapter 3). The difference is that Gottfredson "views vocational choice first as an implementation of the social self and only secondarily as an implementation of the psychological self" (Swanson & Fouad, 1999, p. 86). That is, Gottfredson differs from many career theorists in the attention she pays to the constraints of inheritance and the way that these constraints are played out in, and influence, the habitus of the child.

Conclusion

Curiously, the inheritance principle, and particularly the effects of social structure, innate characteristics, and parental influence, plays little part in most careers textbooks. It plays even less of a part in most popular books that tell us how to plan and conduct our careers. In a society that believes in equal opportunity, it is almost as if we don't like looking at something that implies privilege in life's chances.

But the effects of inheritance can't be ignored, and there are plenty of people who recognize these effects and try to redress the balance through political and social activism. The women's movement, poverty action groups, adult literacy campaigns, and political movements aimed at redistributing wealth are all examples of attempts to improve the career opportunities of those whose only inheritance appears to be debt. Many sociologists and activists believe that inequality is so deeply embedded in society that there is little individuals can do to remove the crushing weight of their inheritance and base their careers on agency. Fundamental, redemptive change in society is necessary, these critics say, before careers can be truly liberated.

I take a slightly different view. Inheritance is a significant factor affecting careers, but it is not the only factor. Most people find that life is too short to wait for fundamental social change to take care of their careers. Many with negative inheritances are nevertheless able to overcome them (see Chapter 4). It may be a good idea at least to know your inheritance, to understand where you come from and what that means, and to look for ways to work with the positives in your inheritance and to strive to look the negatives in the eye and overcome them—or help your children to do so.

Many individuals are able to make fundamental, redemptive changes in their lives that enable them to cast aside negative inheritances and enjoy fulfilling and successful careers. It is hoped that some of the mature, midcareer readers of this book will feel that they have already done so; if not, they are doubtless acquainted with friends who have. Some people, like Nita described earlier in this chapter, go further and make it a personal mission to seek social change that can enhance the career prospects of others. Other chapters in this book balance the account by showing how even good inheritances may be wasted.

Key Points in This Chapter

- Observation of careers shows great inequalities apparently based on different forms of privilege. Careers are often affected by social structures in the wider society, which are balanced against individual action or agency.
- The sociological concepts of field and habitus help to explain how structure affects careers. Fields impose structural constraints on career behavior, and habitus is a worldview that determines how individuals respond to the constraints.
- Careers at all levels can become "prisons," both through their employment structures and through individuals' responses.
- Social class is based on differences in wealth, skills and qualifications, and power. It is inherited in careers and affects them because it is occupationally based and because it tends to persist through different generations of the same family.
- Other structural factors affecting career opportunities are race, education, and gender. Gender segregates careers both vertically and horizontally.
- Careers and career-related opportunities, aptitudes, and attitudes may be passed on in families.
- Gottfredson's theory of circumscription, compromise, and self-creation shows how structural factors are learned in children's concepts of their careers.

Questions From This Chapter

General Questions

1. In Britain, the monarchy is inherited. In the United States, the presidency is elected. But did George W. Bush, elected president 2001–2009, inherit the job from his father George Bush, president 1989–1993? Justify your answer.

2. Identify two or three well-known people you admire. Use the Internet to find out more about their backgrounds. To what extent do you think they inherited their careers?

3. In looking at your own career, past, present, or future, what aspects of field and habitus can you identify?

4. Do you believe career opportunities are becoming more or less affected by structural factors, such as social class, as time goes by? Justify your answer.

5. Think about your family. What aspects of your career, if any, have you inherited, or are you likely to inherit, from them?

6. Overall, do you think your career inheritance is positive or negative? What can you do to build on it or overcome it?

Career Case Study Questions

1. What are the origins of your case person in terms of social class, ethnic origin, gender, and education? How have these affected the case person's career?

2.. Has your case person ever felt imprisoned or constrained in his or her career? How did this come about?

References

Allen, R. E. (Ed.). (1990). *Concise Oxford dictionary* (8th ed.). Oxford, UK: Clarendon Press.

Anand, N., Peiperl, M. A., & Arthur, M. B. (2002). Introducing career creativity. In M. Peiperl, M. B. Arthur, & N. Anand (Eds.), *Career creativity: Explorations in the remaking of work* (pp. 1-11). Oxford, UK: Oxford University Press.

Arthur, M. B., Inkson, K., & Pringle, J. K. (1999). *The new careers: Individual action and economic change.* Thousand Oaks, CA: Sage.

Barak, A., Feldman, S., & Noy, A. (1991). Traditionality of children's interests as related to their parents' gender stereotypes and traditionality of occupations. *Sex Roles, 26,* 511-524.

Bardsley, P., & Sherstyuk, K. (2001). *Rat races and glass ceilings: Career paths in organisations.* Parkville, Victoria, Australia: University of Melbourne.

Blau, P. M., & Duncan, O. D. (1967). *The American occupational structure.* New York: Wiley.

Burke, R. (Ed.). (2001). *Advancing women's careers: Research and practice.* Malden, MA: Blackwell.

Cappelli, P. (2000). A market-driven approach to retaining talent. *Harvard Business Review, 78*(1), 103-111.

Cotter, D. A., Hermsen, J. M., Ovadia, S., & Vanneman, R. (2001). The glass ceiling effect. *Social Forces, 80*(2), 655-681.

Cushman, P. (2005). Let's hear it from the males: Issues facing male primary school teachers. *Teaching and Teacher Education, 21*(3), 227-240.

De Botton, A. (2004). *Status anxiety.* New York: Pantheon Books.

Elder, G. H., Rudkin, L., & Conger, R. D. (1995). Intergenerational continuity and change in rural America. In V. L. Bengston, K. Warner Schaie, & Linda M. Burton (Eds.), *Adult intergenerational relations: Effects of societal change* (pp. 30-60). New York: Springer.

El-Sawad, A. (2005). Becoming a "lifer": Unlocking career thought through metaphor. *Journal of Occupational and Organizational Psychology, 78*(1), 23-41.

Entwisle, D. R., & Alexander, K. L. (1993). Entry into school: The beginning of school transition and educational stratification in the United States. *Annual Review of Sociology, 19,* 401-423.

Featherman, D. L., & Hauser, R. M. (1978). *Opportunity and change.* New York: Academic Press.

Feldman, D.C. (2004). The role of physical disabilities in early career: Vocational choice, the school-to-work transition, and becoming established. *Human Resource Management Review, 14*(3), 247-274.

Fulcher, J., & Scott, J. (2003). *Sociology.* New York: Oxford University Press.

Ghurye, G. (1961). *Caste and race in India.* Bombay, India: Popular Book Depot.

Goldthorpe, J. H., Lewellyn, C., & Payne, C. (1980). *Social mobility and class structure in modern Britain.* Oxford, UK: Clarendon Press.

Goodale, J. G., & Hall, D. T. (1976). On inheriting a career: The influence of sex, values, and parents. *Journal of Vocational Behavior, 8*, 19-30.

Gottfredson, L. S. (1981). Circumscription and compromise: A developmental theory of occupational aspirations. *Journal of Counseling Psychology, 28*, 545-579.

Gottfredson, L. S. (2002). Gottfredson's theory of circumscription, compromise and self-creation. In D. Brown & Associates, *Career choice and development* (4th ed., pp. 85-148). San Francisco: Jossey-Bass.

Hakim, C. (1979). *Occupational segregation.* London: Department of Labour.

Henslin, J. M. (1997). *Sociology: A down-to-earth approach* (3rd ed.). Boston: Allyn & Bacon.

Hicks Stiehm, J. (Ed.). (1996). *It's our military too! Women and the U.S. military.* Philadelphia: Temple University Press.

Higgins, J. M. (2005). Lachlan Murdoch resigns. *Broadcasting and Cable, 135*(31), 6.

Hoffman, J. C., Hofacker, C., & Goldsmith, E. B. (1991). How closeness affects parental influence on business students' career choices. *Journal of Career Development, 19*, 65-73.

Humphrey, J. C. (1999). Organizing sexualities, organized inequalities: Lesbians and gay men in public service occupations. *Gender, Work and Organization, 6*(3), 134-151.

Johnson, M. K. (2001). Changes in job values during the transition to adulthood. *Work and Occupations, 28*, 315-345.

Johnson, M. K., & Mortimer, J. T. (2002). Career choice and development from a sociological perspective. In D. Brown & Associates (Eds.), *Career choice and development* (4th ed., pp. 37-81). San Francisco: Jossey-Bass.

Judge, T. A., & Cable, D. M. (2004). The effect of physical height on workplace success and income: Preliminary test of a theoretical model. *Journal of Applied Psychology, 89*(3), 428-441.

Kanter, R. M. (1977). *Men and women of the corporation.* New York: Basic Books.

Kerckhoff, A. C. (1995). Institutional arrangements and stratification processes in industrial societies. *Annual Review of Sociology, 15*, 323-347.

Kluegel, J. R., & Smith, E. R. (1986). *Beliefs about inequality: America's beliefs in what is and what ought to be.* Hawthorne, NY: de Gruyter.

Kohn, M., & Schooler, C. (1983). *Work and personality: An inquiry into the impact of social stratification.* Norwood, NJ: Ablex.

Ledwith, S., & Colgan, F. (1996). *Women in organizations: Challenging gender politics.* Basingstoke, UK: Macmillan Business.

Lee, V. E., & Bryk, A. S. (1989). A multilevel model of the social distribution of high school achievement. *Sociology of Education, 62*, 172-192.

Marx, K., & Engels, F. (1967). *The communist manifesto.* Harmondsworth, UK: Penguin. (Original work published 1848)

Mayrhofer, W., Iellatchitch, A., Meyer, M., Steyrer, J., Schiffinger, M., & Strunk, G. A. (2004). Going beyond the individual: Some potential contributions from a career field and habitus perspective for global career research and practice. *Journal of Management Development, 23*(9), 870-884.

McDonald, I. (2004). Women in management: An historical perspective. *Employee Relations, 26*(3), 307-319.

Moore, D. P. (2000). *Careerpreneurs: Lessons from leading women entrepreneurs on building a career without boundaries.* Palo Alto, CA: Davies-Black Publishers.

Morgan, R. (Ed.). (2003). *Sisterhood is forever: The women's anthology for a new millennium.* New York: Washington Square Press.

Morrison, A. (1992). *Breaking the glass ceiling.* Reading, MA: Addison Wesley.

Mortimer, J. T., Lorence, J., & Kumka, D. (1986). *Work, family and personality: Transition to adulthood.* Norwood, NJ: Ablex.

Mulholland, K. (2003). *Class, gender and the family business.* New York: Palgrave Macmillan.

Neische, R. (2003). Power and homosexuality in the teaching workplace. *Social Alternatives, 22*(2), 43-47.

Palley, T. (2002). The child labor problem and the need for international labor standards. *Journal of Economic Issues, 36*(3), 601-615.

Parsons, F. (1909). *Choosing a vocation.* Boston: Houghton Mifflin.

Peiperl, M. A., & Arthur, M. P. (2000). Topics for conversation: Career themes old and new. In M. A. Peiperl, M. B. Arthur, R. Goffee, & T. Morris (Eds.), *Career frontiers: New conceptions of working lives* (pp. 1-19). Oxford, UK: Oxford University Press.

Pelham, B. W., Mirenberg, M. C., & Jones, J. T. (2002). Why Susie sells seashells by the sea-shore: Implicit egotism and major life decisions. *Journal of Personality and Social Psychology, 82*(4), 469-487.

Peplau, L. A., & Fingerhut, A. (2004). The paradox of the lesbian worker. *Journal of Social Issues, 60*(4), 719-735.

Persico, J. E., & Powell, C. L. (1995). *My American journey: An autobiography.* New York: Random House.

Powell, G. N., & Graves, L. M. (2003). *Women and men in management* (3rd ed.). Thousand Oaks, CA: Sage.

Rosenbaum, J. E. (1984). *Career mobility in a corporate hierarchy.* New York: Academic Press.

Rosener, J. B. (1997). *America's competitive secret: Women managers.* New York: Oxford University Press.

Scholl, M. B. (1999). A career path tournament: Developing awareness of sociological barriers to career advancement. *Career Development Quarterly, 47*(3), 230-242.

Shawcross, W. (1997). *Murdoch: The making of a media empire.* New York: Touchstone.

Super, D. E. (1957). *The psychology of careers.* New York: Harper & Row.

Swanson, J. L., & Fouad, N. A. (1999). *Career theory and practice: Learning through case studies.* Thousand Oaks, CA: Sage.

Treiman, D. J. (1977). *Occupational prestige in comparative perspective.* New York: Academic Press.

U.S. Bureau of the Census. (2000). *Statistical abstract of the United States.* Washington, DC: U.S. Government Printing Office.

Valcour, P. M., & Tolbert, P. S. (2003). Gender, family and career in the era of boundaryless-ness: Determinants and effects of intra- and inter-organizational mobility. *International Journal of Human Resource Management, 14*(5), 768-787.

Wacquant, L. J. D. (1998). Pierre Bourdieu. In R. Stones (Ed.), *Key sociological thinkers* (pp. 215-229). New York: New York University Press.

Watson, M., & McMahon, M. (2005). Children's career development: A research review from a learning perspective. *Journal of Vocational Behavior, 67*(2), 119-132.

Weber, M. (1978). *Economy and society.* Berkeley: University of California Press. (Original work published 1922)

Weick, K. E. (1996). Enactment and the boundaryless career: Organizing as we work. In M. B. Arthur & D. M. Rousseau (Eds.), *The boundaryless career: A new employment principle for a new organizational era* (pp. 40-57). New York: Oxford University Press.

Weiler, S., & Bernasek, A. (2001). Dodging the glass ceiling? Networks and the new wave of women entrepreneurs. *Social Science Journal, 38*(1), 85-103.

Williams, R. (1965). *American society: A sociological interpretation* (2nd ed.). New York: Knopf.

Wilson, F. (1999). Genderquake? Did you feel the earth move? *Organization, 6*(3), 529-541.

Wilson, W. J. (1981). Race, class and public policy. *American Sociologist, 16,* 125-134.

Wolf, N. (1993). *Fire with fire: The new female power and how it will change the twenty-first century.* New York: Random House.

Women CEOs of Fortune 500 companies. (2005, April). *Money Magazine* [Electronic version]. Retrieved February 8, 2006, from http://money.cnn.com/magazines/fortune/fortune 500/womenceos/

Wright, R. (1997). Occupational gender in women's and men's occupations. *Qualitative Sociology, 20*(3), 437-442.

Young, R. A., & Friesen, J. D. (1992). The intentions of parents in influencing the career development of their children. *Career Development Quarterly, 40,* 198-207.

CHAPTER 3

Careers as Cycles

Not Making It

Fifty-year-old Perry is thinking about his career. He has a career problem. Or has he? The problem he thinks he has is that, in the past 7 years since being promoted to manager of the small claims department at the local branch of the Phoenix Insurance Company, he has been offered no further promotions. Every year, he receives a good performance evaluation from his manager, but never is it suggested—as it always was in the past, every 2 or 3 years—that he is ready for the next step up. Perry long ago set his sights on getting to the top, and now he is beginning to wonder if he will ever make it.

The reason his lack of promotion may not be a problem is that in other ways things are going well for Perry. His present job is congenial, sociable, and not too hard. The company seems secure. His children have grown and left home and are doing well. He and his wife, Josie, a kindergarten teacher, have a nice house and have paid it off. They have a good social life. They go square dancing twice a week and often have friends or family visit for dinner. Perry is also active in local sports groups.

Promotion now would bring Perry more money, but it would also bring more responsibility. He would have to go on out-of-town business trips more often, maybe work late sometimes. His and Josie's social life would suffer. They might even have to move to a different city. Although being bypassed for promotion is kind of humiliating, in a strange way it is also reassuring.

Perry reflects on his past hopes. When he graduated from college, he had fire in his belly. He promised Josie that nothing would stop him from becoming either a rich man or the boss of a big company by the time he was 40 years old. In his 20s, he worked enthusiastically to become self-sufficient, starting off a number of new small businesses, none of which made any money. He loved traveling, and they moved with their family from city to city. In the end, Josie, tired of trying to bring up children while living hand-to-mouth, more or less forced him to take his first job with Phoenix as an insurance salesman, buy the house, and settle down.

He turned out to be surprisingly good at selling and made a lot of money on commission very quickly. But after a few years, he tired of the stress of traveling and selling and resolved instead to climb the corporate ladder. He believed he was a leader and that he could get to the top. But there were others in the company, just as talented as he was, and perhaps even more determined, who seemed to get all the best breaks. Gradually, he lowered his ambitions. And now, here he is, basically not caring if he never gets offered another promotion! The young Perry, he reflects, would probably feel betrayed by the middle-aged Perry's lack of ambition. But the young Perry doesn't exist anymore, and the older Perry is content. Why put that contentment at risk by looking for more?

As Perry ages, his priorities change. In his 20s, he wanted to try new things and grow rich through them. In his 30s, he wanted to get to the top of his company. In his 40s, he developed a taste for a civilized leisure and social life and gradually lowered his career ambitions. As he enters his 50s, he appears to want little except continuation of the same. How typical is Perry of midcareer men, and indeed of midcareer women? How typical was the younger Perry of others of his generation? Will all of us experience burning ambition in our youth, followed by reduced energy and increased compromise as we age? Do we all go through similar cycles of commitment and experience in our careers?

Age/Stage Theory

According to *Webster's Dictionary,* a *cycle* is "a period of time in which a certain succession of events or phenomena is completed" (Thatcher & McQueen, 1981). Examples are the orbiting of the planets and the familiar academic year of enrollments, teaching periods, examinations, and vacations in the universities. The essence of cycles is that they are predictable and repeated. How well does the "cycle" metaphor fit careers?

The cycles that career theorists and researchers have mainly proposed are certainly predictable but not repeated—or at least not repeated in the same individual. Instead, it is suggested that career cycles can be generalized across individuals and that there are certain stages that all, or most, careers go through. In some theories, it is suggested that we can tie particular career stages to particular human ages, in what might be called an age/stage approach to understanding careers.

In thinking about career stages, we need to remember that our work careers are only one aspect of our day-to-day living. A career cycle is, perhaps, just one facet of a broader life cycle. Stages that underlie our careers are represented in other areas of our lives as well. For example, there are age-related patterns of development and decline in our physical strength, agility, fitness, and health, and these affect our careers (Rholes & Simpson, 2004). The traditional family cycle of marriage, child bearing, child rearing, and empty nest is also likely to impose on our careers

(Fitzgerald & Weitzman, 1992). Career cycles most likely arise as by-products of factors in our wider lives.

For many years, psychologists have taken a strong interest in patterns of human development. Initially, they tended to focus on sequences of intellectual, emotional, and social development in children. In the careers area, Walls (2000, p. 137) explored the development of *vocational cognition*—ways of understanding careers—from the 3rd to the 12th grade, and Gottfredson's (1981) theory of circumscription, compromise, and self-creation (Chapter 2) describes an age-related set of stages that children pass through in their thinking about different occupational choices. More recently, a new focus has developed regarding processes of adult and life-span development (Bee & Boyd, 2002; Cronin & Mandich, 2005). Career development is an important part of adult development.

Freudian psychologist Erik Erikson (1959) mapped eight stages of individual development, each with characteristic tasks mostly focused on childhood with some relevant to adult career issues. Erikson posited various dilemmas and tasks that people face at different times of their life. In adolescence, he said, we face an identity crisis as we endeavor to establish a clear sense of who we are: Early choices of education or occupation may well be part of that process, and there are twin risks of excessive confusion and overcommitment to a rigid identity. In our 20s and 30s, we try to resolve competing desires for intimacy and isolation, and again the resolution may be reflected in work-related behavior—for example, in viewing our career as an independent project (discussed in this book in Chapter 4) or as involvement in a network of relationships (discussed in Chapter 8). An important issue running through much of middle and later adulthood is that of stagnation versus generativity, the latter being an interest in developing something for the next generation, which is clearly relevant to the supervision and mentorship of others.

Can we divide our careers into predictable stages taking place at particular ages? If we can, it should make career planning easier. Potentially, the "cycle" metaphor supplements the "inheritance" metaphor (Chapter 2) by further confining the career within particular parameters. Age/stage theories tell us that we have particular ways of approaching our careers at different periods in our lives—for example, that we can expect the greatest desire to explore career options when young, expect major turbulence in our 40s, and then expect a slowing down of our energy and advancement when older. A career thus becomes a predictable sequence of events. Not everything we discover from age/stage theory may be palatable to us, but at least it tells us what to expect. So what do the theorists tell us?

Donald Super: A Theory of Career Development

Many theorists and researchers—for example, Baird and Kram (1983), Hall and Nougaim (1968), Schein (1978), Super (1957, 1990), and Savickas (2002)—have expounded career stage theories. All of these theories divide career development from birth to death into four to six stages. All except Baird and Kram indicated the ages at which the various stages start and finish and in some cases overlap. Most of the theories define the following terms:

- An *exploration* stage, commencing prior to the career
- An *establishment* phase, in which the career gets started
- A *progress* stage, in which the career generally advances
- A *maintenance* stage, when the career continues but progress slows
- A *retirement or disengagement* stage, when the career ends or winds down

Donald Super (1953, 1957, 1990) was the dominating figure in career development research in the 20th century and developed probably the most comprehensive theory of career development. Since Super's death in 1994, Mark Savickas (2002) has guarded, developed, and refined his long-standing and influential theory of vocational development.

Originally developed in a series of 10 propositions (Super, 1953), Super's theory was eventually expanded to 16 (Savickas, 2002, 2005; Super, Savickas, & Super, 1996). Reading these propositions in detail will repay the effort involved. Here, the following summary—based on Savickas (2005)—is offered:

- In Propositions 1–3, Super's theory focuses on the individual's life course through various social roles, such as work versus family. Work roles are focused on occupations, and career patterns through occupations are influenced by both social structure and personal characteristics.
- In Propositions 4–9, the theory focuses on the facts that people differ in vocational characteristics, such as abilities and personalities; that each occupation requires different vocational characteristics; that people seek outlets in their work for their characteristics; and that their satisfaction depends on the extent to which they are able to implement their vocational self-concept. The vocational self-concept is based on people's actions in relevant roles and their observation of the approval of others.
- Propositions 10–12, 15, and 16 describe a process of career construction in more detail. People implement their vocational self-concept by undertaking vocational tasks and through reflection, education, and role enactment. The self-concept changes over time but becomes increasingly stable as the individual progresses through a cycle of stages, labeled growth, exploration, establishment, maintenance or management, and disengagement. This "maxicycle," however, may be disrupted by "minicycles" that cover similar ministages, either between stages or triggered by events such as illnesses, layoffs, and job changes.
- Propositions 13 and 14 describe the constructs of *vocational maturity*— essentially progress through the various stages—and *career adaptability*— readiness to cope with current and anticipated tasks of vocational development.

It should be evident from this that while this chapter focuses on the part of Super's work that defined stages of career development, Super was much more than a theorist of the career cycle. Particularly in Propositions 1–3, his approach also recognized the limiting forces of inheritance and structure (dealt with through the "inheritance" metaphor; see Chapter 2 of this book) and the status of the career as a series of work roles that is part of a wider life space that also includes other roles, such as family roles ("role" metaphor; see Chapter 7). Propositions 4–8 stress the importance of vocational fit between individual and job ("fit" metaphor; see Chapter 5). The whole theory—particularly Propositions 9, 15, and 16—stresses the constructive role of the individual as builder of the career ("action" metaphor; see Chapter 4). So, although most attention has been paid to Super's conceptualization of career stages covered in Propositions 11 and 12, the stages suggested are only a small part of a much more comprehensive theory of career development.

The five stages of career development are summarized in Table 3.1. The essence of these is to enable appropriate ongoing interactions between the individual and the work roles that society creates. Essentially, said Super, the individual is implementing a self-concept by occupying a series of work roles created by society (Chapter 8). But each stage has different goals and different developmental tasks for the individual to undertake.

Table 3.1   Key Features of Career Stages Described by Super (1957) and Savickas (2002)

Age	Stage	Key Features
0–14 years	Growth	Childhood focus on the occupational world; development of concern about future as a worker, greater personal control over career activities, ideas about how to make choices, and confidence to do so
15–24 years	Exploration	Learning what one might become; exploring self (e.g., interests and abilities) and the world of work and occupations in depth and making tentative matches; making occupational choices in line with one's self-concept and actualizing these choices in career behavior; developing skills, experimenting with jobs, stabilizing a job to make it secure
25–44 years	Establishment	Ongoing implementation of self-concept to bring about integration of self, and own values, in society; stabilizing choice within organizational and occupational parameters, adjusting the self-concept if necessary; advancement or transfer to new or higher responsibility; toward the end of the stage, reflecting on the past and the future of the career
45–64 years	Maintenance*	Reflecting on the career and deciding on continuation or change; if change is necessary, recycling through the previous stages; holding steady in position, maintaining performance, conserving what has been accomplished, and remaining interested; renewing and innovating where possible
65 years and older	Disengagement	Adjusting to declining energy, decelerating, delegating to others, withdrawing, retiring, organizing a new life structure in which paid work is not central

Note: *Tentatively renamed "management" by Savickas (2002).

Reflections on Super's Theory

Super gathered plenty of observational data to justify his series of stages, and the idea of predictability in careers is appealing. However, as Arnold (1997) noted, empirical support for the general existence of career stages appears limited perhaps because the proposition that discernible stages exist is hard to test scientifically.

There may be something too rigid about the notion of such clearly defined stages. For example, Bejian and Salomone (1995) argued that under today's more fluid employment conditions there is typically an additional stage between the establishment and maintenance stages. These authors label the additional stage as "renewal" and perceive it as a confluence of Erikson's (1959) generativity versus stagnation and Levinson's (1986) midlife transition stages. More generally, it may be better to think of a career not as a series of discrete stages but as a gradual flow of development, with different tasks gradually acquiring and losing salience at different times. This is actually implicit in much of the writing of Super and Savickas.

The theory also seems idealistic: It seems to be more about the way that careers ought ideally to be or perhaps the way they were 50 years ago when the theory was first formulated rather than the way they are now. Careers nowadays seem more erratic (see Chapter 1). And the theory appears to fit the smooth progression of men through sequences of end-to-end full-time jobs more than the disrupted careers of women struggling to cope with family issues (Larwood & Gutek, 1987).

Against this, Savickas (2002) said that within the broader cycle of a person's overall career, "a mini-cycle of growth, exploration, establishment, management and disengagement occurs . . . each time an individual's career is destabilized by socio-economic and personal events" (Savickas, 2002, p. 156). This gives the theory greater flexibility in enabling cyclic careers to adapt to destabilizing events. It also helps us to see that the idea of cycle can apply to discrete events within the bigger cycle of the whole career, a point to which we will return later.

Most of the other age/stage conceptualizations mentioned earlier are not dissimilar to Super's. However, the greatest strength of his theory may be that it agrees with common sense and everyday observation. It acknowledges that different ages of life bring different challenges; although there are many exceptions, overall, people's careers do seem to start very exploratory and stabilize over time. Careers such as Perry's in the lead case in this chapter are very comprehensible as progressions through the stages, as suggested by Super. As Savickas (2002) stated, the theory thus provides a good retrospective explanation of many careers, and most of us would recognize the phenomena attributed to each stage as being characteristic of many people we know who are at the appropriate age.

Daniel Levinson: The Seasons of a Life

Another well-known protagonist of the age/stage view of careers is the psychologist Daniel Levinson, who with colleagues published *The Seasons of a Man's Life* (Levinson, Darrow, Klein, Levinson, & McKee, 1978; see also Levinson, 1986).

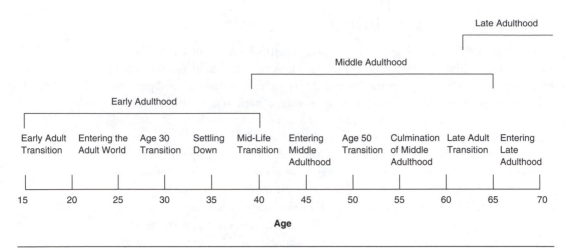

Figure 3.1   Levinson's Theory of Adult Development

Source: From *THE SEASONS OF A MAN'S LIFE* by Daniel Levinson © 1978 by Daniel J. Levinson. Used by permission of Alfred A. Knopf, a division of Random House, Inc.

The choice of "seasons" as a metaphor for human life is interesting, and it is easy to see parallels, in our careers, to the springtime when we sow seeds for the future, the summer of glowing success or parched failure, the fall when we harvest the fruits of the spring sowing, and the winter when our career dies.

The empirical basis for *The Seasons of a Man's Life* (Levinson et al., 1978) was a series of interviews with 40 American men, all between 35 and 45 years of age, 10 from each of four contrasting occupations: business executives, university-employed biologists, novelists, and factory workers. Each man was interviewed at least five times over a period of at least 2 months, and the database consisted of an average of 300 pages of data per man. Levinson was nothing if not thorough! Levinson also studied published biographies, enabling him to get a sense of stages of development of men beyond the age of 45 years.

On the basis of his data, Levinson divided men's lives into four stages—preadulthood, early adulthood, middle adulthood, and late adulthood—each linked to the previous and succeeding stages by a period of transition, as shown in Figure 3.1.

Adulthood is thus composed of relatively stable periods, in which the individual works at building a desired life structure, that alternate with shorter transitional periods of questioning, reappraisal, and often change. Table 3.2 indicates the main characteristics ascribed by Levinson to each period up to age 50 years.

Some features of Levinson's theory (Levinson et al., 1978) require further explanation. The Dream is a personal view of how one wants to live one's life, and what the main values are that one is pursuing. The Dream is often rooted in occupational ambitions. It is an essential preoccupation of early adulthood, a period that culminates, in the late 30s, with the BOOM (Becoming One's Own Man) phase, in which the individual's attempts to fulfill the Dream are particularly intense.

Table 3.2   Key Features of Life Stages Described by Levinson et al. (1978)

Age	Stage	Key Features
17–22 years	Early adult transition	Financial and emotional separation from parents; first attempts at adult roles
23–28 years	Entering the adult world	First stage of early adulthood; exploration of different roles while keeping options open; simultaneously trying to create a stable life structure
29–33 years	Age 30 transition	Reflection and possible redirection; reappraisal of current life structure, concern that it may soon be too late for radical change; focusing one's Dream (see text)
34–40 years	Settling down	Last stage of early adulthood; developing a life structure that supports the Dream; finding one's niche in work, family, and leisure; meeting society's expectations and timetables for career success; culminates in Becoming One's Own Man (BOOM; see text)
41–45 years	Midlife transition	Reappraisal of life structure: "What have I done with my life? What do I truly want?"; focused by observation of progress toward the Dream, perceptions of aging, and other changes in family; often results in personal crisis
46–50 years	Entering middle adulthood	Implementing decisions made in midlife transition

NOTE: This table does not go beyond age 50 years because Levinson did not study men older than that age.

Levinson et al.'s (1978) characterization of the early 40s as being a time of personal crisis resonates with the experiences of many middle-aged people and has entered popular consciousness as the midlife crisis. Levinson believed that such crises are triggered by factors such as feeling physically weaker, worrying about aging parents, and becoming more aware of one's own mortality. Some feel they have failed to fulfill their Dream and need to change. Others have climbed career ladders but worry that they have not made a lasting contribution of value. Similar questions may arise concerning family relationships. Individuals may react to the crisis in radical and sometimes painful ways.

Reflections on Levinson's Theory

Levinson et al.'s (1978) theory has the virtue of placing the work career within a cycle of wider events in the individual's life. The theory emphasizes the psychology of the individual and the internal, subjective career rather than its outward manifestations. That of course makes it possible to interpret the vague internal feelings that people often have in line with the theory, and Levinson and his colleagues may have interpreted somewhat ambiguous data to fit a rather specific theory, rather than making their theory more flexible to accommodate a wide range of data. Another possibility is that this study, like much careers research, involves a lot of retrospective sense making, in which people—in this case Levinson's career participants—organize what has happened to them in the past into much neater patterns than were perhaps apparent at the time. This tendency for career rationalization is considered further in Chapter 10.

In addition, Levinson (Levinson et al., 1978) was rather dogmatic in his insistence that the phases invariably follow one another in the correct order and within, or close to, the specified ages. Although most of us can observe periods of stability and transition in our lives, applying a rigid timetable of dates enabling our unique career to be lumped in with everyone else's in a common format does not seem to be a good expression of reality.

Remember, too, that Levinson et al.'s (1978) theory is based on the experiences of American men in the 1970s. Even if there were real regularities between those people at that time, major changes have taken place in the careers terrain since that time, which may have badly disrupted any such regularities. Also, the theory is an internally driven one, which does not appear to take account of the structural features of the careers environment or major events such as boom–bust cycles and mass layoffs, which constantly buffet many careers (Chapter 1): If you get laid off from a long-term job in the middle of a stable period, how can you avoid going into a transition at that point?

On the other hand, many ideas in Levinson et al.'s (1978) theory—the distinctions between early, middle, and late career and between stable and transitional periods, the life structure, the Dream, BOOM, and the midlife crisis—are ideas that many people can identify in their own lives and in the lives of others. Levinson identified issues and tasks that probably occur in many careers. The trick, perhaps, is to deemphasize the rigid structure that he described and to pay attention to how some of these ideas can be applied more flexibly to specific careers.

Women's Career Stages

Both Super (1990) and Levinson et al. (1978) tended to state that their theories applied to women as well as men, and Levinson reported a second study on women (Levinson & Levinson, 1996). But other researchers considering women's career cycles have resolutely claimed that women's careers have totally different dynamics from men's, partly because of women's special role in bearing and rearing children (e.g., Franz & White, 1985; Gallos, 1989; Gilligan, 1982). Many studies of specific occupations show major disruptions to women's careers compared with men's due to family commitments (e.g., Arun, Arun, & Borooah, 2004; Gjerberg, 2003; Hinze, 2004; Windsor & Auyeung, in press). A study by Ornstein and Isabella (1990) showed little support for either the Levinson or the Super model in relation to women's careers. According to Gallos (1989), women pursue not a dream, as envisaged by Levinson, but a *split dream*, providing a balance between career and family relationships. Bardwick (1980) similarly noted that women face tension in their later child-bearing years as they constantly set career development goals against the tick of the biological clock, marking the years when they are able to bear children.

These authors assert that separate theories of career development stages are needed for women.

According to Levinson, who conducted a study of women similar to his study of men (Levinson & Levinson, 1996), women go through stages similar to those of men in early adulthood, a conclusion supported by other research by Roberts and Newton (1987). In the Levinson research, the main difference between women and men was the clash for women between the roles of homemaker and career woman. Professional women had similar career tasks to those of men but found them difficult due to home commitments. Work career, though important, was less central to their Dream. In general, they had a more complex and ambiguous sense of their place in the world and, hence, greater difficulty in specifying goals. In Levinson's study, depressingly, only a few women "had it all"—successful full-time careers and families; the others were all either single women with careers, married women with careers but no families, or full-time homemakers with no current career. Although child rearing and family undoubtedly disrupt women's career stages, this issue is probably better conceptualized as one of role conflict (i.e., conflict between a woman's work role and her family roles) and is therefore dealt with mainly in Chapter 7.

Pringle and McCulloch Dixon (2003) proposed a theory of women's development with four stages—explore, focus, rebalance, revive—applying not to their work careers so much as to an integration of their work and relationships, with the stages being separated from each other by periods of reflective assessment.

Early to midcareer for many women is a time when, due to domestic responsibilities, they are unable to pursue the advancement of their work careers as much as men can. On the other hand, in their 40s and 50s, with family commitments reduced, many women find that they are able to pursue career and professional accomplishment with considerable self-confidence, almost as if some of the assertiveness of men's establishment phase had been delayed (Gallos, 1989).

Career Stages and the New Careers

How well does age/stage theory fit the new careers characteristic of the changes in economic and managerial fashion in recent years? In Chapter 1, I noted the trends, over the 1980s, 1990s, and into the new century, of the careers environment, which shows employment to be much less stable, with careers being increasingly disrupted by phenomena such as organizational restructuring and layoffs, international displacement of work, rapid development of new information technology, and increased impatience of individuals to reach their career goals. The *New Careers* study conducted in the late 1990s in the wake of major restructurings (Arthur, Inkson, & Pringle, 1999) suggested that modern careers are much more mobile, disrupted, discontinuous, zigzag, improvisational, and anarchical than age/stage theory predicts. This makes the notion of predictable life stages much harder to sustain.

For example, consider the career exploration and establishment of Brett, a 32-year-old plasterer.

Anarchical Exploration

Brett went to college and studied business because he thought he would learn how to get rich. Instead, he drank a lot of beer, did little work, and after 3 years flunked out. He got a job driving a forklift in a factory and learned to do four-wheel skids and smoke pot, but he soon got bored and quit. Next, he tried being unemployed, but that was just as boring.

When his parents hassled him to get a decent job, Brett bought his first suit, had a haircut, and got a job as a clerk in the stock exchange. When he showed promise, his boss gave him a chance as a stock trader. In the cut and thrust of trading, he found he had good bargaining skills and a strong personality, and he did well. But he also realized that the values of his industry were unacceptably materialistic: "the business world, suit world in the inner city . . . wasn't me." Brett was creative—for example, he played in the evenings in a professional rock group, and he took his distress out on his employers creatively, busking on a unicycle at lunchtimes, outside the stock exchange where he knew the bosses could see him. Eventually, the stock exchange experienced a major share market crash and Brett walked out.

Using informal contacts he quickly obtained temporary work helping a friend to paint a boat. The friend was also a plasterer and next invited Brett to help him plaster a house. Brett, who had been expert as a child in building plaster-of-paris models, knew immediately he had found his niche. He loved plastering. The normal 4-year plastering apprenticeship was unnecessary—he was already an expert. When the plasterer offered him another contract, he said no and used his selling skills to solicit plastering contracts of his own. His business prospered, and within a few years he was working only when he felt like it, subcontracting most of his work and specializing personally in ornamental plastering. He even resumed and completed his abandoned business degree in his spare time. In the evenings, his musical and dramatic work had met with success. When interviewed, he was a little bored with plastering and his lifestyle and was beginning, at age 32, to think of going overseas in search of fortune as a performer.

Source: Arthur et al. (1999).

In his late teens and early 20s, Brett went through a phase of exploration, but his method of exploration was trial and error—he threw himself into whatever came up and then checked whether he liked it. Through what appears to be a lucky chance, he was successful, and he certainly started, as the theory predicts, to establish his career in plastering at the right age, 25 years. To *establish* means "to make steadfast, firm, or stable; to settle on a firm and permanent basis" (Thatcher & McQueen, 1981, p. 299): In age/stage theory, the establishment phase is about laying down a firm foundation on which a career can be constructed. The expectation of career establishment, of stabilization, advancement, and even permanence in career at such an early age, may be a heavy burden, and a more flexible approach may be called for.

But in any case, Brett's plastering career now looks problematic, not because of the unstable external environment but because of Brett's changing internal sense of identity. Indeed, Brett appears to be about to reenter the exploration stage. Careers may be less predictable, and more at the mercy of chance, individual change, whim, and the unstable economic system and labor market, than maxicyclic theories, even with built-in minicycles, suggest.

Despite all this, when we authors of *The New Careers* (Arthur et al., 1999) examined all of the data from our 75 career cases and tried to organize it into a good framework, we found that, despite the many cases of individuals behaving outside of type, the general ideas of age/stage theory fit rather well.

Bearing in mind that we examined careers only from the time of the first major job—usually between age 15 and 23 years—and did not consider retirement, we divided our data into three themes, representing three different types of career behavior:

- Behavior driven by the desire for exploration and novelty: for example, career exploration, experimentation, trying new occupations, career entry, seeking and starting new jobs, and learning and seeking change on the job. We labeled this type of behavior *fresh energy: engaging with unfamiliar situations.* Perhaps we could have called it exploration, as Super did.
- Behavior directed at creating career momentum and establishing direction: for example, planning a career, making deliberate choices, linking to an established occupation or organization, and seeking advancement. We labeled this type of behavior *informed direction: pursuing career pathways.* Perhaps we could have called it establishment, as Super did.
- Behavior in which the individual is concerned with continuity, with using previous experience, with maintaining security in a changing world, and with adapting as much as possible to change. We labeled this type of behavior *seasoned engagement: rounding out career experience.* Perhaps we could have called it maintenance, as Super did.

These three types of behavior were broadly age related. The majority of instances of fresh energy came from people mainly up to age 30 years (different from the Super-Savickas model, where the exploration phase, differently conceptualized, ends at age 24 years). Most informed direction was practiced by those in their 30s and early 40s, and most seasoned engagement was practiced by those older than 45 years. But there were spectacular exceptions, such as in the cases of Irene and Vera on the following page.

The broad expectation of a three-stage sequence of early-career exploration, midcareer direction, and late-career maintenance appeals because it fits with observed careers and with other career theories, including Levinson et al.'s (1978) and Super's (1990). Because of the growing tendency for disruption of the cycle, it is probably best, however, not to be too specific about age definitions. A better approach may be to look specifically at some of the key career tasks that each stage in the sequence typically entails.

Out of Phase

Irene was good at science in school but wanted to work with people. A family friend was an optometrist, and she talked with Irene about her work. Irene quickly saw that optometry promised all the things she wanted in her career, including regular hours. At 18 years of age, she enrolled for her degree qualification, and by age 22 had passed it. After a year of professional work in a hospital setting, she was hired as a consulting optometrist by a local partnership. At 25 years of age, her career is well underway, and she looks forward eventually to having an optometry practice of her own. Irene appears to have completed her exploration while still a teenage high school student and is now well down the track of an established career.

Vera, a nurse, was unfairly fired from her job at age 53. Rather than seeking another nursing position, she looked around to see if there were other preferable opportunities. With a friend, she began to experiment with running psychotherapy workshops. But she had also been trying to grow various market vegetables on some land she and her husband owned, and she seemed to be having some success with macadamia nuts. What to do? In a moment of truth one day, she realized that it was the nuts not the psychotherapy that had her attention. She decided to go into the nut business full-time. Within a few years, she had several hundred trees under cultivation and a small factory for processing and packaging. Vera's exploration had taken place in her mid-50s.

Source: Arthur et al. (1999).

Pre- and Early Career Issues

Occupational Choice

Occupational choice is often not so much a single decision as a set of consequential decisions. For example, a person might first decide whether to follow an academic stream or a vocational stream at high school, then choose which degree to pursue in college, then choose from a range of options for postgraduate work or for an initial job. In essence, the person is trying to evaluate him- or herself and the world of work to optimize the match between the two. This process is further described in Chapters 4 and 5.

Career development experts and counselors attribute initial choice of occupation high importance on the assumption that it may frame the career for a long time: Make a bad choice at age 16 years, and you may be stuck with it until you are 60. Much of the literature in this area uses the term *vocation* rather than *occupation,* implying a calling to, and permanence in, a particular occupation. However, many people, like Brett in a previous case, fail to settle in the fields of study or occupation they first choose: In the *New Careers* study, more than 60% of participants had changed occupation at least once in the previous 10 years (Arthur et al., 1999). It has become more common for people to have several changes of occupation in the course of a working life (Jepsen & Dickson, 2003). In such cases, the issue of occupational choice is not confined to early career.

Organizational Entry

In addition to choosing an occupation, individuals also have to choose their first organization, and the process of entry and adjustment to the organization is critical (Wanous, 1992). For example, the amount of challenge given to graduate recruits after initial entry to the organization has been shown to be predictive of their success several years later (Berlew & Hall, 1966).

Organizational entry is made difficult by the fact that the world of full-time, regular employment in a business or other organization is very different from education in college (Greenhaus, Callanan, & Godschalk, 2000). For example, regular attendance and punctuality are not only strongly expected but also often enforced. There are rules about what one should wear and what one is allowed to do. Employees' efforts are expected to be devoted to the organization's business objectives, rather than their own learning or social agendas. Projects, outcomes, rewards, and promotions are less frequent than in the semester system of school.

The new systems, values, and norms are typically maintained in the organization by strong formal systems of rules and procedures and the informal system of organizational culture, whereby the organization provides the individual with numerous cues as to the type of behavior expected (Martin, 1992). The process whereby the new employee learns the organization's ways is known as *socialization*: Through socialization the newcomer not only acquires proficiency in his or her job but also builds relationships and learns the history, traditions, rituals, heroes, goals, values, power structure, informal language, and other norms of the organization (Chao, O'Leary-Kelly, Wolf, Klein, & Gardner, 1994).

Organizational entry, particularly entry to one's first major organization, can come as a major shock. Not only is the new scene likely to be very different from the old, but also the individual, commonly influenced by glossy company recruitment propaganda and the age-old tendency to see what one wants to see, may have quite unrealistic expectations. When reality does not live up to hope, the result can be a major disillusion. The sequence of recruitment, entry, and socialization is part of another cyclic process, this time of engagement and disengagement between individual and organization, which is discussed later in the section titled "Cycles Within Cycles." An example of the combination of socialization and disillusion is provided in the case of Harry.

Harry's First Day

"My first day in the company? I'd have to say it was a bit of a disaster. After all the song and dance they had made about 'we are a people company,' no one seemed to be expecting me! Eventually a secretary saw me looking lost and showed me my office, but no one had cleared it, and I spent the first morning throwing out old files and cleaning it up. My boss found me and gave me a long lecture on the proud history of the company, how honored I should

(Continued)

(Continued)

be to be a member, blah blah blah, but to me everything seemed smaller and pokier than it had looked in the brochures. Then he took me to see the CEO, supposedly a hero who had saved the company from going under, but he seemed ordinary too—he had egg on his tie and kept losing his glasses on his desk. He said to me, 'That's a most interesting shirt, Mr. Peters. Red. Very flamboyant!' And he kind of glared at me. Later someone told me that the company standard was white or pastel colored shirts and dark ties—the CEO thought that was what the customers liked. The worst part was in the afternoon when I had to attend my first product development meeting, and I sat down and then an elderly man came in and sort of stood in the doorway, and he glared at me too and then sat down at the other end of the table looking grumpy, and I found out later that he was the senior engineer and I was sitting where he always sat. Well! How was I supposed to know?"

Midcareer Issues

Managing Career and Family

The work–career cycle inevitably and inexorably interacts with another cycle—the family cycle (Friedman & Greenhaus, 2000; Moen & Sweet, 2004; Parasuraman & Greenhaus, 1997). The family cycle is based on our roles as members of, and contributors toward, various family groups, including parents, siblings, spouse or partner, extended family, and, most crucially, children. Family matters are also commonly based on a sequential pattern of experiences: single adult status; marriage or long-term partnership; bearing and rearing of children through infancy, early childhood, primary, and high school years; departure of children from home (i.e., empty nest); and finally the years in which the children often become more independent and the parents more dependent.

The family cycle affects people most toward the end of early career and throughout midcareer, for that is nowadays the time when child-rearing responsibilities make their strongest competing demands. It affects women more than men because of the continuing, though slightly weakening, tradition that in any partnership the woman carries the major responsibility for child care. Partnership, whether heterosexual or gay, brings the additional problem, whether or not children are involved, of the dual-career couple, where two careers, each one with its own dynamic, must somehow be integrated with each other (Barnett & Rivers, 1996; Hall & Hall, 1979).

Although family, like career, introduces cyclic issues, it is probably best thought of as a matter of different and sometimes conflicting roles—the work role and the family role. This issue is therefore dealt with in more detail in Chapter 7.

Dealing With the Career Plateau

A *plateau* is "a broad flat area of land in an elevated position" (Thatcher & McQueen, 1981, p. 635). A career plateau occurs at the point of a career when the individual has made some progress but the chances of additional hierarchical advancement or increased responsibility are very low (Feldman & Weitz, 1988). Again, the metaphor assists us to see that we may make rapid ascents early in our careers only to find them going flat. Career plateaus are common and may occur at any stage of the career, though they are most common in midcareer and late career (Bardwick, 1986).

The career plateau has organizational, individual, and even familial causes (Tremblay & Roger, 1993). Organizations tend to have pyramidal structures, so there are fewer opportunities as one ascends. Slow organizational growth may exacerbate the problem. The trend of organizations to *delayer*—that is, to simplify their structures by having fewer hierarchical levels—effectively flattens them, providing even fewer opportunities (Thornhill, Saunders, & Stead, 1997). In terms of individual causes, plateauing may be caused by the person's declining energy, increased preoccupation with external matters such as leisure interests, inadequate skills in relation to new technology or managerial responsibilities, or distraction from work due to family commitments (Tremblay & Roger, 1993).

Ambitious people find being plateaued humiliating and frustrating, particularly if they have the expectation, which many organizations encourage, that they can reasonably expect continuing promotions through their career, until they get to the top (Goffee & Scase, 1992). Being plateaued also tends to reduce job satisfaction and work commitment (Lee, 2003; Nachbagauer & Riedl, 2002), though employing organizations may combat this by expanding job assignments and project work (see Chapter 9) or mentoring (Chapter 8) (Rotondo & Perrewe, 2000).

On the other hand, many adapt well to the plateau and accept that there are other means of fulfillment for them, such as continuing to perform their role well and taking more of an interest in their fellow workers and in family and leisure activities (Feldman & Weitz, 1988). Perry, the first case in this chapter, is an example. The employees who pose the greatest problem for the organization and for themselves are those who are "dead wood" (Ference, Stoner, & Warren, 1977)—plateaued, dissatisfied, and ineffective. These employees may need major interventions by themselves, their advisors, or the organization to help them get their careers back into a more satisfactory pattern.

Midcareer Change

The stereotype of the middle-aged man who comes to question the fundamentals of the course of his life—including his career—is a common one, and increasingly it is extended to women. Consider the popular-culture example in the film *American Beauty.*

The American Dream and Midlife Crisis

In the 1999 Oscar-winning film *American Beauty,* from director Sam Mendes, Kevin Spacey plays Lester Burnam, a 40-ish corporate employee with a wife, daughter, and suburban house. Lester has built a solid, conventional life structure but has come to despise both the narrow corporate values of his company and the consumerist values of his own lifestyle, which are epitomized by his wife Carolyn (played by Annette Bening).

Lester's response is to suddenly quit his long-time job with his company. He takes a low-level part-time job in a fast-food outlet, starts jogging and body-building, buys a racy sports car, rejects his wife, and attempts to seduce a glamorous teenage friend of his daughter. It is a return to youth, a total change in lifestyle and goals. Meanwhile, in her attempts to be *supermom*—the modern woman who is successful both as a mother and in her career—Carolyn, a realtor, agonizes over her outfits, her front garden, her deteriorating relations with her husband and daughter, and her lack of success in selling. In a desperate attempt to succeed in both the work and family arenas, she listens to motivational audiotapes and recites them. Then, her own midlife crisis kicks in. She makes friends with a successful local realtor and goes to bed with him. And, to boost her self-confidence, she buys a handgun and learns how to use it. Tragedy is inevitable, and careers are at the heart of the problem.

The case shows how complex interactions between contextual, individual, and family relationships induce dramatic change. But midcareer change may take place in a more planned, career-specific, and gradual manner. Often the move is from employment into self-employment, as when teachers and business executives abandon corporate life to become store owners or self-employed potters. Such transitions are not uncommon (Roborgh & Stacey, 1987).

Midcareer changes can be regarded as the outcome of the career reevaluation and midcareer transition posited by Levinson et al. (1978) and outlined earlier in this chapter. The person may encounter a career plateau, or a major dissatisfaction with work, and cycle back into the career exploration stage looking for alternatives. Downsizing and layoff cause many to look at their lives and make a fresh start to their careers (Jiang & Klein, 2000). The precise causes vary between individuals (Thomas, 1980): For example, Marshall (1995) found that many successful female executives responded to corporate sexism by making a major change. Whatever the causes, there is evidence that the process is a functional one for many individuals. Roborgh and Stacey (1987) studied a sample of midcareer changers in a small town and found that although most of them were worse off financially than they had been previously, they were also much happier with their lives than are the general population.

Late-Career Issues

Holding On

In the late-career maintenance phase (Super, 1990), the individual is concerned, as stated earlier, with holding steady in position, maintaining performance, conserving what has been accomplished, and remaining interested. In the *New Careers* study (Arthur et al., 1999), we identified a pattern among late-career workers in which they achieved a satisfactory and satisfying adjustment to their jobs and sought simply to hold on to them, with little change, until they could afford to retire. These workers sought no new career challenges: They sought merely to continue their jobs, and they hoped that nothing, such as a corporate restructuring or bankruptcy, would cause the loss of their jobs before they were ready. The case of Maria and Stefano provides an example.

Holding On

Maria is 53 years old. She has secretarial and clerical skills, and since her youngest child started school she has always worked, part-time or full-time, as the "office lady" for various small companies. She has done this job for a small manufacturing company located near her home for the past 5 years.

Maria's husband, Stefano, is 6 years older than she is and worked for many years as head storeman at a local factory. It seemed a secure job, but 3 years ago the company was restructured, the factory's production was relocated, and Stefano was laid off. He then found that he was unable to secure another job—it seemed his age and lack of qualifications were against him. About a year ago, Stefano had a minor heart attack. He now gets a small sickness benefit, but his health has deteriorated, and it seems likely he will never work again. Stefano and Maria own their house, but so far they have not saved enough for their retirement.

Being the sole breadwinner has made Maria very nervous about her responsibilities. She always saw her work as secondary to her home life, and she doesn't like being responsible for most of the family income. It is hard to make ends meet, let alone save, from her modest earnings. The industry she is in is volatile. Suppose she loses her job, just like Stefano did? "That's something I don't like to think about. But if I can just hold on for another 10 years, maybe we'll be all right."

People in late career, like Stefano, often face stereotypes that jeopardize their careers: They are typically perceived to be less able and productive, more prone to absenteeism, and less able than their younger counterparts to adjust to change (Warr & Pennington, 1994). As a consequence, organizations may seek to lay off older workers before younger workers or may be more reluctant to employ them if they are displaced. But independent studies of older workers' performance suggest that the stereotypes are seriously wrong: for example, older workers are often either as productive (McAvoy & Cascio, 1989; Parkhouse & Gail, 2004) or slightly more productive than younger workers, and have lower absenteeism (Ali & Davies, 2003; Greller, 1999).

Disengagement and Retirement

A conventional stereotype or myth of retirement is shown in Charlie's case.

How to Retire

Charlie always intended, at age 65 years, to retire totally from his job in the company for which he has worked for many years. He saved and planned with that in mind. He worked productively at his job, as he always had, through his 60s. On his 65th birthday—the compulsory retiring age—a celebration of Charlie's career was held on company premises. Champagne was drunk. Various managers made speeches in honor of Charlie, emphasizing his wonderful service over the years. He was presented with a gold watch, inscribed with his name and that of the company. Then he said a modest goodbye and walked out of the office in midafternoon, while his ex-colleagues returned to their jobs. Charlie was never seen at work again, preferring to relax at home watching television and weeding his garden. A few months later, unable to cope with leisure after all those years of work, he collapsed and died of a heart attack.

Modern retirement is seldom so clear-cut. In many countries, legislation against age discrimination has removed the possibility of compulsory retirement. Instead, it has become much more common—particularly among employees who receive financial settlements for layoff or who have alternative means of income—to retire early. Others prefer to work into their 70s or even 80s. Some organizations offer retirement planning and opportunities for individuals to accept part-time contracts as a way of winding down gradually from full-time employment. More options for part-time work are available, enabling a retirement to be phased in rather than sudden, a concept known as *bridge employment* (Kim & Feldman, 2000). And recently, worries have developed around the demographic trends of increased life expectancy: If too many people retire early or even at the "normal" age, that will leave too many aging people for society to support and too few active workers to support them (Collins, 2003). According to Dychtwald, Erickson, and Morison (2004, p. 48), "it's time to retire retirement."

Retirement is often a major change, and various factors combine to affect the ability of the individual to make a successful adjustment (LaBauve & Robinson,

1999). Nevertheless, many individuals see retirement as a definite, and mostly desired, milestone, a time when they can take life easier and develop new interests outside of the workplace. The evidence suggests that retirement is not generally stressful but rather the reverse (Bosse, Aldwin, Levenson, & Workman-Daniels, 1991). Prior to retirement, retirees may disengage their interest in work. They may actively plan their retirements and may be assisted to do so by their organizations (Kamouri & Cavanagh, 1986). Other things being equal, those in lower status or dull jobs may be more disposed to retire (Hanisch, 1994). Satisfaction with retirement is enhanced by good health and financial support, prior retirement planning, planned hobbies and other postretirement activities, and high self-esteem (Hanisch, 1994; Schmitt, White, Coyle, & Rauschenberger, 1979; Talaga & Beehr, 1989). Levinson and Wofford (2000) characterize retirement as the flexibility phase of the career, when the person has greater freedom of choice of location, time, expenditure, and activities than ever before.

Cycles Within Cycles

At various points in this chapter, it was noted that the 40-year career cycle may have smaller cycles within it: for example, Savickas's (2002) "minicycles" and the cycles of anticipation, entry, socialization, and so forth, pertaining to each job. Many jobs include one-off or repeated projects, each with its project cycle. Nicholson (1984) and others describe *work-role transition cycles*, which take place whenever our work role changes, which may happen without our changing jobs; these important cycles are discussed further in Chapter 7. Calendar cycles, such as the farming seasons, the financial year, the school semester, and the monthly sales report, build additional smaller cycles into our careers.

These smaller cycles provide texture and predictability in our working lives. But they also alert us to the danger of stagnation: A 40-year career may turn out to be not 40 years of experience but one year of experience 40 times over. This may happen if each cycle is essentially the same as the one before it and ends in the same place. In practice, external events often ensure that cycles involve change and learning as well as repetition: for example, doing the same basic job cycle with more sophisticated software packages or learning to do it better.

Hall (2002) argues that "people's careers will increasingly become a series of 'mini-stages' (or short-cycle learning stages) of exploration-trial-mastery-exit, as they move in and out of various product areas, technologies, functions, organizations, and other work environments" (p. 118). In this model, the learning experiences in each cycle enhance the psychological success, or life satisfaction, of the individual and provide a new starting point for subsequent cycles. Hall goes on to argue that careers increasingly "unfold in erratic episodes . . . lasting perhaps 2 to 4 years, during which the person learns about and masters a new area of work" (p. 119). If Hall is right, our focus should perhaps be not on the cycle but on the learning that takes place within it, and the smaller cycles may be best seen not as circles that return to the same place but as spirals moving onward or upward.

Conclusion

I conclude that it is indeed useful to consider the career as a cycle and that understanding the typical dynamics of the cycle increases the predictability of our careers and our control over them. Such regularities have been popularized, at least in middle-class circles in the United States, by Gail Sheehy's (1997) notion of life passages. However, the cycle is complicated by its less predictable interaction with other cycles, particularly the family cycle, and by the disruptions caused by external changes and cataclysms and by human aspirations and capriciousness. But we can still identify career regularities and tasks likely to apply to different stages of our working lives and plan how we can handle them. Cycles are patterns, and they may constrain us, but if we study them and understand them, we may well be able to predict them and use them to help us create a better future for ourselves.

Key Points in This Chapter

- In their career attitudes and aspirations, people change over time. Age/stage theories of career attempt to explain career behavior as part of a life cycle, sometimes considered akin to predictable seasons.
- Psychologists look for patterns of psychological development over the life span. For example, Erikson suggested there were periods of the adult life span when identity, then intimacy, then generativity provided key challenges.
- Super proposed a five-stage theory in which the key stages were exploration in early career, establishment in midcareer, and maintenance in late career. Levinson proposed a life-span theory in which periods of relative stability were predictably linked by more dynamic transitions, including midlife transition. These theories accord with many observed cases but cannot be applied universally.
- Women's careers appear to develop differently from men's. Their patterns are complicated by the dual focus on career and family.
- Key early-career tasks are occupational choice and organizational entry. Key midcareer tasks are managing work and family, dealing with the career plateau, and making midcareer change. Late-career tasks are holding on in a changing world and retiring productively.
- The career cycle often involves minicycles of shorter duration and less impact.

Questions From This Chapter

General Questions

1. Use the theories in this chapter to analyze the career of Perry in the first case. What stages and transitions can you discern?

2. Can you observe any of the stages from your own career or the careers of other people you know?

3. Compare and contrast the theories of Levinson and Super. Which do you find the more convincing?

4. What are the main differences between the typical career cycles of men and women?

5. The chapter described a number of issues that tend to be important at different stages of mid- and late career. Which of them do you expect to be the most important in your own career and what can you do to prepare for them?

6. Provide some examples of career minicycles from your own experience or that of people you know.

Career Case Study Questions

1. Ask your career case person to divide his or her career into not more than five stages, which the case person can differentiate. Ask your case person what the key characteristics of each stage were. Compare the responses with the Levinson or Super model. If you want, show your case person these models. What does he or she think?

2. Ask your case person the following questions: What are your thoughts about your career when you were young? How does that compare with your thoughts about your career now? How do you account for the difference?

3. What key career issues did your case person face in his or her early, mid-, and late careers?

References

Ali, H., & Davies, D. R. (2003). The effects of age, sex and tenure on the job performance of rubber tappers. *Journal of Occupational and Organizational Psychology, 76*(3), 381-391.

Arnold, J. (1997). *Managing careers into the twenty-first century.* London: Paul Chapman.

Arthur, M. B., Inkson, K., & Pringle, J. K. (1999). *The new careers: Individual action and economic change.* Thousand Oaks, CA: Sage.

Arun, S. V., Arun, T. G., & Borooah, V. K. (2004). The effects of career breaks on the working lives of women. *Feminist Economics, 10*(1), 65-84.

Baird, L., & Kram, K. (1983). Career dynamics: Managing the supervisor/subordinate relationship. *Organizational Dynamics, 11*, 46-64.

Bardwick, J. M. (1980). The seasons of a woman's life. In D. G. McGuigan (Ed.), *Women's lives: New theory, research and policy* (pp. 35-55). Ann Arbor: University of Michigan, Center for Continuing Education of Women.

Bardwick, J. M. (1986). *The plateauing trap.* New York: Bantam Books.

Barnett, R., & Rivers, C. (1996). *She works, he works.* New York: HarperCollins.

Bee, H., & Boyd, D. (2002). *Lifespan development* (3rd ed.). Boston: Allyn & Bacon.

Bejian, D. V., & Salomone, P. R. (1995). Understanding midlife career renewal: Implications for counseling. *Career Development Quarterly, 44*(1), 52-62.

Berlew, D. E., & Hall, D. T. (1966). The socialization of managers: Effects of expectations on performance. *Administrative Science Quarterly, 11*, 207-223.

Bosse, R., Aldwin, C., Levenson, M., & Workman-Daniels, K. (1991). How stressful is retirement? Findings from a normative ageing study. *Journal of Gerontology, 46*, 9-14.

Chao, G. T., O'Leary-Kelly, A. M., Wolf, S., Klein, H. J., & Gardner, P. D. (1994). Organizational socialization: Its content and consequences. *Journal of Applied Psychology, 79*, 730-743.

Collins, G. A. (2003). Rethinking retirement in the context of an ageing workforce. *Journal of Counseling and Development, 30*(2), 145-157.

Cronin, A., & Mandich, M. (2005). *Human development and performance throughout the lifespan.* New York: Thomson/Delmar Learning.

Dychtwald, K., Erickson, T., & Morison, B. (2004). It's time to retire retirement. *Harvard Business Review, 82*(3), 48-57.

Erikson, E. H. (1959). Identity and the life cycle. *Psychological Issues, 1*, 1-171.

Feldman, D. C., & Weitz, B. A. (1988). Career plateaus reconsidered. *Journal of Management, 14*, 69-80.

Ference, T. P., Stoner, J. A. F., & Warren, E. K. (1977). Managing the career plateau. *Academy of Management Review, 2*, 602-612.

Fitzgerald, L. F., & Weitzman, L. M. (1992). Women's career development: Theory and practice from a feminist perspective. In H. D. Lea & Z. B. Leibowitz (Eds.), *Adult career development: Concepts, issues and practices* (pp. 124-160). Alexandria, VA: National Career Development Association.

Franz, E. D., & White, K. M. (1985). Individuation and the attachment of personality development: Extending Erikson's theory. *Journal of Personality, 53*, 224-256.

Friedman, S. D., & Greenhaus, J. H. (2000). *Work and family—Allies or enemies? What happens when business professionals confront life choices?* New York: Oxford University Press.

Gallos, J. V. (1989). Exploring women's development: Implications for career theory, practice and research. In M. B. Arthur, D. T. Hall, & B. S. Lawrence (Eds.), *Handbook of career theory* (pp. 110-132). Cambridge, UK: Cambridge University Press.

Gilligan, C. (1982). *In a different voice: Psychological theory and women's development.* Cambridge, MA: Harvard University Press.

Gjerberg, E. (2003). Women doctors in Norway: The challenging balance between career and family life. *Social Science and Medicine, 57*(7), 1327-1341.

Goffee, R., & Scase, R. (1992). Organizational change and the corporate career: The restructuring of managers' aspirations. *Human Relations, 45*, 363-385.

Gottfredson, L. S. (1981). Circumscription and compromise: A developmental theory of occupational aspirations. *Journal of Counseling Psychology, 28*, 545-579.

Greenhaus, J. H., Callanan, G. A., & Godschalk, V. M. (2000). *Career management* (3rd ed.). Fort Worth, TX: Dryden Press.

Greller, M. M. (1999). In search of the late career: A review of contemporary social science research applicable to the understanding of late career. *Human Resource Management Review, 9*(3), 309-348.

Hall, D. T. (2002). *Careers in and out of organizations.* Thousand Oaks, CA: Sage.

Hall, D. T., & Hall, F. S. (1979). *The two-career couple.* Reading, MA: Addison-Wesley.

Hall, D. T., & Nougaim, K. (1968). An examination of Maslow's need hierarchy in an organizational setting. *Organizational Behavior and Human Performance, 3*, 12-35.

Hanisch, K. A. (1994). Reasons people retire and their relations to attitudinal and behavioral correlates in retirement. *Journal of Vocational Behavior, 45*, 1-16.

Hinze, S. W. (2004). Women, men, career and family in the U.S. young physician labor force. *Research in the Sociology of Work, 14,* 185-217.

Jepsen, D. A., & Dickson, G. L. (2003). Continuity in life-span career development: Career exploration as a precursor to career establishment. *Career Development Quarterly, 51*(3), 217-227.

Jiang, J. J., & Klein, G. (2000). Effects of downsizing on IS survivors' attitudes and career management. *Information and Management, 38*(1), 35-45.

Kamouri, A. L., & Cavanagh, J. C. (1986). The impact of pre-retirement education programmes on workers' retirement socialization. *Journal of Occupational Behaviour, 7,* 245-256.

Kim, S., & Feldman, D. C. (2000). Working in retirement: The antecedents of bridge employment and its consequences for quality of life in retirement. *Academy of Management Journal, 43*(6), 1195-1210.

LaBauve, B. J., & Robinson, C. R. (1999). Adjusting to retirement: Considerations for counselors. *Adultspan, 1,* 2-12.

Larwood, L., & Gutek, B. (Eds.). (1987). *Women's career development.* Newbury Park, CA: Sage.

Lee, P. C. B. (2003). Going beyond the career plateau. *Journal of Management Development, 22*(6), 538-551.

Levinson, D. J. (1986). A conception of adult development. *American Psychologist, 46,* 3-13.

Levinson, D. J., Darrow, C. N., Klein, E. B., Levinson, M. H., & McKee, B. (1978). *The seasons of a man's life.* New York: Knopf.

Levinson, D. J., & Levinson, J. D. (1996). *The seasons of a woman's life.* New York: Knopf.

Levinson, H., & Wofford, J. C. (2000). Approaching retirement as the flexibility phase. *Academy of Management Executive, 14*(2), 84-95.

Marshall, J. (1995). *Women managers moving on: Exploring life and career choices.* London: Thomson.

Martin, J. (1992). *Organizational cultures: Three perspectives.* New York: Oxford University Press.

McAvoy, G. M., & Cascio, W. F. (1989). Cumulative evidence of the relationship between employee age and job performance. *Journal of Applied Psychology, 74,* 11-17.

Moen, P., & Sweet, S. (2004). From "work-family" to "flexible careers." *Community, Work and Family, 7*(2), 209-226.

Nachbagauer, A. G. M., & Riedl, G. (2002). Effects of career plateaus on performance, work satisfaction and commitment. *International Journal of Manpower, 23*(8), 716-733.

Nicholson, N. (1984). A theory of work-role transitions. *Administrative Science Quarterly, 29,* 172-191.

Ornstein, S., & Isabella, L. (1990). Age versus stage models of career attitudes of women: A partial replication. *Journal of Vocational Behavior, 36,* 1-19.

Parasuraman, S., & Greenhaus, J. H. (Eds.). (1997). *Integrating work and family: Challenges and choices for a changing world.* Westport, CT: Quorum.

Parkhouse, W., & Gail, G. (2004). Task frequency as a function of age for the powerline technician trade. *Ergonomics, 47*(6), 660-670.

Pringle, J. K., & McCulloch Dixon, K. (2003). Re-incarnating life in the careers of women. *Career Development International, 8*(6), 291-300.

Rholes, W. S., & Simpson, J. A. (Eds.). (2004). *Adult attachment: Theory, research and clinical implications.* New York: Guilford.

Roberts, P., & Newton, P. (1987). Levinsonian studies of women's adult development. *Psychology and Ageing, 2*(2), 154-163.

Roborgh, P., & Stacey, B. (1987). Happiness and radical career change among New Zealanders. *Journal of Psychology, 121*(5), 501-515.

Rotondo, D. M., & Perrewe, P. L. (2000). Coping with a career plateau: What works and what doesn't. *Journal of Applied Social Psychology, 30*(12), 2622-2646.

Savickas, M. L. (2002). Career construction: A developmental theory of vocational behavior. In D. Brown & Associates (Eds.), *Career choice and development* (4th ed., pp. 149-205). San Francisco: Jossey-Bass.

Savickas, M. L. (2005). The theory and practice of career construction. In S. D. Brown & R. W. Lent (Eds.), *Career development and counseling: Putting theory and research to work* (pp. 42-70). Hoboken, NJ: Wiley.

Schein, E. H. (1978). *Career dynamics: Matching individual and organizational needs.* Reading, MA: Addison-Wesley.

Schmitt, N., White, J. K., Coyle, B. W., & Rauschenberger, J. (1979). Retirement and life satisfaction. *Academy of Management Journal, 22,* 282-291.

Sheehy, G. (1997). *New passages: Mapping your life across time.* New York: Bantam Books.

Super, D. E. (1953). A theory of vocational development. *American Psychologist, 8,* 185-190.

Super, D. E. (1957). *The psychology of careers.* New York: Harper & Row.

Super, D. E. (1990). A life-span, life-space approach to career development. In D. Brown, L. Brooks, & Associates (Eds.), *Career choice and development* (2nd ed., pp. 197-261). San Francisco: Jossey-Bass.

Super, D. E., Savickas, M. L., & Super, C. M. (1996). The life-span, life-space approach to careers. In D. Brown, L. Brooks, & Associates (Eds.), *Career choice and development* (3rd ed., pp. 121-178). San Francisco: Jossey-Bass.

Talaga, J., & Beehr, T. A. (1989). Retirement: A psychological perspective. In C. L. Cooper & I. T. Robertson (Eds.), *International review of industrial and organizational psychology* (Vol. 4, pp. 186-211). Chichester, UK: Wiley.

Thatcher, V. S., & McQueen, A. (Eds.). (1981). *The new Webster encyclopaedic dictionary of the English language.* Chicago: Consolidated Book Publishers.

Thomas, L. E. (1980). A typology of mid-life career changers. *Journal of Vocational Behavior, 16,* 173-182.

Thornhill, A., Saunders, M., & Stead, J. (1997). Downsizing, delayering—But where's the commitment? *Personnel Review, 26*(12), 81-98.

Tremblay, M., & Roger, A. (1993). Individual, familial and organizational determinants of career plateau. *Group and Organization Management, 18*(3), 411-435.

Walls, R. T. (2000). Vocational cognition: Accuracy of third-, sixth-, ninth-, and twelfth-grade students. *Journal of Vocational Behavior, 56*(1), 137-144.

Wanous, J. P. (1992). *Organizational entry: Recruitment, selection, orientation and socialization of newcomers.* Reading, MA: Addison-Wesley.

Warr, P. B., & Pennington, J. (1994). Occupational age-grading: Jobs for older and younger non-managerial employees. *Journal of Vocational Behavior, 45,* 328-346.

Windsor, C., & Auyeung, P. (in press). The effect of gender and dependent children on professional accountants' career progression. *Critical Perspectives on Accounting.*

CHAPTER 4

Careers as Action

Seizing the Day

She was born into an Italian Catholic family and grew up in middle America. She had five brothers and sisters. Her mother died when she was 5 years old, and her father, a stern disciplinarian, worked hard to bring her up. She was educated in a nunnery and at one stage wanted to be a nun. But music entered her life: first piano, then dance. At 14 years of age, she enrolled in a dance school and fell under the spell of her dance instructor. He took her to gay clubs, enabling her to see a different way of life. When she danced, people looked at her. And her dance instructor was the first man to tell her she was beautiful.

A straight "A" high school graduate, she enrolled in the School of Music at the University of Michigan, but it wasn't for her, and she moved to New York, intent on succeeding in the entertainment industry. She arrived in Times Square with less than $20. She waited tables, took more dance classes, and danced in clubs, but it wasn't enough: She wanted to sing and act as well, and to be famous. To make ends meet, she modeled nude. She got a break as a backup dancer overseas, but it didn't work out, and she came back to New York.

With a boyfriend, she formed a band and got her first taste of professional singing. She formed another band. She was out in front singing, but it was sporadic: She wasn't really getting anywhere.

She tried to network: dancers, musicians, deejays. She had an in-your-face style but could charm people. She wasn't above using her sexuality to get what she wanted. She and a new boyfriend squatted in the Music Building in Manhattan, a shrine to pop music, full of music companies. She hustled executives for a break, and eventually a woman executive offered to be her manager. The story goes that when the manager entrusted to her the care of the manager's pet poodles, she spray painted rude words on the poodles and took them walking on Fifth Avenue—anything for publicity.

(Continued)

(Continued)

She continued to live hand-to-mouth. She dyed her dark hair blonde. Then she met a club deejay, slept with him, and got him to play a demo tape at his club, where she danced often and had a following in the crowd. The crowd loved the tape, loved *her*! The deejay hawked the tape around the record companies. A few said no, but at last she got a deal. Like his predecessors, the deejay disappeared from the scene, his job done. A record was released. She recorded a video to go with one of the songs, and it went straight to the top of the dance charts. A stellar career had begun. It was 1983. She was 24 years old.

For her professional name, she had dropped her family name, Ciccone. She had kept her first name, Madonna.

Source: Evans (1995).

Perhaps it is no accident that one of Madonna's biggest world tours was called *Blonde Ambition*. Evans's (1995) colorful minibiography of the superstar's early years is a portrayal of huge, vaulting egotism, of an individual with big career ambitions imposing herself relentlessly on the world, much of the time by sheer outrageousness, until she got what she wanted. As she said herself, "It's a great feeling to be powerful. I've been wanting it all my life."

In her early years, Madonna was a prime example of the career as action. Her career did not just happen to her: By her own actions, she made her career happen. She produced it, directed it, and starred in it. It was her own creation.

This chapter is about careers as action. Chapters 2 and 3 emphasized forces such as inherited characteristics, social structure, aging, and family cycles, which exert external power over careers and limit individual action. In contrast, this chapter focuses on people exerting power to create and direct their own careers.

We all exert some influence over our careers. The career of Madonna has been introduced not because it is an especially admirable one but because it appears to be one where her own ambitions and actions dominated and where constraining forces, such as limited family assistance, childhood discipline, and the inhospitable labor market of the entertainment industry, were conspicuously overridden. It is a career in which the careerist was unambiguously in charge. Few people have the talent, the strength of will, or the selfishness to emulate Madonna even in their own fields. But by and large career experts consider that most of us could benefit from greater empowerment and expression of ourselves in our careers (e.g., Hansen, 1997, 2002). It therefore seems worthwhile to pay special attention to the ideas in this chapter.

Agency

Agency means "the state of being in action or exerting power" (Thatcher & McQueen, 1981). Madonna exerts agency over her career because she is exceptionally active and energetic about it and has her own ways of exerting power and making things happen.

Bakan (1966) identified two basic strategies for dealing with life's uncertainties and labeled them communion and agency. *Communion* is a strategy of opening oneself up to the world and other people, accepting them, adjusting to them, and integrating with them.

Agency, introduced as a key concept in the study of careers by Marshall (1989), is a strategy of dealing with the world by independent self-assertion and control. In essence, the individual imposes him- or herself on the world, rather than allowing it to dominate. In agentic career behavior, the individual takes the initiative, attempts to make progress through personal action, applies assertively for new jobs, seeks progression, and attempts to take charge of his or her own career.

Marshall (1989) argued that agency was more characteristic of men than women. In career behavior, agency, if carried to extremes—as in the hard-driving, fast-paced, competitive way of living that stress researchers have labeled Type A behavior—can have negative consequences (including heart disease) for both the agentic person and those with whom he or she deals (e.g., Edwards, Baglioni, & Cooper, 1990).

Nevertheless, there is good reason to believe that without going to extremes individuals can practice agency to improve their careers. For example Boyatzis, McKee, and Goleman (2002) considered the problem of lack of passion for one's job and noted various agentic practices, such as creating reflective structures, learning from a coach or a development program, or searching for new meaning in familiar territory, whereby people can take their own action to reawaken their passion. Employing organizations are becoming less willing to provide either the security or the automatic promotions that might enable members to have successful careers without practicing agency. A catch-cry of recent years has been that organizational careers are declining or even dead and that from now on individuals will have to look after their own careers (e.g., Hall & Associates, 1996; Rifkin, 1995; Stroh, Brett, & Reilly, 1994). In other words, agency is more essential for career development.

The career development movement has always adopted an agency approach to careers. That is, the movement has assumed that if people are empowered to take responsibility for their own careers and are provided with the information and skills to do so, then they will act on their own careers to make decisions leading to greater career satisfaction and success.

Self-Expression

One common form of action in careers is self-expression. *Self-expression* means "the expression of one's feelings, thoughts, etc., especially in writing, painting, music, etc." (Allen, 1990, p. 1098). Madonna's self-expression emerges in her dancing and her singing and is recorded forever in albums, videos, and DVDs: See *Blonde Ambition* and you see not just a marketable product but also Madonna's unique personality.

Those performing in the arts or entertainment industries have special opportunities to express themselves in their work, and the artifacts and performances they create embody their own personalities. For example, consider this statement of career philosophy by a professional ceramic artist:

> The philosophy behind my work is to project something of myself; images held deep within my soul, whether it be those built of the past, or that which surrounds me in the present time. To shut out all that intrudes on my thoughts and take a long and searching look at what I hold important. To dismiss those influences which others would force upon me, whether it be in lifestyle or perception or thought, or, most arrogant of all, the type of work I should produce. (Sue Clifford, in Parkinson & Parker, 1988, p. 21)

Thus, Clifford sees her work as an exercise in self-expression. She literally *is* her work. True, she recognizes the constraints that the outside world tries to place on her art, such as her family demanding that she make a living or customers trying to specify what kind of work she should produce. But she sees these as unwarranted intrusions on the self-expression that constitutes her career. Like Clifford, many people seek to use their careers to express who they are.

But external forces often limit self-expression. Artists whose careers are exercises in self-expression must usually balance this against the realities of a competitive world. They can survive economically only if they can find customers who value the products of their self-expression sufficiently to pay for them. Although art or craft meets the self-expressive values of artists up to a point, their self-expression is limited by commercial pressures (Inkson, 1987).

Likewise, Madonna might much rather not have waited tables, let alone model nude, but was compelled to do so by financial necessity. Unfortunately, there is not a one-to-one match between the selves that people want to express and the jobs that need to be done in the outside world. In some cases, however, we can find ways of sublimating and redirecting our creative energies and bringing them, in disguise, into the apparently more mundane world of work. Julie's case is an example.

Acting It Out

Julie's passion for the theater went back to her childhood. Right through school she loved acting and played every part she could get. When she went to college, she studied drama, took courses in theatrical improvisation, played parts in regional theater productions, and did backstage work at a local professional company. After graduation, she would have loved to make a career in theater, but in this highly competitive industry there were few prospects. To pay her way, she got a part-time job in customer service in an international service company.

Quickly she learned that customer service was a performance skill like acting, and she acquired an excellent reputation. When it became known in the company that she had theater skills, a salesman asked her to coach him on how to do a presentation. With her assistance, he put on a great performance. Her reputation as a coach grew, and she was promoted to a job in the training department. It was through coaching for presentations that she really made her mark.

Julie realized that what she had learned about improvisation could be applied to the corporate world. There were roles to be played, and what made actors believable was their ability to immerse themselves in their roles. She began to apply for senior appointments and treated each interview as a theatrical performance to which her script writing, improvisation, and presentation could be applied. For one successful interview, she served breakfast from her briefcase and used the ingredients as a metaphor for how her talents would fit the job. She based another presentation on baseball and ended by throwing a ball to the recruiting manager, saying, "Put me in, Coach!" It was the beginning of a very successful corporate career.

Source: Inkson & Arthur (2001).

As Julie's story shows, we often can't avoid expressing who we are in our work, whatever our role. One lesson from this story is that parents should not get too concerned when their children seek to involve themselves in school subjects and leisure activities that don't seem to lead to a job. Many career-relevant skills, such as improvisation, the spoken word, self-confidence, presentation, and teamwork, are generic and can be learned in theater and in other nonvocational activities.

For most of us, the world of work provides many opportunities for us to express our identities. But often we must find compromises between the self that we are and want to express and the role that society needs to be filled. How do we get the self to fit the role or the role to fit the self? In Chapter 5 we look at fit and in Chapter 7 at roles.

Theories of Career Development

Some of the theories that appear most to emphasize personal action in careers can be grouped under the heading of *career development*. This is the term of choice used by the careers research and career counseling movements to describe their work (e.g., Brown, Brooks, & Associates, 1984; Niles, 2002; Tiedeman & O'Hara, 1963). However, the word *development* is ambiguous: A thing can develop solely under the influence of external events, or it can be developed by a human agent. Here, the latter meaning is used, the career being developed actively by the individual whose career it is. A number of theorists, including Donald Super, already discussed in Chapter 3, have proposed theories that stress the active role of the individual in determining his or her own career path. These writers focus on internal processes, such as concept formation, learning, and decision making, and the way in which these energize and inform career behavior.

Career Construction Theory

In Chapter 3, I discussed some of the work of Donald Super, the age/stage element of his theories, and the continuation of his work by Mark Savickas. In fact, Super's (1980) theory, although it describes stages of career development, is basically about the career as the implementation of the person's self-concept in his or her working life.

In most of his publications, Super (e.g., 1953, 1980) used the words *vocational development* and *career development* to refer to the study of careers in general and his theory in particular. In his recent formulation of Super's theory, Savickas (2002, 2005) calls it *career construction theory*. Thus, "careers do not unfold: they are constructed" (Savickas, 2002, p. 154). Construction is a form of action. The metaphor of "construction," and the resulting imagery of the career being put together by the actions of the person, and having physical, manufactured form—for example, a hierarchical structure or a delicate work of art—is potent.

The process of career construction is that of developing and implementing a vocational self-concept, an image of what one is like in relation to the various possible contexts of work. We develop a self-concept through our experiences, starting in early childhood, including being aware of physical and psychological attributes, having opportunities to undertake various roles and to watch others do so, and being rewarded for particular forms of behavior. We begin to get a sense of who we might be, what kind of job we might realistically do. As we progress through childhood and adolescence, the vocational concept gradually stabilizes and provides lines of possible continuity for the career. The notion of self-concept explains how and why we can experience a satisfying career by constantly finding work that is a good fit with our developing self-concept (see Chapter 5). Thus, career construction theory embraces both the adult development approach of Chapter 3 and the vocational fit approach of Chapter 5.

But, as shown in Chapter 3, the self-concept may change through the stages of the career or be destabilized by transitions or by external events, and the career stages hypothesized in vocational development/career construction theory involve different career tasks at different stages. The tasks are experienced by individuals as social expectations: For example, there may be an expectation that those in the exploration stage will choose an occupation. However, the term *career task* also indicates that it is the individual's responsibility to accomplish career tasks and complete career stages—that is, to show agency rather than having the occupation chosen or other tasks performed by others. The tasks prompt the individual to perform them and thereby to construct the career (Savickas, 2002).

Another important concept in the theory is career maturity, which is "the level and rate of an individual's development with regard to career matters" (Osipow & Fitzgerald, 1996, p. 114). Career maturity is shown by the ability to master the tasks at each stage. Another concept is career adaptability, or "readiness for coping with current and anticipated tasks of vocational development" (Savickas, 2005, p. 46), which has become increasingly significant in the turbulent career environment of recent years. According to Savickas (2005), adaptive individuals are characterized by four C's:

- *Concern* about their future as a worker
- Increased personal *control* over their future
- *Curiosity* shown in the exploration of future scenarios
- Strengthened *confidence* to pursue their aspirations

This definition goes beyond the advocacy of adaptability in the form of career resilience (London & Stumpf, 1986; Waterman, Waterman, & Collard, 1994)—a reactive ability to stand up to hard knocks—to something more proactive, through which individuals, rather than just "going with the flow," become the active builders and shapers of their own careers.

Maturity and adaptability may be regarded as competencies that provide individuals with the personal skills to engage productively with career tasks as they arise. Because the theory forms an extensive basis for the work of many career counselors, questionnaire measures of such variables are available and continue to be developed (Busacca & Taber, 2002; Crites & Savickas, 1996; Levinson, Ohler, Caswell, & Kiewra, 1998; Perrone, Gordon, Fitch, & Civiletto, 2003; Savickas & Hartung, 1996; Super, Thomson, & Lindeman, 1988).

In his most recent formulation of career construction theory, Savickas (2005) extended the theory to embrace the idea of social constructionism (see Chapter 10), which suggests that, rather than phenomena such as careers existing in objective form, individuals create their own reality, including careers, through shared social experiences. The idea of self-concept is extended into the notion that our careers can be seen as personal, subjective narratives of our lives, and contextual structures (Chapter 2) are identified as narratives of our society, such as progress or inequality, in relation to which we continue to act our stories out. This innovation extends the theory of career construction across the boundary between careers as objective entities and careers as mental and social constructions framed by people. Although career theorists are still a long way from developing a single integrated theory of careers that explains all career phenomena, career construction theory, whose 16 key propositions (Savickas, 2005, pp. 45–46) are derived from the original formulation by Super (1957), may be as close as we can currently get.

Social Learning Theory

Social learning theory is based on the observation that career behavior is learned behavior, which can be explained to a considerable extent by the theories of learning. You have probably heard of instrumental learning, where people are reinforced (e.g., by praise) for particular responses and punished (e.g., by ridicule) for others: The rewarded behavior tends to increase so that a child whose parents and teachers and internal psychology reward him or her for activities connected with biology, healing, and high-level educational performance may develop a desire to be a doctor. Another form of learning, association, contributes, too—for example, when positive stimuli, such as enjoyable medical television dramas are paired with more neutral stimuli, such as hospitals. In a third type, vicarious learning, individuals learn through observation and imitation of others, who are career role models. These different types of learning are incorporated into John Krumboltz's social learning theory of career choice (Krumboltz, 1979; Mitchell & Krumboltz, 1996).

Mitchell and Krumboltz (1996) acknowledged the influence of four factors over the career paths that individuals choose. Two of them we have already dealt with in Chapter 2: innate human characteristics and environmental conditions and events. The third is the learning experiences outlined earlier. The fourth is what Mitchell and Krumboltz call task approach skills—background attitudes, habits, and thought processes that the individual brings to the learning task.

Mitchell and Krumboltz (1996) stated that people make worldview generalizations about the context—for example, the generalization that opportunities in certain occupations may be limited because of sex discrimination. More directly related to occupational choice, people also make self-observation generalizations about themselves through observation of, and learning from, their day-to-day experiences (e.g., "I'm better with machines than I am with people"), an idea apparently not far removed from Super's (1980) notion of self-concept.

These generalizations may be explicitly stated or may simply represent the person's internal awareness. They are constantly adapted as the person learns from experience, and at the same time they determine career behavior—for example, when a child with a self-observation generalization that he or she is good at carpentry attempts to make a piece of furniture and modifies the generalization on the basis of the observed results. Krumboltz (1994) suggested that attraction to an occupation will be influenced, through learning, by success at tasks typical of the occupation, observation of role models being rewarded for such tasks, and positive statements made about the occupation by others.

Although the theory was introduced as an example of agency (it is active responses that the person learns, through which the person can impose his or her will on the environment), it also, like all learning theories, reminds us uncomfortably that our own careers can perhaps be controlled, particularly when we are young and impressionable, by rewards and punishments administered by others: for example, by the sexist teacher, who says to a girl, "You can't do that—that's a boy's job." Krumboltz and Henderson (2002) outlined a more positive approach, in which learning theory is applied to the task of career counselors, who can focus not so much on the reinforcing of specific choice responses of their clients as on their clients' learning of such broad and useful career behaviors as self-reflection, open-mindedness, and creativity in the use of unplanned career events.

Social Cognitive Career Theory

A limitation of learning theories applied to human decision making is that they may downplay the importance of the individual's thought processes. In making career decisions, we think about things: about ourselves and our interests, abilities, and goals; about the world of work and the various opportunities that may be available; and about the outcomes we may expect from putting ourselves into these opportunities.

Social cognitive career theory (Lent & Brown, 2002; Lent, Brown, & Hackett, 1994, 2002) is based on Bandura's (1986) well-known general social cognitive theory. It attempts to provide the following:

A unifying framework for understanding the processes through which people develop vocational interests, make (and remake) occupational choices, and achieve varying levels of career success and stability. . . . [The theory] high-lights people's capacity to direct their own vocational behavior (i.e. human agency) yet it also acknowledges the many environmental influences . . . that serve to strengthen, weaken or even over-ride human agency in career development. (Lent et al., 2002, p. 277)

Key to understanding the theory are two central variables through which the theorists say individuals regulate their career behavior:

- *Self-efficacy beliefs* are a person's judgments of their abilities to carry out particular actions or activities. These beliefs are learned through the various learning forms referred to under social learning theory. The belief that one is competent, or potentially competent, to carry out a particular job is likely to have a big influence over a career's direction toward or away from such jobs. People who have low self-efficacy beliefs across a range of different activities may have difficulty finding career options.
- *Outcome expectations* are a person's expectations about what will happen—what the outcomes will be—if he or she follows a particular course of action. Thus, a person with good artistic ability and interest might feel capable of embarking on a career as an artist but might also think that the outcome of such a choice would be financial insecurity. Outcome expectations are influenced by self-efficacy beliefs.

Social cognitive career theorists incorporate self-efficacy beliefs and outcome expectations into a complex model in which they act together to determine first the individual's broad interests (e.g., hobbies, favorite school subjects); next, his or her choices, first in goals and second in actions (basically the choice of an occupation); and last, performance attainments in that occupation. The full model is shown in Figure 4.1.

Note that as interests lead to goals, goals lead to actions, and actions lead to performance, self-efficacy and outcome expectations continue to influence people at each stage in the process. Also, contextual variables relating to the person's career inheritance and the external environment may continue to affect the process at any stage.

On page 87 is a career case study analyzed in terms of social cognitive career theory.

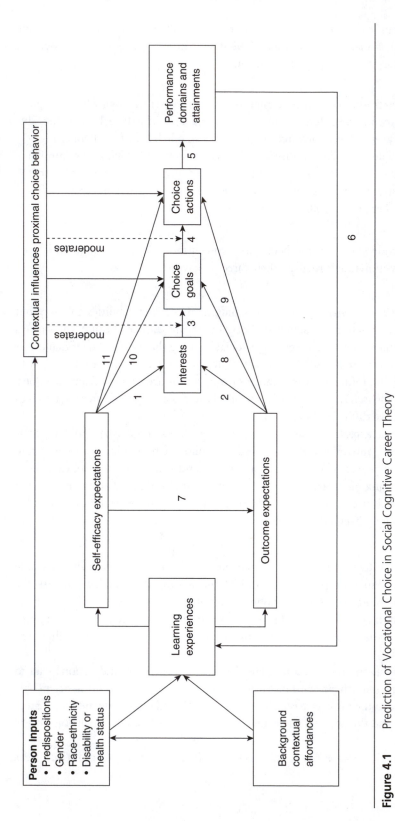

Figure 4.1   Prediction of Vocational Choice in Social Cognitive Career Theory

Source: Reprinted from *Journal of Vocational Behavior*, Vol. 45, No 1, R. W. Lent, S. D. Brown and G. Hackett, Towards unified social cognitive theory of career and academic interest, choice and performance, pages 79-122. Copyright © (1994) with permission from Elsevier.

Finding Her Way

Leslie attended public schools in a predominantly White suburban area. Her father was a lawyer and her mother had some college education and was active in community organizations. They were supportive of Leslie's education, and she did well, particularly in math (where she gained tutoring experience) and science. But she did not get career guidance at school or from her parents and found it difficult to make choices. Unsure whether she could be successful at university, she enrolled instead for a general course including math and chemistry at her local community college, where most of her friends had also chosen to study. After a year, however, she transferred to a state university, not for educational reasons but because she had a boyfriend there.

At college, she chose courses that kept her options open. She considered math, engineering, creative writing, psychology, and medicine. But her father wanted her to do business, a subject she did not like, and her mother wanted her to get a good education but assumed she would soon marry and it would not matter. She continued to vacillate.

In her advanced math class, where she was the only student, she found that the professors singled her out for her mistakes. Psychology would require extensive graduate training, which she did not feel motivated toward, and in engineering her professors told her that it was difficult to combine engineering with looking after a family. Her final decision, to major in secondary education with an emphasis on math education, was based on her interest and ability in math, her belief that teaching and raising a family could easily be combined, and the fact that postgraduate work would not be necessary. Over the next few years, she developed an initially enjoyable and successful career in math teaching.

Source: Swanson & Fouad (1999). This excellent source provides information on the development of Leslie's career up to the age of 35 years and analyzes Leslie's case from six additional theoretical viewpoints, including those of Gottfredson (Chapter 2 of this book), Super (Chapter 3), Krumboltz (this chapter), and Holland (Chapter 5). Using diverse approaches to consider a single case is an excellent way of learning career theories.

Swanson and Fouad (1999) provided an analysis of this case from the standpoint of social cognitive career theory. They focused on the special influence of self-efficacy beliefs and outcome expectations on Leslie's career choices, in particular her initial choice of community college over university and, second, her deliberate avoidance of postgraduate academic work.

Swanson and Fouad (1999) pointed out how early experiences—for example, doing math tutoring while still at school—provide a basis for Leslie's feelings of self-efficacy in math and teaching but noted that she may have lacked challenging role models or encouragement at school to pursue demanding courses: A lack of belief in her ability to do challenging academic work may have caused her initial choice of the easier community college curriculum and her later avoidance of postgraduate work. At college, areas of potential self-efficacy were removed from her range of choice by others' actions, and as a result she was unable to see positive outcomes from pursuing advanced academic work. It is likely that she was better able to see a secure positive outcome in the familiar local community college among her friends than in the unknown setting of a university with its higher standards. Her occupational choice of math teaching combined a strong self-efficacy belief in her capabilities with an appreciation of likely positive outcomes in terms of both career success and satisfaction and later opportunities to combine career with family.

Career Success

In any discussion of human agency the following questions arise: "What for? With what end in view?" If people are indeed seeking to exercise influence over their own careers, what goal is it that they are pursuing? In terms of career construction theory (Chapter 3), what self-concept are they trying to express? In terms of social learning theory, what rewards do they find reinforcing? In terms of social cognitive career theory, what are their career goals? In terms of normal human discourse, what are their career ambitions?

According to Reardon, Lenz, Sampson, and Peterson (2006), "Almost every college student working through a career problem or decision is really pursuing a vision of 'having a successful career'" (p. 82). But students will find the concept of success fuzzy, and insofar as they can define it each is likely to define it differently.

Traditional measures of career success relate to the objective career (see Chapter 1): status on an organization ladder, amount earned in salary, reputation in one's profession. This is also what the general public understands as success. The occupational hierarchies outlined in Chapter 2 carry success connotations, but within each occupation and within many organizations there are further hierarchies to be climbed. But other definitions of success are possible. For example, Derr (1986) identified five measures of career success:

- Getting ahead: advancing in terms of traditional status hierarchies
- Getting secure: having an established and secure position
- Getting high: being inspired and motivated by the nature of the work being done
- Getting free: achieving autonomy and control over one's own work environment
- Getting balanced: achieving a balance of work and nonwork interests

In considering career satisfaction, Reardon et al. (2006) recommended paying attention also to the subjective career: "It may be appropriate to substitute the word *satisfying* for the word *successful*" (p. 83). Indeed, the contrast between objective career success in terms of status and salary and subjective success in terms of career satisfaction is a current preoccupation of careers research (Adamson, Doherty, & Viney, 1998; Gunz & Heslin, 2004; Ng, Eby, Sorenson, & Feldman, 2005). Mirvis and Hall (1994) used the term *psychological success* to refer to internal career satisfaction. Hall (2002, pp. 152–153) suggested that personal and external definitions of success may be quite different and implicitly advocated the pursuit of psychological success as defined by the career actor. Arthur, Khapova, and Wilderom (2005) argued that in a world of increasingly common boundaryless careers, marked by more transitions across institutional boundaries, broader and more individualized definitions of career success are necessary.

Each individual is likely to have his or her unique and personal definition of career success. The following cases provide examples.

Redefining Success

Michelle Buck and her colleagues studied the working lives and careers of 82 managers who had deliberately shown agency by seeking "reduced-load" work arrangements in their jobs: that is, in order to achieve a better balance between non-work and work in their lives they had opted to work part-time for reduced pay. This in itself denotes a creative departure from "normal" careers, an overt proclamation of Derr's "getting balanced." But the reduced-load workers tended also to have redefined their notions of career success, as these quotes show:

> I couldn't make a lot of money and not enjoy what I was doing. Like, I would have to have both. I don't need the prestige and power, I just, I am able to contribute, lead, make a difference in the team environment. So, I mean I have not desired to be president of (the company).

> Career success? It has got to do with making a contribution to the organization that I am in and the company at large, really having an impact, feeling that something I'm doing isn't just pushing a pencil but that there are things that I can see and touch and feel and know

that I contributed to making them what they are. And then there is a personal element of it, too, which is that I do it in a way that is really very honorable. That I keep my work, that I am a person of commitment, that I fulfill my commitments, that I treat people fairly.

> If you really enjoy the people you are working with, everybody is learning and growing and you're having fun. Which is pretty much all the jobs I've had have been like that. And I never really had a plan, ever. I never had a plan to get a PhD. It just felt good at the time, I was having a good time, I was really interested in what I was doing.

Thus, the first speaker defines success in terms of contribution to a team, the second in terms of contribution and reputation, and the third in terms of personal enjoyment. The authors of the paper comment that "knowing where one belongs and clearly knowing one's priorities can lead to creative alternatives that may not be predictable or traditional, but that meet one's priorities" (Buck, Lee, & MacDermid, 2002, p. 90).

Source: Buck et al. (2002).

Career success and satisfaction are not the same as job success and satisfaction, which can be momentary. One of the defining characteristics of the career is its continuity over a long period. Reardon et al. (2006) suggested that it is probably best to "think of the career as a journey, a path, a process, rather than a destination or prize" (p. 83). Career success in this view is determined not just by where the career gets to but also by satisfaction and feelings of self-efficacy along the way. At the same time, the person may deliberately make sacrifices of success and satisfaction in the short term to create the opportunities for long-term career benefit—for example, when someone enrolls in a long, arduous program of study or takes a relatively low-level job with the knowledge that it will provide long-term opportunities to meet his or her career goals.

Career Planning and Management

The idea of suffering short-term career pain to bring about long-term career gain raises the question of career planning. Contemporary accounts suggest that many individuals are uncertain how to further their careers (Mallon & Walton, 2005). If we can indeed exercise agency, should we not try to do so in a planned way, using our power over our careers strategically to bring us the career success we want? The theory and practice of business management (e.g., Fayol, 1949) tell us that the first step in a management process is planning. An organization first plans where it wants to get to, for example, by setting goals for several years into the future; it then organizes itself to get there and motivates its members to energize it in its quest. Finally, it sets up a system of control, which enables it to check its progress and keep itself on track. It benefits from this process in terms of having clear direction and increased chances of success. Can people apply the same type of thinking to the management of their own careers?

Career management is essentially career self-management (King, 2004). In career self-management, the individual applies principles of planning and management to his or her own career in pursuit of self-defined objectives. Career self-management has always been the model for the career development movement (e.g., Reardon et al., 2006): Even when people require career guidance and counseling, part of the objective is likely to be to provide them with the skills and information to manage their own careers independently in the future.

Careers experts have developed models of the career decision-making process that are prescriptive—that is, they prescribe optimum ways for individuals to go about the process for maximum personal benefit (Greenhaus, Callanan, & Godschalk, 2000; Reardon et al., 2006). Career planning models such as these make the assumption that we can actively determine our own futures. In this book, they are discussed in greater detail in Chapter 11.

Schemes for planning our own futures are based on agency but add rationality. Ideally, they lead to the notion of career design, the planned specification of the career as in an engineering blueprint. Of course, the factors affecting careers are often more uncertain and variable than those affecting physical structures, so the planning process is typically complex and continuous. If we adopt similar approaches to other facets of our lives, such as finance, family, and leisure interests, then we may be able to integrate the management of our own lives, as in integrative life planning (Hansen, 2002). Career self-management certainly seems to offer a promising model for taking better control of our own lives.

By and large, career counselors recommend the components of career self-management, such as gathering information about ourselves and the world of work in an organized way, setting goals, ensuring feedback loops, and measuring progress (Wehmeyer et al., 2003). There is empirical support that strategies such as goal setting and career self-management are associated with career satisfaction (e.g., Murphy & Ensher, 2001). Bookstores tend to be thick with self-help books, telling you how to take control of your life by planning your career rather than leaving it to chance, and in many cases these books provide you with helpful self-appraisal inventories and goal-setting forms to help you do so (Bolles, 2003; Love, 2002). A case study of a person who altered his career for the better by using simple techniques of career goal setting and planning is provided in the case of Barry.

Writing It Down

Barry learned basic career relevant skills while still at school: helping in his parents' vegetable shop taught him about profit margins, negotiation with suppliers and customers, and general running of a business. But he drifted into selling on commission and might never have found his way to a top management position if it had not been for his manager, who said to him one day, "What are you going to do with your life? What do you want to be?" Barry looked at the manager and replied, off the top of his head, "A sales manager." The manager asked him to go away and make a plan. Exactly how was he going to do it?

For the first time in his life, Barry sat down and thought about his goal and what he needed to do to achieve it. He wrote a two-page statement of what he needed to do. It focused on improving his education, his personal skills, and his understanding of business. And he found, as many do when they put effort into crystallizing their goals and plans by writing them down, that the exercise did not just make the plan clearer: It also increased his psychological commitment to the plan.

Eight years later, he achieved his goal. He went on to become the CEO of a major organization.

Source: Robbins, Bergmann, & Stagg (1997).

The main argument against career planning is that it may be too formulaic, too organized, to apply to the real uncertainties of today's careers. Planning for the future depends on being able to predict the future, and as we saw in Chapter 1, in the fast-changing world of work that appears to be increasingly problematic. We might fear that excessive planning leads to paralysis by analysis, where we become rigidly locked into the detail of the plans we made and are unable to respond properly to unexpected opportunities or to act creatively in relation to our careers.

To some people, the essence of career satisfaction is not to plan but to be spontaneous and do one's best to create opportunities and take them when they seem right. Ibarra (2003) even went so far as to suggest that major career changes may—and sometimes should—often be made on the basis of acting first, then reflecting later. A compromise between rigorous planning and leaving the career to unfold as it will may be planned happenstance: By managing your career in a systematic way, you can increase your chances of the fortunate coincidences—for example, your chance of meeting someone socially who is looking to hire someone exactly like you—on which many successful careers depend (Mitchell, Levin, & Krumboltz, 1999). Thus, we may be able to plan to maximize the likelihood of fortunate chances and to act decisively to take them when they occur (Krumboltz & Levin, 2002; Mitchell, 2003).

We might sum up by saying that every career actor should at least consider the opportunities offered by systematic career planning, by reading more about it or asking experts. Systematic career self-management suits some better than others and probably is easier to apply to short-term career goals than to long-term ones. As the organized application of agency by the right people, to the right career issues, career planning has much to offer.

Crafting Careers

Consideration of career planning and career management raises the issue of a whole new set of metaphors to understand how we use agency to enact our careers: the metaphors of "science," "technology," "art," and "craft."

Is there a science of careers? Arguably there is: Many of the theories and principles of careers outlined in this book were developed through the scientific process modeled on the physical sciences, including theory development, the collection of empirical data about careers, and the testing of hypotheses. From that base, a technology, or applied science, of careers was developed, including the following:

- The scientific understanding of how goal setting works is routinely built into career goal-setting exercises used by counselors.
- Scientifically based psychometric tests of relevant psychological characteristics, such as career maturity (Super et al., 1988), career interests (Harmon, Hansen, Borgen, & Hammer, 1994), psychological barriers to career accomplishment (Krumboltz, 1991), and suitability for specific occupations (Holland, Fritzsche, & Powell, 1994) can be used by counselors and others to provide quantitative information about the individual's current characteristics relevant to career decision making.
- Methods of career counseling (e.g., Gysbers, Heppner, & Johnston, 1998) have been scientifically validated.

Thus, a powerful science and technology of careers is potentially available for individuals to use in their own career agency. This technology includes preplanning, measurement, goal setting, design, and systematic management. However, it may be relatively inaccessible to those who do not have the assistance of expert psychometricians and advisors.

An alternative metaphor to science and technology for developing one's career is that of "art." Definitions of *art* include "a human creative skill or its application . . . human skill or workmanship as opposed to the work of nature" (Allen, 1990, p. 60). What happens if we conceptualize career development as art? Art can incorporate science and technology, as when a painter or potter gathers technical information about different oils or glazes. It can employ planning and design, as when the artist makes a preliminary sketch or even imagines the work that he or she intends to create. But art allows for creativity, intuition, and improvisation in a way that science and technology do not.

A good compromise metaphor for the individual's skilled construction of his or her career may be "craft." That is, at a personal level career development may be skilled, purposeful behavior. A craft, such as weaving or carpentry, incorporates good technology but ensures that it is sympathetic to the characteristics and skills of the craftsperson. It produces outputs that are functional as well as artistic.

Poehnell and Amundson (2002), in their concept of CareerCraft, which they describe as a "complementary paradigm to career management" (p. 120), emphasized the functionality, skill, and creativity inherent in effective individual behavior relating to careers. They related it to the work of Csikszentmihalyi (1991) in the way that skilled individual action produces "flow" or "optimal experience" through proactive engagement with the world. In flow, the task energizes and empowers, and performance becomes smooth and apparently effortless.

How can ordinary people become skilled creators of their own careers? We can get some ideas by looking at the ways in which craftspeople such as carpenters learn their trade. They go to college perhaps 1 day a week to acquire the theory and science of what they are doing. They use vicarious learning by observing the work of skilled experts. But most of all, they have to engage actively with the work, all the time reflecting on what they have done and seeking to make their performance ever more skilled. Overall, the "craft" metaphor appears to be a good one to summarize the agency of career actors.

Career Self-Direction: The Protean Career

To complete our review of careers as action, we lastly consider Tim Hall's (1976, 2002; Hall & Associates, 1996) concept of the protean career. Again, metaphor is important in the genesis of this idea. Proteus was a mythical Greek sea creature who could change shape at will, and the literal, dictionary meaning of the word *protean* is "variable, taking many forms, versatile" (Allen, 1990, p. 961). In 1976, writing about managerial careers in organizations, Hall noted the tendency of organizations to want to manage members' careers for them (see Chapter 9). In contrast, Hall stated,

the protean career is one in which the person, not the organization, is managing. It consists of all the person's varied work experiences in education, training, work in several organizations, changes in occupational field, etc. (p. 201)

No doubt we would all like to be able to change shape at will to meet changing career tasks and opportunities. The idea of acquiring career adaptability and versatility through a variety of experiences is a good one. Elsewhere, I wrote that "the strength of the Proteus metaphor [is] its unusual vividness, the empowerment that it provides to the heroic career actor, and the value in today's rapidly changing careers arena of being able to quickly improvise new ways of working" (Inkson, 2002, p. 23).

In further developing the protean career construct, Hall (2002; see also Briscoe & Hall, in press), while retaining adaptability as a key valuable characteristic of 21st-century careers (Hall & Moss, 1998), focused on two other aspects of proteanism—self-direction and identity. The difficulty with an individual practici ng infinite self-direction and adaptability in his or her career is that the person may become skilled at adjusting to change but lose a sense of overall direction. According to Hall (2002), in today's turbulent circumstances the protean career actor needs a "compass"—another metaphor!—to provide direction. The compass comes, says Hall, from the individual's sense of identity—understanding who he or she is and knowing his or her values, needs, goals, and interests. The idea of the protean career is interesting as a potential model for career survival and development in the turbulent career context of this century (Hall & Associates, 1996), but given that the dictionary definition of *protean* is merely "versatile," we need to realize that the concept involves much more than adaptability (Inkson, in press).

Here is an exemplar protean career. Note how Mary Robinson's constant adaptability to new challenges is based on her clear identity as a lawyer, politician, and activist; her deeply rooted and consistent values, and her own direction of her own career.

Mary Robinson: A Protean Career

Mary served from 1997 to 2002 as the United Nations High Commissioner for Human Rights. How did she rise to such an exalted position?

Mary was born Mary Bourke in Ballin, County Mayo, in the Republic of Ireland, in 1944. She was Roman Catholic but had family relations who were Anglicans as well as ancestors who had fought for rebel causes against the British monarchy. The daughter of two medical doctors and academically gifted, Mary studied law at Trinity College in Dublin. Such was her brilliance that she was appointed in 1969, at the young age of 25, as Reid Professor of Constitutional Law. The same year she commenced her political career when she was elected to the Irish Senate as an independent candidate. In 1970, despite opposition from her family, she married Nicholas Robinson, a lawyer and conservationist: They later had three children.

From the beginning of her career, Mary was an activist, in a then deeply conservative country, for women's issues: for example, the right of women to serve on juries, their right to continue in civil service jobs after marriage, and the right to contraception. The last of these causes earned her many enemies, as well as "smear" campaigns and abusive mail. She also campaigned for homosexual law reform and battled (unsuccessfully) against Dublin Corporation over its plans to build an office block over a historic Viking site.

In 1975, Mary relinquished her independent status in the senate and joined the Labour Party. But soon after Labour entered into a coalition government in 1982, she resigned from the party in protest against an agreement between her government and that of British Prime Minister Margaret Thatcher: Although she was herself a Catholic, Mary felt that the rights of Northern Ireland's protestants had not been sufficiently considered.

By 1989, many of the causes for which Mary had fought had been won, and she decided not to seek reelection to the senate. But in 1990, at the controversial invitation of the Labour Party, she stood as a candidate for the position of president of Ireland. Assisted by a scandal involving her main opponent and the very positive impression she made as a potential "reforming" president, Mary was elected and became Ireland's first Labour candidate and first woman to win the presidency.

Mary had major assets for the job she had to do: legal knowledge, political experience, high ethical values, commitment to the underprivileged, and strong interpersonal skills. She broke a long period of cool relations between Ireland and Great Britain by being the first Irish president to visit the queen at Buckingham Palace. She worked to develop relations between her country and the Irish migrants scattered round the world and placed a special symbol for them on public view in her window. In Northern Ireland, she met with politicians of all shades of opinion. She invited many groups to visit her in her residence—for example, gay rights groups. She visited famine-stricken Somalia in 1992 and Rwanda in the aftermath of its terrible civil war—then became emotional about it at a subsequent press conference. She raised the presidency to a new level and was remarkably popular with her people, reaching an unheard-of popularity rating of 93%.

Mary's outstanding record as president, her legal background, her commitment to human rights and her lifelong pursuit of justice and equality resulted in 1997 in her being appointed to the position of United Nations High Commissioner for Human Rights, a position she held until 2002. Her outspoken views on such topics as the plight of Afghans in the War on Terror and the suppression of ethnic minorities in China made her enemies in superpower countries, but Mary remains defiantly true to her principles. Among the many other positions she holds or has held are chancellor of her old university, Trinity College; chair of the Council of World Women Leaders; and honorary president of Oxfam International. At the time of writing, she is also a professor at Columbia University and heads the Ethical Globalization Initiative with a goal of bringing human rights standards into the globalization process, particularly as it affects Africa.

Conclusion

Despite the career predictabilities brought about by career inheritances and social structure (Chapter 2), and by patterned sequences of human development and aging (Chapter 3), much of our career behavior and success depends on our own actions. Understanding human psychology, particularly concepts such as motivation, learning, cognition, intention, and self-efficacy, and applying them to careers, provides a basis for us to increase our agency and control over our careers. Proactive career behavior and the practices of self-direction, and adaptability around clear identity and values as in the protean career ideal, enable understanding to be put into action. Practices of goal setting and career management can assist.

Key Points in This Chapter

- Careers result not just from social structure and natural human cycles but also from deliberate action by the person concerned. The term *agency* represents the idea that people are agents determining their own careers.
- Many careers are determined by self-expression—the individual's wish to express his or her identity or talents.
- Various career development theories indicate the processes underlying career action. Career construction theory presents career behavior as being based on the implementation of the individual's changing self-concept. Social learning theory shows how people learn career behavior in social settings. Social cognitive career theory indicates the psychological processes that people go through when making their career decisions and choices.
- Career success is a criterion for career action, but people define success differently.
- Career management is a semiformal process through which an individual can apply general management principles to the self-management of his or her career.
- A craft model of career development combines advantages of a science model and an art model.
- The protean career combines adaptability, self-direction, and values and is a good model for career self-management in contemporary conditions.

Questions From This Chapter

General Questions

1. Consider the careers of well-known people. Find out more about them on the Internet if you need to. To what extent do you think they have succeeded because of their personal actions?

2. If your career were to be based purely on the principle of self-expression, what would you do? How realistic is this? Can you see ways in which your expression of yourself might have application to different types of opportunity?

3. Write or draw a simple model of career development that includes the key elements from career construction theory, social identity theory, and social cognitive theory.

4. Write your own definition of *career success*. Now ask other people for their definition. Is there consensus? Do you think it is realistic to have multiple competing objectives (e.g., money, satisfaction, balance)?

5. Can you apply the idea of career planning to your own career, even at the level of your career as a student trying to move toward your work career and maximize your academic performance? How would you go about planning the next 3 years of your career?

6. Think of someone you know who may show protean career characteristics and write how they meet the definition.

Career Case Study Questions

1. Ask your case person to describe his or her self-identity in careers and how it might have influenced various career choices (career construction theory) and ask to what extent the case person thinks he or she learned personal career behavior from others (social learning theory).

2. Ask your case person whether any parts of his or her career were planned and, if so, what kind of planning techniques were used and how the case person was able to implement the plans.

3. Evaluate your case person's career against the criteria for the protean career.

References

Adamson, S. J., Doherty, N., & Viney, C. (1998). The meaning of career revisited: Implications for theory and practice. *British Journal of Management, 9*(4), 251-259.

Allen, V. (Ed.). (1990). *The concise Oxford dictionary of current English.* Oxford, UK: Clarendon Press.

Arthur, M. B., Khapova, S. N., & Wilderom, C. P. M. (2005). Career success in a boundaryless career world. *Journal of Organizational Behavior, 26*(2), 177-202.

Bakan, D. (1966). *The duality of human existence.* Boston: Beacon.

Bandura, A. (1986). *Social foundations of thought and action: A social cognitive theory.* Englewood Cliffs, NJ: Prentice Hall.

Bolles, R. (2003). *What color is your parachute? 2004: A practical manual for job hunters and career changers.* New York: Tenspeed Press.

Boyatzis, R., McKee, A., & Goleman, D. (2002). Reawakening your passion for work. *Harvard Business Review, 80*(4), 86-94.

Briscoe, J., & Hall, D. T. (in press). The interplay of the protean and boundaryless careers: Combinations and implications. *Journal of Vocational Behavior.*

Brown, D., Brooks, L., & Associates. (1984). *Career choice and development.* San Francisco: Jossey-Bass.

Buck, M. L., Lee, M. D., & MacDermid, S. M. (2002). Designing creative careers and creative lives through reduced-load work arrangements. In M. Peiperl, M. B. Arthur, & N. Anand (Eds.), *Career creativity: Explorations in the remaking of work* (pp. 77-99). Oxford, UK: Oxford University Press.

Busacca, L. A., & Taber, B. J. (2002). The Career Maturity Inventory-Revised: A preliminary psychometric investigation. *Journal of Career Assessment, 10*(4), 441-455.

Crites, J. O., & Savickas, M. L. (1996). Revision of the Career Maturity Inventory. *Journal of Career Assessment, 4,* 131-168.

Csikszentmihalyi, M. (1991). *Flow: The psychology of optimal experience.* New York: HarperCollins.

Derr, B. C. (1986). *Managing the new careerists: The diverse career success orientations of today's workers.* San Francisco: Jossey-Bass.

Edwards, J. R., Baglioni, A. J., Jr., & Cooper, C. L. (1990). Stress, type-A, coping and psychological and physical symptoms: A multi-sample test of alternative models. *Human Relations, 43*(10), 919-956.

Evans, D. (1995). *Glamour blondes: From Mae to Madonna.* London: Britannia Press.

Fayol, H. (1949). *General and industrial management.* London: Pitman.

Greenhaus, J. H., Callanan, G. A., & Godschalk, V. M. (2000). *Career management* (3rd ed.). Orlando, FL: Dryden.

Gunz, H. P., & Heslin, P. (2004). Reconceptualizing career success. *Journal of Organizational Behavior, 26*(2), 105-111.

Gysbers, N. C., Heppner, M. J., & Johnston, J. A. (1998). *Career counseling: Process, issues, and techniques.* Boston: Allyn & Bacon.

Hall, D. T. (1976). *Careers in organizations.* Glenview, IL: Scott Foresman.

Hall, D. T. (2002). *Careers in and out of organizations.* Thousand Oaks, CA: Sage.

Hall, D. T., & Associates. (1996). *The career is dead—Long live the career: A relational approach to careers.* San Francisco: Jossey-Bass.

Hall, D. T., & Moss, J. E. (1998). The new protean career contract: Helping organizations and individuals adapt. *Organizational Dynamics, 26*(3), 22-37.

Hansen, L. S. (1997). *Integrative life planning—Critical tasks for career development and changing life patterns.* San Francisco: Jossey-Bass.

Hansen, L. S. (2002). Integrative life planning (ILP): A holistic theory for career counseling with adults. In S. G. Niles (Ed.), *Adult career development: Concepts, issues and practices* (3rd ed., pp. 59-78). Tulsa, OK: National Career Development Association.

Harmon, L. W., Hansen, J. C., Borgen, F. H., & Hammer, A. C. (1994). *Strong interest inventory: Applications and technical guide.* Palo Alto, CA: Consulting Psychologists' Press.

Holland, D. C., Fritzsche, B. A., & Powell, A. B. (1994). *The self-directed search: Professional users' guide.* Odessa, FL: Psychological Assessment Resources.

Ibarra, H. (2003). *Working identity: Unconventional strategies for reinventing your career.* Boston: Harvard Business School Press.

Inkson, K. (1987). Re-skilling and the integration of work: A study of potters. *Human Relations, 40,* 163-176.

Inkson, K. (2002). Thinking creatively about careers: The use of metaphor. In M. Peiperl, M. B. Arthur, R Goffee, & N. Anand (Eds.), *Career creativity: Explorations in the remaking of work* (pp. 15-34). Oxford, UK: Oxford University Press.

Inkson, K. (in press). Protean and boundaryless careers as metaphors. *Journal of Vocational Behavior.*

Inkson, K., & Arthur, M. B. (2001). How to be a successful career capitalist. *Organizational Dynamics, 31*(3), 48-61.

King, Z. (2004). Career self-management: Its nature, causes and consequences. *Journal of Vocational Behavior, 65*(1), 112-133.

Krumboltz, J. D. (1979). A social learning theory of career decision making. In A. M. Mitchell, G. D. Jones, & J. D. Krumboltz (Eds.), *Social learning and career decision making* (pp. 19-49). Cranston, RI: Carroll.

Krumboltz, J. D. (1991). *Manual for the Career Beliefs Inventory.* Palo Alto, CA: Consulting Psychologists Press.

Krumboltz, J. D. (1994). Improving career development theory from a social learning perspective. In M. L. Savickas & R. W. Lent (Eds.), *Convergence in career development theories* (pp. 9-31). Palo Alto, CA: Consulting Psychologists Press.

Krumboltz, J. D., & Henderson, S. J. (2002). A learning theory for career counselors. In S. G. Niles (Ed.), *Adult career development: Concepts, issues and practices* (3rd ed., pp. 41-57). Tulsa, OK: National Career Development Association.

Krumboltz, J. D., & Levin, A. S. (2002). *Planned happenstance: Making the most of chance events in your life and your career.* Atascadero, CA: Impact.

Lent, R. W., & Brown, S. D. (2002). Social cognitive career theory and adult career development. In S. G. Niles (Ed.), *Adult career development: Concepts, issues and practices* (3rd ed., pp. 77-97). Tulsa, OK: National Career Development Association.

Lent, R. W., Brown, S. D., & Hackett, G. (1994). Towards a unifying social cognitive theory of career and academic interest, choice and performance. *Journal of Vocational Behavior, 45,* 79-122.

Lent, R. W., Brown, S. D., & Hackett, G. (2002). Social cognitive career theory. In D. Brown & Associates (Eds.), *Career choice and development* (4th ed., pp. 255-311). San Francisco: Jossey-Bass.

Levinson, E. M., Ohler, D. L., Caswell, S., & Kiewra, K. (1998). Six approaches to the assessment of career maturity. *Journal of Counseling and Development, 76*(4), 475-482.

London, M., & Stumpf, S. A. (1986). Individual and organizational career development in changing times. In D. T. Hall (Ed.), *Career development in organizations* (pp. 21-49). San Francisco: Jossey Bass.

Love, N. (2002). *The pathfinder: How to choose and change your career for a lifetime of satisfaction and success.* New York: Fireside.

Mallon, M., & Walton, S. (2005). Career and planning: The ins and outs of it. *Personnel Review, 34*(4), 468-487.

Marshall, J. (1989). Re-visioning career concepts: A feminist invitation. In M. B. Arthur, D. T. Hall, & B. S. Lawrence (Eds.), *Handbook of career theory* (pp. 275-291). Cambridge, UK: Cambridge University Press.

Mirvis, P. H., & Hall, D. T. (1994). Psychological success and the boundaryless career. *Journal of Organizational Behavior, 15,* 365-380.

Mitchell, K. E. (2003). *The unplanned career: How to turn curiosity into opportunity.* San Francisco: Chronicle Books.

Mitchell, K. E., Levin, A. S., & Krumboltz, J. D. (1999). Planned happenstance: Constructing unexpected career opportunities. *Journal of Counseling and Development, 77*(2), 115-124.

Mitchell, L. K., & Krumboltz, J. D. (1996). Krumboltz's learning theory of career choice and counseling. In D. Brown & L. Brooks (Eds.), *Career choice and development* (3rd ed., pp. 233-280). San Francisco: Jossey-Bass.

Murphy, S. E., & Ensher, E. A. (2001). The role of mentoring support and self-management strategies on reported career outcomes. *Journal of Career Development, 27*(4), 229-246.

Ng, T. W. H., Eby, L. T., Sorenson, K. L., & Feldman, D. C. (2005). Predictors of objective and subjective career success: A meta-analysis. *Personnel Psychology, 58*(2), 367-408.

Niles, S. G. (Ed.). (2002). *Adult career development: Concepts, issues and practices* (3rd ed.). Tulsa, OK: National Career Development Association.

Osipow, S. H., & Fitzgerald, L. (1996). *Theories of career development* (4th ed.). Boston: Allyn & Bacon.

Parkinson, C., & Parker J. (1988). *Profiles: 24 New Zealand potters.* Auckland, NZ: David Bateman.

Perrone, K. M., Gordon, P. A., Fitch, J. C., & Civiletto, C. L. (2003). The Adult Career Concerns Inventory: Development of a short form. *Journal of Employment Counseling, 40*(4), 172-180.

Poehnell, G., & Amundson, N. (2002). CareerCraft: Engaging with, energizing and empowering career creativity. In M. Peiperl, M. B. Arthur, & N. Anand (Eds.), *Career creativity: Explorations in the remaking of work* (pp. 105-122). Oxford, UK: Oxford University Press.

Reardon, R. C., Lenz, J. G., Sampson, J. P., & Peterson, G. W. (2006). *Career development and planning: A comprehensive approach* (2nd ed.). Mason, OH: Thomson.

Rifkin, J. (1995). *The end of work.* New York: Putnam.

Robbins, S. P., Bergman, R., & Stagg, I. (1997). *Management.* Englewood Cliffs, NJ: Prentice Hall.

Savickas, M. L. (2002). Career construction: A developmental theory of vocational behavior. In D. Brown & Associates (Eds.), *Career choice and development* (4th ed., pp. 149-205). San Francisco: Jossey-Bass.

Savickas, M. L. (2005). The theory and practice of career construction. In S. D. Brown & R. W. Lent (Eds.), *Career development and counseling: Putting theory and research to work* (pp. 42-70). Hoboken, NJ: Wiley.

Savickas, M. L., & Hartung, P. J. (1996). The career development inventory in review: Psychometric and research findings. *Journal of Career Assessment, 4,* 171-188.

Stroh, L. K., Brett, J. M., & Reilly, A. H. (1994). A decade of change: Managers' attachments to their organizations and their jobs. *Human Resources Management, 33,* 531-548.

Super, D. E. (1953). A theory of vocational development. *American Psychologist, 8,* 185-190.

Super, D. E. (1957). *The psychology of careers.* New York: Harper & Row.

Super, D. E. (1980). A life-span, life-space approach to career development. *Journal of Vocational Behavior, 16,* 282-298.

Super, D. E., Thomson, A. S., & Lindeman, R. H. (1988). *Adult Career Concerns Inventory: Manual for research and exploratory use in counseling.* Palo Alto, CA: Consulting Psychologists Press.

Swanson, J. L., & Fouad, N. A. (1999). *Career theory and practice: Learning through case studies.* Thousand Oaks, CA: Sage.

Thatcher, V. S., & McQueen, A. (Eds.). (1981). *The new Webster encyclopaedic dictionary of the English language.* Chicago: Consolidated Book Publishers.

Tiedeman, D. V., & O'Hara, R. P. (1963). *Career development: Choice and adjustment.* Princeton, NJ: College Entrance Examination Board.

Waterman, R. H., Waterman J. A., & Collard, B. A. (1994). Towards a career resilient workforce. *Harvard Business Review, 72*(4), 87-95.

Wehmeyer, M. L., Lattimore, J., Jorgenson, J. D., Palmer, S. B., Thompson, E., & Schumaker, S. M. (2003). The self-determined career development model: A pilot study. *Journal of Vocational Rehabilitation, 19*(2), 79-87.

CHAPTER 5

Careers as Fit

A Match Made in Heaven

Philip is not academically or intellectually gifted. He has no qualifications beyond a high school education. But he is practical and good with his hands. He loves constructing and repairing things. He is also sociable, has good interpersonal skills, and enjoys meeting people. Since his conversion to the Christian religion a few years ago, he has developed strong altruistic values and a desire to express his faith in his work. He has also cast aside his previous materialistic values. Last, he is not very literate, hates routine, and has a real antipathy to filling in forms and doing other administrative work. What job can he find that simultaneously requires manual and social abilities and religious and altruistic, but not administrative, interests?

Philip found just the job! He was appointed to a manager/caretaker position at a camp facility that specializes in catering for small conventions and retreats organized by Christian church groups. He and his wife, Martha, and small son Jonathan live on the premises in a small chalet. Philip loves it. There is plenty of manual work to be done in developing the facility and keeping it smart and well maintained. Hosting the client groups requires ongoing interaction with pleasant people who share his religious views. True, the job is very poorly paid, but then he doesn't care about that anymore. After all, it is God's work he is doing.

But what of the administrative side? The job requires supplies to be ordered, bookings to be confirmed, space allocations to be planned and recorded, letters to be written, financial records to be kept. Here, too, Philip found a solution. Martha shares Philip's religious beliefs, has a background in office administration, and enjoys that kind of work. So Philip delegates her all the administrative work, which she does unpaid on a part-time basis while also looking after Jonathan. The camp owner doesn't mind, as long as the work is done. In fact, he gets two employees for the price of one. As for Philip, he feels both he and Martha have indeed found the "perfect fit."

n expressing his satisfaction with his new job, Philip is reflecting a career ideal that most of us can identify with: that however complex and demanding we may be in our expectations of the job we want, somewhere out there is a job that fits like a glove, requiring exactly the abilities that we have and offering exactly the rewards and satisfaction that we want. The obverse—not fitting—is represented by the common metaphor "you can't fit a square peg in a round hole," which conjures imagery of a lot of "pegs" (people) walking around a field full of "holes" (jobs) looking for the right one to fit into. Extending the notion to careers, we have to recognize that over time the pegs are likely to change in size and shape (Chapter 3) and so are the jobs (Chapter 1). How far then can we apply the "fit" metaphor to careers?

Recall from Chapter 1 that in 1909 Frank Parsons published *Choosing a Vocation,* the first-ever book on career choice and guidance. The term *vocation* implied that careers should be defined by occupations. Parsons wanted to ensure that people made good choices of occupation. They should then use reason to relate their knowledge of themselves to the jobs available and thereby choose jobs with a good fit. In its essentials, Parsons's formulation is still the philosophy of much career guidance today.

The advent of the Internet has given new opportunities for the selling of the "fit" metaphor by those who think they can help us find the perfect fit. Consider the case of CareerMatch.

Searching for a Fit

Here is an excerpt from a Web site called CareerMatch*:

Are you stuck in a job that doesn't fit you?

Are you trying to find a good career and don't know where to start?

Do you want to know where you would fit in?

Use CareerMatch's unique package of assessments to match yourself against the world of work.

Let CareerMatch help you to find the best job for *who you are* and *what you would like to do.* Don't delay! You owe it to yourself to make an *investment* in yourself and *your future* now. Use CareerMatch for 30 days for $29.95. It could change your life forever!

Using this type of advertising, Career-Match offers immediate assessments of your "interests, motivations, activities, abilities, skills and knowledge." All you have to do is complete the online questionnaires. Career-Match's computer systems will score them automatically. "Your profile will then be matched against 500 different occupations and an assessment will be made of your suitability for each one."

Do you like the sound of it? Do you think that CareerMatch may be able to help you? Do you want to go immediately to your computer and send CareerMatch money? If so, read the rest of this chapter first: There may be strengths in what CareerMatch offers, but there are weaknesses, too.

*To avoid seeming to endorse an unproven Web site, the name of the site and some minor details of its approach have been changed.

In this publicity material, CareerMatch implies the following statements—the basis of most applications of the "fit" image of careers:

- People are different. They have different characteristics. Therefore, each person is suited to different occupations.
- Like people, each occupation has its own profile—characteristics that indicate what kind of people are suited to it.
- Through its process of assessment, CareerMatch is able to measure accurately people's individual characteristics that are relevant to their occupational choices.
- CareerMatch can use the information from the assessments it makes of different people to advise them of their suitability for different occupations.
- People can choose an occupation that is a good match for them—if possible, the "perfect match."

Thus, CareerMatch claims to establish the degree of congruence between each person and his or her career choices. Find a good fit, according to the Web site and the metaphor, and you will have a happy and successful career.

Work Adjustment Theory

An important theoretical application of the "fit" metaphor to people at work is called, variously, the theory of work adjustment (Dawis & Lofquist, 1984) and person-environment correspondence theory (Dawis, 2002). The latter heading is a nice summary of the precepts of the "fit" metaphor.

This theory consists of a series of formal propositions relating to people's adjustment to their work. The key variables and relationships in the theory are shown in Figure 5.1.

The theory is based on the correspondence or noncorrespondence of individuals with their jobs. Both individuals and jobs are complex, but like many psychologists and others interested in individual differences, Dawis and Lofquist (1984) believed that this complexity can be reduced to a finite set of variables:

- With respect to individual people, there is a set of variables labeled "abilities." These are the person's capacities and aptitudes relevant to specific skills that may be required to do a job: Abilities represent what the person is capable of doing.
- There is also a set of variables labeled "values" that express outcomes that the individual might seek to obtain from the job. Six crucial values defined by Dawis and Lofquist (1984) are achievement, comfort, status, altruism, safety, and autonomy. These indicate what needs the individual wants from the job.
- Corresponding to the person's abilities are ability requirements of the job— the abilities that are needed to perform the job well. A close correspondence between abilities and ability requirements brings satisfactoriness (i.e., the individual performs the job well).
- Corresponding to the person's values are reinforcer patterns—the rewards that are available from the job. A close correspondence between values and reinforcements brings job satisfaction.

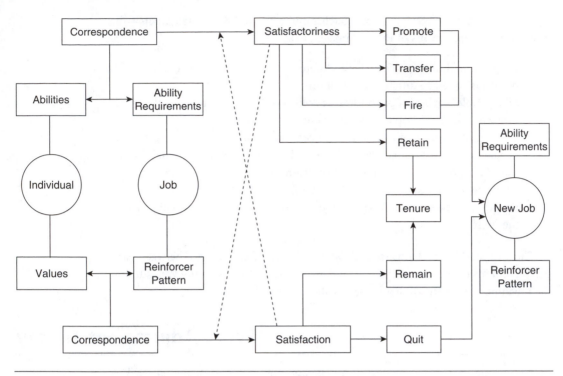

Figure 5.1   Prediction of Work Adjustment

Source: Copyright © Dawis and Lofquist (1984). Reprinted with permission of John Wiley & Sons, Inc.

Because employing organizations have an interest in their employees' satisfactoriness, and the employees seek maximum satisfaction, ensuring close correspondences between people and their jobs is presumed to be functional for both.

Figure 5.1 also shows some possible consequences of satisfactoriness, satisfaction, and their opposites. High or moderate satisfactoriness or satisfaction, or both, normally leads to the individual remaining in the job. But high satisfactoriness can lead to promotion, low satisfactoriness to being fired. Either can lead to transfer. Low satisfaction can lead to quitting. All these outcomes mean that the cycle recommences, with the individual seeking to find a new correspondence between his or her abilities and values and a new job.

However, these relationships are, according to the theory, moderated by other forces. People who are dissatisfied don't necessarily leave the job. For a start, some people are more flexible or more persistent than others and able to tolerate noncorrespondence for longer. Also, the theory is called a theory of work *adjustment:* There are ways the individual can adjust to increase his or her correspondence with the job. Dawis and Lofquist (1984) mentioned active modes of adjustment where the individual adjusts by changing the ability requirements or reinforcement patterns of the environment—for example, by altering the job description or seeking additional rewards. In reactive modes of adjustment, the individual alters the person rather than the environment—for example, by taking new training courses to increase abilities or by altering personal priorities to change values. Suzanne's case is an example of active adjustment to noncorrespondence.

Making Adjustments

Suzanne was a graduate biological scientist with several years' work experience in a consultancy company offering technical services to the food industry. Her job was to develop product inspection programs according to U.S. Food and Drug Administration (FDA) requirements, and to work with client companies to study their requirements and ensure that the applications were customized to their needs. Suzanne was technically competent and had a strong intellectual interest in the software, but she was also somewhat extroverted. Her day-to-day work was as a laboratory scientist, with a lot of detailed technical testing to do but without much contact with other people. She felt envious of the company's sales and service people, who were on the road a lot of the time, dealing with clients. She worried that she was failing to develop as a person and might eventually find herself consigned to a long future in boring technical roles. She was also missing out on the people experience, and the networks, that might eventually lead to promotion or transfer to a managerial position. She decided she needed a more social job.

Without telling her employer, Suzanne went for interviews for sales and client liaison positions with other companies in her industry. But it didn't work: Her skills were very specialized, and she had no other relevant experience. There was no market for her skills, and she was offered no jobs. What should she do? Perhaps she should try to train herself in new skills? But then, she thought, why should she? Apart from the routines of her job, she really liked working for her current employer—it was a good company, with understanding bosses, in a convenient location, and she was well paid.

So Suzanne went to her manager, confessed her discomfort, and talked the problem over with him. The manager was sympathetic, especially because he had been concerned about Suzanne's apparent isolation and lack of self-confidence. He didn't want to lose a good employee. Eventually, they agreed on a solution—to redefine her role in such a way that she took over part of the client liaison work for a number of the applications she was developing; and to appoint a new graduate to assist Suzanne and others on the technical side. So Suzanne received a fresh job description, and the change was made. That was 6 months ago. Suzanne's job satisfaction and sense of self-efficacy have dramatically increased due to the redefinition of her work to better fit her interests. She has also increased her performance and value to the organization. Her new job is a much better fit.

In the example, the noncorrespondence was mainly between Suzanne's values and the organization's reinforcement patterns. Suzanne's immediate reaction was to quit, but with the help of her manager she was able to make an appropriate active adjustment that brought the job into correspondence with her values.

Work adjustment theory can also provide a framework for understanding occupational choice. The process is shown in Figure 5.2 on the next page (Dawis, 1996).

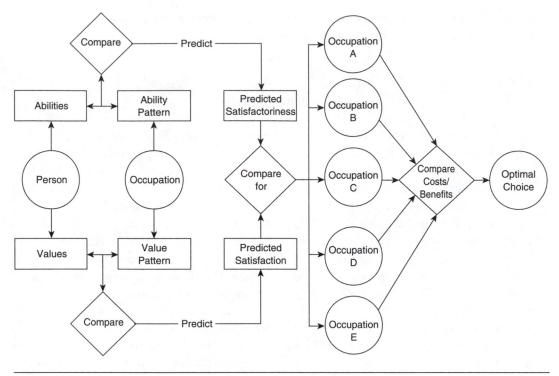

Figure 5.2 Using the Theory of Work Adjustments in Career Choice

Source: Copyright © Dawis (1996). Reprinted with permission of John Wiley & Sons, Inc.

In this process, the correspondence has to be with an occupation. The idea of occupation implies that even though every job is unique, jobs in the same occupation are sufficiently similar to enable us to figure out the ability requirements and reinforcement pattern of the whole occupation: "A teacher is a teacher is a teacher." An occupation can therefore be profiled in terms of its required abilities and reinforcement patterns. Individuals who are considering an occupation, or being considered for it, can also be profiled to see if they are congruent. This comparison enables the prediction of satisfactoriness and satisfaction. In this way, individuals can compare themselves with a range of different occupations, compare the costs and benefits in satisfactoriness/satisfaction terms, and make the optimal choice. Organizations or employment consultants who wish to can apply similar principles to their personnel selection tasks, choosing those applicants who have a close correspondence with the occupations available.

Both the theory and the practice of these principles require the identification of the traits of both people and occupations that are important in determining correspondence and a means of measuring the traits thus identified. If we do not measure the characteristics of the career aspirant, and those of the occupations he or she is interested in, how can we assess congruence, predict the outcome, and offer advice?

In common with many adherents—theorists and practitioners—of the "fit" metaphor, Dawis and Lofquist (1984) are strong on measurement. They measure a person's abilities using a test battery known as the General Aptitude Test Battery, they measure values using the Minnesota Importance Questionnaire, and they measure required abilities and reinforcement patterns using Occupational Aptitude Patterns. They also have standard measures of satisfactoriness and satisfaction. All of these measures assess a number of different dimensions within the broad categories of abilities, values, and so forth. All were developed systematically according to good psychometric principles. They enable systematic tests of the work adjustment theory to be developed, with results moderately favorable to the theory (Dawis & Lofquist, 1984: Rounds, Dawis, & Lofquist, 1987).

Personal Traits and Occupational Choice

Dawis and Lofquist (1984), not to mention Parsons (1909), advocated consideration and measurement of both individual and occupational characteristics as a means of assessing congruence or correspondence. But the greatest emphasis in career assessment has always been on measuring people's characteristics. Much of the impetus came from the work of early psychologists, such as James Cattell (1890), Alfred Binet (1911), and Charles Spearman (1923), who were interested in the nature of human capacities and the measurement of individual differences in human ability, and who developed the first intelligence tests, which were used in the early 20th century to determine students' fitness for various forms of education.

The distinction made by Dawis and Lofquist (1984) between abilities (what the individual is capable of) and values, needs, or interests (what the individual wants to do) was recognized early, and the first test of vocational interests, the Strong Vocational Interest Blank, appeared in 1927. The approach came to be known as trait-and-factor theory (see Chapter 1) because of its focus on different human traits and its use of the statistical technique known as factor analysis to discover the constructs or traits defined by the statistical associations contained in mass test data (Betz, Fitzgerald, & Hill, 1989).

The Second World War saw the beginnings of the massive application of the "fit" metaphor and trait-and-factor theory in the mass testing of millions of military personnel in the interests of assigning them efficiently to tasks that suited them (e.g., Stewart, 1947). After the war, the science of industrial psychology applied the same kind of thinking to personnel selection in large organizations. Many new tests were developed to test a wide range of aptitudes, including verbal and numerical reasoning; spatial, clerical, and scientific skills; and various forms of manual dexterity (e.g., Thurstone, 1955).

In the United States and Europe, clear possibilities began to be seen for offering advice—and sometimes direction—to young people who were unsure about their career choices and for using a range of assessment devices to gather information about the traits of these clients. With the emphasis on satisfaction as well as satisfactoriness, tests were broadened to include more assessments of values and interests. To some extent, the career counseling movement was driven not just by the wish to assist people to make good career decisions but also by a burgeoning technology of paper-and-pencil tests of human traits that made it possible to measure a wide range of relevant variables. Particular attention was given to the measurement of apparently directly applicable vocational interests—for example, in the Kuder's (1966) Occupational Interest Survey, the Holland (1979) Self-Directed Search, and the Strong Interest Inventory (Harmon, Hansen, Borgen, & Hammer, 1994).

Such techniques were validated by reference to the occupation side of the balance in the sense that occupations can be analyzed to determine whether they contain the kind of content included in the scales or whether people working in particular occupations report specific "normative" profiles of interests. Research on the validation of interest inventories led Betz et al. (1989) to conclude that "regardless of the method used to construct interest inventories, there is evidence that the congruence of interests with career choices is related to subsequent satisfaction and tenure in the job" (p. 30). Tracey and Hopkins (2003) stated that "interests and abilities . . . have a high level of correspondence with occupational choice" (p. 178). And although it is the area of vocational interests that has stimulated most interest and activity in the careers guidance movement, a range of valid tests of deeper assessments of both ability (including achievements, special aptitudes, and self-efficacy) and personality characteristics is also available. Crites and Taber (2002) provide an authoritative review.

John Holland: Vocational Personality Theory

Over many years, American researcher and former career counselor John Holland (1973, 1985, 1997) developed an important conceptual scheme, with supporting research and assessment techniques, for classifying individuals and jobs according to what Holland called "vocational personality." Holland's scheme is based on a huge volume of research conducted over several decades and provides not just an important theory of occupational fit but also a series of assessment devices and practical techniques to assist individuals in putting theory into practice.

Holland's system is a typology in the sense that it classifies individuals and occupations into specific types. For a detailed description of each type, interested readers are referred to Holland's own work and to more extensive reviews of it (e.g., Gottfredson, 1999; Spokane, Luchetta, & Richwine, 2002). Table 5.1 sketches a brief summary description of each type.

The hexagon shown in Figure 5.3 represents a space around which the different types are arranged. This means that, in a sense, different types are considered opposites—that is, Realistic is the opposite of Social, Investigative the opposite of Enterprising, and Artistic the opposite of Conventional. Individuals high on a particular type are also likely to be above average on adjacent types—for example, those strongest on the Artistic dimension may also have relatively high scores on Social and Investigative. Nevertheless, it is possible—though rare—for people to be high on two opposite types.

An individual's correspondence with each of the six types can be measured using an instrument called the Self-Directed Search (SDS), which is available from test agencies in a number of countries, or—for a fee—on the Internet

Table 5.1   Holland's Types

Type	Key Characteristics
Realistic	Like practical and physical activities, tend to dislike social interaction or the expression of feelings; task oriented
Investigative	Interested in ideas, logic, research, and problem solving; rational, scholarly, not particularly interested in social interaction
Artistic	Creative; enjoy unstructured situations and self-expression and autonomy and dislike regulation
Social	Enjoy working with and helping others, tend to be idealistic and skilled in interpersonal relations; warm and caring
Enterprising	Enjoy working with others, interested in leading others to achieve goals through persuasion, management, and so on; action oriented
Conventional	Interested in structure, planning, and organization; value security and control; like detail work

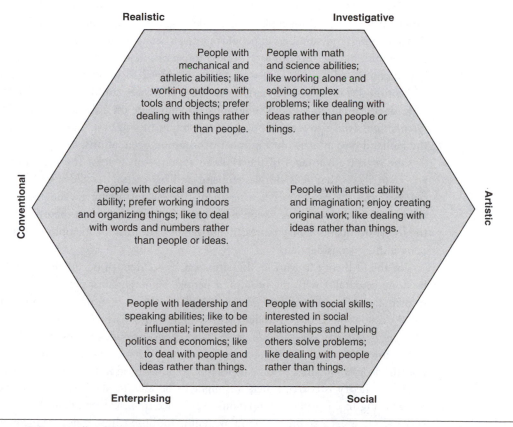

Figure 5.3   Holland's RIASEC Hexagon

Source: Reproduced by special permission of the publisher, Psychological Assessment Resources, Inc. 16204 North Florida Avenue, Lutz, FL 33549, from *Making Vocational Choices,* 3rd Edition. Copyright © 1973, 1985, 1992, 1997 by Psychological Assessment Resources, Inc. All rights reserved.

(www.selfdirectedsearch.com). The SDS asks questions about jobs you think you might like (even if you haven't the ability to do them), activities you enjoy or dislike, self-estimates of competence in specific activities and in more general areas, and even your occupational daydreams. When the test is scored, it provides you with an indication of the three types for which you score highest, each indicated by its first letter. For example, SEA would indicate that the individual's strongest area is Social, followed in order by Enterprising and Artistic. Full information about the SDS and a range of related assessment products is available in Reardon and Lenz (1998).

Holland (1997) was interested in other characteristics of people's profiles. For example, the degree of differentiation where there is a very clear distinction between their likes and dislikes; the degree of consistency, or internal coherence, in their responses to adjacent types in the conceptual scheme; and their degree of identity—the clarity and stability of their interests. Holland believed that high differentiation, consistency, and identity should make it easier for people to find occupations that suit them.

For the theory to be applicable, occupations as well as individuals must be able to be scored in relation to the relevant dimensions. There should be specific occupations considered most suitable for an SEA type, an ESA type, an AES type, and so on. Over the years, Holland (1997) and other researchers administered his inventory to large numbers of people from a wide range of occupations. Holland argued that surveying large numbers of people in a given occupation and noting their types enabled him to compute, for each occupation, a profile that represents the best fit. If you completed the test, you would be encouraged to think about occupations with profiles close to your own: For example, SEA types could also consider ESA, SAE, or SEI occupations. You could look up your type on a document called the *Occupations Finder* to see what occupations might fit you best. Table 5.2 indicates the Holland type attached to a number of common occupations.

One of the advantages of the Holland system—or at least the measurement aspect of it—is that it is simple. Holland and his colleagues did a good job of demystifying the psychometric assessment process and making validated assessments accessible to ordinary people. User satisfaction is high. On the other hand, the list of occupations may represent an oversimplification of the options that the person might consider.

For the fit theory to work in this situation, assessment of occupations needs to be done in parallel with the profiles of people. Here, Holland provides plenty of information. The *Occupations Finder* included with the SDS provides more than 1,000 occupations grouped under their RIASEC codes. The *Dictionary of Holland Occupational Codes* (Gottfredson & Holland, 1996) provides three-letter RIASEC codes for more than 12,000 occupations. The *Position Classification Inventory* (Gottfredson & Holland, 1991) enables jobs to be assessed in terms of their code.

If the theory is correct, then we ought to be able to show that people who are working in congruent occupations experience more career satisfaction, more success, and greater stability of employment than those whose types are incongruent with their work. Also, people who are in occupations with a poor fit to their vocational personality should presumably move over time into something more congruent, as the Work Adjustment theory predicts. Is this what happens?

Table 5.2   Holland Types for Some Common Occupations

CES	Accountant	RAS	Landscaper
CSI	Accounts Clerk	EIS	Lawyer
ASE	Actor	ESC	Manager
ASI	Artist	RSE	Massage Therapist
AIE	Architect	ISR	Medical Doctor
CSE	Bank Officer	ASI	Musician
SIC	Career Counselor	SRC	Nurse
RIA	Carpenter	ISR	Optometrist
CSR	Checkout Cashier	ISC	Physical Therapist
RSA	Chef	RIC	Pilot
ICR	Computer Programmer	RSI	Police Officer
CRI	Data Entry Operator	ISC	Psychologist
RAC	Dental Technician	RCS	Sailor
EAR	DJ	ESC	Sales Manager
CRA	Draftsperson	ESA	Salesperson
IRE	Engineer	IRS	Scientist
RCI	Factory Assembler	CSI	Secretary
RIE	Farmer	CRS	Shop Assistant
AIS	Fashion Designer	SIA	Social Worker
SEC	Funeral Director	SAR	Teacher
RSE	Hairdresser	CSE	Travel Agent
ESC	Human Resource Manager	RIA	Welder
ARE	Jeweler	ISC	X-ray Technician
AEI	Journalist		

As is usual in such situations, the answer is complex. Some reviews of research suggest that there is a moderate relationship between congruence and outcome variables, such as satisfaction (De Fruyt, 2002; Spokane, 1985; Spokane, Meir, & Catalano, 2000), and that people are often able to increase their congruence by adjusting their interests or by moving to a different occupation. However, other reviews suggest there is little relationship between congruence and career outcome variables (Tranberg, Slane, & Ekeberg, 1993). Researchers continue to refine and improve Holland's model to improve its predictions of career outcomes, but Bright and Pryor (2005) used Arnold's (2004) conclusion that Holland's notion of congruence accounts for less than 4% of the variance in occupational choice to conclude that the scientific prediction of fit is too difficult and that counselors might be better off paying attention to the more dynamic and unpredictable notions of chaos theory.

Again, because of factors such as the wide range of jobs within specific occupations and the large number of other factors in addition to vocational type that may affect the fit of a person with his or her work situation, it is not realistic to expect a strong relationship. The most useful contribution of the SDS may be the stimulus it gives the individual to do some systematic thinking about the potential fit between his or her potential career decisions, both in terms of relevant aspects of the self and in terms of initial exploration of possible choices.

Edgar Schein: Career Anchors

Edgar Schein was a business school professor who in 1978 published a book called *Career Dynamics: Matching Individual and Organizational Needs.* The subtitle is revealing because Schein used the term *matching* and thereby the "fit" metaphor, but he was interested in matching people not to occupations but to organizations.

Schein (1978) put forward a conceptual scheme based on what he called career anchors. His definition of *career anchors* was "enduring constellations of self-perceived, career-relevant, talents, motives and values" (Schein, 1978, p. 128). This represents a wider view than Holland's because in addition to vocational interests it involves values and abilities. "Anchors" provide another obvious metaphor, with connotations of heaviness and stability, apparently implying that like a ship held fast by its anchor, impervious to stormy conditions, a career must have a means of being held in place and a limited range of movement. Schein (1993) believed that even when people's careers seem quite varied and changing, their predominant anchors provide a consistent sense of purpose and direction. A summary of the anchors is shown in Table 5.3.

Schein's (1978) interest in organizational fit—the matching of a person's anchors with the values, competencies, systems, management, rewards, and so on of the employing organization—suggested that good matching could be facilitated by organizational management, where systems of employee development, transfer, promotion, and rewards could take anchors into account. Thus, in Table 5.3 the column labeled "Reward Valued" is similar to Dawis and Lofquist's (1984) concept of reinforcer pattern in indicating how the context can provide a good fit with the individual. But this is not about occupations; instead, it shows employer rewards offered can be tailored to individual anchors, regardless of occupation.

Like Holland, Schein (1985a, 1993) developed a questionnaire—the Career Orientation Inventory (COI)—to measure individuals' anchors. The COI has been used in a number of studies. However, the research conducted on career anchors lacks both the volume and the rigor of that on Holland's types. Also, rather than arguing as Holland had that each person's interests are arranged in a hierarchy of importance, Schein (1993) tended to insist that for most people one career anchor has enduring primacy over all the others, helping to keep careers stable over long periods.

That perhaps suggests a high degree of stability in careers, but in changing times people perhaps need a solid anchor to provide them with a clear sense of identity and direction. And there is more than one type of anchor. Not all anchors are massive steel constructions designed to keep a ship immobile in the fiercest of storms; some are smaller anchors towed behind the ship and used as stabilizers rather than

Table 5.3   Schein's Career Anchors

Career Anchor Name	Summary of Characteristics	Reward Valued
Technical/functional competence	Use of skills in specific work; focus on technical work rather than management	Recognition for skills
Managerial competence	Orientation to management of others, including accountability and interpersonal competence	Promotion, responsibility
Autonomy/ independence	Freedom from organizational rules, control over one's own work	Increased autonomy
Security-stability	Feeling security for the future, in employment, industry, location; predictable work	Recognition for loyalty
Entrepreneurial creativity	Personal innovation (e.g., in organization, products); achievement of something worthwhile; being prominent	Income, profitability of organization
Service/dedication to a cause*	Doing work that meets personal values (e.g., service to others)	Helping others, organizational mission
Pure challenge*	Achieving results against the odds, solving difficult problems	Novel or challenging work
Lifestyle*	Integrating work demands with other demands (e.g., family responsibilities), balancing expenditure of time	Job flexibility (e.g., flex-time, parental leave)

Note: *These three anchors were not in Schein's (1978) original five-anchor schema but were added in a later revision (Schein, 1985a).

foundations. If a person believes, said Schein, that "I know who I am and where I want to go," that person should not lightly give away such a valuable guide (E. Schein, personal communication, 2001).

Measuring Career-Related Traits

The past 50 years have seen the development of many questionnaires and diagnostic instruments, each designed to measure supposedly important human traits related to careers. Some of the instruments, such as the SDS, were painstakingly developed and improved over many years, tested and validated through well-constructed research, and used extensively and with good effect by professional career counselors, who may then be able to recommend to clients which occupations they appear to be suited to. This has been called the test-and-tell method of counseling (see Chapter 12). The tests are generally quantitative, measuring individual behavior against predetermined constructs, though recently there has been growing interest in the use of qualitative methods used by trained counselors (McMahon & Patton, 2002).

Other measures have been relatively casually developed by people with no particular qualifications or insight to do so. Many—though not all—devices sold on the Internet or through the popular media may be of this type. If you seek career-related assessments to assist your own decision making, you should always ask questions about these instruments' origins, the extensiveness of their use in the past, and their validity as demonstrated by good research.

The following key questions are raised by the "fit" metaphor: What human characteristics and what work characteristics make a difference? What should we measure to determine fit? For example, the CareerMatch Web site mentioned "interests, motivations, activities, abilities, skills, and knowledge." Holland measured interests, Schein, anchors. Clearly there is some overlap, but it is not complete.

A basic distinction, noted earlier, in relation to work adjustment theory is that between abilities and personality, values, and interests.

Abilities

As indicated in the discussion of work adjustment theory, the term *abilities* refers to what we are able to do, what we can do when we are working at our best. For example, we may be able to solve mathematical equations, write grammatically correct English, dismantle and clean a motor, or persuade others to change their minds about something—each of these indicating a potentially valuable ability or even a directly relevant skill, for at least some occupations. Employers tend to pay a lot of attention to such capabilities when they are deciding whom to hire for a particular job.

Abilities range from general intelligence—the famous "g" factor, which is thought to underlie all other human abilities (Spearman, 1923)—to special aptitudes, such as numerical and mechanical ability, to specific occupationally relevant skills, such as mastery of a foreign language or a particular software program, to achievements on specific jobs. Tests of abilities are inherently controversial due to concerns that they are culturally biased against certain groups (Casillas & Robbins, 2005), and in the United States their use in personnel selection is legally limited to situations where good relationships to job performance can be demonstrated. Over a range of different occupations, these relationships have been shown to be moderate to high (Hunter, 1986; Schmidt, 2002).

Because of their focus on job performance, many employing organizations use techniques such as aptitude and skill tests, manual and dexterity tests, work simulations, in-basket tests, assessed group discussions, and assessment centers to assess ability to do a job (Jackson & Schuler, 2000). The accuracy of such measures may be affected by factors such as the anxiety of candidates, but tests are part of the careers landscape, and people seeking new jobs should be prepared for them.

Tests tend to measure raw ability. Work experience turns raw ability into specific skills, which may be quite specialized. Although some work performance tests exist, performance may have to be measured in much less structured ways—for example, by information provided in a job or interview or guidance session, self-assessments by the person, and references from previous employers. In many situations, employers gauge applicants' skills by considering their previous experience in similar work, and testimonials.

Personality, Values, and Interests

The terms in the heading, in contrast, refer to what we are disposed to do (i.e., what we typically prefer to do or how we characteristically behave). For example, we may like attending concerts, socializing with other people, messing with motorcycles, or ensuring that things are well organized.

The broadest type of disposition is *personality*: "an individual's unique constellation of behavioral traits" (Weiten, 2001, p. 486). Personality theory assumes a degree of consistency in our behavior—that is, we carry traits such as extroversion or adaptability with us and display them in different situations so that they are bound to influence any behavior, including career behavior. In the past, there was considerable debate as to which are the key human personality variables, but nowadays there is a consensus among many psychologists that much of the personality variation between people can be attributed to their degree of five identifiable traits—extroversion, neuroticism, openness to experience, agreeableness, and conscientiousness (Wiggins & Trapnell, 1997). These factors can be measured using a questionnaire called the NEO Personality Inventory (Costa & McCrae, 1992; McCrae & Costa, 2003).

We can see intuitively how some personality characteristics might be related to fit with specific occupations. For example, extroversion might have a good fit with people jobs, such as teaching or sales. Conscientiousness might be better for jobs involving analysis and organizing, such as computer programming or inventory control. Suggestions for the use of the NEO Personality Inventory in career counseling are available (Costa, McCrae, & Kay, 1995). However, personality characteristics are so broadly conceptualized that only low associations with occupational fit are likely (Crites & Taber, 2002). On the one hand, personality characteristics may have some relationship to career success. Boudreau, Boswell, and Judge (2001) and Seibert and Kraimer (2001) found extroversion positively related to and neuroticism negatively related to career success, as they predicted. On the other hand, counter to prediction, agreeableness and openness were negatively related to extrinsic measures of career success such as salary. Do nice guys finish last after all?

Another much-used personality inventory is the Myers-Briggs Type Indicator (MBTI) (Myers & McCaulley, 1985), which measures people on four dimensions according to how they process information and make decisions: introversion versus extroversion (whether people draw their energy from the external world or from within themselves); sensing versus intuition (getting information from their five senses or from intuitive sources); thinking versus feeling (making decisions based on logic or based on values and emotions); and judging versus perceiving (preferring to live in an organized or in a spontaneous way). Between them, the four dimensions enable people to be classified into 16 different personality types, useful for determining a person's work preferences (Kummerow, 1991).

Values represent abstract outcomes that individuals seek to attain. In one formulation (Katz, 1993), 10 categories of value are income, prestige, independence, helping of others, security, variety, leadership, work in your main field of interest, leisure, and early entry (to an occupation). The potential to affect career behavior is clear: A helping others person is more likely to seek work as a poorly paid teacher or social worker, whereas a high-income person may make salary a major criterion of the job sought. Values thus provide much of the motivation for career-related actions. Brown (2002) pointed out that values have special importance because they typically differ as a result of the person's cultural background. Brown developed a theory and some evidence predicting occupational choice and fit from the assessment of values.

Interests are more specific than values. They are about what we like and dislike, what we choose to spend our time doing when given a choice. Concrete examples of interests are stamp collecting, carpentry, camping (rather specific), handicrafts, and active outdoor activity (rather general). Interests are derived from a range of sources (e.g., values, family, class, education), and like abilities they develop and become more specific over time.

Of course, interests are often related to abilities, as in the case of Stephanie, which also gives an idea of how generalized traits become refined and more specific through consistent application in jobs. Note how Stephanie's abilities were developed through different learning experiences and became more specialized.

Messing About With Motors

Stephanie was apparently blessed from an early age with the ability to understand machines, the manual dexterity to work with them, and a strong interest in doing so. In her childhood, encouraged by her parents, she helped her father fix the family car and motor mower. By her teens, she had her own motorcycle and enjoyed stripping it, cleaning it, fixing it, and tuning its motor almost more than she enjoyed riding it. She refined her skills by undertaking a mechanic's apprenticeship. After some years of working in repair companies specializing in high-performance sports cars, she obtained a job with a professional auto racing team and became highly expert in the team's cars.

Assessing Individuals

The traditional concept of occupational fit is simple: know yourself, know the world of work, and put the two together logically. Unfortunately, both people and the world of work are much more complicated. Given the complexities of human psychology epitomized by the huge number of theories, tests, and measures of human ability, interests, and so on, and the even greater complexities in the world of work, is it possible for us to know what we need to know and to make good choices for ourselves? Many would argue that although career choices are ours to make, most of us need periodic help from skilled practitioners who understand the processes of choice, are able to assess people on critical dimensions, and are skilled in the art of counseling. An example of what career professionals may be able to offer in terms of assessment is provided in the case of Leslie.

Assessing Leslie

Swanson and Fouad (1999) provided a worked-through example of the kind of thorough assessment of career-related dispositions that sophisticated theory-based measuring instruments can bring about. The case of Leslie was previously considered in Chapter 4. Leslie is a high school math teacher, 35 years of age, who is dissatisfied with her job and wishes to make a career change.

To gather background information about Leslie, Swanson and Fouad (1999) administered six questionnaire inventories to her. In an appendix to their book, they included Leslie's profile on all of these. They also provided an interpretation of her results. A summary of the questionnaires Leslie completed and the results observed by the investigators are as follows.

The SII, a version of the Strong Vocational Inventory (Harmon et al., 1994), contains 317 different items and was used to assess Leslie's interests on the six Holland interest types. Leslie's profile was SCI (Social, Conventional, Investigative). Another part of the questionnaire assessed her in relation to 25 clusters of vocational interests, indicating, for example, her strong interests in math and data management, as well as teaching, religious activities, and social service. Her interests were compared to the norms of people in 100 different occupations and were similar to those of actuaries, chemists, programmers, analysts, and other groups. A last part of the questionnaire indicated her preferences in personal style—for example, that she felt fine about working alone, enjoyed practical over academic learning, and did not like taking risks.

The Skills Confidence Inventory (Betz, Borgen, & Harmon, 1996) measures the same six themes but differentiates between the client's interest in an area and the client's confidence that he or she can complete tasks in the area. In Leslie's three main areas, her scores showed that in the social area her interests were higher than her confidence, in the investigative area her confidence was higher than her interest, and in the conventional area there was no difference.

The Minnesota Importance Questionnaire (Rounds, Henley, Dawis, Lofquist, & Weiss, 1981), mentioned earlier in association with work adjustment theory, assesses 21 needs divided among six values categories. Leslie showed especially high moral, ability utilization, achievement, and social service values but low authority and independence values.

The Myers-Briggs Type Inventory (Myers & McCaulley, 1985) was described earlier. Leslie was typed as an ISTJ—Introverted, Sensing, Thinking, Judging—type. Swanson and Fouad (1999) say this means that she is "task oriented, structured, and orderly in her work style, and values a work environment that offers stability and security and that contains other hardworking people" (p. 35).

The Adult Career Concerns Inventory (Super, Thomson, & Lindemann, 1988) is based on Super's notion of career stages (Chapter 3) and shows the client's degree of concern for tasks typically within the respective exploration, establishment, maintenance, and disengagement stages. Leslie's highest score was for the exploration stage.

The Career Beliefs Inventory (Krumboltz, 1991) has 96 items and is designed to identify illogical beliefs that may interfere with the process of making logical career decisions. Leslie's answers provide a range of possible barriers to her decision making, including her desire for others' approval, her wish not to relocate, and her need for a structured environment.

In considering Leslie as a career counseling client, Swanson and Fouad (1999) provide considerable additional "soft" information of the type that would be obtained through interview methods—for example, Leslie's career history, qualifications, and domestic circumstances as well as her own verbalizations of her interests, values, and so on. They also show how various important theories of career development can be used to further understand her case. The detailed account of her profile as assessed by inventory is provided only to indicate the sophisticated and intensive nature of the information that is potentially available to clients through their counselors, as they seek to understand themselves and to make good decisions.

On the other hand, many people claim that using such tests and questionnaires is applying spurious quantitative measurement to something that is not measurable in this way or is using a sledgehammer to crack a nut. For example, instead of having people fill in complex inventories of interests, it might be simpler to ask them what they are interested in, which some argue is equally valid (Borgen & Seling, 1978). A complex information-gathering process apparently requires the intervention of a career professional trained to choose, administer, and score the inventories and to interpret them for the client. Of course, there is much more to career guidance than this: A good advisor integrates knowledge of the person with understanding of the psychology of career choice, knowledge of occupations, and skills to help the client to make, and own, good career decisions. An alternative narrative process of career guidance based on qualitative, historical data has gained popularity in recent years (Chapter 12). But many people have to make important career decisions but do not have the opportunity, the inclination, or the money to invest in professional advice.

How well are we able to assess ourselves? Studies comparing self-assessments with independent assessments suggest that although we tend to overestimate ourselves, there is reasonable agreement between the rankings of people based on self-assessment and independent assessment (Mabe & West, 1982). Most likely, we can make a better stab at assessing ourselves on specific skills and interests, such as word processing or crossword puzzle solving, than on broad traits, such as general intelligence or agreeableness. In making our self-assessments, we usually have a lot of evidence to go on: for example, our educational achievements, our job performance, our evaluations at work, the feedback we get from relations and friends, and our day-to-day observation of our own behavior. Web sites such as CareerMatch and self-help books with built-in self-assessments are available, too. One approach recommends a wide range of do-it-yourself assessments (Clawson, Kotter, Vaux, & McArthur, 1992).

A resource available from the U.S. Department of Labor, at www.onetcenter .org, is the set of information packages and self-completion inventories known as O*NET. O*NET enables you to match yourself to as many as 20,000 different occupations and provides information about tasks, skills required, salaries, long-term prospects, and a host of other things. Thus, O*NET seeks to move beyond the assessment of job seekers to enable those job seekers—and other interested parties, such as employers, human resource managers, educators, and career counselors—to consider how the "pegs" match with the various "holes" available.

Assessing Jobs and Occupations

The other side of assessment is the assessment of jobs—the "holes" in our central metaphor. As shown in the case of Leslie, some assessment devices incorporate information about occupations that match particular individual profiles. However, there are major differences in type of work within the same general occupation—for example, the many specialties within medicine, such as surgery, orthopedics, pediatrics, psychiatry, and general practice—which may suit very different profiles. There are also major differences between organizations, such as size, location, financial health, future outlook, facilities, organizational culture, and social life. There are differences between specific jobs within the same occupation, such as responsibility, variety of tasks, physical setting, stress, independence, and management. All these mean that we need to be cautious in generalizing about jobs.

Also, as indicated in Chapter 1, there is the labor market to consider. In the end, employment is an economic transaction: However congruent you are with your chosen occupation, someone has to want to hire you, at a wage you are able to live on. Many would-be dancers, sports players, entertainers, divers, private eyes, and the like who have excellent interest in, and motivation and talent for, their lines of work, and in some cases excellent and expensive qualifications, find in the end that there are simply too many able people chasing a very small number of opportunities. Fortunately, much information is available on the Internet and elsewhere about numbers of persons employed in different occupations, areas of shortage and of oversupply, and prospects for expansion in the years ahead. See, for example, Reardon, Lenz, Sampson, and Peterson (2006).

Assessment of the job market can take a variety of forms: for example, scanning job vacancy columns and recruitment Web sites, visiting relevant organizations and recruitment consultants, talking with people employed in or knowledgeable about the kind of jobs you are interested in, going to career information centers and exhibitions, and reading reference books, company reports, and publicity and business news.

Career Decision Making

Assessing self and assessing context are only Steps 1 and 2 of the "fit" model. Step 3 is using what Parsons (1909) called true reasoning to make choices based on the comparison. By true reasoning, Parsons meant reasoning based on rationality. If you can accurately assess both yourself and the job or occupation in terms of goodness of fit, then, following work adjustment theory, you are able to predict satisfaction and satisfactoriness. We would probably consider a person choosing between three career options rational if he or she chose the one most likely to lead to optimum satisfaction.

Unfortunately, truly rational decision making depends on a number of conditions that are unlikely to exist (Huber, 1993). Our assessments of self and environment may be better than guesswork, but they will not be 100% accurate. Our prediction of future outcome may be just that—a prediction with a limited likelihood. Unanticipated events—an illness in the family, a new manager in the organization—may change the situation. True rationality is only possible with perfect prediction. In the world of careers, every decision, no matter how rigorously researched, involves risk.

Moreover, basic limitations in human psychology mean that each of us has limited capability to judge with full logic the wide range of factors and contingencies inherent in complex decisions (Simon, 1976). Simon's theory of bounded rationality asserts that in these situations we typically resort to simpler but less rational strategies, such as acting on intuition rather than reason (Behling & Eckel, 1991), making choices based only on the most salient information (Tversky & Kahneman, 1983), and "satisficing" (i.e., choosing the first plausible alternative rather than continuing to search for the best alternative). Psychological conditions such as depression may further interfere with effective decision making (Saunders, Peterson, Sampson, & Reardon, 2000).

For all these reasons, making decisions about best fit may be far from rational. Phillips, Friedlander, Pazienza, and Kost (1985) described three common decision-making styles:

- The *rational,* based on careful collection and analysis of information, with a long-term perspective, as outlined earlier
- The *intuitive,* based on emotional factors and imagination, often immediate rather than long term
- The *dependent,* where the decision is allowed to be based on random events (fatalism) or to be taken by other people (compliance)

The last style is the only one where the individual does not accept responsibility for his or her own actions and is apparently the least likely of the three to result in success. Surprisingly, Arnold (1997) stated that the other two styles may both be effective under the right circumstances, which may mean when being used by the right people—for example, those rated intuitive rather than sensing on the Myers-Briggs Type Index discussed earlier may make good decisions using an intuitive style, which recognizes deep feelings about the alternatives (Behling & Eckel, 1991).

Organizational Choice

This chapter is largely about the fit of people with their occupations. But Betz et al. (1989) held a different view of the fit metaphor as applied to careers:

> Optimal career outcomes for both the individual and the organization can best be facilitated through a congruence between the individual's characteristics and the demands, requirements and rewards of the organizational environment. (p. 26)

Note Betz et al.'s (1989) term *organizational environment.* It may well be important for individuals to achieve congruence not just with their jobs and occupations but also with their organizations: For example, the importance of fitting in to organizational culture—the predominant set of values and norms in the organization—is recognized (Argyris, 1957; Schein, 1985b). Schneider (1987) and Schneider, Kristof-Brown, Goldstein, and Smith (1997) applied the fit metaphor to the notion of organizational fit: They argued that individuals are differentially attracted to organizations on the basis of the organization's character and its fit with their personality. Organizations select those whom they too perceive to fit. Later, those who manage to find their way into the organization but do not properly fit in tend to leave or be asked to leave (O'Reilly, Chatman, & Caldwell, 1991). Thus, over time, the homogeneity of the organization steadily increases. The mechanisms involved are similar to those described in work adjustment theory. Unfortunately, methods of assessing individuals' fit with their organizations have not been much developed.

Conclusion

The use of the "fit" metaphor in theory and practice has much to commend it. It is based on a simple, commonsense view of life: Most of us have been in jobs that we felt "fit" or "didn't fit" us. The metaphor reflects the undeniable diversity of both people and jobs and attempts to systematize this diversity. It has enabled the development of an impressive technology of measurement of people and occupations to enable individuals and their advisors to make well-informed decisions. Last, it has stood the test of time well: Parsons's initial 1909 formulation, or something close to it, still forms part of the underlying system of beliefs of many current experts on careers.

Against these strengths we must set some undoubted weaknesses. The characteristics of human beings and of work contexts are difficult to measure. The way the metaphor is typically applied seems to suggest that occupations are homogeneous, when within occupations jobs may vary greatly. Some uses of the metaphor tend to ignore the realities of the labor market. Finally, the metaphor may lead to stereotyping of individuals as having particular characteristics permanently. As other chapters in this book show, no one remains the same forever, and jobs, too, change over time. Nevertheless, as a cornerstone of understanding careers and providing tools to enable people to improve their career satisfaction and success, the "fit" metaphor continues to prove its worth.

Key Points in This Chapter

- A common approach and ideal for careers is to ensure that there is a good fit between people and the work they do. This can be done by assessing people, assessing work, and logically matching them.
- Work adjustment theory suggests that if there is congruence between workers' abilities and values with their occupations' requirements and rewards,

their satisfaction and performance increase. The theory also suggests that people change jobs to achieve greater congruence.

- Practice based on the "fit" metaphor is assisted by psychometric assessments.
- Holland's vocational personality theory is based on six dimensions of vocational interest such that an individual's pattern can be matched against different occupations using the Self-Directed Search. Schein's theory of career anchors uses a typology of eight clusters of values, interests, and abilities.
- Career-relevant assessments of individuals' abilities, personality, values, and interests provide a structure of key traits and enable accurate professional measurement.
- Assessing the context of work opportunities is also important, but methods are more informal and less well developed.
- Career decision making in pursuit of a good fit aims to be rational but is affected by other factors.

Questions From This Chapter

General Questions

1. Find at least one Web site offering a service of personal assessment and information on suitable careers. As far as you are able to judge, how worthwhile and professional a service does it offer?

2. Consider the job or program of study you are currently engaged in. What "fit" process took place in your selection of this experience? How congruent do you feel it is? Can you change things by altering either the "peg" or the "hole"?

3. When you have to make a career decision, what do you think are the most important traits for you to know about yourself? Why? How could you go about gathering the necessary information?

4. Compare and contrast the work adjustment theory of Dawis and Lofquist, the vocational personality theory of Holland, and the career anchors theory of Schein. What similarities and differences do you see among them?

5. Make a list of some of the traits mentioned and defined in this chapter. Assess yourself on each one (e.g., much higher than average, higher than average, average, lower than average, much lower than average). If possible get a friend or relative who knows you well to assess you in the same way. Compare the results. What types of occupations are suggested?

6. Think of an occupation that you don't know much about but that interests you. Gather information about the occupation—for example, read job advertisements, research the job on the Internet, find out about related educational programs, and talk to people who do that job. Prepare a specification of the traits required by that occupation and assess its fit with your own traits.

Career Case Study Questions

1. Ask your career case person about the fit of some of his or her jobs. Were there times when the fit seemed poor? How did the person resolve the issue? What can you learn from this?

2. Discuss Holland's six dimensions with your case person. Try to estimate your case person's profile. (If you can afford the money and time, have the person complete the SDS online.) What did you learn from this activity?

References

Argyris, C. (1957). *Personality and organization.* New York: Harper & Row.

Arnold, J. (1997). *Managing careers into the twenty-first century.* London: Paul Chapman.

Arnold, J. (2004). The congruence problem in John Holland's theory of vocational decisions. *Journal of Occupational and Organizational Psychology, 77*(1), 95-113.

Behling, O., & Eckel, N. L. (1991). Making sense out of intuition. *Academy of Management Executive, 5*(1), 46-54.

Betz, N. E., Borgen, F. H., & Harmon, L. W. (1996). *Skills Confidence Inventory.* Palo Alto, CA: Consulting Psychologists Press.

Betz, N. E., Fitzgerald, L. F., & Hill, R. E. (1989). Trait-factor theories: Traditional cornerstone of career theories. In M. B. Arthur, D. T. Hall, & B. S. Lawrence (Eds.), *Handbook of career theory* (pp. 26-40). Cambridge, UK: Cambridge University Press.

Binet, A. (1911). Nouvelles recherches sur la mesure du niveau intellectuel chez les enfants d'ecole [New research on the measurement of the intellectual level of schoolchildren]. *L'Annee psychologique, 17,* 145-201.

Borgen, F. H., & Seling, M. J. (1978). Expressed and inventoried interests revisited: Perspicacity in the person. *Journal of Counseling Psychology, 25,* 536-543.

Boudreau, J. W., Boswell, W. R., & Judge, T. A. (2001). Effects of personality on executive career success in the United States and Europe. *Journal of Personality and Social Psychology, 58*(1), 53-81.

Bright, J. E. H., & Pryor, R. G. L. (2005). The chaos theory of careers: A user's guide. *Career Development Quarterly, 53*(4), 291-305.

Brown, D. (2002). The role of work values and cultural values in occupational choice, satisfaction and success. In D. Brown & Associates (Eds.), *Career choice and development* (4th ed., pp. 465-509). San Francisco: Jossey-Bass.

Casillas, A., & Robbins, S. B. (2005). Test adaptation and cross-cultural assessment from a business perspective: Issues and recommendations. *International Journal of Testing, 5*(1), 5-21.

Cattell, J. B. (1890). Mental tests and measurements. *Mind, 15,* 373-380.

Clawson, J. G., Kotter, J. P., Vaux, V. A., & McArthur, C. C. (1992). *Self-assessment and career development* (3rd ed.). Englewood Cliffs, NJ: Prentice Hall.

Costa, P. T., & McCrae, R. R. (1992). *NEO PI-R professional manual.* Odessa, FL: Psychological Assessment Resources.

Costa, P. T., McCrae, R. R., & Kay, G. G. (1995). Persons, places, and personality: Career assessment using the revised NEO Personality Inventory. *Journal of Career Assessment, 3,* 123-139.

Crites, J. O., & Taber, B. J. (2002). Appraising adults' career capabilities: Ability, interest and personality. In S. G. Niles (Ed.), *Adult career development: Concepts, issues and practices* (pp. 121-138). Tulsa, OK: National Career Development Association.

Dawis, R. V. (1996). The theory of work adjustment and person-environment-correspondence counseling. In D. Brown, L. Brooks, & Associates (Eds.), *Career development and choice* (3rd ed., pp. 75-120). San Francisco: Jossey-Bass.

Dawis, R. V. (2002). Person-environment correspondence theory. In D. Brown & Associates (Eds.), *Career choice and development* (4th ed., pp. 427-464). San Francisco: Jossey-Bass.

Dawis, R. V., & Lofquist, L. H. (1984). *A psychological theory of work adjustment.* Minneapolis, MN: University of Minneapolis Press.

De Fruyt, P. (2002). A person-centered approach to PE fit questions using a multi-trait model. *Journal of Vocational Behavior, 60*(1), 73-90.

Gottfredson, G. D. (1999). John L. Holland's contributions to vocational psychology: A review and an assessment. *Journal of Vocational Behavior, 55*(1), 74-85.

Gottfredson, G. D., & Holland, J. L. (1991). *The Position Classification Inventory: Professional manual.* Odessa, FL: Psychological Assessment Resources.

Gottfredson, G. D., & Holland, J. L. (1996). *Dictionary of Holland occupational codes.* Odessa, FL: Psychological Assessment Resources.

Harmon, L. W., Hansen, J. C., Borgen, F. H., & Hammer, A. C. (1994). *Strong Interest Inventory: Applications and technical guide.* Palo Alto, CA: Consulting Psychologists Press.

Holland, J. L. (1973). *Making vocational choices.* Englewood Cliffs, NJ: Prentice Hall.

Holland, J. L. (1979). *Professional manual for the Self-Directed Search.* Palo Alto, CA: Consulting Psychologists Press.

Holland, J. L. (1985). *Making vocational choices* (2nd ed.). Englewood Cliffs, NJ: Prentice Hall.

Holland, J. L. (1997). *Making vocational choices: A theory of vocational personalities and work environments* (2nd ed.). Odessa, FL: Psychological Assessment Resources.

Huber, G. P. (1993). *Managerial decision making.* Glenview, IL: Scott Foresman.

Hunter, J. E. (1986). Cognitive ability, cognitive aptitudes, job knowledge, and job performance. *Journal of Vocational Behavior, 29,* 340-362.

Jackson, S. E., & Schuler, R. S. (2000). *Managing human resources: A partnership perspective.* Cincinnati, OH: South-Western College Publishing.

Katz, M. (1993). *Computer-assisted career decision making: The guide in the machine.* Mahwah, NJ: Erlbaum.

Krumboltz, J. D. (1991). *Manual for the Career Beliefs Inventory.* Palo Alto, CA: Consulting Psychologists Press.

Kuder, G. F. (1966). The Occupational Interest Survey. *Personnel and Guidance Journal, 45,* 72-77.

Kummerow, J. E. (1991). Using the Strong Interest Inventory and the Myers-Briggs Type Indicator together in career counseling. In J. E. Kummerow (Ed.), *New directions in career planning and the workplace* (pp. 61-93). Palo Alto, CA: Consulting Psychologists Press.

Mabe, P. A., & West, S. G. (1982). Validity of self-evaluation of ability: A review and meta-analysis. *Journal of Applied Psychology, 67,* 280-296.

McCrae, R. R., & Costa, P. T. (2003). *Personality in adulthood: A five-factor theory perspective.* New York: Guilford.

McMahon, M., & Patton, W. (2002). Using qualitative assessment in career counselling. *International Journal of Educational and Vocational Guidance, 2*(1), 51-66.

Myers, I. B., & McCaulley, M. H. (1985). *Manual: A guide to the development and use of the Myers-Briggs Type Indicator.* Palo Alto, CA: Consulting Psychologists Press.

O'Reilly, C. A., Chatman, J., & Caldwell, D. F. (1991). People and organizational culture: A profile approach to assessing the person-organization fit. *Academy of Management Journal, 34,* 487-516.

Parsons, F. (1909). *Choosing a vocation.* Boston: Houghton Mifflin.

Phillips, S. D., Friedlander, M. L., Pazienza, N. J., & Kost, P. P. (1985). A factor analytic investigation of career decision-making styles. *Journal of Vocational Behavior, 26,* 106-115.

Reardon, R. C., & Lenz, J. G. (1998). *The Self-Directed Search and related Holland career materials: A practitioner's guide.* Odessa, FL: Psychological Assessment Resources.

Reardon, R. C., Lenz, J., Sampson, J., & Peterson, G. (2006). *Career development and planning: A comprehensive approach* (2nd ed.). Mason, OH: Thomson Custom Solutions.

Rounds, J. B., Dawis, R. V., & Lofquist, L. H. (1987). Measurement of person-environment fit and the prediction of satisfaction in the theory of work adjustment. *Journal of Vocational Behavior, 31,* 297-318.

Rounds, J. B., Henley, G. A., Dawis, R. V., Lofquist, L. H., & Weiss, D. J. (1981). *Manual for the Minnesota Importance Questionnaire.* Minneapolis: University of Minnesota.

Saunders, D. E., Peterson, G. W., Sampson, J. P., Jr., & Reardon, R. C. (2000). Relation of depression and dysfunctional career thinking to career indecision. *Journal of Vocational Behavior, 56*(2), 288-298.

Schein, E. H. (1978). *Career dynamics: Matching individual and organizational needs.* Reading, MA: Addison-Wesley.

Schein, E. H. (1985a). *Career anchors: Discovering your real values.* San Francisco: University Associates.

Schein, E. H. (1985b). *Organizational culture and leadership.* San Francisco: Jossey-Bass.

Schein, E. H. (1993). *Career anchors: Discovering your real values* (Rev. ed.). London: Pfeiffer.

Schmidt, F. L. (2002). The role of general cognitive ability and job performance: Why there cannot be a debate. *Human Performance, 15*(1/2), 187-210.

Schneider, B. (1987). The people make the place. *Personnel Psychology, 40,* 437-453.

Schneider, B., Kristof-Brown, A. S., Goldstein, H. W., & Smith, D. B. (1997). What is this thing called fit? In N. Anderson & P. Herriott (Eds.), *International handbook of selection and assessment* (pp. 393-412). London: Wiley.

Seibert, S. E., & Kraimer, M. L. (2001). The five-factor model of personality and career success. *Journal of Personality and Social Psychology, 58*(1), 1-21.

Simon, H. A. (1976). *Administrative behavior* (3rd ed.). New York: Free Press.

Spearman, C. (1923). *The nature of "intelligence" and the principles of cognition.* London: Macmillan.

Spokane, A. R. (1985). A review of research on person-environment congruence in Holland's theory of careers. *Journal of Vocational Behavior, 26,* 306-343.

Spokane, A. R., Luchetta, E. J., & Richwine, M. H. (2002). Holland's theory of personalities. In D. Brown and Associates (Eds.), *Career choice and development* (4th ed., pp. 373-426). San Francisco: Jossey-Bass.

Spokane, A. R., Meir, E. I., & Catalano, M. (2000). Person-environment congruence and Holland's theory: A review and reconsideration. *Journal of Vocational Behavior, 57*(2), 137-187.

Stewart, N. (1947). AGTC scores for Army personnel grouped by occupation. *Occupations, 26,* 5-41.

Super, D. E., Thomson, A. S., & Lindeman, R. H. (1988). *Adult Career Concerns Inventory: Manual for research and exploratory use in counseling.* Palo Alto, CA: Consulting Psychologists Press.

Swanson, J. L., & Fouad, N. A. (1999). *Career theory and practice: Learning through case studies.* Thousand Oaks, CA: Sage.

Thurstone, L. L. (1955). *The differential growth of mental abilities* (Psychological Laboratory Report No. 14). Chapel Hill: University of North Carolina.

Tracey, T. J. G., & Hopkins, N. (2003). Correspondence of interests and abilities with occupational choice. *Journal of Counseling Psychology, 48*(2), 178-189.

Tranberg, M., Slane, S., & Ekeberg, S. E. (1993). The relation between interest congruence and satisfaction: A meta-analysis. *Journal of Vocational Behavior, 42*(3), 253-264.

Tversky, A., & Kahneman, D. (1983). Extensional versus intuitive reasoning: The conjunction fallacy in probability judgment. *Psychological Review, 90*, 283-315.

Weiten, W. (2001). *Psychology: Themes and variations* (5th ed.). Belmont, CA: Wadsworth/ Thomson Learning.

Wiggins, J. S., & Trapnell, P. D. (1997). Personality structure: The return of the big five. In R. Hogan, J. S. Johnson, & S. R. Briggs (Eds.), *Handbook of personality psychology* (pp. 737-764). San Diego, CA: Academic Press.

CHAPTER 6

Careers as Journeys

The Long Walk to Freedom

Nelson Mandela was born in 1918 in a village near Umtala, Transkei, South Africa. Born into a high-ranking African family, he was groomed in childhood to become a chief. But Mandela was keen, even at an early age, to help his people free themselves from apartheid and oppressive White South African regimes. So he resolved to become a lawyer. He completed a BA and then an LLB degree and entered practice. But it was political activity that was to dominate his career.

In 1942, Mandela joined the African National Congress (ANC). He was one of a new group of young Africans attempting to transform a polite, select pressure group dominated by old men into a mass movement of all Africans. They infiltrated senior positions in the ANC and were able to have policies of boycott, strike, and civil disobedience accepted as ANC policy. In 1952, Mandela was elected leader of a mass disobedience campaign and traveled the country organizing opposition to discriminatory laws. About the same time, in partnership with Oliver Tambo, he opened South Africa's first Black legal practice: Most of their clients were Black peasants who had been ejected from their land.

Through the 1950s, Mandela continued to lead Black resistance: Issues included protection from removal, Bantu education, the creation of a Freedom Charter, labor exploitation, pass laws, the segregation of the universities, and the establishment of segregated Bantustans for Africans. All the time, he struggled against bans, arrests, and periods of imprisonment. In 1961, as South Africa prepared to establish a republican constitution, he led a mass strike of Africans. He had to live apart from his family and adopt disguises to escape arrest. But in 1962 he was imprisoned for having left the country illegally—to undertake military training in Algeria—and then, at the famous Rivonia Trial, he was convicted of incitement to strike and sabotage (his group targeted installations, not people).

Mandela spent the next 28 years—from age 45 to age 73 years—in prison, most of it in the notorious Robben Island Prison near Cape Town. He underwent hard labor,

(Continued)

(Continued)

kept himself physically fit and psychologically active, and turned Robben Island Prison into a center for education. In the 1970s, he refused offers of remission of sentence if he agreed to recognize the legality of the Transkei Bantustan. In the 1980s, he refused to renounce the use of violence in return for his freedom.

By 1990, the political climate in South Africa had changed, and the government sought an accommodation with the ANC and its Black population, of which Mandela, even after so long in prison, was still the recognized leader. On February 11, 1990, Mandela was released from prison and immediately suspended the armed struggle of his people and entered into discussion of a new constitution for his country. In 1993, he was awarded the Nobel Peace Prize, and in 1994 he was inaugurated as the first democratically elected state president of South Africa.

Mandela titled his 1994 autobiography *Long Walk to Freedom*. In the book's conclusion, he looked back on the main part of his career and forward to what remained:

> I have walked that long road to freedom. I have tried not to falter; I have made missteps along the way. But I have discovered the secret that after climbing a great hill, one only finds that there are many more hills to climb. I have taken a moment here to rest, to steal a view of the glorious vista that surrounds me, to look back on the distance I have come. But I can rest only a moment, for with freedom come responsibilities, and I dare not linger, for my long walk has not yet ended. (p. 751)

Like many people, Mandela conceptualizes his career as a journey—a "long walk." His journey has clear characteristics. It has a destination: freedom. He had that destination from his earliest years. He travels in an upward direction. He experiences false destination as he finds that each hill he crests has another hill beyond it. He is able, for a moment, to look back and enjoy what he can see. Yet, at well over 70 years of age, he is still in a hurry.

As used by Mandela, the "journey" metaphor is a wonderful, vivid way of understanding his career. We can almost see this amazing, dignified man climbing the dry, dusty hills through the veldt, perhaps using a stick, with millions of his people walking behind him. At the same time, the idea of "journey" provides Mandela with a sense-making device that enables him to link the past, present, and future of his life and guides his actions.

Journey Metaphors

The first recorded meaning of the word *career* was "racecourse" and "the charge of a horse, in a tournament or battle." It is from that that the term has derived its sense of progress along a course (Chantrell, 2002, p. 84), and it is therefore not surprising that people think of careers in terms of progression and journeys.

The "journey" metaphor is common. In asking people around the world for metaphors of their career, I have found that more than 50% of people nominate some kind of journey. But they tend to say more than just "journey"—usually their metaphors tell what kind of a journey it is:

- A train journey
- A hard road
- A roller-coaster ride
- An expedition; a safari
- Flying
- Stuck; trying to get out of a swamp
- Like whitewater rafting

Thus, people think of their careers as having movement, as getting them from place to place. Baruch (2003) noted differences between careers viewed as rowing down a river (no way back); climbing a mountain (upward, clear destination, many potential routes); navigating at sea (no path, not necessarily a destination, unknown obstacles); and wandering in space (no map, lost).

We also use "journey" metaphors in everyday talk about careers. Sometimes they tell us the type of route: career *path*, career *ladder*, fast *track*, career *plateau*. Sometimes they talk about the destination: What *direction* do you want to take? Where do you want to *get to*? They might describe the destination as getting to *the top*, new *territory*, and fresh *fields*. Sometimes they describe what the journey is like: *climbing* the mountain, on the *escalator*, job *hunting*, job *hopping*, *bailing* out, *cruising*, facing a *brick wall*, and *stuck*.

These are powerful, evocative images. They tell us something about what a person's career journey is like. They enable us to identify instantly with the person's experience.

The images are also varied. Each is different. Some travelers have clear destinations; others are venturing into the unknown. Some follow predictable, well-trodden paths; others change direction unexpectedly. Some have a clear sense of momentum or upward progression; others appear stuck or lost. Some involve being constantly on the move; others include long periods of rest, reflection, and planning. Such differences make each journey unique. And it is quite possible for someone to experience several different types of journey during a single career.

Despite the diversity in career journeys, the "journey" metaphor has the potential to help us think productively about careers. Every journey can be evaluated in terms of its destination or aimlessness; its speed; its trajectory—upward, downward, sideways, random; its route—linear, winding, random; and its purpose—exploration, the experience of "getting there," enjoyment along the way. Thinking about the characteristics of your journey in these terms may be helpful (Inkson & Amundson, 2002).

A common "journey" metaphor is "career path." But how are career paths created? Do you follow a unique career path that you choose for yourself, creating it as you go, or do you allow institutions to lay the path down for you? Formal mechanisms such as degree regulations, professional requirements, and company promotion systems are used to prescribe and control the paths people follow. They provide clarity and security, and some career travelers are constantly looking for clear, paved pathways along which they may travel more safely. But because of the dynamism and change in the economic and organizational terrain through which career travelers journey (Chapter 1), much career travel nowadays has to take place along improvised or personal pathways.

Direction and Destination

Career travelers are often expected to have a sense of destination, or at least of direction. Children are asked, "What are you going to be when you grow up?" Adults are encouraged to think about their futures and to set career goals (McCaskey, 1977). This kind of talk implies that in our career journeys we should always be moving toward a destination.

Getting to the Top

One favored destination is "the top." In occupational careers, we tend to conceptualize occupations in terms of the status hierarchies described in Chapter 2. We look for ways to enter superior occupations, and then we try to gain higher responsibility and better paying positions within them. Organizations' hierarchies of salary, status, and authority provide even clearer cues to the expected direction of a career. We are encouraged to be interested in whether we and others are moving up, sideways, or down (Veiga, 1981). Society's expectation—at least in most developed countries—is that the route should never take us downward. Researchers and practitioners add to the structure of the metaphor by talking about career gradients, indicating the steepness of the ascent; career milestones, marking off the precise point reached; and career timetables, indicating when different milestones should be reached if the career is to be considered "on track" (Lawrence, 1984). People who are content to stay at the same level are stigmatized as "dead wood" (Veiga, 1981).

A problem with upward career paths within institutions—whether professions or organizations—is that institutions tend to be the wrong shape to accommodate them. Organizations are typically pyramid shaped (Galbraith, 1987). This means that there are only a few jobs at the top of the organization and many at the bottom. If everyone at the bottom wants to be the chief executive officer (CEO), most of them are going to be disappointed. Organizations can grow in size and thereby create more top jobs, but the tendencies to downsize and flatten in recent years have created the opposite effect (Hendricks, 1992; Inkson, 1995). Most career travelers find it hard in any case to devote the requisite energy to their journeys consistently over a 40-year period to ensure constant upward progress. Many indeed end up on a career plateau (Chapter 4). Others make rapid progress initially but eventually burn out due to the stresses of sustained speedy travel (Cordes & Dougherty, 1993; Pines & Aronson, 1988).

Alternative Destinations

Another problem with upward-moving journey routes is that they refer almost exclusively to the observable objective career goals rather than to the subjective career (see Chapter 1). But as seen in Chapter 4, individuals may define career success in terms of subjective satisfaction rather than objective position (Mirvis & Hall, 1994). The destination may therefore not be a specific job but something more intangible, such as satisfaction or peace of mind. As we saw in earlier chapters, groups such as Super's (1990) late-career maintainers (Chapter 3) and the increasing number of people interested in Schein's (1996) lifestyle anchor (Chapter 5) ensure a diversity of career directions. Herb Shepard (1984), in a memorable "journey" metaphor, talked about "the path with a heart," where the destination meets one's central values in life—for example, job satisfaction, social service, creation of beauty, or balance.

One implication of this is that career journeys should be judged less by the destination than by the enjoyment of traveling. As Robert Louis Stevenson (1907) said, "I travel not to go anywhere, but to go. I travel for travel's sake."

Topography and Climbing Frames

Topography is the "detailed description, representation on a map, etc., of the natural and artificial features of a town, district, etc." (Allen, 1990). Career journeys take place along routes with distinctive topography— the general shape and contour of the land, the observable barriers, and so forth. The topography provides a structure of career opportunities and barriers (Chapter 2)—for example, gender barriers, organizational gradients, paved pathways, and job locations. The journey through the topography results from individual action (Chapter 4).

In seeking to persuade us that action and structure—traveler and topography— are equally important and are interdependent, Gunz (1989) replaced the familiar metaphor of the "career ladder" with that of the "career climbing frame." A climbing frame allows for a variety of different types of career moves. Climbers can move from one frame to another and can choose their own movements. They can go up, sideways, or down. They are not necessarily trying to reach the top. Frames may be differently shaped from each other, and the shapes may change over time (e.g., in organizational flattening). Most intriguing of all, Gunz noted that as people clamber on the climbing frames they become part of it and change it, renewing the structure as they go. Structure may influence action, but action also changes structure.

This is one of the wonderful things about career journeys: They are recursive. We do not leave unaltered the climbing frames over which we clamber and the landscapes through which we pass. As we travel, we work, and our work has effects. Organizational shapes alter, career footpaths are trodden firm or carved out in new locations, and new structures grow. As people enact their careers, "they create the materials that become the constraints and opportunities that they face" (Weick, 1995, p. 30). For example, someone who, against the odds, succeeds in growing a successful, new, nonhierarchical division in a bureaucratic organization changes the organization and also changes the careers of the division's employees and those who come after.

Career Maps

Travelers need maps. Career maps—what Reardon, Lenz, Sampson, and Peterson (2006, p. 34) call "knowing about my options"—provide a representation to career travelers of topography, terrain, and direction. They include formal, written information—such as lists of occupations and industries, job advertisements and descriptions, rules for professional accreditation, organizational charts, formal career plans, and informational Web sites. They also include informal mental maps carried in one's head.

Good maps are vital, but frequently career travelers set out with inadequate maps or no maps. I have met graduates who spent years taking courses to qualify for occupations they felt passionate about and in which they believed there were plenty of opportunities but who eventually found that the labor market for their specialist skills was very restricted. Others rely on misleading maps. For example, a university prospectus might state that a degree in communication studies is a "gateway to a wide range of new career opportunities in industries such as advertising, public relations, journalism, media, and entertainment." This is a map of sorts but one drawn by an institution with a vested interest in encouraging the reader to take a particular route (see Chapter 10 for material on career rhetoric).

Learning where to find, or how to draw, accurate maps of career landscapes is an important skill of the career traveler. Some authorities recommend career exploration, including a thorough investigation of different occupations, industries, organizations, required skills and qualifications, job availability, and typical routes taken (Greenhaus, Callanan, & Godschalk, 2000; Reardon et al., 2006). Maps may also include information from explorers and travelers who have traveled over the terrain. For example, a recently published map of routes for women seeking success in entertainment industry careers is based on reports from those who have gone before (Ensher, Murphy, & Sullivan, 2002).

Maps may be based on information from libraries; educational institutions; professional, occupational, and industry agencies; employment companies; the Internet; help wanted columns; personal networks; and many other sources (Reardon et al., 2006). A particular problem caused by the typical long duration of most career journeys is that the information on which maps are based tends to become obsolete quickly, requiring constant rechecking and redrawing of the map to reflect the changed situation. Further information on career maps, particularly related to access of information about specific occupations, is provided in Chapter 11.

Career Types

How can we make sense of the wide range of types of journey observable in people's careers? One way is to look at real career journeys, their typical patterns and routes. Can we discern any main types of career?

A feature of many career journeys is that they are restricted within boundaries. Boundaries are important in careers and help to remind us who we are, and where we are "at home" careerwise. Two common types of journey are the occupational and the organizational career. In an occupational career, the person may cross many boundaries but sticks with the same occupation. In an organizational career, the career journey takes place within organizational boundaries.

Driver (1979) distinguished four types of career concept:

- In the *linear* career concept, the individual chooses a specialist field or organization early and executes a plan for upward movement (a bounded, upward journey).
- In the *steady-state* career concept, the individual chooses a single work role or occupation and spends his or her career in it (a bounded nonjourney).
- In the *spiral* career concept, the individual moves from area to related area on a cyclic basis (a planned, boundaryless journey).
- In the *transitory* career concept, the individual moves from job to job with no particular pattern (an unplanned, boundaryless journey).

Kanter (1989) distinguished three major career patterns, each driven by its own logic of career opportunity:

- In *professional* careers—careers defined by professional occupations—there is a logic of acquisition of socially valued knowledge and expertise within professional boundaries, which again enables the key career rewards to be accessed.
- In *bureaucratic* careers—Kanter's term for organizational careers—there is a logic of advancement, or status, in a single organization, through which major career opportunities—in earnings, responsibility, power, and challenge—can be accessed.
- In *entrepreneurial* careers—a new type—there is a logic of growth, as the individual grows territory, or adds value, beneath her or him. An entrepreneurial career is characteristic of the ambitious owner-managers of small businesses but is not confined to them. The principles of the entrepreneurial career can be used, according to Kanter, in any job setting.

In this typology, Kanter (1989) focused on higher level careers. Those in mass occupations such as sales, customer service, and clerical and manual work, and those whose careers are not consistently directed toward status, professional development, and growth, tend to be neglected. Nevertheless, in essence, Kanter defined some of the key routes for career journeys.

Occupational Careers

Occupations differ from each other in social status, in market value, and in exclusiveness (Chapter 2). Many occupations—for example, professions such as medicine, law, and teaching—are restricted, in terms of entry, to those who have acquired specialist qualifications and training and are accredited by a licensing authority. To put themselves in a good position to gain entry to some professions, young people may have to choose specific college degree programs and even high school subjects. In such occupations, there are strong professional associations that guard the interests and reputation of the profession to ensure that jobs in the occupation are confined to qualified people, that standards are high, that numbers in the occupation do not grow too quickly, and that those in the occupation remain loyal to it (Downs, Damrosch, Flanigan, & Gutierrez, 2005). Other occupations, for example sales, computer programming, and management, are less restrictive, though those seeking to make progress to positions of higher responsibility may well find later that credentials are helpful.

An occupational career journey takes place along a route that can involve much geographical and interorganizational mobility. A sense of progress is denoted by the kind of work being done, which typically retains its occupational focus but becomes progressively more responsible or more specialized as the person gains experience. These journeys therefore have something of the effect of traveling along deep valleys: Travelers may find a valley congenial and make good progress along it, but if they change their minds, it is difficult to go back or to climb into another valley.

Barbara's case is an example of an occupational career.

Variations Around a Theme

Barbara qualified in her early 20s as a physical therapist. Her early career included a number of jobs working in this field in various hospital settings. Barbara found that because her qualifications were recognized in other countries, she was able to travel while continuing to practice her occupation and gain more expertise. During her travels, she met the man who became her husband, and eventually they returned to her home city and started a family.

During her children's preschool years, Barbara continued to work part-time as a physical therapist in a local hospital. She found that having a career and a role other than mother was important to her. She identified strongly with her profession. However, she also broadened her skills by undertaking training as a play center supervisor.

When Barbara was in her late 30s, her husband's company transferred him to another city. The family moved, and Barbara looked for another job. She found one in a local maternity hospital, using physical therapy to help pregnant women prepare for childbirth. She found the work fulfilling, acquired teaching skills, and completed a postgraduate diploma in women's health.

After 7 years, Barbara decided to leave her job. She felt the work had become routine, and the long hours were interfering with her family responsibilities. Thinking about what she might do instead, Barbara found herself, for the first time in her life, considering possibilities outside physical therapy. Perhaps a major change would do her good. She applied for a job as a receptionist but was told she was overqualified. She applied to take nursing training but got "cold feet" and withdrew.

Then she heard about a part-time vacancy for a physical therapist in a rest home for elderly people. Now she works there, finding great fulfillment in the work. As she looks to the future, she finds it less likely that she will ever work outside the occupation that she loves.

Source: Arthur, Inkson, & Pringle (1999).

Barbara's career has been focused by a single occupation. It provides a secure anchor for her. Not only has she never left that occupation, but she has also found herself drawn back when she considered leaving and has not moved into the managerial ranks. Yet she gained several different types of experience within the occupation, and she was able to move between work and home, between different organizations, between different sectors of the health industry, and between geographical locations to fit her family requirements. Her occupation became the anchor point of a quite mobile career.

Another issue connected with occupational careers is the ongoing obsolescence of their knowledge bases. A degree or basic training, or both, in an occupation such as nursing, surveying, law, or medicine provides you with a starting point. It is rather like having the basic equipment to commence your journey. But knowledge acquisition must continue as you progress. Not only do you need improved expertise as you aspire to higher levels of the occupation, but the knowledge base you set out with will quickly go out of date. Even if all you want to do is stay in the same place, you will have to acquire new expertise.

Some occupations go out of business altogether due to technological change. If you had chosen to be a barrel maker in the year 1900, you might have found enough business to use all of your skills, but by 1920, with your career only half-finished, you would probably have found that barrel making had been overtaken by technology. Twenty-five years ago occupations such as computer programmer, software engineer, motorcycle courier, one-on-one fitness coach, life coach, and laser surgeon hardly existed; now they are commonplace, creating opportunities to commence or move into quite new occupations.

Organizational Careers

Much interest has centered on organizational careers—career journeys that take place within the boundaries of a single, usually large, organization. I provide another example from my own family in the case of Henry Wilson.

Loyal Company Servant

My maternal grandfather was Henry Wilson. He lived his life in Aberdeen, Scotland. He was born in 1880 and did well in school. When he was about 11 years old, his father took him to an accounting firm in Golden Square, Aberdeen, and had him taken on as an office boy. With quill pen, ink bottles, and handwritten ledgers, Henry progressed to accounts clerk and then ledger clerk. When the First World War broke out, he volunteered for the army but was too old to serve. He became senior clerk, a trusted company servant. He was thrifty and was able to buy his own house, within a 5-minute walk of Golden Square. In the Depression, his wages were reduced, but there was never any question that he would lose his job. Eventually, things got better. The Second World War came and went. By now, the firm had progressed to using typewriters and adding machines. In 1951, Henry retired at age 70 years. He had spent nearly 60 years working in the same office.

Henry Wilson epitomized the traditional linear, organizational career: He worked in the same industry, the same organization, the same type of work, the same location, even the same office, for 60 years. The only boundaries he crossed in his journey were those of status, responsibility, and technology.

Organizational careers are determined to a considerable extent not by individuals but by organizations, as a means of recruiting, retaining, and developing the overall human resource on which organizations' profitability or achievement of other organizational goals are based. Thus, from the organizational perspective, the career is not a journey by the employee but a resource for the organization. The implications of considering careers as resources are dealt with in Chapter 9: Here I note only some of the consequences for career journeys within organizations.

Organizations develop career systems (Weber, 1947) through which the individual can progress to higher levels of status, responsibility, and salary, while retaining high security of employment. The potential career rewards are substantial but tend to be delayed so that the individual can only qualify for them by restricting his or her career journey within the organization. This leads to the danger of overspecialization—that is, a person may become highly expert and valuable in certain work of the organization, but will this specialist organizational expertise be relevant elsewhere?

Additionally, the restructurings of recent years (Chapter 1) have made organizational careers increasingly problematic (Bridges, 1995; Hall & Associates, 1996). Many organizations spent the 1950s to the 1970s building structures suitable for traditional organizational careers. But they found in the 1980s and 1990s that under more competitive business conditions such arrangements could not be maintained. Organizational career journeys are only sustainable if the organization is stable or expanding in an orderly manner. When the organization merges, downsizes, or restructures—as many have been compelled to do—staff have to be laid off, demoted, or transferred. The effects on individuals' careers may be catastrophic. Sam's case is an example.

Journey to the Scrap Heap

Sam was an immigrant, had accounting qualifications, and immigrated directly into a job in management with a company called Vertex. On arrival, he found the organization primitive and the branch he had come to manage totally disorganized. For several years, Sam invested a huge amount of energy getting the branch on the right track. Obsessed with getting things right, he worked long hours, sometimes until 3 or 4 in the morning. He felt it was worth it to help get his branch on the right track and safeguard his own career. He also invested socially in the company by basing his social life around the employees. But after 6 years, the company suddenly restructured and closed his branch. Vertex tore up Sam's contract but offered him another job, at a lower status and salary, which he was not prepared to accept. Since then he has been able to secure only part-time clerical work. He is very bitter about Vertex.

Source: Arthur, Inkson, & Pringle (1999).

In many organizations and countries, the disruption to the workforce caused by restructuring has fractured the careers of many employees, left promises of long-term employment in ruins, and reduced the level of employer–employee trust—an essential factor in organizational careers (Brockner, Grover, Reed, & DeWitt, 1992). In "journey" terms, employees' career paths were bulldozed out of existence. In consequence, they had to pick themselves up and start a quite different journey. Overall, although some people continue to have successful organizational careers (Gunz, Evans, & Jalland, 2002), and in some countries and companies "the firm's career management practices still mark the careers of employees [and] serve as benchmarks for making sense of career" (Dany, 2003, p. 821), it is apparent that this type of journey is increasingly problematic as a career mode.

Entrepreneurial and Self-Employment Careers

Kanter (1989) described the entrepreneurial career as "one in which growth occurs through the creation of new value or new organizational capacity" (p. 516). Although Kanter made it clear that on the basis of this definition it is possible to have an entrepreneurial career as a corporate employee, this usually involves crossing the boundary into self-employment and traveling alone or without the security that traveling as an employee may bring.

In most developed economies, a significant portion of the workforce is self-employed rather than employed. For example, in the United States in 2004 there were 10.3 million self-employed people—more than 8% of the workforce. Self-employed people can range from the entrepreneurial owners of ambitious new dot-com startups to people who have bought lawn-mowing franchises or small retail stores to people who make and sell their own products working from home. About a quarter of the workforce will have self-employment as their main means of livelihood at some point in their career, and many others engage in forms of self-employed work separate from their main job. Therefore, self-employment is a key component of many careers.

Why do people choose to pursue their careers, or parts of their careers, in self-employment? Research suggests that in general such people seek autonomy from an employing organization and have a high need for achievement, an internal locus of control, tolerance for ambiguity, risk-taking propensity, and a self-concept as entrepreneurs (Brockhaus, 1982; Feldman & Bolino, 2000). These predisposing personal characteristics may be triggered by external situational factors, such as dissatisfaction with one's work, loss of one's job, or business conditions favorable to the new venture.

Self-employment has special appeal to those who feel restricted and controlled by the demands of working in an authority system for someone else. Feldman and Bolino (2000) found that key reasons offered in favor of self-employment were the opportunity to make more money, to achieve greater autonomy, to generate personal wealth, and to escape organizational bureaucracies. On the other hand, the reality of self-employment is often not wealth but financial insecurity. Autonomy may come at the cost of social isolation, flexibility of hours at the cost of long total hours, and escape from the organization at the cost of constant control by the market (Eden, 1973; Feldman & Bolino, 2000; Peel & Inkson, 2004).

To steer your career journey into self-employment, therefore, you need both a product and a market. In most cases, those interested in self-employment need to spend time in employment first, to figure out a business idea and learn the necessary skills. Typically, self-employed people need a wider range of expertise—for example, they need to do their own selling, accounting, and administration, particularly in the early stages of their business. If they grow beyond being one-person businesses, they will have to manage their own staff. Even more important is the external demand for the products or services the person is supplying. Working from home—for example, as a Web designer or craftsperson—can provide a secure, happy, and integrated career very much under the person's control and integrated with his or her family life (Sayers & Monin, 2005). On the other hand, those whose skills or services are not especially in demand or can easily be supplied by others may find that self-employment is a route to relative marginalization from the workforce (Peel & Inkson, 2004).

Boundaryless Careers

In the early and middle 20th century, careers conducted within clear boundaries were probably relatively common. Nowadays, boundary crossing—to new jobs, new occupations, new industries, new employers, new employment status (e.g., self-employment), new geographical locations, even new countries—is common. The boundary between work and home life has also become more blurred and is crossed more frequently. In the 1990s, new forms of career journey began to be talked about: careers along routes that had greater mobility and greater flexibility than either of the "traditional"—occupational and organizational—career forms.

The *new careers*, as they have been called (Arthur et al., 1999), are a response to new economic and business conditions and new forms of organization described in Chapter 1. As society attempts to develop flexibility in its work arrangements, people more frequently depart from traditional career paths and look for different routes. Sometimes the change is involuntary, enforced by restructuring. Sometimes it is a voluntary move, a search for a better opportunity in a changing environment. Alternatives to full-time employment in a single, permanent job have become more available: part-time work, shift work, temporary work, contract work, project work, telecommuting work, moonlighting, self-employment, and informally arranged jobs completed in the black economy to avoid regulations or taxes (Crompton, Gallie, & Purcell, 1996). These alternatives enable career travelers to experiment, perhaps even to travel along, more than one path simultaneously.

A term that is heard with increasing frequency is *boundaryless career* (Arthur & Rousseau, 1996). According to the originators of the term, a boundaryless career is one that is not confined to a single employment setting but takes place in a number of settings through the individual's crossing of boundaries and associated barriers. The following boundaries may be crossed by individuals:

- Level of job (e.g., seeking and accepting a promotion)
- Geographical (e.g., moving to a new city)

- Occupational (e.g., a mechanic becoming a salesperson)
- Organizational (e.g., leaving one's job at Exxon and getting a job with Shell)
- Industry (e.g., moving from a job in the heavy engineering industry to one in financial services)
- Employment status (e.g., leaving employment and becoming self-employed)
- International (e.g., emigrating and resuming one's career in a new country)
- Work-home (e.g., giving up a professional practice to be a stay-at-home parent)
- Psychological (e.g., moving to a new job one is afraid of)

As the environment of work becomes less stable and less clear, the normal career boundaries become more permeable, and we become more willing, in our career journeys, to cross them (Arthur & Rousseau, 1996). An important element of the boundaryless career, and one it shares with the protean career (Chapter 5), is the implicit responsibility it places on people for their own career choices and career development.

Arthur and Rousseau (1996, p. 6) mentioned six specific types of meaning for the boundaryless career:

- Movement across the boundaries of separate employers
- Validation from outside the present employer
- External networks or information that sustain the career
- Breakthrough of traditional organizational career boundaries
- Rejection of traditional career opportunities for personal or family reasons
- Perception of a boundaryless future regardless of structural constraints

Arthur and Rousseau (1996) stated, in particular, that the boundaryless career is "the opposite of the organizational career" (p. 5)—that is, it is *inter*organizational. But it may cross other boundaries as well and is clearly predicated on a boundaryless attitude by the person concerned. Boundaryless careers therefore have a subjective as well as an objective side. People in boundaryless careers have career goals, expertise, and networks that go beyond their current employer and can therefore build their careers across a range of settings. Examples described in the research of Arthur and others include research and development careers in the semiconductor industry of Silicon Valley (Saxenian, 1996) and careers in the world of temporary projects that is the modern film industry (Inkson & Parker, 2005; Jones, 1996). In both of these cases, the industries tend to be based on temporary rather than permanent structures, to which boundaryless careers seem especially well suited.

Proponents of the boundaryless career argue that these industries are extreme examples of a general loosening of boundaries in the world of work. Boundaryless careers have become more common (Ackah & Heaton, 2004). The new careerist finds it progressively easier to transcend boundaries and determine his or her own career direction as a free agent. Accounts of the boundaryless career create images of talented men and women, liberated from the crushing constraints of organizational life, moving freely and autonomously between exciting opportunities for them to develop ever more interesting and prosperous careers.

The boundaryless career ideal has been criticized. One argument concerns the term *boundaryless.* Most people agree that in recent times boundaries have become more permeable. But they still exist, and for that reason the term *boundary-crossing career* might be more suitable. Every career stays within some boundaries. Boundaryless career proponents focus on the crossing of boundaries between organizations, but why should these boundaries be considered more important than, say, occupational boundaries, industry boundaries, or geographical boundaries (Inkson, in press)? All careers have boundaries, and it may even be that the more one crosses one type of boundary, such as organizational, the more one is constrained by others, such as occupational (Bagdadli, Solari, Usai, & Grandori, 2003; Gunz et al., 2002).

A focus on boundaryless careers may also mask the deprivation and marginalization of a large section of the workforce—those with low status in terms of background, gender, and skills. These people may seem boundaryless, or at least highly mobile between jobs, in their career behavior, but they may be bound instead by the crushing structural constraints mentioned in Chapter 2. If you are a female doing occasional sewing work on contract, at minimum price, for whichever local company needs it at the time, it may be little consolation to know that you have a boundaryless career. By making the individual totally responsible for his or her career and by applying market forces logic at the level of the individual, boundaryless careers arguably assist those with skills in demand only at the expense of those on the margins of the workforce. It may therefore be a narrower career type than it looks (Pringle & Mallon, 2003).

Despite these drawbacks, the boundaryless career type provides us with a model of career development that appears to have some advantages over traditional occupational or organizational models. In a changing environment, it encourages mobility, flexibility, the development of currently valued knowledge, the development of networks, and the taking of responsibility for one's own career. It also resonates effectively with the temporary organizational structures (Cappelli, 1999) and knowledge workers (Horwitz, Chang Teng Heng, & Quazi, 2003) becoming characteristic of the new century. And there is evidence that it is associated with career success and marketability, both inside and outside the organization (Eby, Butts, & Lockwood, 2003).

Transitory Careers

In a variant of the boundaryless career model, French researcher Loic Cadin and his colleagues (Cadin, Bailly-Bender, & de Saint-Giniez, 2000), in a telling metaphor, describe a substantial portion of French workers as nomads. Literally, nomads are desert dwellers who travel from place to place in search of pasture. Cadin et al. provide the following definition of *career nomads:*

> [Career nomads are] people who experience frequent and radical transitions without being tied to any organization . . . they are the sole managers of their careers and usually cultivate a strong feeling of autonomy. They break away from traditional paths and have to seize various opportunities. (p. 241)

Such people are experiencing Driver's (1979) transitory career concept. When we talk about occupational, organizational, entrepreneurial, and boundaryless careers, we tend to consider travelers at the privileged end of the spectrum. They are travelers with a sense of direction, travelers who have skills to sell as they go, travelers for whom there is likely to be a meal and a place to sleep at each port of call. Not everyone is so fortunate. Many people live out their careers on the margins of employment, apparently unable to get a secure enough footing to make much progress on their journey. Gilles is an example of this type of traveler.

A Career Nomad

Gilles left school at 14 years of age and undertook an apprenticeship in sales, which he did not like. During the 1960s, it was not too difficult to find another job. Gilles became a manual worker, learning on the job and changing employment when working conditions no longer suited him. Eventually, he passed an exam in welding and for the following 11 years was a contingent worker, finding jobs through temporary agencies. In 1988, Gilles wanted to change and gained a license to drive trucks. For the next 7 years, he worked for many different employers, mostly "off the books." Eventually, an accident compelled him to give up this kind of work. After a year's unemployment, the job center offered him a training program, and he decided to become an electrician. Since training, he has been doing sporadic jobs in his new field for the past two years.

Source: Cadin et al. (2000).

Gilles has no stable employers. All his jobs are manual, and he is therefore especially susceptible to aging processes, illness, and accident. He works frequently on the margins of mainstream, often in temporary and semi-illegal situations. He is unable to settle in any occupation. His living is frequently insecure. There seems no principle providing direction to his career journey, beyond changing occupations periodically and moving on frequently. His career situation is now precarious. Furthermore, this is not just a response to tough economic conditions—Gilles's career was aimlessly mobile even when he was young and jobs were plentiful. But now there is additional insecurity. The primary concern must be "putting bread on the table," and career development would be considered an unnecessary indulgence.

Many other workers—for example, sweatshop factory employees, low-level workers in the catering industry, and the long-term unemployed—are even worse off, unable to achieve any kind of traction for career development. When we observe such cases, we need to remember that our original definition of *career* (Chapter 1), which enabled everyone to be viewed as having a career, perhaps gives a false impression of Gilles, some of his fellow nomads, and other dispossessed groups. Is it fair to say that they have "careers" as most people understand them? Their traveling seems desultory, short term, and directionless.

Portfolio Careers

A career journey does not necessarily take place along a route defined by a sequence of one-at-a-time full-time jobs. The fragmentation of work and organizations that has come to characterize much economic life means that more careers consist of fragments—temporary jobs, casual jobs, part-time jobs, projects, small part-time businesses, odd jobs for friends, evening work in supermarkets or restaurants, spare-time Internet trading or tutoring at home, consulting work for employers—the list is endless. Some people's careers are made up of constantly changing sequences of such jobs. They are called portfolio careers because, like portfolios of shares, the makeup of the portfolio constantly changes. Portfolio careers tend to be less secure than the main forms of career, but they provide special opportunities for those who seek to spend some of their working hours in leisure or family activities or in education or the development of a business (Platman, 2004). Portfolio careers may have the advantage of broadening the individual's perspectives on career and making him or her more flexible (Borgen, Amundson, & Reuter, 2004).

International Careers

My grandfathers confined their careers to one city, and my father stayed within one country, but my career has been in several countries, and my children's careers may be more so. More career journeys now cross international boundaries.

How has this come about? In the process of globalization, conventional organizational forms are giving way to strategic alliances with other firms, affecting the career locations of millions of people (Thomas, 2002). New multinational companies retain control and disseminate expertise by transferring employees to subsidiaries in foreign settings (Osland, 1995; Thomas, 1998). Countries solve labor shortages and build their reservoirs of talent and expertise by opening their borders to immigrants with suitable backgrounds, creating "brain drains" of talent journeying toward better opportunities (e.g., Beine & Docquier, 2001). Political refugees seek a better life abroad. Young people from developed countries seek new cultural experiences involving employment (Inkson, Arthur, Pringle, & Barry, 1997; Vance, 2005). Business travel multiplies. Increasingly, career journeys take us across international boundaries. University academic staff members are involved in international academic communities, and many take the opportunity to seek positions in foreign countries and develop their careers in an international labor market (Richardson & McKenna, 2003). Increasingly, careers are global (Thomas, Lazarova, & Inkson, 2005), and national boundaries become matters of indifference to global career travelers (Suutari, 2003).

International career journeys involve three types of travel: expatriate assignments (EAs), self-initiated foreign experiences (SFEs), and permanent migration.

- EAs are organized by multinational organizations as a means of managing far-flung subsidiaries and developing their staff internationally (Black, Gregersen, Mendenhall, & Stroh, 1999). This type of travel is mainly restricted to the professional and managerial staff of large multinationals. The large research literature on EAs tends to see them as an exercise in career management by the organization rather than career self-development by the expatriate (Thomas, 1998).

- SFEs are working experiences abroad initiated by the individual, usually for purposes of broadening cultural experiences rather than for career advancement, although SFEs may nevertheless have career benefits. In my country, New Zealand, between 14% and 20% of the potential workforce are outside the country at any given time, including many of the most qualified and talented citizens (Bryant & Law, 2004; Hugo, Rudd, & Harris, 2003). In a small and geographically isolated country, foreign experiences are very important to young people and bring them substantial career benefits in terms of increased self-confidence, interpersonal skills development, and cross-cultural understanding (Inkson & Myers, 2003). More generally, many professional people initiate employment overseas as part of their normal career development (Suutari & Brewster, 2000).

- Permanent migrants travel overseas with the intention of settling in a new country. Frequently, they encounter cultural difference, discrimination, lack of recognition of their qualifications, and career disruption because their skills go unrecognized in their new country (Mahroum, 2000). Acculturation processes are necessary to enable them to adapt to their new situation (Berry, 2001). Later, some may move on to new destinations or, disappointed, return to their home country (McHugh, Hogan, & Happel, 1995).

All of these types of journey contribute to the growth of a group of travelers who see themselves more often as global citizens or citizens of the world—people who have no firm national identity and will pursue their lives and careers wherever the best opportunities are in terms of their priorities. They do so in pursuit of a range of goals—economic security, political freedom, cultural betterment, career improvement, and prospects for family members (Carr, Inkson, & Thorne, 2005). Note the mix of economic, cultural, ideological, and family motivations in the example of David.

A Rolling Stone

David is in his mid-60s, married with four grown children, and currently living in Canada. He was born and brought up in New Zealand, but when he was 24 he left New Zealand on a self-initiated foreign experience in the United Kingdom, a normal excursion for young New Zealanders (Inkson & Myers, 2003). He stayed in the UK for 18 months, making enough money to go to Canada for a year on the way back to New Zealand. He had a return ticket, and on his return to New Zealand he married. He struggled to settle, finding his country "a parochial, narrow-minded place" with exorbitant tax rates. (Not everyone agrees, and that was a long time ago!) He moved to Canada for 2 years, working as a tax accountant in a large firm, before taking a job with the United Nations in Zambia. But after 3 years "it was time to get the kids back into the real world." He returned to Canada and has been living there since. He is currently considering retirement in either Australia or New Zealand.

Source: Carr, Inkson, & Thorn (2005).

Mixed Career Journeys

Few people nowadays have full-blown occupational or organizational careers. Most of us have mixed careers—career journeys linked together in a series of episodes such that we cannot describe them as being any single type. Most people move on after a while. Jo's case is an example.

Jo: A Career of Changing Priorities

Jo completed a community college qualification in computer science and by age 23 years had gathered some good work experience in her hometown. Finding her skills were in good demand, and wanting to get away from home, she began to travel. She was able to find good job or project opportunities in each city she selected and was careful to stay up-to-date in her specialist programs and packages.

As Jo's self-confidence grew, she felt she could do better by working for herself. At the age of 28 years, with two business partners, she established a computer consulting business in a major city. For a time, things went well, and the business grew. But Jo was finding, as CEO of the fledgling company, that although she still enjoyed the core business of computer work, she was unable to avoid the associated duties of finance, accounting, marketing, selling, and general management.

After a few years, there was a dip in the market. Jo, now 32 years old, was pregnant with the child of her long-term boyfriend, Marcus. Another change was called for, and Jo sold her share in the business to her partners, getting back less money than she had

originally put in. A few months later, Jo's daughter, Marie-Louise, was born and Jo, entranced with the child, settled down as a full-time homemaker. Marcus was a successful realtor and more than able to provide the income to support the family.

But within 2 years, Jo had become bored with the routines of family life and worried that she would never be able to catch up the years she had lost from her career. Now 34 years old, she decided to go back to work. She got a temporary, part-time job on a 1-year project in the information systems department of a major utility and found child care for Marie-Louise. After a few weeks, the project leader suffered a serious illness, and Jo had to replace him. But the project was very successful, and after its completion her manager called her to his office. He offered her a drink, a bonus, and a promotion. "I want you to be a project manager," he said. "And with your skills, you should be able to move on from that within 2 years. This is a big company, and it's growing. For someone with your talent, the sky's the limit. But there's a catch. You'd have to go full-time."

Jo is only 34 years old, but already her career is a hybrid of different types. She swings through her career in a series of jobs and transitions—freelance programmer, business owner-manager, at-home parent, contingent worker, prospective company star—that give her career journey a unique dynamic and resistance to stereotyping. We can see the occupational career in her initial work as a programmer and the entrepreneurial career in her brief time as a consultant. Then there was a hiatus of family time. Her boss is now offering her a long-term organizational career. Sometimes the changes in Jo's career were externally driven, by market conditions or organizational encouragement, sometimes internally, by the desire to try something new, the need for a break, boredom at home, or an unexpected opportunity. Each time, Jo took charge of her career and set her journey's course in a new direction to resolve the issue. There are surely many who would like to have Jo's confidence in ordering their own lives and the variety of early-career experiences that she was able to sample and compare.

One way of thinking about Jo's career and that of others is as a "knowledge journey," in which what is important is not the places traveled but the knowledge acquired in the traveling. Jo, for example, in starting her own business added knowledge about a range of functions to her base knowledge of computer programming, and the combination later assisted her to take advantage of a prospective project management role. In a memorable metaphor, Bird (1996) described careers as repositories of knowledge, with much of the knowledge being tacit (Polanyi, 1966), experience based, and internalized. Career journeys can thus create a key resource for individuals as they progress on their journeys, a resource that can be exploited by their employers or by the individuals themselves. Perhaps a good traveler will always ask the questions, at each possible stage along the way, "What will I learn from this and how valuable will the knowledge be? What unique combination of competencies is my journey giving me?"

Modern societies are mobile, and if there are key principles that provide careers with their patterns, they may be more subtle than the observable ideas of occupational and organizational membership. Elements in our personal makeup, such as our values or career anchors (Chapter 5), may give us the stability that we need in a rapidly changing scene, but they allow us plenty of scope in our expression of them. Increasingly, as I show in Chapter 9, the "journey" metaphor may be superseded by the metaphor of the career as a repository of personal knowledge capital, with our journeying being only a means to that end.

Conclusion

If our careers are indeed journeys, we all need to give some thought to what sort of journey they are likely to be, whether that is what we truly want and how we can best prepare to travel. The "journey" metaphor enables us to tease out some characteristics of many careers in terms of the routes traveled and to show some main types. But overall, we are left with the impression of immense variety in the routes that individual people choose, or are forced, to follow.

It seems that much of the terrain over which career journeys must be traveled is rough, uncertain, and unexplored. Under such circumstances, much travel must be improvisational. Success is defined by the experience and knowledge gained from travel as well as by the outcome of "getting there." Industrial society had industrial careers, organizational society had organizational careers, and they provided stability and development to both the employees who lived them and to the institutions that sponsored them. Postindustrial society will have postindustrial careers, and the career actors will travel them:

The life of men and women of our time is very much like that of tourists-through-time: they cannot and will not decide in advance what places they will visit and what the sequence of stations will be; what they know for sure is that they will keep on the move, never sure whether the place they have reached is their final destination. (Bauman, 1995, pp. 268-269)

In the world of the new careers, no job is a permanent home for world-weary travelers or even a long-term guest house for visitors. These images are too static for the new realities. If the word *journey* implies destination, then perhaps careers are not journeys at all. Perhaps they are, purely and simply, travel.

Key Points in This Chapter

- People commonly use the metaphor of "journey" to describe their career. But there are many different kinds of journey, in terms of destination, speed, ground covered, and so on.
- The notions of destination (e.g., "getting to the top"), topography (e.g., gradients and barriers), and career maps (e.g., occupational information) may usefully be applied to career journeys.
- Careers may be classified into different types.
- Occupational careers take place within occupational boundaries but must be revitalized by appropriate knowledge. Organizational careers usually involve upward movement but are sometimes put at risk by restructuring. Entrepreneurial careers provide autonomy but not necessarily wealth or security.
- Boundaryless careers involve the crossing of occupational, organizational, industry, work-home, and other boundaries. They are attractive to those in possession of scarce skills who are prepared to be mobile. They have a counterpart in transitory careers, which are also mobile but in a less planned way, and may be subject to marginalization. An increasing trend, driven by globalization, overseas assignment, self-initiated travel, and permanent migration, is for career journeys to cross international boundaries.
- Most people follow careers that, looked at in their totality, are not of any one type but involve elements from all types.

Questions From This Chapter

General Questions

1. Which is more important to you in your career—the destinations you reach or the experiences you have getting there? Can you justify your answer?

2. Find out about the careers of some members of the prior generations of your family. In terms of the various types of career described in the chapter, what types did these relatives have?

3. Outline the benefits and the drawbacks of organizational careers, occupational careers, and entrepreneurial careers. Which of these forms is most attractive to you, and why?

4. Are you aware of career boundaries that you experience now or may experience in the future? If so, what are they and how strong do they feel? How do you feel about crossing them?

5. How attractive to you is the idea of a boundaryless career? Why? In a world of boundaryless careers, who wins and who loses? Why?

6. Should people like Gilles be left to get on with their transitory and marginal careers, or should they be directed or assisted to follow better career paths? Justify your answer. If you think they should be assisted, how?

Career Case Study Questions

1. Consider your case study career as a journey. To what extent does it show the characteristics of predetermined pathways, destination and direction, knowledge expeditions, and movement into management? Were there maps? Can you describe some of the terrain and topography traveled through or any climbing frames involved?

2. Consider the various types of career boundaries listed in the chapter. Which ones did your case person cross and which did your case person stay inside? With the benefit of hindsight, how does your case person feel about these boundaries now?

References

Ackah, C., & Heaton, N. (2004). The reality of the "new careers" for men and women. *Journal of European Industrial Training, 2*(4), 141-158.

Allen, V. (Ed.). (1990). *The concise Oxford dictionary of current English.* Oxford, UK: Clarendon Press.

Arthur, M. B., Inkson, K., & Pringle, J. K. (1999). *The new careers: Individual action and economic change.* Thousand Oaks, CA: Sage.

Arthur, M. B., & Rousseau, D. (Eds.). (1996). *The boundaryless career: A new employment principle for a new organizational era.* New York: Oxford University Press.

Bagdadli, S., Solari, L., Usai, A., & Grandori, A. (2003). The emergence of career boundaries in unbounded industries: Career odysseys in the Italian New Economy. *International Journal of Human Resource Management, 14*(5), 788-808.

Baruch, Y. (2003). *Managing careers: Theory and practice.* Englewood Cliffs, NJ: Prentice Hall.

Bauman, Z. (1995). *Life in fragments: Essays in postmodern morality.* Oxford, UK: Blackwell.

Beine, M., & Docquier, F. (2001). Brain drain and economic growth: Theory and evidence. *Journal of Development Economics, 64*, 275-340.

Berry, J. W. (2001). A psychology of immigration. *Journal of Social Issues, 57*, 615-631.

Bird, A. (1996). Careers as repositories of knowledge: Considerations for boundaryless careers. In M. B. Arthur & D. M. Rousseau (Eds.), *The boundaryless career: A new employment principle for a new organizational era* (pp. 150-168). New York: Oxford University Press.

Black, J. S., Gregersen, H. B., Mendenhall, M. E., & Stroh, L. K. (1999). *Globalizing people through international assignments.* New York: Addison-Wesley.

Borgen, W. A., Amundson, N. E., & Reuter, J. (2004). Using portfolios to enhance career resilience. *Journal of Employment Counseling, 41*(2), 50-59.

Bridges, W. (1995). *JobShift: How to prosper in a workplace without jobs.* London: Allen & Unwin.

Brockhaus, R. H. (1982). The psychology of the entrepreneur. In C. Kent, D. Sexton, & H. H. Vesper (Eds.), *Encyclopaedia of entrepreneurship* (pp. 39-57). Englewood Cliffs, NJ: Prentice Hall.

Brockner, J., Grover, S., Reed, T. F., & DeWitt, R. L. (1992). Layoffs, job insecurity and survivors' work efforts: Evidence of an inverted-U relationship. *Academy of Management Journal, 35*, 413-425.

Bryant, J., & Law, D. (2004). *New Zealand's diaspora and overseas-born population* (Working Paper 04/13). Wellington: New Zealand Treasury.

Cadin, L., Bailly-Bender, A.-F., & de Saint-Giniez, V. (2000). Exploring boundaryless careers in the French context. In M. Peiperl, M. B. Arthur, R. Goffee, & T. Morris (Eds.), *Career frontiers: New conceptions of working lives* (pp. 228-255). Oxford, UK: Oxford University Press.

Cappelli, P. (1999). *The new deal at work.* Boston: Harvard University Press.

Carr, S. C., Inkson, K., & Thorn, K. (2005). Talent flow and global careers: Reinterpreting "brain drain." *Journal of World Business, 40*(4), 386-398.

Chantrell, G. (Ed.). (2002). *Oxford dictionary of word histories.* Oxford, UK: Oxford University Press.

Cordes, C. L., & Dougherty, T. W. (1993). A review and integration of research on job burnout. *Academy of Management Review, 4,* 621-656.

Crompton, R., Gallie, D., & Purcell, K. (Eds.). (1996). *Changing forms of employment.* London: Routledge.

Dany, F. (2003). "Free actors" and organizations: Critical remarks about the new career literature, based on French insights. *International Journal of Human Resource Management, 14*(5), 821-838.

Downs, B., Damrosch, J., Flanigan, M., & Gutierrez, M. (Eds.). (2005). *National trade and professional associations of the United States.* Washington, DC: Columbia Books.

Driver, M. J. (1979). Career concepts and career management in organizations. In C. L. Cooper (Ed.), *Behavioral problems in organizations* (pp. 79-139). Englewood Cliffs, NJ: Prentice Hall.

Eby, L. T., Butts, M., & Lockwood, A. (2003). Predictors of success in the era of the boundaryless career. *Journal of Organizational Behavior, 24*(6), 689-708.

Eden, D. (1973). Self-employed workers: A comparison group for organisational psychology. *Organisational Behavior and Human Performance, 9*(2), 186-197.

Ensher, E. A., Murphy, S. E., & Sullivan, S. E. (2002). Boundaryless careers in entertainment: Executive women's experiences. In M. Peiperl, M. B. Arthur, R. Goffee, & N. Anand (Eds.), *Career creativity: Explorations in the re-making of work* (pp. 229-254). Oxford, UK: Oxford University Press.

Feldman, D. C., & Bolino, M. C. (2000). Career patterns of the self-employed: Career motivations and career outcomes. *Journal of Small Business Management, 38*(3), 53-67.

Galbraith, L. R. (1987). Organization design. In J. W. Lorsch (Ed.), *Handbook of organizational behavior* (pp. 343-357). Englewood Cliffs, NJ: Prentice Hall.

Greenhaus, J. H., Callanan, G. A., & Godschalk, V. M. (2000). *Career management* (3rd ed.). Fort Worth, TX: Dryden.

Gunz, H. (1989). The dual meaning of managerial careers: Organizational and individual levels of analysis. *Journal of Management Studies, 26*(3), 225-250.

Gunz, H. P., Evans, M. G., & Jalland, R. M. (2002). Chalk lines, open borders, glass walls and frontiers: Careers and creativity. In M. Peiperl, M. B. Arthur, R. Goffee, & N. Anand (Eds.), *Career creativity: Explorations in the re-making of work* (pp. 58-76). Oxford, UK: Oxford University Press.

Hall, D. T., & Associates. (1996). *The career is dead: Long live the career.* San Francisco: Jossey-Bass.

Hendricks, C. E. (1992). *The rightsizing remedy.* Homewood, IL: Irwin.

Horwitz, F. M., Chang Teng Heng, F. M., & Quazi, H. A. (2003). Finders, keepers? Attracting, motivating and retaining knowledge workers. *Human Resource Management Journal, 13*(4), 23-44.

Hugo, G., Rudd, D., & Harris, K. (2003). *Australia's diaspora: Its size, nature and policy implications.* Canberra: Committee for Economic Development of Australia.

Inkson, K. (1995). The effects of changing economic conditions on managerial job change and careers. *British Journal of Management, 6,* 183-194.

Inkson, K. (in press). Protean and boundaryless careers as metaphors. *Journal of Vocational Behavior, 67*(1).

Inkson, K., & Amundson, N. E. (2002). Career metaphors and their application in theory and counseling practice. *Journal of Employment Counseling, 39*(3), 98-108.

Inkson, K., Arthur, M. B., Pringle, J., & Barry, S. (1997). Expatriate assignment versus overseas experience: Contrasting models of human resource development. *Journal of World Business, 14*(4), 151-168.

Inkson, K., & Myers, B. (2003). "The big O.E.": International travel and career development. *Career Development International, 8*(3), 170-181.

Inkson, K., & Parker, P. (2005). Boundaryless careers and the transfer of knowledge: A "Middle Earth" perspective. *Higher Education Policy, 18,* 313-325.

Jones, C. (1996). Careers in project networks: The case of the film industry. In M. B. Arthur & D. M. Rousseau (Eds.), *The boundaryless career: A new employment principle for a new organizational era* (pp. 58-75). New York: Oxford University Press.

Kanter, R. M. (1989). Careers and the wealth of nations: A macro-perspective on the structure and implications of career forms. In M. B. Arthur, D. T. Hall, & B. S. Lawrence (Eds.), *Handbook of career theory* (pp. 506-521). New York: Cambridge University Press.

Lawrence, B. S. (1984). Age grading: The implicit organizational timetable. *Journal of Occupational Behavior, 5*(1), 23-35.

Mahroum, S. (2000). Highly skilled globetrotter: Mapping the international migration of human capital. *R & D Management, 30,* 23-31.

Mandela, N. (1994). *Long walk to freedom.* London: Bantam.

McCaskey, M. B. (1977). Goals and direction in personal planning. *Academy of Management Review, 2,* 454-462.

McHugh, K. E., Hogan, T., & Happel, S. (1995). Multiple residence and cyclical migration: A life course perspective. *Professional Geographer, 47*(3), 251-267.

Mirvis, P. H., & Hall, D. T. (1994). Psychological success and the boundaryless career. *Journal of Organizational Behavior, 15,* 365-380.

Osland, J. S. (1995). *The adventure of working abroad: Hero tales from the global frontier.* San Francisco: Jossey-Bass.

Peel, S., & Inkson, K. (2004). Contracting and careers: Choosing between self- and organizational management. *Career Development International, 9*(6), 542-558.

Pines, A. M., & Aronson, E. (1988). *Career burnout: Causes and cures.* New York: Free Press.

Platman, K. (2004). Portfolio careers and the search for flexibility in later life. *Work, Employment and Society, 18*(3), 573-599.

Polanyi, M. (1966). *The tacit dimension.* London: Routledge & Kegan Paul.

Pringle, J. K., & Mallon, M. (2003). Challenges to the boundaryless career odyssey. *International Journal of Human Resource Management, 14*(5), 839-853.

Reardon, R. C., Lenz, J. G., Sampson, J. P. Jr., & Peterson, G. W. (2006). *Career development and planning: A comprehensive approach* (2nd ed.). Mason, OH: Thomson Custom Solutions.

Richardson, J., & McKenna, S. (2003). International expertise and academic careers: What do academics have to say? *Personnel Review, 32*(6), 774-795.

Saxenian, A.-L. (1996). Beyond boundaries: Open labor markets and learning in Silicon Valley. In M. B. Arthur, & D. M. Rousseau (Eds.), *The boundaryless career: A new employment principle for a new organizational era* (pp. 23-39). New York: Oxford University Press.

Sayers, J., & Monin, N. (Eds.). (2005). *The global garage: Home-based business in New Zealand.* Melbourne, Australia: Thomson Dunmore Press.

Schein, E. H. (1996). Career anchors revised: Implications for career development in the 21st century. *Academy of Management Executive, 10*(4), 80-88.

Shepard, H. A. (1984). On the realization of human potential: The path with a heart. In M. B. Arthur, L. Bailyn, D. J. Levinson, & H. A. Shephard (Eds.), *Working with careers* (pp. 25-46). New York: Graduate School of Business, Columbia University.

Stevenson, R. L. (1907). *Travels with a donkey in the Cevennes.* London: Chatto & Windus.

Super, D. E. (1990). A life-span, life-space approach to career development. In D. Brown, L. Brooks, & Associates (Eds.), *Career choice and development* (2nd ed., pp. 197-261). San Francisco: Jossey-Bass.

Suutari, V. (2003). Global managers: Career orientation, career tracks, lifestyle implications and commitment. *Journal of Managerial Psychology, 18*(3), 185-207.

Suutari, V., & Brewster, C. (2000). Making their own way: International experience through self-initiated foreign assignments. *Journal of World Business, 35*(4), 417-436.

Thomas, D. C. (1998). The expatriate experience: A critical review and synthesis. *Advances in International Comparative Management, 12,* 237-273.

Thomas, D. C. (2002). *Essentials of international management: A cross-cultural perspective.* Thousand Oaks, CA: Sage.

Thomas, D. C., Lazarova, M. B., & Inkson, K. (Eds.). (2005). Global careers: New phenomenon or new perspectives? *Journal of World Business, 40*(4), 349-440.

Vance, C. M. (2005). The quest for building global competence: A taxonomy of self-initiating career path strategies for gaining business experience abroad. *Journal of World Business, 40*(4), 374-385.

Veiga, J. F. (1981). Plateaued versus nonplateaued managers: Career patterns, attitudes and path potential. *Academy of Management Journal, 24,* 566-578.

Weber, M. (1947). *The theory of social and economic organization.* New York: Free Press.

Weick, K. E. (1995). *Sensemaking in organizations.* Thousand Oaks, CA: Sage.

CHAPTER 7

Careers as Roles

A Multifaceted Career

Christopher Reeve was born in New York City in 1952. From a very early age, he was interested in the theater, and by the time he left school he had already played many parts in school musical productions and participated in the school orchestra, choral group, and hockey team. By age 15 years, he had played in professional theater and by 16 he had an agent. At Cornell, he studied music, English, and theater, and by the time he graduated he had played a number of parts professionally. From Cornell he won a scholarship to study under John Houseman at the Juilliard School of Performing Arts in New York, and he was soon performing on stage with the great Katherine Hepburn. Aided by striking good looks and a strong physique, he seemed destined for a fine theatrical career.

In 1976, Reeve auditioned for the lead role in the 1978 movie *Superman* and won the part. As Reeve remarked, Superman was not just one movie role but two: the superhero and the modest everyday guy Clark Kent. Said Reeve, "There must be some difference stylistically between Clark and Superman, otherwise you just have a pair of glasses standing in for a character." He also became irritated with people who behaved towards him as if he were Superman: "As far as I'm concerned, there is Superman and there is Christopher Reeve, and I'm not interested in having them merge. What I'm interested in is acting. . . . I wasn't Superman before, and I don't plan to be Superman after."

The film *Superman* was a major success and made Reeve famous. He continued in his acting career, eventually appearing in a total of 17 films, including *Superman II;* about 150 plays; and numerous television programs. But he resisted playing to his Superman type, preferring to appear on stage, where possible, rather than on film, and playing challenging, offbeat parts. Off-stage and off-screen he had a close personal relationship with executive Gae Exton and their children. After he and Exton parted in 1987, he met and eventually married Dana Morosini in 1992.

(Continued)

(Continued)

Reeve was multiskilled and had multiple interests. A political activist since the anti–Vietnam War protests of his student days, he was also actively involved with charities such as Amnesty International and Save the Children. In 1988, he received an award for work on behalf of oppressed writers in Chile and addressed the United Nations on the environmental effects of drift net tuna fishing. For recreation, he composed and played classical piano music, flew a small plane solo across the Atlantic, and was expert in scuba diving, skiing, and horse riding.

In 1995, Reeve suffered a major accident while riding, fracturing his spine and almost losing his life. He was rendered quadriplegic, unable to move either his legs or his arms and was confined to a special electric wheelchair that he operated by means of blowing and sucking on a straw. He was now highly dependent on others to fulfill his everyday needs and at major risk for illness.

However, throughout the trauma he was determined to remain a loving husband and father and to rebuild his life anew. His celebrity status and determination soon enabled him to take on formidable new challenges, particularly as an activist on behalf of disabled people. He began to accept speaking engagements around the country, including the 1996 Oscars, the Paralympics, and the Democratic National Convention. Soon he was speaking at charity events all over the country. As an activist, he fought for reform of insurance laws covering paralysis, chaired the American Paralysis Association, and founded a research center and foundation focused on the disabled. His iconic status and example brought inspiration to many disabled people. He wrote his biography and lobbied for research on the use of embryonic stem cells to assist nerve regeneration. He even narrated an award-winning TV documentary on spinal injury and directed the film *In the Gloaming,* starring Glenn Close. And with the help of therapy, he regained sensation in parts of his body and the ability to move parts of one hand.

His dream continued to be that he would walk again. But it never eventuated. On October 10, 2004, Christopher Reeve died of heart failure. He was 52 years old.

Careers such as Christopher Reeve's fill us with awe. How could one man have excelled at so many things? How was he able to continue his career following the apparent loss of its main base and, indeed, go further to bring it to new heights?

One way of understanding Reeve's career is to see it as a set of different roles. According to the *Concise Oxford Dictionary* (Allen, 1990, p. 1043) a *role* is (1) "a person's or thing's characteristic or expected function" or (2) "an actor's part in a play, film, etc."

In terms of the first of these definitions, Reeve played a wide range of roles: for example, son, student, lover, husband, father, stage actor, screen actor, celebrity, sportsman, speaker, activist, fundraiser, political lobbyist, trust manager, film director. Some of these roles he played consecutively, others simultaneously. In terms of the second definition, Reeve was indeed a professional actor, and within his acting career there were literally hundreds of other discrete roles. He appeared to move from role to role effortlessly yet without abandoning key values: In this sense, his career was certainly protean (Chapter 4).

Reeve's life contains one of the great riddles of career: role versus self; playing a part versus being oneself. On the one hand, Reeve's actions were dictated by the life roles and acting roles in which he found himself. When he was on stage or on camera, for example, he might bring a personal interpretation to his role, but basically, like any actor, he had to say the words that the writer had written and follow the instructions that the director provided. Even when he was being a son, a father, or a protester, he was expected by others to behave in ways appropriate to that role. Yet Reeve was a unique human being with specific physical features, abilities, dispositions, attitudes, and interests. Whatever role he was playing, he applied himself and his own values and dispositions consistently to his life, always knew who he was, and maintained a steely determination and ideals of self-sufficiency. In short, no matter what role he was playing, he remained himself—Christopher Reeve.

It seems that Reeve was acutely aware of the importance of retaining identity while in different roles: Despite going from the role of Superman to the role of quadriplegic, he revealingly titled his autobiography *Still Me* (Reeve, 1999). From his comments about Clark Kent and Superman and his approach to the selection of acting roles, he appears to have been sensitive to the unique personality within each theatrical role. And as best he could, he used the many roles available to him to live a uniquely fulfilling and effective life.

All of us, to some extent, in life and in career, face the problem of remaining ourselves while discharging roles to the satisfaction of others. Careers demand that we play multiple roles, which are not always compatible with each other and which may in some way threaten our sense of who we are—our identity. Reeve handled these conflicts extremely well. Most of us have less challenging dilemmas. How do we deal with them?

Roles and Work

In the definition of *role* provided earlier—"a person's characteristic or expected function"—the word *function* reminds us that when we discharge a role it is for a purpose. The word *expected* tells us that purpose may be defined by the expectations of others (Fondas & Stewart, 1994). If we were to divide a career into the jobs of which it is composed, each job would have a purpose or function. Indeed, many would also have a formal job description describing the tasks expected of the job occupants. Consider the sample job description for a personal assistant.

Position Description: PA (Personal Assistant) to the CEO (Chief Executive Officer), Amethyst Industries

Day-to-Day Activities

Open mail and distribute it to CEO and other designated staff.

Screen phone calls to the CEO according to the CEO's specification.

Support the MD as required.

Register invoices daily into accounts payable system.

Set up the boardroom for all presentations for both CEO and sales staff, ordering meals and refreshments as necessary.

Make all boardroom and meeting room bookings.

Travel: Arrange all staff travel directly with agent or airlines, according to manual of procedures.

Assist management team with contracts and correspondence of a personal nature.

Ensure maintenance of office buildings in terms of any necessary electrical or plumbing work, repairs.

Maintenance of the cleaning contract and weekly liaison with the contractor.

Order stationery and ensure stocks are up-to-date.

Orient new employees and supply them with office/telephone/IT equipment and stationery.

Order staff uniforms and ensure stocks are up-to-date.

Order printing requirements and negotiate best quotations.

Monthly

Take minutes at national managers' meetings and divisional managers' meetings.

Distribute all minutes.

Complete monthly statistics at the end of each month and submit to parent company.

Compile and complete shipping line rebate claims.

Type all new contracts of employment.

Maintain HR system, including all contracts, work records, leave forms, and related documentation.

It is clear from this job description that the role of the PA is tightly prescribed by the employing organization. In this type of job, it is likely that in addition to the formal requirements specified there will be standardized procedures as well as company norms and expectations, which provide precise rules not just for what tasks are to be done but also for how they are to be done. For example, the employee may be conceptualized as a helper or support person who fulfills the formal aspects of the job as described earlier but is also willing to participate in various unspecified ways. There may be an organization culture in which particular emphases are specified for all roles (e.g., personal customer service), further guiding the behavior of the PA. The CEO and other managers may additionally use their authority to specify other duties and methods of operating in the job. Looked at in this way, a career is a series of roles whose content is determined not by the person having the career but by the organizations in which he or she is employed. Part of the price we pay for the wages and conditions we receive from employers may be a degree of subservience to them and the recognition that our time and effort, which they pay for, is theirs, not ours.

In addition, there may be legislative requirements mandating, for example, hours of work and safe and healthy working conditions, which further limit the job. Each job represents an occupation, often denoted by the job title—for example, engineer, social worker, hairstylist—which may also specify professional or trade methods and standards and engender particular public expectations (Hickson & Thomas, 1969). Then there are more general roles, such as professional, loyal company servant, and unionist, which may represent individuals' own values and aspirations or the values and expectations others expect of individuals. Can we then understand careers largely as combinations and sequences of roles dictated by employers and others?

Roles and Society

An early explication of the social framing of careers through social roles, identity, and associated mechanisms came from the Chicago School of Sociology, a group of scholars at the University of Chicago working in association with Everett Hughes (1937, 1958). An excellent review of the work of this group is provided by Barley (1989).

In 1937, Hughes wrote the following:

A career consists, objectively, of a series of statuses and clearly defined offices.
. . . Careers in our society are thought very much in terms of jobs, for these are the characteristic and crucial connections of the individual with the institutional structure. But the career is by no means exhausted in a series of business and professional achievements. There are other points at which one's life touches the social order. (p. 413)

The idea of "statuses and clearly defined offices" indicates the importance of roles in this view of careers. The work of the Chicago School embedded the notion of career in a range of theories also concerned with self and identity (individual-level constructs) and with organizations and institutions (collective constructs), with role providing a key link. The Chicago group believed that by studying careers they could treat them as microcosms of society, and they developed ethnographic techniques for studying the careers of distinct occupational groups (e.g., Becker, 1951; Becker, Geer, Hughes, & Strauss, 1961). In noting that careers extend beyond the work sphere and that it is possible, for example, to talk about the "career" of a hospital patient (Roth, 1963), these sociologists were perhaps ahead of their time.

To a considerable extent, roles are representations of the social structures and institutions referred to in Chapter 2. They bring us face-to-face with the reality that other groups and individuals have an interest in our careers and express that interest by trying to define our roles for us. We need to recognize, too, the following facts:

- Each job involves multiple roles, and these change over time.
- Roles are defined by us, by others, by the organizations in which we work, and by the social institutions in which our careers are embedded.
- The work career is affected by nonwork roles.
- Maintaining and developing our identity through this plethora of roles and role changes are major career tasks.

Role Expectations and Role Conflict

Roles provide guidance as to how to conduct our careers, but they also create difficulties. Jobholders may not be able, or want, to do the job in the way prescribed or expected by others. Different people involved with our job, such as our boss, colleagues, subordinates, coworkers, and customers, and perhaps even family and friends, may have their own ideas of how we should do the job, and these views will not necessarily agree with each other. Jobholders therefore find that discharging their role effectively is often complicated. Then there is the fact that a job is only one of the many roles that jobholders have: Other roles, such as holder of a second or even third job, parent, partner, relation, spouse, consumer, sportsman or sportswoman, voluntary organization member, and so forth, all provide their own roles and expected behavior, which again may conflict with the job role. Last comes the problem of role change—taking up and learning new roles, adapting to roles as they change, and relinquishing roles.

One way of understanding roles is to use two subsidiary concepts: role set and role expectations—terms used by Katz and Kahn (1966). A role set is a set of other people who attempt to define parts of the role of a focal person. For example, if the focal person is an office manager, the role set may consist of the focal person's subordinates, secretary, direct boss, spouse, the manager of an adjacent department, and perhaps one or two major customers. Each member of the role set has role expectations regarding how the focal person will discharge his or her role and communicates these expectations directly and indirectly to the focal person. From this, the focal person receives a perception of what the required role behavior is and complies or resists in his or her behavior.

The role expectations of members of a role set lead to various complications for a role member. The expectations may not be clearly defined, leading to role ambiguity. They may conflict with personal values held by the focal person, leading to person–role conflict. (The discussion of work adjustment theory in Chapter 5, and particularly the case of Suzanne, clearly demonstrate person–role conflict caused by lack of fit between individual characteristics and role requirements.) The expectations of various members of the role set may be different and incompatible, leading to intrarole conflict. Two different roles held by the same person, for example, jobholder and family member, may get in the way of each other, leading to inter-role conflict. Finally, the sum total of expectations inherent in a particular role may be more than the focal person can handle, leading to role overload. Such difficulties can cause significant stress (Aneshensel, 1992). Marcie's case is an example.

Role Conflict

Marcie is supervisor of a small department in a "rag trade" clothing factory. She supervises seven women machinists and performs some machining herself. For years she has found herself mediating between her subordinate machinists and her boss, Mr. Bennett, over the role of the machinists. The machinists find their work hard and boring. Several of them are extroverts, and they discharge their energy by gossiping, joking, horseplaying, and sometimes singing. Mr. Bennett is a strict disciplinarian who believes that his employees should work every minute of every paid hour and should maintain a quiet, productive atmosphere in the factory.

Marcie finds that she is the "meat in the sandwich." Mr. Bennett constantly reminds her that it is her job, not his, to ensure that the machinists meet his standards. The machinists remind her that she is one of them—she was a machinist herself for 15 years—and that she should stand up for them in the face of Mr. Bennett's unreasonable expectations. Marcie tries to reason with each side, tactfully requesting each to try to compromise its attitude a little. But she feels under stress.

Recently, Mr. Bennett has asked her to institute disciplinary action against the noisiest woman, who is also an old friend of Marcie's—action that could lead to the woman's eventual dismissal. Marcie recognizes that he has a good case: Her friend's behavior has often gone over the top, including occasional instances of drinking on the job. But, on the other hand, what Mr. Bennett is suggesting is directly contrary to her own value of loyalty to one's friends. This has put Marcie under real stress—she doesn't know what to do.

When she confides in her husband, Joe, about the problem, however, he is very clear about what she should do. "I know you've been preoccupied with this," he says. "You haven't been sleeping properly. You're not any fun with the family the way you used to be. Frankly, you don't need it. In fact you don't need the job. You have two choices. One is to tell Bennett you don't want to be supervisor any more. It simply isn't worth the extra money. Tell him you want to go back on the factory floor as a machinist. The other is to walk away. Find another job. Find one where *you* are in charge of your own life."

And so Marcie's career may undergo an important change due to a mixture of intrarole conflict (different messages from different role senders), person–role conflict (Marcie's values vs. what she is expected to do), and inter-role conflict (Marcie as a supervisor vs. Marcie as a family member). Her predicament comes about not just because of pressures put on her by those around her but also by fundamental characteristics of her social situation, for example, the level of authority possessed by her boss, and societal definitions of what roles such as supervisor and friend entail.

Marcie's husband recognizes that people can become imprisoned by their roles and advises her to engineer her own liberation. In so doing, he is echoing a frequent criticism of role theory and the consequences of institutions, organizations, and individuals defining other people's roles:

> One of the most objectionable aspects of role theory is that it assumes that all people must adjust to society. There is no historical vision of a society which changes to fulfill people's needs. Role in society is taken to be analogous to roles in a play. Details of how a dramatic role is to be played are indicated by writer, producer, the stage setting and other actors; and the words are written down and actions prescribed. The actor merely conforms to expectations . . . it is sometimes even asserted that an individual is no more than the sum of the roles s/he plays: Mary, for example, is mother, daughter, wife, and housewife. Apart from that, Mary as a thinking, feeling being with potential for development, does not exist. (Sargent, 1994, p. 84)

Sargent (1994) made it clear that she is arguing chiefly against prescriptive roles being used in a consensual way (i.e., with the implication that there is only one way to conduct a role) and in a political way (i.e., by powerful institutions using roles to impose their will on individuals). And it is certainly true that much of what we do in our career roles is prescribed in considerable detail. Fortunately, there is another concept—identity, an intrapersonal counterpart of role—that enables us to take a more balanced view.

Identity

Identity represents one's sense of individuality and personality—who one is. It is important because it provides values and gives a sense of direction. The psychologist Erikson (1959) considered that the search for identity is the major task of adolescence, but maintaining a sense of identity is a lifelong process. Defining who we are enables us to ascribe new meanings to our lives: for example, "I am a medical student," "I am a doctor," "I am a heart surgeon" and also "I am a totally honest person," "I am a go-getter," "I am a Moslem." Regardless of what job descriptions and company expectations say, most individuals inject their own identity into the situation by "being themselves" to a greater or lesser extent, and by taking on roles in which they can express that identity, such as leader, joker, and workaholic or, indeed, greaser, dictator, or petty bureaucrat.

Many career theories include a concept such as identity to represent the basis for individuals imposing themselves on their choices of roles and the way they choose to enact roles. For example, Super's (1990) career development theory (Chapter 4) talks about career as the implementation of a self-concept, and Dalton (1989) noted that "the establishment and a maintenance of self identity is a critical dimension of personal development" (p. 100). Hall (2002) referred to the career subidentity as a component of a broader identity and regarded this identity as "an internal compass . . . in the midst of all the turbulence" (p. 32). In Chapter 10, I develop the idea that identity is a key element in the stories we tell about our careers.

We derive our identity partly from the roles we enact, but, in a corresponding manner, those roles are often chosen on the basis of identity and provide the opportunity for further identity development. The case of Sara is an example.

Defining an Identity

Sara Ford, BS, Mathematics and Computer Science, 2001:

I am a software design engineer in Test for the Microsoft Corporation, working on the Visual Studio Core Team. Visual Studio is a development environment assisting everyone, from the "Introduction to Computer Science" student to the professional software engineer, to write programs and develop software. I graduated with a double major in computer science and mathematics and a minor in French. Yet I put all my emphasis on my mathematics degree during the interview.

Mathematics teaches you logical thinking and problem solving skills—skills all employers look for in new candidates. While interviewing at Microsoft, I introduced myself as a problem solver. What made me so special, in comparison with other applicants? My answer was simple: "I have a mathematics degree."

Mathematics builds the foundation for learning how to problem solve. A chemical engineer is a chemical engineer, a biologist is a biologist, but a mathematician can learn how to become either one. I never took a college course on how to test software, and yet I was hired as a software tester. The recruiter understood that someone with a mathematics background has the discipline and the analytical way of thinking it takes to test new types of software.

One of my job descriptions is to automate testing. Automation is a code that simulates what a user might want to experience when interacting with a program and records any unexpected or undesired results as failures. . . . In this ever-changing world, the issue of figuring out how to best test or automate these new technologies is never solved. Testers always search for better methods and approaches . . . that require less time and effort to find failures and bugs. Having a strong background in mathematics is essential to creating these new testing methodologies, since this is problem solving in its purest form.

The best thing I ever did for my career was declaring a double major in mathematics and computer science.

Source: Sara Ford, personal communication.

People's interpretations of their own careers inevitably vary according to their audience and purpose (Chapter 10): This one is from the Web site of the Mathematics Association of America (MAA) and presumably has the objective of engendering interest in mathematics as a career training. Nevertheless, Sara provides a rationale for having a nested set of roles derived from her core identity as a mathematician. Her software tester role is a form of a broader problem-solving role, and she chose these roles because of her identity as a graduate in mathematics and discharges them with her mathematics training and her problem solver identity acting as a compass for her present work and her career. Most likely, Sara also identifies nowadays as a software engineer and as a member of the Microsoft organization. Most likely, too, her identity will shift as her career takes her into new roles.

Note that, although identity is individual, it is often derived from reference groups that provide rules, role models, and even a language for understanding one's situation and identity. Sara understands her career as part of the collective groups of mathematicians, software testers, and Microsoft employees. Thus, identity and role can become very close to each other. Faced with a role change or career change—for example, the opportunity for promotion into a managerial job or a job opportunity in another company—Sara would have to consider whether the new role was compatible with her mathematician–problem solver–Microsoft identity and either decline the role, seek to change the role in line with her identity, alter her identity to suit the role, or live with the incongruence of the two. Many career decisions represent triumphs of identity over role, notably when someone leaves a job because the duties required by the role are incompatible with the person's core values.

This discussion of identity and role echoes some of the considerations in the "fit" metaphor (Chapter 5). Consistently having to practice role behavior that is inconsistent with one's identity results in stress. An example is the increasingly common expectation of emotional work by employees in personal services, such as air cabin crew, who have to consistently smile and maintain pleasant cordial relationships with customers, even though, for all sorts of reasons—some of them personal—the crew members may be feeling miserable (Morris & Feldman, 1997; Williams, 2003). Even more extreme are cases where individuals become so preoccupied with their roles that they lose their true identity. Peter Sellers provides another theatrical case.

Many Roles, No Identity

The famous British character actor Peter Sellers was, from his childhood, a talented mimic. It was said he could imitate almost any voice he heard and make a telephone listener believe he was the real person. He gained early fame in Britain through his wonderful voice characterizations on the anarchic radio program *The Goon Show,* in which he played multiple characters. But he soon showed that his talent extended to physical characterization, and he embarked on an extensive film career in which he played a wide range of characters of both sexes, all ages, and many different nationalities and types. For example, in Stanley Kubrick's *Doctor Strangelove,* Sellers played three parts: the fussy U.S. President Merkin Muffley, the eccentric ex-Nazi intellectual Dr. Strangelove, and the "stiff-upper-lip" British Air Force Officer Lionel Mandrake. However, he proved unable to master the Texan accent required of the extroverted bomber pilot Major "King" Kong, and another actor was used in that role.

Sellers was an immense talent, loved in his own country and respected worldwide for his skills. Yet in his personal life he was often insensitive and capricious. He often took on roles from his acting career into his personal life or invented them and used them in his interactions with others. He frequently complained that he had no identity of his own and could survive in the world only by being the characters whom he played. As he said, "I have no personality of my own. . . . I'm a character actor. I couldn't play Peter Sellers the way Cary Grant plays Cary Grant, say—because I have no concrete image of myself. . . . When I'm doing a role I feel as if it's the *role* doing the role. . . . When I finish a picture I feel a horrible sudden loss of identity" (Peter Sellers, quoted in Lewis, 1994, p. xiii). His final screen role, in *Being There,* was that of Chauncey Gardner, a man who had no personality or identity of his own and onto whom others therefore projected the identity that they wanted to see.

SOURCES: Lewis (1994); Sikov (1998).

Role Transitions

If careers are considered as sequences of roles, then an important feature of careers may be the process of transition between roles: for example, entering one's first job, moving between education and employment, being promoted, being laid off, leaving voluntarily to move to a career opportunity in another organization, or retiring. Most people in describing their careers use role transitions as the key marking points, and they are often direction changing and stressful.

Nicholson and West (1988) define *work-role transition* as "any move into and/or out of a job, any move between jobs, any major alteration in the main duties and activities" (p. 48). Thus, they include changes within the present role, where, for example, new duties are added or the nature of the role is altered by reorganization or technology.

It is difficult to generalize about work-role transitions because the term includes so many different types of change. As seen in the previous chapter, transitions may be made within the current organization or to a new one, at the current level or to a new one, within the current occupation or function or to a new one, or to new industries, geographical locations, even countries. Boundaryless careers (Chapter 6) involve many transitions between different roles across the boundaries that separate them.

Perhaps the most important characteristic of role transitions is whether the change is deliberately sought by the individual or is inadvertent due to some (usually negative) external circumstance: for example, being laid off, fired, demoted, or transferred, or having an accident or illness that makes it impossible to continue in the present role. Alternatively, job changes may be actively sought by individuals as a means of escaping a disliked role, finding more interesting and challenging work, changing career direction, gaining higher status or rewards, or addressing family circumstances (Nicholson & West, 1988).

Nicholson (1984) outlines a four-stage process that individuals typically go through in making their transitions. The four stages are preparation, encounter, adjustment, and stabilization.

Preparation

In preparation, the change is anticipated and expected, and the individual seeks to be ready for it. Part of this process is saying goodbye to the job one is leaving, a process often involving the severing of familiar routines and personal ties, which may cause something close to grief (Adams, Hayes, & Hopson, 1976). In terms of looking ahead, a common problem is that people tend to be optimists rather than pessimists, and their expectations—possibly influenced by the "sales pitch" of a new employer or boss—may be unrealistic in terms of what the job actually offers. The onus is on both individual and organization to maximize prior information about each other, possibly through the realistic job previews described in Chapter 9 (Wanous, 1989, 1992).

Encounter

This is the initial experience of a new role, in which the individual encounters and comes to terms with the requirements and expectations of the new situation. Employers often provide a range of information to assist newcomers to learn their roles quickly—for example, technical information concerning the role, expectations of other employees, and organizational norms, as well as feedback on the newcomer's initial performance and behavior (Morrison, 1993). Sophisticated organizations often employ strong orientation programs, in which the individual is indoctrinated into not only his or her own job but also the position of a knowledgeable and committed member of the new organization. For example, the Disney organization is well known for its meticulous initial training to newcomers in the history, traditions, and core values of their new employer (Martinez, 1992).

The range of ways in which individuals learn their new roles and how those new roles fit their new organizations are diverse and include both organization-managed and informal, individual components (Van Maanen & Schein, 1979). In Chapter 3, we looked at the case of Arthur, in which Arthur, on his first day in his new organization, encountered various new expectations of him, including the expectations that he would wear light-colored shirts and would avoid sitting in the senior engineer's favorite chair. Through the combination of formal induction/orientation and informal feedback, people learn what is expected, even if they do not necessarily like it. The process is called socialization, and it is an important source of assistance to individuals in their personal career development (Chao, O'Leary-Kelly, Wolf, Klein, & Gardner, 1994).

Adjustment

In this phase, the individual adapts his or her behavior and perhaps even identity to accommodate the new role or attempts to enact or alter the role in such a way as to accommodate his or her own identity and motivation (Nicholson & West, 1989). While the term *adjustment* has connotations of emotional well-being and is generally thought to be a good thing, there may be difficulties in store for both individuals and organizations if the individual slips too easily into a role, does not question or change it in any way, and continues to remain similarly adjusted forever: Eventually, such a person might be regarded as moribund, to the detriment of both person and organization. There is evidence that strong orientation and socialization practices by the organization encourage acceptance of, and commitment to, the organization, but they may limit innovative behavior (Ashforth & Saks, 1996)—a matter to be followed up on in the next section. In contrast, the latter possibility of the individual adjusting the role rather than adjusting *to* the role reminds us that roles are not always fixed and that individuals acting with autonomy may escape potential enslavement by roles.

Stabilization

In this phase, the adjustment becomes stable—the individual is in balance with the organization. However, there are many forces that may disturb this state: individual boredom, stagnation or poor performance, and organizational change. This stage, of course, may never be reached. Indeed, many of today's employees may well feel that they are so bedeviled by changes to organization structure, new reporting relationships and job descriptions, and major technological and system changes that their role never stays stable long enough for them to adjust, let alone stabilize.

The conditions of technological and structural change in today's organizations make role transitions frequent and substantial, even for those employees who remain loyal to a particular organization or even a particular job. For those pursuing boundaryless careers, major role transitions inevitably become part of their lives and are often found to be enjoyable and energizing. It may be that the personality characteristic of flexibility or adaptability is becoming ever more critical in careers as the sources of transition increase (Ebberwein, Krieshok, Ulven, & Prosser, 2004).

Role Innovation

Formal roles in organizations do not need to be accepted exactly as they are. Role innovation (Schein, 1971) and crafting one's job (Wrzesniewski & Dutton, 2001) imply that individuals can, literally, carve out a role for themselves in their work by adding things to the role that are not in their job description or that they can at least deliberately change in desired directions the role they have. Schein (1971) distinguished between custodians, who do their jobs according to traditional job descriptions and do not innovate; content innovators, who accept the purpose of the role but change the detail of how it is done; and *role innovators,* who change the whole nature of their role. Jenny's case is an example of role innovation.

By Her Own Bootstraps

Jenny, bored with high school, left at age 16 years. With good typing skills and a pleasant personality, she secured a job as a typist in an advertising agency. As one of the most junior people in the organization, her role was very limited: She was expected to stick to the information-recording tasks in her job description and to take orders from most of the professional staff in the agency. However, she took an active interest in the content of what she was typing, in the interactions of other staff, and in the overall business of the agency. She quickly became fascinated: Advertising was wonderful! She also realized that sometimes she could see things more clearly than some of her superiors could.

Jenny began to speak up, as tactfully as she could, in executive and account meetings at which she was taking the minutes. Initially, the professional and managerial staff members were surprised to hear her voice, and on one occasion her direct superior advised her to remember that speaking up was not her job. Using the latitude her job description allowed, she made friends with the other staff, joined them for lunch, and talked informally with them about her ideas. Gradually, her contributions became accepted and then, as it became clear that she knew what she was talking about, encouraged. The professional staff began to see her almost as one of them. Within a year it was clear that she was wasted as a typist. Her boss brought her to the attention of the CEO, who appointed her to a position as media planner, with time off to pursue a relevant educational qualification. Thus commenced Jenny's rapid rise to senior positions in the industry. Sometimes, a job description need be a constraint only if the person lets it.

Jenny's transformation appears to be to the advantage of both Jenny and her employing organization. But clearly as she sought to innovate there was some uneasiness in the organization as to whether that was appropriate. Much depends on the organization's tolerance of people who go outside their formal role and its encouragement of creativity (Oldham & Cummings, 1996). At the extreme is a story of a new employee in an especially open-minded organization who came to work on his first day and asked his supervisor what his job was. "Walk around and find something useful to do," said the supervisor. "I'll come and look for you in a couple of weeks" (Manz & Sims, 1991).

Role innovation may be built around learning opportunities. One concept is the self-designed apprenticeship (Arthur, Inkson, & Pringle, 1999, pp. 68–70). In a formal apprenticeship, the new learner sacrifices higher earnings by accepting a very low pay rate, mundane work, and a subservient role and learns skills from skilled practitioners or teachers in the organization or in college until he or she is qualified as a skilled practitioner. In the self-designed apprenticeship, the same principles apply, except the apprentice designs the curriculum and chooses the teachers, and there is not necessarily a formal qualification. For example, in *The New Careers* (Arthur et al., 1999), a young unemployed engineering graduate improvised: He offered to work as a bartender for no pay for 2 weeks in return for being taught bar skills. When the 2 weeks was up, he had made himself indispensable and was offered a full-time job. Within 2 years, he had worked his way up to bar manager at night, regained daytime employment based on his engineering qualifications, and now had the option of a career in engineering or as a bar owner.

Work–Life Balance

The phrase *work–life balance* is nowadays heard increasingly (Greenblatt, 2002; Sturges & Guest, 2004). Work–life balance reminds us that each of us has other life roles in addition to our work role.

Super (1992) used the metaphor and visual stimulus of a life-career rainbow (Figure 7.1) to illustrate the multiple work and nonwork roles occupied by each individual over his or her life span.

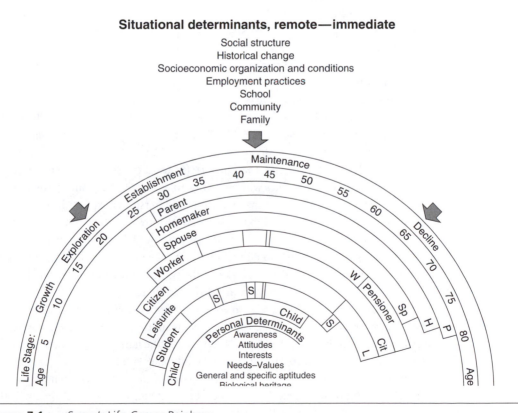

Figure 7.1   Super's Life-Career Rainbow

Source: Reprinted from *Journal of Vocational Behavior*, Vol. 16, No. 1, D.E. Super, "A life-span, life-space approach to career development." Copyright (1980) with permission from Elsevier.

The rainbow diagram includes the following elements:

- The internal, personal determinants of career behavior, such as attitudes, aptitudes, and interests
- External determinants, such as social structure, employment practices, and family
- The five life stages in Super's age/stage theory (Chapter 3), paralleling age changes
- Eight roles that tend to operate in the individual's life and that become active and inactive at different ages so that all are simultaneously active for much of the life: child, student, leisurite (e.g., hobbyist, sports player, volunteer worker), citizen, worker, spouse, homemaker, and parent; on this basis, "worker"—the major career role—complements, or competes with, a wide range of other roles

Chief among these other roles are family roles, such as the role of son, daughter, brother or sister, spouse or partner, parent, grandparent, and caregiver. To many people, their family roles as partners and parents are particularly important, perhaps even more important than their work roles. Indeed, the chief point of work roles for some may be the opportunity they give to provide money for the well-being of the family. Although much of the focus on work–life balance has been on the competing demands of work and family, the real problem for many people may be that early in their careers the pursuit of career success (Chapter 4) draws them into the habit of working harder and for longer hours than is good for them (Sturges & Guest, 2004).

An unfortunate feature of the phrase *work–life balance* is its apparent implication that work is not part of life but rather something separate from life, perhaps even something opposed to life, something akin to being dead. In reality, work is very much part of life, and many people gain immense liveliness and pleasure through their work. *Work–nonwork balance,* or possibly *work–family balance,* is a better alternative.

Nevertheless, it is quite true that there is, for most people, a problem of balancing the demands of work roles with nonwork roles, particularly family roles. A person's contract of employment may state that the person is expected to work for a company from 9 a.m. until 5 p.m., Monday through Friday: But if the person receives a phone message at work at 10 a.m. on Tuesday stating that the person's 12-year-old son was injured in an accident, was taken to hospital, and is asking for the person, he or she knows which takes priority. In this type of situation, the work role is normally compromised in favor of the family role.

Historically, this problem was solved in nuclear families by having one adult member, invariably the man, take on the breadwinning work role, while the woman stayed home and discharged all the roles relating to the family. The wholesale entry of most women into the workforce (Chapter 1) did away with that solution, spread both women and men much more thinly in relation to their family responsibilities, and created a major problem, especially for women, of competing devotions (Blair-Loy, 2003).

Greenhaus and Beutell (1985) provided a model of the problem of work–family role incompatibility (Figure 7.2). In this model, role expectations from the work domain and the family domain conflict with each other in three areas.

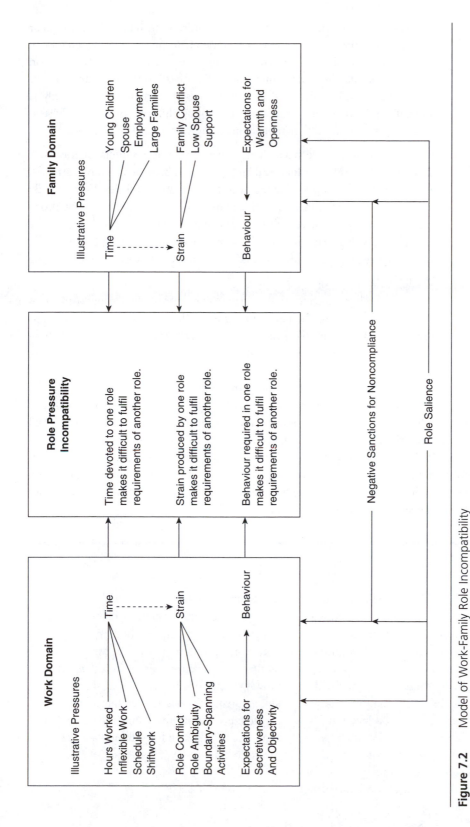

Figure 7.2 Model of Work-Family Role Incompatibility

Source: From Greenhaus, J. H., & Beutell, N. J. (1985). *Academy of Management Review*, 10, p. 78. Reprinted with permission of the Academy of Management.

1. In respect to time, many jobs nowadays require both regular and irregular hours. For example, an employee may work late to clear a backlog, take work home, attend evening or weekend meetings, work irregular shifts, or be on call 24 hours a day in case of emergency. All of these conditions can interfere with normal family time, and the problem is exacerbated if the family is large; if family members are infants, very young children, or frequently sick; and if other adult family members, including partners, also have jobs.

2. In respect to strain, we have already seen how role conflicts in the work domain, such as role overload and ambiguity, can provide their own stresses, even without the complicating factor of family responsibilities. In the family situation, too, various factors, such as family size, children's behavior problems, and lack of spousal support, can likewise be stressful. Under these circumstances, it is hard not to take work-related stress home to the family and family-related stress to work and as a result fail to discharge either role satisfactorily.

3. Behavior, such as competitive or aggressive actions or strong control of emotions—which may be part and parcel of the work role—may be inappropriate in the family role, just as family behavior such as warmth and affection may not sit well in the work role.

Greenhaus and Beutell (1985) noted that the outcome of these conflicts is moderated by role salience. For some family members, often men, work roles may have higher salience; for others, often women, family roles have higher salience, and these predispositions provide guidance as to how to solve the problems (Frone & Rice, 1987). In practice, this often means that when family demands are high, women modify their work arrangements to "be there" for their family when needed. In the case of Elsie, note how she constantly builds her career around her family's needs, rather than vice versa.

Family First

Elsie is an office administrator who constantly tries to protect her home life from interference from her work role. Early in her career, she moved between companies to pursue opportunities. But after she married and had children, family matters were always the primary criterion for career decision making. When her job was moved to a location less convenient to her home and the hours were extended and interfered with her family life, she resigned, remaining unemployed for several months as she sought local part-time work during a recession. She finally obtained her present job only 7 minutes' drive from her home: a very big plus. Her children have now grown up and left home, but her career orientation has not changed. Her primary objective now is quality of life with her husband. The key recurring themes in her talk about her career are location and hours of work. For Elsie, work is second to family—a minor means to a major—family—end.

Source: Arthur et al. (1999).

Women—and some men—with families constantly juggle aspects of their hours and type and location of work to ensure they meet their family commitments (Arthur et al., 1999). For example, some husband-wife duos work different shifts so that one can always be home with the family: This may be good for the family but may put a strain on the husband–wife relationship. Working parents frequently try to arrange shortened hours of work so that they can drive their children to school in the morning and home from school at night. Part-time work is often preferred, particularly by women, because of the additional time it releases for family commitments (Gottlieb, Kelloway, & Barham, 1998). Another solution is to telework or start a home-based business (Riley & McCloskey, 1999) so that young children always have a parent with them. Of course, all these options typically mean, as in Elsie's case, that the person is compromising his or her career opportunities to serve a higher priority. And despite the supposed new equality of the sexes, women continue to take primary responsibility for child care and housework, in addition to the career roles that they occupy (Friedman & Greenhaus, 2001).

The limitation of family on career is compounded for women during pregnancy and their children's young years. At this time, women often feel that the energy required by their family roles is so great that they cannot consider taking even a part-time job at the same time. As discussed elsewhere in this book, women's careers as a result tend to be more interrupted, less linear, and (by conventional measures of career success, such as salary and status advancement) less successful than men's. Women in this situation may of course continue to acquire career-relevant skills through their work in managing the home and through voluntary activities, such as at school and at the Red Cross. However, these skills tend to be undervalued by employers when women return to the workforce. Although some women such as Elsie make a conscious choice to downplay their careers, it seems that the conflict of work and family roles has the effect, for many others, of severely limiting work careers.

A key factor in determining work limitations is the existence, or not, of family-friendly policies by employers (Schwartz, 1996). That is, employers may assist parents to reduce the negative impact of competing family roles on their careers by putting suitable arrangements in place. This is not just a matter of being understanding and providing some latitude in cases of family emergency. It also includes formal procedures for maternity and other leave without financial or career penalty; flexible working hours; opportunities for part-time, job-sharing, or contract options; and the provision of child care facilities at the place of work (Arnold, 1997). Such policies are not just the responsibility of employing organizations but also need to be encouraged by a supportive state framework of policies, laws, and regulations (Hantrais & Ackers, 2005).

Indeed, some argue that if organizations are to capitalize on the new diverse workforce of female as well as male professionals and knowledge workers, they must redesign organizational processes to take account of these workers' dual roles (Bailyn, 1993). Although some employers may say that it is not their function to cater to the family arrangements of employees, and that to do so is against their own financial interests, there is increasing evidence that such arrangements enable the retention of good employees and the maintenance of staff morale and thereby have indirect bottom-line benefits (Lambert, 2000; Perry-Smith & Blum, 2000).

Although the issue of work–family balance is the main area of contention in the broader work-nonwork arena, we should not forget that work roles (and therefore careers) can also become unbalanced in relation to leisure and other nonfamily activities (Schein, 1996). Organizations seek to maximize their employees' commitment and have become better at arranging work conditions, corporate norms, and work and career incentives in such a way as to encourage commitment. Many people work long hours, and the phenomenon of workaholism—addiction to one's job, even to the extent of risking one's health—is well known (Fassel, 1990; McMillan & O'Driscoll, 2004). This possibility may be exacerbated by management pressures for individual and organizational performance (White, Hill, McGovern, Mills, & Smeaton, 2003).

Although individuals differ hugely in their "natural" balance of work and nonwork, many could probably find a better balance than they currently have. The practice of downshifting (Ghazi & Jones, 2004)—deliberately seeking a new, less demanding work role or reducing the role one has to achieve a better quality of life—is increasingly attracting interest. Mainiero and Sullivan (2005) drew attention to the opt-out revolution of women who deliberately choose not to aspire to conventional career success. These women, the authors claim, develop "kaleidoscopic careers" and "shift the pattern of their careers by rotating different aspects in their lives to arrange their roles and relationships in new ways" (Mainiero & Sullivan, 2005, p. 106).

The trend to greater flexibility in working arrangements—for example, part-time work, temporary work, and contracting—changes the dynamics of work–life balance (De Bruin & Dupuis, 2004). A frequent benefit of the new flexibility in employment arrangements is that these newly favored options can be used to create opportunities for achieving a more satisfactory balance and freeing up more time for family commitments, vacations, tertiary study, hobbies, voluntary work, and home-based small businesses or business startups (Inkson, Heising, & Rousseau, 2001; Peel & Inkson, 2004). Although temping—working temporarily with different employers through an agency—has rightly been criticized for its tendency to spread insecurity and marginalize workers (Hardy & Walker, 2003; Henson, 1996), enterprising workers with skills in demand can use the flexibility and freedom entailed in temping to become lifestyle temps, with a good, self-chosen balance between paid work and other activities (Alach & Inkson, 2004).

A last point concerns gender. Work–life balance is frequently thought of as an issue affecting women's careers. But let us not forget that men too often face work–life balance issues, particularly in relation to the expectations attached to their primary breadwinner role. As women increasingly extend their activities across workplaces, there are signs that men too are taking more of an interest in their nonwork roles, particularly as family members.

Dual-Career Couples

A special case of work–family conflict is that of the dual-career couple: two people in a loving and usually cohabiting relationship who are also conducting their own separate careers, which may come into conflict not only with nonwork roles but also with each other—for example, if one seeks to advance his or her career by transferring to a new location. How does a relationship survive when the career ambitions and behaviors of its partners become incompatible (Friedman & Greenhaus, 2001; Hall & Hall, 1979)? When does a dual-career couple find time for a social life or even for the proper maintenance of their living relationship?

Dual-career couples typically face many of the problems of work–life balance, particularly if they also have children. However, there is no evidence that the development of children of working women suffers unduly compared with the children of nonworking women (Spitze, 1988). But other problems may surface, such as career competition and jealousy between the partners and issues of role identity by men who seek to be providers or women who cherish their roles as nurturers (Greenhaus, Callanan, & Godschalk, 2000).

Keeping a relationship healthy under such circumstances requires open communication between the partners, support for each other's career—what has been called a "we" orientation rather than a "me" orientation—recognition that the two careers function interactively within a wider family system, and the conscious development of mutually agreed strategies for dealing with the issues. Here, some of the role sending/role behavior ideas discussed earlier may be relevant: Partners can adjust their role expectations of their partner, redefine their own roles, or try to work smarter or work to different standards to try to accommodate the wider demands of the two-career situation (Hall & Hall, 1979).

Careers as Theater

From the notion of careers as roles it is a natural extension to think of careers in terms of theatrical metaphors. Gioia and Poole (1984) discussed the powerful effects of scripts, which enable people to understand what is going on in the organization and guide appropriate behavior. However, Gioia and Poole's concept of scripts is more flexible and subtler than the straightforward notion of job description. For example, scripts may be weak (i.e., specifying only general behaviors) or strong (i.e., specifying specific behaviors in a specific order). Behavior can range from highly scripted (but possibly mindless) performance of learned behaviors to unscripted behavior (e.g., in novel situations where no script exists). But there are also career scripts (Arthur et al., 1999; Barley, 1989) through which institutions such as employing organizations, educational institutions, and industry bodies want individuals to follow in the interests of workforce control. But in the increasingly turbulent careers context, predetermined scripts are often questioned.

Sequences of roles, including careers, may have to be relearned and innovated. Formal education tends to focus the career actor on linear learning. For example, a student may reason, "If I want to be a surgeon, I have to first get into medical school and learn to be a doctor. To do that, I need a strong background in the physical and biological sciences, so I'd better sign up for those." This planning arranges roles in a predictable and functional sequence. But the aspiring surgeon may, in the event, find the arts more interesting than the sciences, may miss out on getting into medical school, may get an unexpected job offer in a nonmedical field, or may have a baby and feel unable to undertake full-time study.

For all sorts of reasons, people innovate in their roles and change their roles, and as they do careers zigzag rather than remain linear. It has been suggested that if the institutional arenas where careers take place are theaters, then in terms of the changing nature of the employment scene, we may be moving from classical theater to improvisational theater:

> The Industrial State . . . was centralized, scripted theater, where the producers supplied big production funds, the writers wrote elegant scripts, and the directors coached the cast to perfection on a predetermined plan. . . . The New Economy, in contrast, is improvisational or street theater. Ideas are decentralized, and can come from anywhere—even from a theatergoer. The boundaries around the roles of producer, writer, director, actor, stage manager, lighting designer are disappearing. People can use their own initiative to take charge. Scripts are loose, team-written, and changeable. Drama school and actors' networks celebrate spontaneity ahead of technique and role. Career actors improvise around a mutually agreed theme, or experiment with a new interpretation. They take on temporary roles in order to learn new skills, and then move on. (Arthur et al., 1999, pp. 16–17)

If this is correct, then the functioning of roles in our careers—at least for those with the labor market power to dictate the terms of their roles—is changing. Future organizations may find—as some already do—that rather than saying to employees, "Here is the role we want you to fulfill; do exactly what the job description says," they will be saying, "Tell us what you are good at and would like to do: we'll try to find a way to turn that to advantage" (Miles & Snow, 1996). In other words, the role becomes the individual's invention, not the employer's.

Conclusion

When roles are expressed in their standardized form, as job descriptions, they are curiously lifeless and can make even the most interesting jobs seem dull. It is when we start exploring the complexities of informal role expectations and roles, the congruence or conflict of role with identity or with nonwork roles, and the endless possibilities of role innovation, role improvisation, and role transition that we understand how role analysis can reflect much of the dynamism associated with modern careers. Reflecting on the roles we have had, the roles we have now, and the roles we seek in the future, and on how these roles were defined and changed, and by whom, is an exercise well worth doing.

Key Points in This Chapter

- A career can be considered as a succession of work roles. Individuals have many other roles (e.g., son or daughter, parent, consumer, friend). These may overlap or conflict with work roles.

- Work roles incorporate both formal expectations, such as a job description, and informal expectations, such as others' expectations. Discordant roles may result in role conflict.
- Identity is a personal recognition of who one is and is often expressed in the roles that the individual takes on and owns. People can find identity in occupations, job titles, and social roles such as leader.
- Role transitions, such as moving from one job to another, are an important part of the career process. Role transitions involve stages of preparation, encounter, adjustment, and stabilization.
- Individuals may modify their roles through role innovation.
- The coexistence of competing work and nonwork roles can lead to problems of work–life balance or work–family balance, which may need to be dealt with by forms of adjustment, including career adjustment, by the individual. In dual-career couples, mutual adjustment to each other's career roles may be necessary.
- The metaphor of theater enables us to understand how work roles are changing and the increasingly improvisational nature of careers.

Questions From This Chapter

General Questions

1. Think about two or three people you know well and investigate their life histories and lifestyle. What different roles do (and did) they occupy, and how have they fit these roles into their lives?
2. Identify any of the following factors in your own life and write a few lines about them: role senders, role expectations, role ambiguity, intrarole conflict, inter-role conflict, conflict between identity and role.
3. Consider the quote by Sargent critical of the whole idea of set roles. Do you agree? Why, or why not?
4. Identify the different stages of role transition in relation to a transition you have experienced (e.g., from high school to college). How effectively do you think you handled the transition?
5. Think of one or more of your current roles. What are the role expectations and how much scope is there for going outside them? In what ways have you role innovated or could you role innovate?
6. Consider whether your life is balanced between work (or education) roles and other roles. What could you and others do to help you achieve a better balance?
7. How do you feel about the general prospect of improvising your own career rather than basing it on responses to roles defined by others?

Career Case Study Questions

1. What have been the main nonwork roles of your case person? How have these complemented or conflicted with the case person's work roles and how have they affected the case person's career?

2. How does the career case person identify himself or herself? How do these identities fit with each other and which is most central? How has the case person's identity changed over time?

3. Ask your case person to describe an important role transition and an example of role innovation during his or her career. Are you able to identify the different stages of role transition? What did you learn about role innovation from the example?

References

Adams, J. D., Hayes, B., & Hopson, B. (1976). *Transition: Understanding and managing personal change*. London: Martin Robertson.

Alach, P., & Inkson, K. (2004). The new office temp: Alternative models of contingent labor. *New Zealand Journal of Employment Relations, 29*(3), 37-52.

Allen, R. E. (Ed.). (1990). *Concise Oxford dictionary*. Oxford, UK: Clarendon Press.

Aneshensel, C. S. (1992). Social stress: Theory and research. *Annual Review of Sociology, 18,* 15-38.

Arnold, J. (1997). *Managing careers into the twenty-first century*. London: Paul Chapman.

Arthur, M. B., Inkson, K., & Pringle, J. K. (1999). *The new careers: Individual action and economic change*. Thousand Oaks, CA: Sage.

Ashforth, B. E., & Saks, A. M. (1996). Socialization tactics: Longitudinal effects on newcomer adjustments. *Academy of Management Journal, 39,* 149-178.

Bailyn, L. (1993). *Breaking the mold: Women, men and time in the new corporate world*. New York: Free Press.

Barley, S. R. (1989). Careers, identities and institutions: The legacy of the Chicago School of sociology. In M. B. Arthur, D. T. Hall, & B. Lawrence (Eds.), *Handbook of career theory* (pp. 41-65). Cambridge, UK: Cambridge University Press.

Becker, H. S. (1951). The career of the Chicago public schoolteacher. *American Journal of Sociology, 57,* 470-477.

Becker, H. S., Geer, B., Hughes, E. C., & Strauss, A. L. (1961). *Boys in white*. Chicago: University of Chicago Press.

Blair-Loy, M. (2003). *Competing devotions: Career and family among women executives*. Cambridge, MA: Harvard University Press.

Chao, G. T., O'Leary-Kelly, A. M., Wolf, S., Klein, H. J., & Gardner, P. D. (1994). Organizational socialization: Its content and consequences. *Journal of Applied Psychology, 79,* 730-743.

Dalton, G. W. (1989). Developmental views of careers in organizations. In M. B. Arthur, D. T. Hall, & B. Lawrence (Eds.), *Handbook of career theory* (pp. 89-109). Cambridge, UK: Cambridge University Press.

De Bruin, A., & Dupuis, A. (2004). Work-life balance? Insights from non-standard work. *New Zealand Journal of Employment Relations, 29*(1), 21-37.

Ebberwein, C. A., Krieshok, T. S., Ulven, J. C., & Prosser, E. C. (2004). Voices in transition: Lessons on career adaptability. *Career Development Quarterly, 52*(4), 292-308.

Erikson, E. H. (1959). Identity and the lifecycle. *Psychological Issues, 1,* 1-171.

Fassel, D. (1990). *Working ourselves to death: The high costs of workaholism, the rewards of recovery*. San Francisco: HarperCollins.

Fondas, N., & Stewart, T. (1994). Enactment in managerial jobs: A role analysis. *Journal of Management Studies, 31*(1), 83-103.

Friedman, S. D., & Greenhaus, J. H. (2001). *Allies or enemies? How choices about work and family affect the quality of men's and women's lives.* New York: Oxford University Press.

Frone, M. R., & Rice, R. W. (1987). Work-family conflict: The effect of job and family involvement. *Journal of Occupational Behavior, 8,* 45-53.

Ghazi, P., & Jones, J. (2004). *Downshifting: The bestselling guide to happier, healthier living.* London: Hodder & Stoughton.

Gioia, D. A., & Poole, P. P. (1984). Scripts in organizational behavior. *Academy of Management Review, 9*(3), 449-459.

Gottlieb, B. H., Kelloway, E. K., & Barham, E. (1998). *Flexible work arrangements.* Chichester, UK: Wiley.

Greenblatt, E. (2002). Work-life balance: Wisdom or whining? *Organizational Dynamics, 32*(2), 177-193.

Greenhaus, J. H., & Beutell, N. J. (1985). Sources of conflict between work and family roles. *Academy of Management Review, 10*(1), 76-88.

Greenhaus, J. H., Callanan, G. A., & Godschalk, V. M. (2000). *Career management* (3rd ed.). Fort Worth, TX: Dryden Press.

Hall, D. T. (2002). *Careers in and out of organizations.* Thousand Oaks, CA: Sage.

Hall, F. S., & Hall, D. T. (1979). *The two-career couple.* Reading, MA: Addison-Wesley.

Hantrais, L., & Ackers, P. (2005). Women's choices in Europe: Striking the work-life balance. *European Journal of Industrial Relations, 11*(2), 197-212.

Hardy, D. J., & Walker, R. (2003). Temporary but seeking permanence: A study of New Zealand temps. *Leadership and Organizational Development Journal, 24*(3), 141-152.

Henson, K. D. (1996). *Just a temp.* Philadelphia: Temple University Press.

Hickson, D. J., & Thomas, M. W. (1969). Professionalization in Britain: A preliminary measurement. *Sociology, 3*(1), 37-43.

Hughes, E. C. (1937). Institutional office and the person. *American Journal of Sociology, 43,* 404-443.

Hughes, E. C. (1958). *Men and their work.* Glencoe, IL: Free Press.

Inkson, K., Heising, A., & Rousseau, D. M. (2001). The interim manager: Prototype of the twenty-first century worker? *Human Relations, 54*(3), 259-284.

Katz, D., & Kahn, R. L. (1966). *The social psychology of organizations.* New York: Wiley.

Lambert, S. J. (2000). Added benefits: The link between work-life benefits and organizational citizenship behavior. *Academy of Management Journal, 43*(5), 801-813.

Lewis, R. (1994). *The life and death of Peter Sellers.* London: Century.

Mainiero, L. A., & Sullivan, S. E. (2005). Kaleidoscope careers: An alternate explanation for the opt-out revolution. *Academy of Management Executive, 19*(1), 106-123.

Manz, C. C., & Sims, H. P. (1991). SuperLeadership: Beyond the myth of heroic leadership. *Organizational Dynamics, 19*(4), 18-35.

Martinez, M. N. (1992). Disney training works magic. *HR Magazine, 37*(5), 53-57.

McMillan, L. H. W., & O'Driscoll, M. P. (2004). Workaholism and health: Implications for organizations. *Journal of Organizational Change Management, 17*(5), 509-519.

Miles, R. E., & Snow, C. C. (1996). Twenty-first century careers. In M. B. Arthur & D. M. Rousseau (Eds.), *The boundaryless career: A new employment principle for a new organizational era* (pp. 97-115). New York: Oxford University Press.

Morris, J. A., & Feldman, D. C. (1997). Managing emotions in the workplace. *Journal of Managerial Issues, 9,* 257-274.

Morrison, E. W. (1993). Newcomer information-seeking: Exploring types, modes, sources and outcomes. *Academy of Management Journal, 36,* 557-589.

Nicholson, N. (1984). A theory of work-role transitions. *Administrative Science Quarterly, 29,* 172-191.

Nicholson, N., & West, M. A. (1988). *Managerial job change: Men and women in transition.* Cambridge, UK: Cambridge University Press.

Nicholson, N., & West, M. A. (1989). Transitions, work histories and careers. In M. B. Arthur, D. T. Hall, & B. Lawrence (Eds.), *Handbook of career theory* (pp. 181-201). Cambridge, UK: Cambridge University Press.

Oldham, G. R., & Cummings, A. (1996). Employee creativity: Personal and contextual factors at work. *Academy of Management Journal, 39*(3), 607-634.

Peel, S., & Inkson, K. (2004). Contracting careers: Choosing between self- and organizational management. *Career Development International, 9*(7), 542-558.

Perry-Smith, J. E., & Blum, T. C. (2000). Work-family human resource bundles and perceived organizational performance. *Academy of Management Journal, 43*(6), 1107-1117.

Reeve, C. (1999). *Still me.* New York: Ballantine Books.

Riley, F., & McCloskey, D. W. (1999). Telecommuting as a response to helping people balance work and family. In S. Parasuraman & J. H. Greenhaus (Eds.), *Integrating work and family: Challenges and choices for a changing world* (pp. 133-142). Westport, CT: Quorum.

Roth, J. A. (1963). *Timetables: Structuring the passage of time in hospital treatment and other careers.* Indianapolis, IN: Bobbs-Merrill.

Sargent, M. (1994). *The new sociology for Australians.* Melbourne, Australia: Longman Cheshire.

Schein, E. H. (1971). The individual, the organization and the career: A conceptual scheme. *Journal of Applied Behavioral Science, 7,* 401-426.

Schein, E. H. (1996). Career anchors revisited: Implications for career development in the 21st century. *Academy of Management Executive, 10*(4), 80-88.

Schwartz, D. B. (1996). The impact of work-family policies on women's career development: Boon or bust? *Women in Management Review, 11,* 5-19.

Sikov, E. (1998). *Mr. Strangelove: A biography of Peter Sellers.* London: Sidgwick and Jackson.

Spitze, G. (1988). Women's employment and family relations: A review. *Journal of Marriage and the Family, 50,* 595-618.

Sturges, J., & Guest, D. (2004). Working to live or living to work? Work/life balance early in the career. *Human Resource Management Journal, 14*(4), 5-20.

Super, D. E. (1990). Career and life development. In D. Brown & L. Brooks (Eds.), *Career choice and development* (2nd ed., pp. 197-261). San Francisco: Jossey-Bass.

Super, D. E. (1992). Toward a comprehensive theory of career development. In D. H. Montross & C. J. Shinkman (Eds.), *Career development: Theory and practice* (pp. 35-64). Springfield, IL: Charles C Thomas.

Van Maanen, J., & Schein, E. H. (1979). Toward a theory of organizational socialization. *Research in Organizational Behavior, 1,* 209-264.

Wanous, J. P. (1989). Installing a realistic job preview: Ten tough choices. *Personnel Psychology, 42,* 117-143.

Wanous, J. P. (1992). *Organizational entry: Recruitment, selection, orientation, and socialization of newcomers.* Reading, MA: Addison-Wesley.

White, M., Hill, S., McGovern, P., Mills, C., & Smeaton, D. (2003). High-performance management practices, working hours and work-life balance. *British Journal of Industrial Relations, 41*(2), 175-195.

Williams, C. (2003). Sky service: The demands of emotional labor in the airline industry. *Gender, Work and Organization, 10*(5), 513-550.

Wrzesniewski, A., & Dutton, J. E. (2001). Crafting a job: Revisioning employees as active crafters of their work. *Academy of Management Review, 23*(2), 179-201.

CHAPTER 8

Careers as Relationships

Individualism and Connectedness

Stanley Kubrick (1928–1999) was one of the 20th century's greatest film directors. Films such as *Paths of Glory* (1957), *Spartacus* (1960), *Dr. Strangelove* (1964), *2001: A Space Odyssey* (1968), *A Clockwork Orange* (1971), *The Shining* (1980), *Full Metal Jacket* (1987), and *Eyes Wide Shut* (1999) made their mark among critics and the public, not just as superb visual spectacles but as mature, thoughtful commentaries on the human condition.

Kubrick was a noted individualist. As a director, he saw each film as the embodiment of his own total vision for what it was to be. For example, in his first full-length film, *Fear and Desire* (1953), he wrote the script, directed the action, operated the camera, edited, and did almost everything else except the acting. Although later in his career Kubrick was forced to work with or hire more professional associates, such as producers, screenwriters, art directors, lighting experts, cameramen, sound technicians, editors, and the like, and although these people were the best in the business in terms of skill and professionalism, Kubrick tended to see them as mechanical functionaries—there not to work with him to produce a satisfactory combined product but rather to execute his instructions. He saw his films as direct reflections of his own work and worth. He was a perfectionist and would certainly be classed nowadays as a "control freak."

Yet careful scrutiny of Kubrick's career—the career of someone apparently more introverted, more independent, and more self-confident than most—shows multiple influences from other people. Throughout his early career—as throughout his whole career—Kubrick struggled to achieve balance between his own assured independent vision and the possibly unwelcome necessity of employing and working with others.

Kubrick was born and raised in New York. For his 13th birthday, his parents gave him a large Graflex camera. Kubrick became an avid hobby photographer. His school friend Martin Traub also had a camera and a darkroom in his home, further stimulating young Stanley's interest. At the age of 16 years, he took a photograph he was particularly proud of to show to Helen O'Brian, a picture editor at *Look!* magazine.

(Continued)

(Continued)

Not only did she pay him $25 for the picture, but she also offered him a job as a *Look!* photographer. A career in the visual arts was born, though in the end only moving pictures would do for Kubrick. His parents, his friend Martin Traub, and Helen O'Brian all played their part in this start.

At school, the isolated, somewhat "arty" Kubrick was not popular, but two like-minded friends subsequently helped him to launch his career. Kubrick recognized that he had limitations as a writer and drafted his friend Howard Sackler, an aspiring novelist, to write the initial screenplays for *Fear and Desire* and his next film, *Killer's Kiss.* Even more important was the "school intellectual," Alex Singer, who was later to become a movie director. He persuaded Kubrick to make his first short movie, *Day of the Fight* (1951), a reprise of one of his photo essays for *Look!,* and helped Kubrick direct it. Later, Singer persuaded Kubrick to educate himself by reading books on film technique. He remained connected to Kubrick, doing the still photographs for *Killer's Kiss* and serving as assistant director for *The Killing* (1956). Most important, Singer introduced Kubrick to a man named James B. Harris who he had met while in the Signal Corps' Photographic Center in Long Island. Harris had a family background in the financing and distribution sides of the movie industry—just the kind of contact the artistically driven and impecunious Kubrick needed. Harris soon recognized the emerging genius that Kubrick's early films showed. The two quickly became close friends and business partners in Harris-Kubrick films. Over the next few years Harris was to play a vital part in the financing and managing of Kubrick's career as producer of several of his most significant films.

Source: Baxter (1998).

Although Kubrick's early career was set in the exotic and uncertain world of the movie industry, and his movements after his early employment as a photographer were project to project rather than job to job, he, like any other careerist, built his career through relationships. Indeed, we might argue that his career was a series of relationships and that it was these relationships that gradually resulted in Kubrick's massive accomplishments.

The popular stereotype of Kubrick and other movie directors is that they are great individualists, who, like Madonna and other cases in Chapter 4, act as individuals who carve out their own careers and impose them on the world. In reality, they are largely dependent on their interactions and relationships with others: Reread the Madonna case to appreciate the way that she used contacts, networks, and reputation to advance her career. In the movie industry, an even more spectacular example is the Spanish Almodovar brothers—the film producer Agustin and the director Pedro, whose careers are symbiotic, or interdependent, and who proceed from film project to film project working together so that neither career can be understood on its own but only in terms of its interaction with the other (Alvarez & Svejnova, 2002). Likewise, New Zealander Peter Jackson, producer/director of *The Lord of the*

Rings trilogy and the remake of *King Kong,* has, in becoming one of the most sought-after directors in the world, created and been nourished by a local network of movie-making experts that has won dozens of Oscars and is, in effect, a major national industry. The career of Jackson and the growth of the industry are best considered in relation to each other (Inkson & Parker, 2005).

It is a paradoxical aspect of our view of careers in the Western world that we tend to view them as individual projects resulting in individual rewards and achievements, even though in many respects they are social. Hofstede (1980) noted that one of the key cultural factors differentiating societies was individualism-collectivism and that individualism to the degree found in North America and Northwestern Europe is in fact extreme (see Chapter 1). In many other societies—for example, societies in Asia, Africa, and South America—collectivism is powerful, meaning that individuals view aspects of behavior, including career behavior, from the perspective of groups, including the family, of which the individual is a member, rather than from the individual's own perspective (Thomas & Inkson, in press). Granrose and Chua (1996), in their careful analysis of global boundaryless careers in Chinese family businesses, showed how careers may be viewed from a quite different perspective—that is, as the property of the family or wider kin group of which the individual is a member. Such groups provide career opportunities and resources to all family members, so it makes more sense in these cases to consider family career systems rather than individual careers.

Even in Western societies, it is difficult to see some careers as having any meaning outside the relationships that embody them. A familiar career stereotype is the "mom-and-pop" business run by a husband and wife: a grocery store, perhaps, or a garage where the husband fixes the cars and the wife does the administration. Generation-to-generation family businesses enmesh careers irretrievably into family relationships, making it difficult to consider the career other than as one facet of a series of developing personal relationships. In another form, two work colleagues, or even a group of colleagues, may have a business idea that they can work on together and may form their own company.

More generally, if we think back over our careers, what we often see is not a succession of jobs but a succession of people with whom we worked, people who made a big difference, for good or bad, in our careers: bosses, colleagues, subordinates, work groups, committees, clients, professional associates. Our careers are profoundly affected by relationships (Flum, 2001). Careers are social.

Networks and Networking

One way to understand social influences on careers is to think about three different levels of social phenomena potentially affecting careers. At the lowest level, we have social encounters, in which chance meetings of individuals enable them to influence each other and sometimes collaborate to mutual benefit, usually in the short term. At a higher level, encounters solidify into relationships so that the individuals develop a longer term association enabling them to influence each other and collaborate on a repeated or ongoing basis. But relationships are combined into complex networks, in which, for example, A has a relationship with B, who in turn is a friend of C, D, and E, who in turn is employed by F, and so on. Although social encounters and relationships can be used to provide major input for careers, it is the broader notion of networks that provides the greatest potential (e.g., Gibbons, 2004).

Consider, for example, the account of Sarah, a recently unemployed journalist, and her networking activities at a party given by her friend Craig, also a journalist.

Partying

Craig is a bit of a snob and very upwardly mobile and his taste in music is too highbrow for me, but when he invited me to his party I jumped at the chance because I knew there would be some very influential people there. When I got there, I was as nice as pie to Craig and asked him to introduce me to a few people. First he introduced me to his friend Dorinda, who is an assistant editor of *The Press*. Well, we exchanged a few pleasantries, but there's no point beating around the bush, so after a few minutes I explained my situation and asked her point-blank if *The Press* had any vacancies. It didn't work. I don't know what I did wrong, but she couldn't back off fast enough. She was like "nothing at the moment" and almost "how can you be so rude as to ask?" I know when I'm beat, but people like that can be really useful in the long term, so I listened sympathetically while she went through her stories about her attempts to get *The Press* to change its editorial policies, and I must have sounded like I really cared because at the end she surprisingly said, "We might have a freelance job or two. Can you call me next week?" and gave me her card. Well, that was a good start. Then I saw Jacko Jacobsen, one of my tutors at journalism school. We got

along really well, but I hadn't seen him for years, so I grabbed another drink and had a yarn with him, catching up on the old crowd. Jacko knows everyone who is anyone in feature journalism, and he genuinely seems to want to help his students. So he was asking what I had done, what I thought my strengths were, and so on. He said that right now he didn't think there were many openings in the city but that if I were willing to go out of state he could think of some publications that seemed to be growing quickly. He said, "Send me your vita and portfolio, and I'll make some calls." But then he tried to make a date with me, and when I said I was already in a relationship, he was, sort of, "you might have told me!" That really worried me. Maybe he's only interested in what he can get. Anyway, he was a bit drunk by this stage, so I said I'd call him next week and moved on. I spent the rest of the evening talking to some people in one of the big PR companies. PR is not my cup of tea, but I've learned to take an interest in all sorts of odd industries and people and to always get their cards and always write some notes about them when I get home. After all, you never know when someone like that is going to come in useful, do you?

Although Sarah may seem somewhat calculating and self-serving in her social interactions, her networking activities are based on her appreciation of the realities of job seeking and job finding. Against the frequent view that the process whereby people find jobs is a formal one involving things like job descriptions, newspaper advertisements, formal shortlists, rational comparison of candidates, and equal employment opportunities, research shows that the majority of jobs are never advertised but instead are filled by means of network connections. That is, they go to people who are personally known to the recruiter. Those who are not involved in appropriate networks have little chance of getting such jobs.

For example, in a classic study by Granovetter (1974), 56% of a sample of professional, technical, and managerial workers found their current jobs by means of personal contacts, compared with 19% who found jobs by formal means, 19% who applied directly to the employer, and 7% who found jobs in miscellaneous other ways. Furthermore, those who found their jobs through personal contacts were on the whole more satisfied with them and were earning higher salaries, possibly because they were older and had had more time to build up networks. The results of this and many other studies appear to bear out the old dictum that, in finding a job, "it's not what you know but who you know that counts." The results suggest that networks are important mediators of careers and that networking techniques such as Sarah's have, from the individual's point of view, much to commend them (Cross, 2004). For example, an Australian study suggested that women seeking to access senior management and corporate board positions, even if they could overcome the common resistances to the employment of women at these levels, were unlikely to succeed unless they were seen to have valuable business contacts (Sheridan, 2002).

Networking is therefore seen by many as a key skill for careerists and was shown to be related to career success (Forret & Dougherty, 2004). For example, in one formulation of career competencies, the three key competencies were "knowing-why" (motivation and values), "knowing-how" (skills and expertise), and "knowing-whom" (relationships and networks) (DeFillippi & Arthur, 1996). Networking involves deliberately building contacts and reputation to "get the success you want by tapping into the people you know" (Darling, 2003, front cover). Many do-it-yourself books have been written about "how to win friends and influence people" (Carnegie, 1981, front cover).

There are plenty of self-help books on how to network. It can be a complex business. Darling (2003), for example, wrote about network planning, inventories of networks, network evaluation, network accessories (business cards, cell phones, etc.), networking locations, conversation guidelines, network etiquette, handshakes, VIP meetings, follow-up for contacts, and so on. In this approach, networking becomes much more than simply taking advantage of the contacts you happen to have built at work and elsewhere: It makes networking an important career self-management strategy, as systematic and thought through as a business plan. Many people may decide that they are not careerists—people who are predominantly concerned with personal career advancement (Feldman, 1985; Feldman & Weitz, 1991)—and that this sort of obsessive socializing is not something they want to get into.

Although networking to access jobs is well known, this is not the only career-related function they perform. Networks—particularly networks of like-minded people, such as those in the same organization, occupation, and industry—can provide reassurance, support, motivation, and knowledge relevant to the individual's career development. For example, when young people in one study were asked who had influenced them most in their employment choices and how they had influenced them, the most common responses were that the influential people had given encouragement, support, and advice; had modeled behavior (particularly through their own work); and had provided information, inspiration, and further contacts of their own. Additionally, in some cases, they had "hassled" the individual into showing greater career energy or changing direction (Dupuis, Inkson, & McLaren, 2005).

Networks have additional characteristics:

- Networks of individual contacts can be influenced by individual action but do not come about solely because of personal sociability. To a large extent, larger social structural forces, such as those discussed in Chapter 2, dictate networks. The network contacts we make are often dictated by things such as the organization we are in; the level we are at; our circle of other employees, clients, and suppliers; the industry; the geographical location; and our family and social connections. Contacts developed and built in these networks further strengthen the networks. They make available the knowledge and learning of the wider network to individuals within it, but that learning is likely to have a specific focus determined by the location and extent of the network.

- Connections can be developed purposely, on a planned calculative basis, as in the case of Sarah, or they can come into being serendipitously as a by-product of people's natural sociability. Often, contacts built up casually or in contexts apparently unconnected with the career turn out to be valuable. For example, someone might say, "My next-door neighbor had been through a similar experience in a different industry and was able to recommend a program of study that was exactly right." People who network naturally, purely because of their sociability and interest in others, may unintentionally build a major resource for their careers.

- Networking is a continuous process. It is not something that one takes up suddenly to solve a problem and then discards when the problem is solved— for example, when a person who has been laid off tries to set appointments with all the human resource managers in the area. In real networking, the contacts and relationships are built over a long period so that when the person is laid off there are lots of potentially useful contacts whom the person can call. As a career strategy, networking is therefore proactive, rather than reactive.

- Networks are reciprocal. That is, network members put energy into the network as well as take energy out, and members also offer help to others and seek help from them (Gouldner, 1960). In the case of Sarah, if she continues to be interested in contacts only for the assistance they might give her rather than for anything she might do for them, she runs the risk of appearing selfish and manipulative. If this happens, she will find it harder to access network resources. Of course, inexperienced lower status networkers tend to have less to offer than their senior counterparts, so giving back may have to be extended over a long period and be based on a generalized desire to help others.

- Networks function not just through direct interactions between people but also on the basis of reputation. Network members know others they have never met. Employers and corporate recruiters with good networks know who may be available on the job market and what their strengths and weaknesses may be (Finlay & Coverdill, 2000). But reputation is a projection not just of the real person but also of the subjective and sometimes self-interested evaluations of that person by other network members and the images presented by the person, which can cause reputations to be misleading (Gowler & Legge, 1989).

- Networks often provide spectacular examples of planned happenstance (Mitchell, Levin, & Krumboltz, 1999), where people are able to take advantage of chance meetings and transform them into career development opportunities. Social and community life present many such unplanned events. The happenstance is planned in the sense that every contact we make becomes a new possible opportunity that may come back to us later in an apparently chance situation. We can't plan how particular contacts may be useful to us, but we can plan to behave socially to make lots of contacts.

Networks and Chance

I recognized this guy on the street whom I'd worked with 15 years ago and hadn't seen since I left the old company. Howard! Straight away he said, "Come and have a drink." We got to talking, and it turned out that he was still there but thinking of leaving. I remembered how creative and reliable he had been when I worked with him, and the projects he had done since seemed right on par. And I liked him. I thought about the problems my own company was facing and eventually said to him, "The company I work with now needs someone exactly like you." Really, the job was no more than a gleam in my boss's eye, but when I talked to him about Howard, he requested a meeting with Howard. Then he set up a formal interview—only for Howard; the job was never advertised. Before the interview, I went to Howard's place and coached him. He didn't make one mistake. He started with us the following month. After all, that's what friends are for.

Social Capital

A term that is used with increasing frequency to emphasize the importance of networks is *social capital* (e.g., Adler & Kwon, 2002; Bourdieu, 1986; Israel, Beaulieu, & Hartless, 2001; Mouw, 2003). Put simply, our social capital is the resources we are able to access through our contacts. The notion of *capital*— "wealth owned by a person or organization or invested, lent, or borrowed"

(Allen, 1990, p. 207)—emphasizes the idea, which will be pursued more completely in Chapter 9, that each of us possesses different amounts and types of career capital, which we are able to invest, if we wish, in our own career development.

Social capital is an important part of career capital that can only be accessed through contacts. Social capital also enables us to build other forms of career capital, such as motivational energy, knowledge, and skills. However, Mouw (2003) suggested that "much of the effect of social capital in the existing literature reflects the tendency for similar people to become friends rather than a causal effect of friends' characteristics on labour market outcomes" (p. 868). In other words, some of the apparent effects of social capital on career development may be simply a reflection of social structural variables, as detailed in Chapter 2.

Social capital also provides a potential asset for employers, who may hire new workers not just for the skills they possess but also for the social connections they bring to the job: Investing in the social capital of employees may bring a firm significant economic returns (Fernandez & Castilla, 2000). Of course, companies seek to build their social capital by developing contacts with agencies and individuals who can undertake special projects for them, source new customers or new employees, or broker relationships leading to joint ventures (Jones, 2002). Such activities provide clear employer-initiated opportunities for individuals to receive the right career invitations by moving actively in the right circles, increasing their social capital as they go. And the contacts who count may not be the contacts who offer direct opportunities but the contacts who can influence others who offer such opportunities.

Types of Networks

Career-relevant networks are often limited to a specific focus or membership. For example, the initial career network for most young people is the family, and, for some, the family continues to exercise influence throughout the career. Employing organizations or departments, professional bodies, industry associations, and trade unions often have memberships, information, and professional goals that give them considerable potential value to members seeking to develop their careers.

Parker and Arthur (2000) used the term *career communities* to describe member-defined communities from which people draw career support. Career communities can be developed around the notion of an industry, an occupation, a region, an ideology (e.g., a charity), a project, a set of alumni, an informal support group, a family, or an organization. Churches, sports clubs, and hobby organizations can all function as career networks, even though this is not their primary purpose. Parker and Arthur also noted a new trend toward virtual communities, such as career chat rooms, which exist without their members being in direct contact with each other.

Career communities typically involve the shared development, by members, of meanings and priorities for working life that will assist them to make sense of their careers and undertake new learning related to their careers. Each community has its own career priorities. For example, in one study achievement was an important career value for three different communities, but each defined achievement differently: A community of victim support workers saw achievement as the collective accomplishment of social change; a community of temporary project managers saw it as project completion and reputation with clients; a group of ethnic-minority public servants saw it as the collective advancement, not of themselves but of their ethnic group. There were numerous other distinctive differences between the communities that played out significantly on the way members developed their own careers (Parker, Arthur, & Inkson, 2004). These contrasts show how the social milieu or network in which an individual shares career-related knowledge is likely to generate its own norms about how to conduct one's career (Gibbons, 2004). Of course, as we saw in Chapter 7, many individuals occupy positions in more than one network or community simultaneously, and this can lead to conflict and ambivalence as to appropriate career direction.

Networks and communities vary not just in focus but also in power, density, and relevance. Some networks are immensely powerful in terms of potential benefit to one's career, whereas others are weak. A young person whose main career community is his or her family, and whose family members are largely unemployed or in low-status jobs, may be hindered more than helped in his or her career by the contacts.

Regarding density, a *dense network* is one where many of the contacts are also contacts of each other—for example, an organizational network where everybody knows each other—whereas a *sparse network* contains a wider range of contacts with little overlap. Granovetter's (1974) concept of "the strength of weak ties" and research on the difference between acquaintanceships compared with closer friendships suggests, surprisingly, that people with many weak ties are more successful in accessing jobs through these contacts than are people with only strong ties to an immediate group whose members also have ties with each other. Weak ties put people in touch with others who are socially distant, thereby creating new opportunities to progress in one's career by moving outside of one's habitual networks. People who are "weak ties" have their own strong ties: The weak tie relationship thus provides "a crucial bridge between two densely knit clumps of close friends" (Granovetter, 1982, p. 106) and as such is important in the flow of information among groups. Weak ties thus assist in accessing information about jobs and finding them (Granovetter, 1973; Raider & Burt, 1996).

It appears therefore that much depends on the heterogeneity of network contacts: Those whose contacts are in widely dispersed, low-density networks (i.e., each network contact has many other network contacts) are better placed than those in high-density networks in which network contacts overlap and have relatively limited external associations (Burt, 1992). Familiar, high-density networks that are limited (e.g., to one's family or one's employing organization) may—however comfortable and supportive they seem—be bad for one's career. Consider the network limitations of Clyde in the following case.

A Driving Ambition

Clyde is 28. His career so far has been totally in the transportation industry. Clyde's grandfather was a truck driver. His father is a truck driver who has won prizes in truck-driving competitions. His uncles and his sister are also truck drivers. Clyde knew from an early age that what he wanted to do when he grew up was to drive trucks.

Clyde has had five jobs, all in transportation companies. The first, when he was too young to have a license to drive tucks, was as a truck loader. His last four jobs have all been truck-driving jobs. The first two were arranged for Clyde by his father, in companies he worked for. But eventually Clyde decided that "it was time to hop out of my father's shoes." He wanted to start long-distance driving. An owner-driver contact, who had seen what Clyde could do, offered him a good job, but said the job wouldn't be available for him for a year, and in the meantime directed him to a suitable job with another company. After a year, he left that company and joined his contact, as previously arranged. He was well paid and well treated. He drove a high-quality truck and won a major truck competition. He wanted to be recognized not just as a driver but as a high-quality driver.

But after three years his employer was bought out by a larger company. Clyde was kept on the staff, but he found things had changed, the personal treatment was gone, "at the end of the day you were just a number." A friend at another long-distance company got him an interview, and he was offered a job immediately. Clyde says all good drivers get their jobs by word of mouth.

Clyde is proud of his expertise and is clear about the benefits he provides to his employer. He says, "I think I've taught them a lot—axle loadings for weights, restraining loads which I basically learned when I was loading trailers. There was hardly anyone at [the company] who knew how to load a truck properly. So I've taught a number of drivers to be more professional in their working environment."

Clyde's involvement with truck driving and truck drivers extends far beyond the sphere of work. His and his family's lives revolve around the trucking industry. Most of his friends are drivers. He and his wife go to parties with other drivers and their wives. They go to truck shows, where, like his father, Clyde has started to win prizes. He has helped several of his friends to get jobs at his company. His pre-school daughters play with toy trucks.

In looking to the future, Clyde says he may eventually give up driving. The nights away from home don't suit family life. But he will remain in the industry: "move into the office, every now and then I help the office with dispatching. But I wouldn't want to be a dispatcher, I would rather be a fleet manager."

Source: Arthur, Inkson, & Pringle (1999, p. 138).

In this case, Clyde's career networks are exceptionally important. His entire career has been mediated by his family, work, leisure activities, and social connections. Every job he has had was gained by means of personal contacts and recommendations. He has begun to reciprocate, feeding his growing expertise back into the network. Clyde's communities—family, occupational, social, and organizational—overlap in a dense network, with few apparent connections with any other industries, occupations, or wider opportunities. Clyde is expert but highly specialized. He has a strong sense of building his career in an industry he knows well and loves and has done well so far. But his eggs are very much in a single (transportation industry) basket, and he apparently has few "weak ties" to assist him should anything go wrong. The social milieu in which he conducts his career nourishes him and gives his life meaning and direction. It will continue to be a huge asset in his developing career—so long as he continues to wish to stay within the trucking and transportation industry. Should he wish, or be forced, to move into a new field, the same network could turn out to be a major handicap.

This type of analysis suggests that the most helpful types of career networks may be wide and diverse, rather than tight and focused. This is especially true in current times, when all sorts of social institutions—families, companies, jobs—are becoming more fragmented and uncertain and less able to be trusted to provide a secure, long-term future.

Although networking within one's organization is related to career success in that setting (Bozionelos, 2003), building networks only within one's employing organization, and relying on only those contacts to ensure a successful organizational career, may be a risky strategy. It is common nowadays for organizations to encourage employees to consider the organization itself as their key network and to rely on their bosses and other organization members to supply them with all the social capital they may need. Some organizations use the metaphor of "family" to encourage their employees to see the company as a warm, nurturing, secure place where a lifelong commitment by the employee will be reciprocated in a worthwhile career (Casey, 1999). In becoming ideal, loyal "family" members, employees may cut themselves off from other contacts. How many of today's organizations can expect to survive and thrive and to provide continuing opportunities for all of their current and new members? The problem is particularly acute for employees who are located close to the "core" of the organization and have few external contacts: Those in regular contact with suppliers, clients, customers, and associated organizations may be able to develop more diverse contacts.

In fields such as film making (Jones, 1996, 2002), television (Ensher, Murphy, & Sullivan, 2002b), semiconductors (Saxenian, 1996), and biotechnology (Higgins, 2002), there are emerging and fluid industry structures, collaborative as well as competitive relationships between firms, geographical proximity of "industry regions," the use of finite projects rather than permanent employment to organize work, and the blurring of boundaries between work and nonwork. These characteristics are reflected in dynamic new patterns of career in which strong networks at least within the industry are vital. For example, according to Higgins (2001), the greater the diversity of a person's network, the more job offers he or she will receive during a job search and the greater the likelihood of changing careers.

Brown and Duguid (1991) and Wenger (1998) used the term *communities-of-practice* to designate the phenomenon of collaborative learning for mutual career advantage by like-minded people cast together in groups. The Silicon Valley networks of young information technology professionals described by Saxenian (1996) enable traditional career structures based on long-term organizational or occupational affiliation to be replaced by informal project-to-project career improvisation requiring sociability, constant learning, flexibility, and interfirm mobility in equal measure.

Interpersonal Influence

The value of relationships and networks to individuals' careers lies not just in having them but also in how they are used. It is of little value to your career to talk to lots of people at parties if you consistently make a bad impression on them or to be in the same golf club as the chief executive officer (CEO) of the company you want to work for if you aren't willing to steer the conversation in the direction of jobs and your career. Psychology has provided us with an understanding of many techniques for influencing others: for example, researching them beforehand to find out what is likely to "work," flattering them, communicating positive expectations, using confident body language, maintaining eye contact, listening, asking questions as well as making statements, communicating associations with people you know will be well thought of (e.g., "I'm a friend of your associate Julie"), negotiating desired outcomes, and reinforcing desired behavior (e.g., by gratitude or praise).

Much of this networking behavior is aimed at what is called *impression management*—"the process through which individuals manipulate information about themselves so that others perceive them as they desire to be viewed" (Schenkler, 1980, reported in Bratton & Kacmar, 2004, p. 291). In the process of applying for a job, for example, a candidate might prepare his or her vita in such a way as to emphasize favorable college grades, might wear a classy new outfit, and might ingratiate him- or herself by deliberately flattering the interviewer. Here is another example from the film *Wall Street* (Stone & Weiser, 1987).

Breaking the Ice

The film *Wall Street* opens with a classic case of impression management in pursuit of career success. Tired of his life as a low-level Wall Street stockbroker, Bud Fox, played by the young Charlie Sheen, decides to try to break into the big time and become a major, and successful, player on the market. To do so, he figures he needs the patronage of Gordon Gecko (played by Michael Douglas), a highly successful broker. The problem he faces is that everyone wants Gecko's time and

attention. Gecko is protected in his office by a personal assistant (PA) and sees people only by appointment. How can Fox get even a few minutes of Gecko's time? And if he does, how can he persuade Gecko to take him on as a protégé?

Fox first researches Gecko. Studying the great man in gossip columns, he finds that Gecko has a penchant for a particular rare brand of Cuban cigars. He also discovers Gecko's birthday and purchases a box of the cigars, wrapping them as a birthday gift. In the days leading up to the birthday, Fox constantly calls Gecko's PA, flattering and sweet-talking her on the telephone. On the day of the birthday, he turns up at Gecko's office with the cigars but says he is only willing to give the gift if he is allowed to deliver it personally. He is kept in the waiting room for hours, but eventually he is granted 5 minutes in Gecko's presence—5 minutes to sell himself! But being in Gecko's office is a nightmare—the phone rings every few moments with more deals that Gecko must attend to. Fox has gone in with carefully considered stock tips he thinks may interest Gecko, but Gecko dismisses them out of hand: "Tell me something I don't know!" But in the end, Fox at last says something of interest to Gecko, and a passing acquaintanceship becomes a relationship and, indeed, a mentorship.

It is evident from this case that the use of impression management, designed as it is to promote image rather than reality, is open to abuse and even untruth—for example, when people claim they left their company voluntarily when they were really fired or when they forge references. Further, excessive impression management can result in the unfair denigration of others (Cialdini, 1989). Bratton and Kacmar (2004) noted that unacceptable impression management is likely to be used in *extreme careerism,* defined as "the propensity to pursue career advancement power or prestige through any positive or negative nonperformance-based activity that is deemed necessary" (p. 291). On the other hand, candidates deserve the opportunity to present themselves at their best, and indeed such self-presentation can become a self-fulfilling prophecy by enhancing work performance (Eden, 1991). Each individual has his or her own standard in terms of the tactics used in career self-promotion.

Mentorship

A *mentor* is "an experienced and trusted advisor" (Allen, 1990, p. 742). In the context of careers, a mentor is normally understood as being an older, more experienced person who is able on the basis of that experience to provide help to a younger person in developing his or her career through its early stages. Many people in the exploration and establishment phases of their careers want and can benefit from the counsel of those who have been through the process in their time.

The Mentor Who Made a Difference

I was 22 years old, a master's student of organizational psychology, knowing my career would probably be academic but not knowing what that meant. He was about 30 years old, a young assistant professor still completing his own PhD. Despite his own

(Continued)

(Continued)

youth, he was street-smart, socially skilled, and committed to his students. Though I scarcely knew what a mentor was and wouldn't have called him that, he became a mentor for a number of us.

What did he do for me?

- He involved me and others in conversation. We talked about our discipline, the outside world, and our careers. In conversation, we put the world right. He helped us feel that we were doing something worthwhile.
- Using his own contacts in town, he arranged for a series of practical projects in local companies, enabling me to develop expertise and self-confidence. He even got me paid for my work!
- He provided wonderful role modeling in the way he went about his job, both teaching and research. The way he went about his doctoral thesis was a model that I still value, 40 years later.

- I got the choice of a "community college" professorship or a job as research assistant in a prestigious academic project. The college job paid double, and I was keen to get married and buy a house. He glared at me and said, "Do you want to be a hack teacher all your life? Go and do something worthwhile." After that, I didn't consider the college job or any other like it. As it turned out, he was absolutely right.

I left the program for the research assistant job and lost contact with him. Nearly 40 years later, I was in his city, found where he was, and wrote to him, thanking him very belatedly. Now about 70 years of age, he wrote back, and we had lunch in a local restaurant. He hadn't changed at all. He seemed happy with what I had done. But he had no more advice to give. It was wonderful.

Source: Kerr Inkson, personal reminiscence.

A mentor may be informal or formal. Informal mentoring occurs naturally due to a relationship between the mentor and the protégé—for example, when parents act as career mentors to their own children or when a senior manager finds a young staff member likeable and promising and takes the employee under his or her wing. Formal mentoring is arranged by institutions—for example, universities, business organizations, professional bodies—to assist the development of their own junior members by attaching them formally to senior members and providing a formal basis for mentoring activity—for example, formal pairing of mentors and protégés, regular meetings following specific formats, and training in how to benefit from mentorship (Cranwell-Ward, Bossons, & Gover, 2004).

What does a mentor do? Kram (1985) described two functions, which she labeled *career* and *psychosocial*. Career functions are instrumental and directly related to career development—for example, offering advice as to career direction, coaching for a job interview, introducing to a new business contact. Psychosocial functions are about background support and affirmation of the protégé's worth. In combination, the two facets of mentoring can provide support for individual career development that takes it beyond career problem solving and makes it a potentially rich and supportive development process.

A mentor familiar with a protégé's current occupation or organization can facilitate his or her rapid learning of work methods, norms, typical hassles, and strategies for overcoming barriers. Influential mentors can make a difference in the jobs the protégé is able to obtain or the projects the protégé is assigned to. Empathetic mentors can act as confidants, sounding boards, and counselors to the protégé about work and career issues. Mentors who are not the direct boss of the protégé can provide independent and confidential advice on how to deal with current issues. All mentors may act as role models. In light of women's orientation to seek communion rather than to pursue agency in their work (Marshall, 1989; see Chapter 4), and their common marginalization within employing organizations, mentoring may have special value to women (Ragins & Cotton, 1991; Tharenou, 2005). Presumably because of these functions discharged by mentors, various studies have shown that mentorship often results in better protégé motivation, work performance, and career advancement (Aryee & Chay, 1994). Small wonder it has been claimed that everyone needs a mentor (Clutterbuck, 1993). Multiple mentors in diverse networks may be even better and may be consciously sought by the individual (de Janasz, Sullivan, & Whiting, 2003).

Mentoring may also bring advantages to the mentor. Psychologist Erik Erikson (1959; see Chapter 3) highlighted the concept of generativity, which he believed characterized many adults. Generativity is about handing one's knowledge and experience to the younger generation and, as it were, living beyond death (or, in this case, more prosaically, beyond retirement from work) through the accomplishments of others. Seeing the protégé develop can bring its own rewards. Developing a protégé may bring its own new challenges. Moreover, mentors can become colearners with their protégés—particularly in situations where the rules of the game have changed since the mentors were younger (Hall, 2002)—and can learn new skills or attitudes from their protégés.

The advantages of career mentoring are so apparent that many organizations nowadays have developed formal schemes to ensure that mentorship is provided—at least for their elite, young professional groups—within the ambit of the company on a regular and regulated basis, with senior managers assigned as mentors (Armstrong, Allinson, & Hayes, 2002; Ragins, Cotton, & Miller, 2000). However, not every manager necessarily has the attributes best suited to mentoring (Van Emmerik, Baugh, & Euwema, 2005), and organizations may have to be careful when setting up mentor–protégé partnerships (Armstrong et al., 2002). The quality of the relationship between mentor and protégé appears to affect job and career attitudes more than the category of mentorship does (i.e., formal vs. informal; Ragins et al., 2000).

Organizational mentoring systems can be coordinated with other aspects of the company's human resource management (see Chapter 9) to maximize both personal and organizational development (Desimone, Werner, & Harris, 2002). Such schemes enable organizations to facilitate a professional model of mentoring, involving clear goals, systematic selection and training of mentors, and integration with the organization's other human resource systems. They may also maximize the synergy between the protégé's career and the organization's goals. By the same token, they may provide a limited, organizational view of career, in which it may be taken for granted that the protégé seeks progress only by advancement within the current organization. Baugh and Fagenson-Eland (2005) reported, however, that organizational mentors tend to provide more support to protégés than do mentors from outside the employing organization. It is important for many individuals that they obtain career mentorship from people with varying viewpoints.

In this context, the concept of mentorship can be widened beyond the notion of a one-to-one relationship between an older mentor and a younger protégé. For example, in considering the mentorship experiences of a sample of women in the entertainment industry, Ensher, Murphy, and Sullivan (2002a) reported that many relied on their peers rather than on senior people for support: "Many of our women took mentoring wherever they could get it" (p. 243). Many people like talking with others about their careers and find that good ideas, advice, and support do not need to come from an "older head" or a trained counselor. Thus, the ethnic minorities considered by Thomas (1990) and Thomas and Higgins (1996) found support lacking within their organizations and developed wider community networks beyond the organization for social and instrumental support in their careers. Developing the idea further, Higgins and Kram (2001) reconceptualized the notion of mentoring as a developmental network involving inputs from a range of sources, which moreover may have more significance for long-term career success than does a relationship with a primary mentor (Higgins & Thomas, 2001).

Conclusion

In Western societies, the career is conceptualized as being essentially an individual project for which each person is personally responsible. Yet the evidence in this chapter makes it clear that in practice it is impossible to separate any career from the social contexts in which it is conducted. Family, education, position in the social structure (Chapter 2), nonwork roles (Chapter 7), as well as employing organizations all provide us with contacts and network connections that can crucially affect our careers. In other societies organized on a more collective basis, the effects may be even stronger.

It therefore behooves individuals pursuing a career, or those interested in the careers of others, to at least pay close attention to their network of relationships and contacts because the network is a crucial potential asset for career development. However, the issue of how far to go in cultivating relationships solely for the purpose of personal career benefit (rather than occasionally using relationships developed for other reasons) is a delicate one for each individual to resolve in his or her own way.

Key Points in This Chapter

- Careers are powerfully facilitated and mediated by work relationships and social connections, even in cases like film directors, where the career seems highly individualistic.
- Career transitions are frequently mediated by personal networks, making networking a key career attribute or skill.
- Networking may be done spontaneously or deliberately for career purposes. Effective networking needs to be done continuously and reciprocally. Reputation can be enhanced through networks.

- Social capital consists of the resources we are able to access through our contacts.
- Careers may be enhanced through participation in career communities, based for example on educational, occupational, or organizational networks where career-related issues are discussed.
- For career development, networks involving diverse "weak ties" may have advantages over those with more narrowly focused "strong ties," such as those in close-knit organizations.
- Techniques of impression management can be used to enhance interpersonal influence—particularly for career advancement—but raise issues of personal ethics.
- Mentorship is a form of career-related social connection between more experienced mentors and younger protégés seeking career development. Sometimes mentorship is formally organized.

Questions From This Chapter

General Questions

1. Make a list, or draw a diagram, of your own major social connections—for example, family, friends, tutors, employers, and work colleagues. Which ones, if any, have had, or are likely to have, the most influence on your career? How diverse do you think your networks are?

2. How good do you think you are at networking? Is this of concern to you? What could you do to improve your networks and networking skills?

3. Do you think it is right to cultivate relationships to use them to benefit your career?

4. Are you a member of any groups—career communities—that discuss careers? How helpful is this? If you wanted to get some advice on your career, whom would you go to?

5. Have you observed other people using impression management techniques to try to influence others? What techniques did they use? Do you think this is effective?

6. Have you had, or do you have, any mentors? How much have they helped you?

Career Case Study Questions

1. Ask your case person to list the other people who were most influential in his or her career and indicate the nature of the relationships and their effects.

2. Ask your case person to indicate other people whose careers he or she affected and describe how the careers were affected.

3. Describe the concepts of impression management and mentorship to the case person and ask whether these played any part in the person's career.

References

Adler, P. A., & Kwon, S. (2002). Social capital: Prospect for a new concept. *Academy of Management Review, 27*(1), 17-40.

Allen, R. E. (Ed.). (1990). *The concise Oxford dictionary* (8th ed.). Oxford, UK: Clarendon Press.

Alvarez, J. L., & Svejnova, S. (2002). Symbiotic careers in movie making: Pedro and Agustin Almodóvar. In M. A. Peiperl, M. B. Arthur, & N. Anand (Eds.), *Career creativity: Explorations in the re-making of work* (pp. 183-208). Oxford, UK: Oxford University Press.

Armstrong, S. J., Allinson, C. W., & Hayes, J. (2002). Formal mentoring systems: An examination of the effects of mentor/protégé cognitive styles on the mentoring process. *Journal of Management Studies, 39*(8), 1111-1137.

Arthur, M. B., Inkson, K., & Pringle, J. K. (1999). *The new careers: Individual action and economic change.* Thousand Oaks, CA: Sage.

Aryee, S., & Chay, Y. W. (1994). An examination of the impact of career-oriented mentoring on work commitment attitudes and career satisfaction among professional and managerial employees. *British Journal of Management, 5,* 241-249.

Baugh, S. G., & Fagenson-Eland, E. A. (2005). Boundaryless mentoring: An exploratory study of the functions provided by internal versus external organizational mentors. *Journal of Applied Social Psychology, 35*(5), 939-955.

Baxter, J. (1998). *Stanley Kubrick: A biography.* New York: HarperCollins.

Bourdieu, P. (1986). The forms of capital. In J. Richardson (Ed.), *Handbook of theory and research for the sociology of education* (pp. 241-258). New York: Greenwood.

Bozionelos, N. (2003). Intra-organizational network resources: Relation to career success and personality. *International Journal of Organizational Analysis, 11*(1), 41-66.

Bratton, V. K., & Kacmar, M. (2004). Extreme careerism: The dark side of impression management. In R. W. Griffin & A. M. O'Leary-Kelly (Eds.), *The dark side of organizational behavior* (pp. 291-308). San Francisco: Jossey-Bass.

Brown, J. S., & Duguid, P. (1991). Organizational learning and communities of practice: Toward a unified view of working. *Organizational Science, 2,* 40-57.

Burt, R. S. (1992). *Structural holes.* Cambridge, MA: Harvard University Press.

Carnegie, D. (1981). *How to win friends and influence people.* New York: Pocket Books.

Casey, C. (1999). "Come, join our family": Discipline and integration in corporate organizational culture. *Human Relations, 52*(2), 155-178.

Cialdini, R. B. (1989). Indirect tactics of image management: Beyond basking. In R. A. Giacalone & P. Rosenfeld (Eds.), *Impression management in the organization* (pp. 45-56). Mahwah, NJ: Erlbaum.

Clutterbuck, D. (1993). *Everyone needs a mentor: Fostering talent at work* (2nd ed.). London: Institute of Personnel Management.

Cranwell-Ward, J., Bossons, P., & Gover, S. (2004). *Mentoring: A Henley review of best practice.* New York: Palgrave Macmillan.

Cross, R. (2004). *The hidden power of social networks: Understanding how work really gets done in organizations.* Boston: Harvard Business School Press.

Darling, D. C. (2003). *The networking survival guide.* New York: McGraw-Hill.

DeFillippi, R. J., & Arthur, M. B. (1996). Boundaryless contexts and careers: A competency-based perspective. In M. B. Arthur & D. M. Rousseau (Eds.), *The boundaryless career: A new employment principle for a new organizational era* (pp. 116-131). New York: Oxford University Press.

de Janasz, S. C., Sullivan, S. E., & Whiting, V. (2003). Mentor networks and career success: Lessons for turbulent times. *Academy of Management Executive, 17*(4), 78-91.

Desimone, R. L., Werner, J. M., & Harris, D. M. (2002). *Human resource development* (3rd ed.). Mason, OH: Thomson South-Western.

Dupuis, A., Inkson, K., & McLaren, E. (2005). *Pathways to employment: A study of the employment related behavior of young people in New Zealand* (Report No. 2005/1, Labour Market Dynamics Research Programme). Auckland, New Zealand: Massey University.

Eden, D. (1991). Applying impression management to create productive self-fulfilling prophecy at work. In R. A. Giacalone & P. Rosenfeld (Eds.), *Applied impression management: How image-making affects managerial decisions* (pp. 13–40). Newbury Park, CA: Sage.

Ensher, E. A., Murphy, S. E., & Sullivan, S. E. (2002a). Boundaryless careers in entertainment: Executive women's experiences. In M. A. Peiperl, M. B. Arthur, & N. Anand (Eds.), *Career creativity: Explorations in the re-making of work* (pp. 229-254). Oxford, UK: Oxford University Press.

Ensher, E. A., Murphy, S. E., & Sullivan, S. E. (2002b). Reel women: Lessons from female TV executives on managing work and real life. *Academy of Management Executive, 16*(2), 106-119.

Erikson, E. H. (1959). Identity and the lifecycle. *Psychological Issues, 1*, 1-171.

Feldman, D. C. (1985). The new careerism: Origins, tenets, and consequences. *Industrial Psychologist, 22*, 39-44.

Feldman, D. C., & Weitz, B. A. (1991). From the invisible hand to the gladhand: Understanding a careerist orientation to work. *Human Resource Management, 30*, 237-257.

Fernandez, R. M. & Castilla, P. M., (2000). Social capital at work networks and employment at a phone center. *American Journal of Sociology, 105*(5), 1288-1356.

Finlay, W., & Coverdill, J. E. (2000). Risk, opportunism, and structural holes: How headhunters manage clients and earn fees. *Work and Occupations, 27*(3), 377-405.

Flum, H. (2001). Dialogues and challenges: The interface between work and relationships in transition. *Counselling Psychologist, 29*(2), 259-270.

Forret, M. L., & Dougherty, T. W. (2004). Networking behaviors and career outcomes: Differences for men and women? *Journal of Organizational Behavior, 25*(3), 419-437.

Gibbons, D. E. (2004). Friendship and advice networks in the context of changing professional values. *Administrative Science Quarterly, 49*(2), 238-262.

Gouldner, A. W. (1960). The norm of reciprocity: A preliminary statement. *American Sociological Review, 25*, 161-178.

Gowler, D., & Legge, K. (1989). Rhetoric in bureaucratic careers: Managing the meaning of management success. In M. B. Arthur, D. T. Hall, & B. S. Lawrence (Eds.), *Handbook of career theory* (pp. 437-453). Cambridge, UK: Cambridge University Press.

Granovetter, M. (1973). The strength of weak ties. *American Journal of Sociology, 78*, 1360-1380.

Granovetter, M. (1974). *Getting a job: A study of contacts and careers.* Cambridge, MA: Harvard University Press.

Granovetter, M. (1982). The strength of weak ties: A network theory revisited. In P. Marsden & N. Lin (Eds.), *Social structure and network analysis* (pp. 105-130). Beverly Hills, CA: Sage.

Granrose, C. S., & Chua, B. L. (1996). Global boundaryless careers: Lessons from Chinese family business. In M. B. Arthur & D. M. Rousseau (Eds.), *The boundaryless career: A new employment principle for a new organizational era* (pp. 201-217). New York: Oxford University Press.

Hall, D. T. (2002). *Careers in and out of organizations.* Thousand Oaks, CA: Sage.

Higgins, M. C. (2001). Changing careers: The effects of social context. *Journal of Organizational Behavior, 22*(6), 595-618.

Higgins, M. C. (2002). Careers creating industries: Some early evidence from the biotechnology industry. In M. A. Peiperl, M. B. Arthur, & N. Anand (Eds.), *Career creativity: Explorations in the re-making of work* (pp. 280-297). Oxford, UK: Oxford University Press.

Higgins, M. C., & Kram, K. E. (2001). Reconceptualizing mentoring at work: A developmental network perspective. *Academy of Management Review, 26*(2), 264-288.

Higgins, M. C., & Thomas, D. A. (2001). Constellations and careers: Toward understanding the effects of multiple developmental relationships. *Journal of Organizational Behavior, 22*(3), 223-247.

Hofstede, G. (1980). *Culture's consequences.* Beverly Hills, CA: Sage.

Inkson, K., & Parker, P. (2005). Boundaryless careers and the transfer of knowledge: A "Middle Earth" perspective. *Higher Education Policy, 18,* 312-325.

Israel, G. D., Beaulieu, L. J., & Hartless, G. (2001). The influence of community and family social capital on educational achievement. *Rural Sociology, 66*(1), 43-68.

Jones, C. (1996). Careers in project networks: The case of the film industry. In M. B. Arthur & D. M. Rousseau (Eds.), *The boundaryless career: A new employment principle for a new organizational era* (pp. 58-75). New York: Oxford University Press.

Jones, C. (2002). Signaling expertise: How signals shape careers in creative industries. In M. A. Peiperl, M. B. Arthur, & N. Anand (Eds.), *Career creativity: Explorations in the re-making of work* (pp. 209-228). Oxford, UK: Oxford University Press.

Kram, K. E. (1985). *Mentoring at work: Developmental relationships in organizational life.* Glenview, IL: Scott Foresman.

Marshall, J. (1989). Re-visioning career concepts: A feminist invitation. In M. B. Arthur, D. T. Hall, & B. S. Lawrence (Eds.), *Handbook of career theory* (pp. 275-291). Cambridge, UK: Cambridge University Press.

Mitchell, K. E., Levin, A. S., & Krumboltz, J. D. (1999). Planned happenstance: Constructing unexpected career opportunities. *Journal of Counseling and Development, 77,* 115-124.

Mouw, T. (2003). Social capital and finding a job: Do contacts matter? *American Sociological Review, 68*(6), 868-898.

Parker, P., & Arthur, M. B. (2000). Careers, organizing, and community. In M. A. Peiperl, M. B. Arthur, R. Goffee, & T. Morris (Eds.), *Career frontiers: New conceptions of working lives* (pp. 99-121). Oxford, UK: Oxford University Press.

Parker, P., Arthur, M. B., & Inkson, K. (2004). Career communities: A preliminary exploration of member-defined career support structures. *Journal of Organizational Behavior, 25,* 489-514.

Ragins, B. R., & Cotton, J. L. (1991). Easier said than done: Gender differences in perceived barriers to gaining a mentor. *Academy of Management Journal, 34,* 939-951.

Ragins, B. R., Cotton, J. L., & Miller, J. S. (2000). Marginal mentoring: The effects of type of mentor, quality of relationship and program design on work and career attitudes. *Academy of Management Journal, 43*(6), 1177-1194.

Raider, H. J., & Burt, R. S. (1996). Boundaryless careers and social capital. In M. B. Arthur & D. M. Rousseau (Eds.), *The boundaryless career: A new employment principle for a new organizational era* (pp. 187-200). New York: Oxford University Press.

Saxenian, A.-L. (1996). Beyond boundaries: Open labor markets and learning in Silicon Valley. In M. B. Arthur & D. M. Rousseau (Eds.), *The boundaryless career: A new employment principle for a new organizational era* (pp. 23-39). New York: Oxford University Press.

Schenkler, B. R. (1980). *Impression management: The self-concept, social identity and interpersonal relations.* Pacific Grove, CA: Brooks/Cole.

Sheridan, A. (2002). What you know and who you know: "Successful" women's experiences of accessing board positions. *Career Development International, 7*(4), 203-210.

Stone, O. (Writer/Director), & Weiser, S. (Writer). (1987). *Wall Street* [Motion picture]. United States: Twentieth Century Fox.

Tharenou, P. (2005). Does mentor support increase women's career advancement more than men's? The differential effects of career and psychosocial support. *Australian Journal of Management, 30*(1), 77-109.

Thomas, D. A. (1990). The impact of race on managers' experiences of developmental relationships. *Journal of Organizational Behavior, 11*, 479-492.

Thomas, D., & Higgins, M. (1996). Mentoring and the boundaryless career: Lessons from the minority experience. In M. B. Arthur & D. M. Rousseau (Eds.), *The boundaryless career: A new employment principle for a new organizational era* (pp. 268-281). New York: Oxford University Press.

Thomas, D. C., & Inkson, K. (in press). Careers across cultures. In M. Peiperl & H. Gunz (Eds.), *Handbook of career studies*. Thousand Oaks, CA: Sage.

Van Emmerik, H., Baugh, S. G., & Euwema, M. C. (2005). Who wants to be a mentor? An examination of attitudinal, instrumental and social motivational components. *Career Development International, 10*(4), 310-324.

Wenger, A. (1998). *Communities of practice: Learning, meaning, and identity.* New York: Oxford University Press.

CHAPTER 9

Careers as Resources

The Company Man

John R. Patrick has had a company career. His company has been information systems giant IBM.

John earned a bachelor's in electrical engineering from Lehigh University and a master's in management from the University of South Florida. He started with IBM in 1967 as a marketing trainee in Bethlehem, Pennsylvania. Soon he was a marketing representative selling and installing IBM systems.

In 1969, he began the only substantial break in his career outside IBM, when he was drafted into the United States Army and took military leave of absence from the company. During this time, he also earned a law degree from LaSalle University. But in 2.5 years he was back as an IBM marketing representative in Bethlehem.

In 1975, John was promoted to regional marketing representative in Philadelphia. In 1976, he became a marketing manager, managing a team focused on the insurance industry. Between 1977 and 1979 he served as executive assistant to the regional manager in IBM's mid-Atlantic headquarters. Then he returned to Philadelphia as branch manager for IBM's distribution and utilities customers.

A long sequence of other IBM jobs followed: financial consultant at corporate headquarters, director of pricing for IBM credit corporation, division controller for the IBM National Marketing Division in Atlanta, and coordinator of IBM's acquisition of Rolm Corporation. By 1987, John was a 20-year IBM veteran, with a significant notch on his belt in the form of his success in developing financial models that allowed the company to get into new financing markets. At this point, he became a company vice president of finance, in the National Services Division based in Franklin Lakes, New Jersey, which made him chief financial officer for IBM's maintenance and services business. In 1988 he became group director of planning for the Information Systems Group in Ryebrook, New York, doing finance and planning for North American field operations, and in 1990 he became a vice president for operations based in Milford, Connecticut. Later jobs—too numerous to enumerate—were all at the vice president level and involved marketing and communications. As vice president of marketing for Personal Systems, he was the senior executive responsible for the introduction of the ThinkPad brand.

About 1994, John became aware of the huge commercial potential of what was then a new and very minor part of IBM's business: the Internet. This effort was described in a *Harvard Business Review* article by Hamel (2000). John secured the protection of IBM chief executive officer (CEO) Lou Gerstner to run an "evangelizing" promotion of the Internet—against some groups at IBM who felt threatened by the Internet—at the grassroots level in the company. Says John, "Lou Gerstner's air cover enabled me to spread the word and build a team that had significant impact." IBM went on to become the leader in Internet technologies. John established a reputation as an Internet guru. He was named a world leader in innovation and networking by various journals.

John was vice president for Internet technology for about 4 years—easily the longest he had held any job in his career. He was closely involved in IBM's backing of the Linux movement. In November of 2001, he published a book about the Internet titled *Net Attitude*.

Shortly afterward, John officially retired—or, as he called it, he "e-tired"—from IBM, where he had had 23 different jobs in 34 years. But John wasn't finished with his career or with IBM. Instead, he entered what he calls Phase 2 of his career—the founding and direction of a new one-person company, Attitude LLC. From within Attitude LLC, he continued his relationship with IBM—this time as a consultant. Nowadays he runs a popular personal blog (http://patrickweb.com), serves on seven boards, writes, and speaks at conferences worldwide.

In his early career John benefited, he says, from the breadth of the experience IBM gave him—technical sales, marketing, finance, staff positions—enabling him to build a wide range of skills. Throughout his career, John was supported by IBM, which sent him to many training courses, ranging from one-on-one e-learning to executive coaching. He also built a huge network of contacts within IBM, and an executive program he attended at the Kellogg School of Management in 1985 extended his network to executives in many other companies and countries.

In the middle part of his career, IBM experienced tough times and downsized substantially, but he kept moving on, always, in his own words, "being in the right place at the right time." His job was never under threat. Throughout it all, he remained totally loyal to IBM. In the 1990s, during the Internet "bubble," his expertise led to major opportunities to move up to the CEO level in Silicon Valley companies, but he never wavered. His dedication and enthusiasm for the organization that gave him so much, and to which he has given so much, accompanied him into his "e-tirement."

What do we make of John Patrick's career? Its basis was his relationship with IBM: John's career was very much a *company* career. Second, it was a managerial career, covering a wide range of management functions—for example, marketing, finance, planning, innovation—as well as a number of general management roles. Third, it was characterized by steady upward mobility, with the various jobs, from the initial marketing traineeship to extremely powerful vice presidencies, carrying increasingly greater responsibility, Fourth, it involved strong elements of networking and company politics based on John's contacts and reputation in IBM and demonstrated particularly in his Internet campaign. Fifth, even though it was a one-employer career, it was a geographically mobile career, with jobs held in many different IBM locations along the eastern side of the United States. Last, the career, which lasted 38 years in the world's most rapidly changing industry, spanned a number of huge technological revolutions: The Internet technology in which John made his greatest contribution in recent years had not begun to be dreamed about by the marketing cadet of 1967. John's career was therefore a learning career and a knowledge-based career.

One way of understanding John's career is to think of it as a resource. A *resource* is "the means available to achieve an end, fulfil a function" or "a stock or supply that can be drawn on" (Allen, 1990, p. 1025). Careers are useful—they can be drawn on to achieve other purposes. The notion of employees as human resources to be drawn on for the achievement of organizational goals is now commonplace in business and managerial circles (e.g., Cascio, 2003; Denisi & Griffin, 2005). To IBM, John Patrick was not just a person and an employee; he was a resource to draw on to sell more laser printers, develop the ThinkPad, and make profits from Internet business.

Increasingly, too, we realize that in what is now a knowledge economy, the main resource that people bring to their organizations is not their physical labor but their knowledge and expertise. Because this knowledge is not an inherent quality of people but develops over time as a result of education, training, development, and experience, it is not just the person but the career that is the resource. People and their organizations invest time, money, and expertise over a long period into growing that resource to the maximum value possible, and they try to ensure that the knowledge being acquired is relevant and valuable in a changing world. A career is therefore a *repository of knowledge* (Bird, 1996) and as such is a key potential resource for both resource-hungry organizations and ambitious individuals.

John Patrick's career can be looked at as a series of investments. John invested his time, energy, abilities, and skills into IBM. IBM invested money in John's salary, benefits, development, and the salaries of those who helped him. The investments were therefore mutual. In many cases of this type, the process works well for both parties, and people live out their careers interdependently with, and harmoniously in, the organizations that succor them and that they in turn succor. In evaluating our current employment, it is worthwhile to consider the reciprocities involved, that is, the benefits exchanged between self and employer and the long-term accrual of those in our career (Arthur & Kram, 1989; Weick, 1996). Some benefits, such as salary, are immediate, whereas others, such as knowledge or expertise, may pay off over many years. In the same way, the employer may gain instant advantage from some employee inputs, such as work performed before receipt of salary, but will benefit over many years from others, such as long-term programs implemented by the employee across the organization (Arthur, Inkson, & Pringle, 1999). John Patrick may no longer be an IBM employee, but both he and IBM continue to benefit from things they did together many years ago.

Organizations naturally seek to maximize their investment by ensuring that the knowledge that employees acquire is maximally relevant to the organization's present and future needs (Desimone, Werner, & Harris, 2003). They seek to protect their investment in these employees by doing all they can to keep them within the organization long term rather than allowing them to leave to work for another organization, perhaps even a competitor. For example, employers offer long-service rewards, company benefits, stock options, and pension arrangements. Conversely, employees often develop extraordinary loyalty and commitment to organizations that look after them in this way and seek to develop and use their own careers largely for the benefit of the organization (Whitener, 2001).

This is a system of interdependence that can work well for organizations. In recent years, this idea has become embodied in what used to be called personnel management or staff management and is now, significantly, known as *human resource management* (HRM). Human resource management tends to define career management as management of employees' careers by the organizations in which they are employed: Career management in this sense is part of an overall approach to staff management that also includes areas such as personnel selection, training and development, remuneration, and performance evaluation, which are integrated with each other and with the general strategic plan of the organization. For full textbooks about HRM see Cascio (2003), Denisi and Griffin (2005), or Dessler (2004).

It should be clear from all this that the "resource" metaphor of careers was developed largely by organizations as a way of conceptualizing their ability to combine human inputs with, for example, plant and financial inputs to provide goods and services and make a profit. But are humans—and their careers—resources? What are the implications of considering them as such? Is there a danger that ready acceptance of this metaphor encourages the appropriation of individuals' personal resources for corporate gain? Although organizational and individual goals may sometimes be congruent, they are seldom identical. The "resource" metaphor raises important issues concerning the ownership of the career.

The Resource-Based View

The idea that careers can and should be managed by organizations can be sourced to a theoretical position in business studies known as the resource-based view of the firm (Barney, 1991; Boxall & Purcell, 2003). The resource-based view is a theory of company strategy. Some approaches to strategy suggest that good strategy is based on taking appropriate action in relation to external conditions, such as market opportunities and competitors (Porter, 1985). In contrast, the resource-based view stresses the internal constitution of the company, particularly its human resources—for example, the strategic vision and team dynamics of its managers and the skills, knowledge, network contacts, and other attributes of its staff—as a major basis of its success that enables it to make appropriate responses to external conditions. Although human resources—based on employees—are not the only resources organizations employ, they are unique in the extent that appropriate investment in them can add value to them and also in that, unlike money or technology, human resources can walk away from the organization if they wish (Boxall & Purcell, 2003).

Companies can build and sustain competitive advantage (Barney, 1991) by developing core competencies (Hamel & Prahalad, 1994), such as cutting-edge expertise in a new technology, that their competitors cannot rival. Therefore, to succeed in competition business organizations must have a vision of the core competencies they need to succeed and must either capture these from outside the organization or develop them inside the organization.

The competencies of an organization are embodied in the expertise of its employees, which is developed from their career experiences. So organizations seeking to succeed have a very good reason to intervene actively to influence the careers of their employees. They do this by inducing outsiders with key knowledge to join the organization, inducing insiders with key knowledge to remain within the organization, and developing and deploying these people's expertise as desired by management according to its strategy. Most likely, the intention behind the many transfers of John Patrick within IBM was not only to get important jobs done but also to ensure John's personal development as an ever more versatile and valuable company resource, well able to assist its continuing competitiveness.

The competencies involved go beyond the individual skills and capabilities that particular employees may bring, and extend to the integration of these capabilities with others' capabilities and the broader organization—for example, through teamwork, managerial systems, and company culture (Leonard, 1998). For example, according to Nonaka and Takeuchi (1995), experience in cross-functional (interdisciplinary) teams, and the development of interdepartmental rather than specialized careers (like John Patrick's), are among the means of developing an overall human resource with greater long-term value to the company. Sophisticated organizations will therefore try to engineer their employees' careers to have these features. Social capital (internal and external relationships; see Chapter 8) can also be fostered by organizations through their employees' networks (Fernandez & Castilla, 2000). Lengnick-Hall and Lengnick-Hall (2003) noted too how effective human resource management in fostering boundary-spanning careers can be used to build the amount of social capital available to the organization.

Organizational Career Management

According to Jeffrey Sonnenfeld (1989), "a career does not exist in a social vacuum but is in many ways directed by the employer's staffing priorities" (p. 202). Business organizations therefore develop a strong interest in developing, controlling, and exploiting the careers of employees for commercial advantage. Public sector organizations seeking efficiencies often follow the same route. Because it is easier to predict and control what is happening inside the organization than outside it, this gives them an interest in developing an internal labor market, that is, filling vacancies from within the organization and developing staff so that they are ready to fill these vacancies. The focus in sophisticated organizational career management is not so much on individual vacancies and placements as on the development of a career system to process and direct the combined resource embodied in employees' careers toward meeting organizational goals (Sonnenfeld, 1989). Career planning for the individual can be done using principles of strategic management and assisting the individual while "satisfying the dynamic and strategic human resource needs of the organization" (Duffus, 2004, p. 144). Thus, the employing organization becomes an active, and possibly controlling, participant in the individual's career.

Sociologist Max Weber (1922/1947), in his analysis of bureaucratic organization structures, referred to career systems in which individuals could join the organization at the bottom and advance hierarchically through their careers by progressively developing specialist skills in their area of work and filling positions above them as these positions became vacant. According to Osterman (1987), management may develop or constrain employees' careers within the organization by using rules of (1) job definition (e.g., specialization vs. multiskilling); (2) career development (e.g., favored career tracks for those with management potential); (3) job security (e.g., pension and other benefits encouraging long service); and (4) nature of payment (e.g., graduated salary scale versus payment-by-results). Where there is a thoroughgoing internal labor market, careers tend to become organizational as well as (or instead of) occupational.

In the second half of the 20th century, the development of powerful internal labor markets, particularly for staff in technical, professional, and managerial roles, became popular, particularly among large companies such as IBM. To encourage loyalty among staff, companies strove to reinforce attractive arrangements for remuneration, development, security, and promotion with strong, appealing organizational cultures (Deal & Kennedy, 1982; Schein, 1985) that encouraged the individual psychologically and socially to be part of the greater enterprise. The model reached its high point in the great Japanese organizations, such as Honda and Mitsubishi, in which young individuals entering the organization were offered lifetime employment (Ouchi, 1981). They could look forward to a career under paternalistic management, in which their continuing employment, regular promotions, and generous pensions were guaranteed; generous assistance in areas such as health, housing, and family education was offered; and a "happy family" metaphor of company life offered further inducements to a company career.

Benefits at Boeing

The giant Boeing organization is typical of many corporations that seek to build employee loyalty and career commitment by offering long-term employee benefits. Just look at the Boeing Web site: The benefits cover the whole life cycle, and the organization appears to be trying to compete in benefits to acquire the best staff and compete commercially:

At Boeing, we know there is a whole world outside of work, and we endeavor to provide you with programs that help you make the most of it. No matter how your life changes, from getting married to having children to caring for an aging parent, Boeing offers resources that protect

(Continued)

(Continued)

you and your family, help you ease transitions in trying times, or help you to grow both professionally and personally. From health, savings and retirement plans to our educational and training programs, travel services and employee discount programs, you will find Boeing's benefits to be among the most progressive in the industry. (Boeing, n.d.)

The listed benefits include vacations and holidays; medical plans that include prescription drugs, dentistry, vision care, mental health programs, and substance abuse treatment; insurance that covers health, life, accidents, and disabilities (with Boeing paying most of the premiums); a savings plan in which the company matches a proportion of employee contributions; a pension plan guaranteeing a stable retirement income; a credit union; a recreation program in company facilities; discount travel to sports events, theme parks, and vacation accommodations; access to state-of-the art-fitness centers; support to attend educational programs; free assistance to access suitable child care; employee assistance programs with trained counselors available in case of financial, emotional, or addiction problems; and commuter assistance programs.

Why would anyone ever leave?

Internal labor markets provide the opportunity for organizations to plan in advance how their total human resource should be developed and deployed. For example, Schein (1978) provided a model of a "human resource planning and development system" (p. 191) (Figure 9.1). Schein's model intertwines organizational activities such as workforce assessment and human resource planning with individual activities such as self-assessment and personal career planning. Through a series of matching processes—performance appraisal, talent identification, jointly negotiated development programs, and so forth—an appropriate integration may be arrived at in which both individual and organizational needs are accommodated for mutual benefit. Twenty-five years since Schein, sophisticated organizational career systems can be integrated within wider corporate systems and strategies (Baruch, 2003).

Large organizations are nowadays assisted in their planning relevant to their members' careers by huge human resource information systems (Mayfield, Mayfield, & Lance, 2003). Further, wider Internet-based systems controlled by external consultants enable organizations and job seekers to connect and find a fit with each other across continents.

Good organizational careers may also be found in organizations where there is not necessarily a sophisticated human resource and career development system. Some employers simply recognize that if they expect loyalty and commitment from their employees, then they too must give it in return and that laying off people once they are no longer economically viable may be counterproductive because the layoffs alienate the remaining staff (Gutknecht & Keys, 1993). In addition, they may

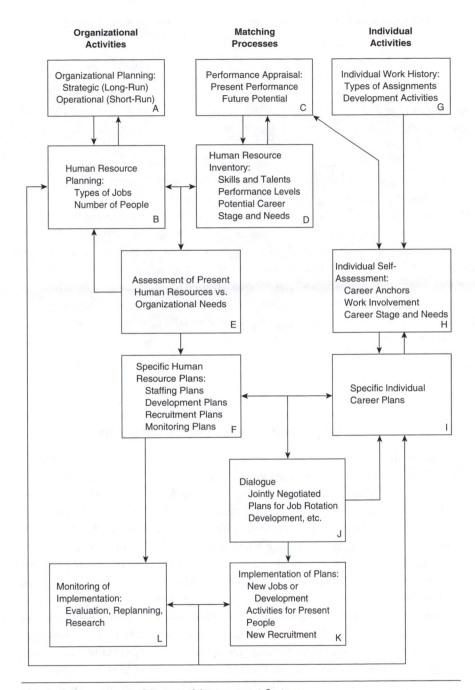

Figure 9.1   Human Resource Management System

Source: Reprinted from Schein, E. H., *Career Dynamics* © 1978, P. 191. Reprinted with permission of Pearson Education, Inc, Upper Saddle River, New Jersey.

feel a moral imperative to look after their people, almost as they would family members (see the case of Piers, next page). However, this is not something any employee can rely on.

Looking After Staff

Piers is 54 years old, has no qualifications, and has always done manual work. At 38 years of age, he was hired by a company called Metalco as a machine operator. The job required exceptional hand–eye coordination. Most workers who tried the job were unable to reach a satisfactory standard, but it turned out that Piers was one of the few who could. He took great pride in his skills and provided Metalco with good service over a number of years.

But 5 years ago Piers's eyesight began to deteriorate. He found he was no longer able to do the job satisfactorily. His manager decided that he needed to be replaced. Operating his machine was Piers's only real skill. But his managers did not lay him off. Instead they created a new role for him, as a supervisor of the machinists. It was really a nonjob, and Piers, who also prided himself on his strong work ethic, found that there wasn't enough for him to do, so again he asked for a change. This time the company gave him a job as a store man.

Piers enjoys his job. "There are no hassles. I do my own thing." He sees himself as a company man and accompanies the company football team to its matches. "I make my employer happy; we look after each other." He is confident that if he ever needed another job, Metalco would find one for him. He expects to stay there until, at a time of his own choosing, he retires.

Source: Arthur et al. (1999).

Problems With Organizational Career Management

The strategic human resource management view puts an interesting spin on the whole question of career development. Whereas the "inheritance" metaphor (Chapter 2) emphasizes the role of social structure in determining career outcomes, and several of the other metaphors, particularly the "action" metaphor (Chapter 4), suggest that individuals control their own career outcomes, the "resource" metaphor, as embodied in corporate HRM, suggests that employing organizations can and should endeavor to influence, and even capture, employees' careers for their own as well as the employees' advantage. Is this practical, or desirable?

The cases cited earlier, of large organizations offering major incentives and a good working lifestyle and corporate culture to loyal employees, certainly suggest that powerful organizations can indeed exercise significant control over employees' careers but can also offer them considerable security and opportunity. But the use of the term *human resource* suggests that the person is part of the company's stock, which can be drawn on, but also developed, for organizational ends. Ask yourself whether you like being thought of as a resource rather than as a person. "Resource" depersonalizes the individuals who make up the resource: It suggests a homogeneous supply of expertise divorced from the individual personalities who provide that expertise. "Resource" also disempowers, reducing potentially self-determining people to ciphers of the company. For example, Cascio (1995) stated, "A career is not something that should be left to each employee: instead it should be managed by the organization to ensure the efficient allocation of human and capital resources" (p. 310).

If the managers of organizations have this outlook, an interesting question arises as to the ownership of the career: Is the career the property of the individual or the organization? Employing organizations buy employees' services, but they do not buy their lives. Fortunately, in a second iteration of the previous passage, its author took a more enlightened view: "A key feature of the new concept is that the company and the employee are *partners* in career development" (Cascio, 1998, p. 308, italics added).

And in a third version, Cascio (2003) moved on again: "A career is not something that should be left to chance. Instead, in the evolving world of work it should be shaped and managed *more by the individual than by the organization*" (p. 373, italics added). This last view makes it much easier for career management to be based on a proper sense of individual ownership of the career and on the recognition that most careers are *inter*organizational. On the other hand, it raises major problems for organizations as they grapple with the problem of building an organization based on careers that they are not able to manage.

The Decline in Organizational Careers

The previous critique of organizational career management is based on the view that excessive control by organizations of their employees' careers can be undesirable. But, as it has turned out, the reliance by many organizations on organizational careers has also proven, in recent years, to be impractical.

The fashion for organizational careers peaked in the 1980s, followed in the 1990s by claims—possibly exaggerated (Dany, 2003)—that the (company) career was dead (Hall & Associates, 1996; Inkson, 1999). The problem with internal labor markets, clear company hierarchical structures, lifetime employment, and even strong organizational cultures had been that their permanence created rigidities that in the long-term reduced competitiveness and organizational performance.

The globalization process of the latter part of the 20th century created fierce competitive pressures for cost reduction and rationalization in organizations. From the 1980s in many organizations staff numbers were reduced (downsizing), whole hierarchical levels of organizations were removed (delayering), work was removed from permanent employees and jobbed out to competitive contracts (outsourcing), and permanent full-time staff were replaced by temporary and part-time—"casual"—workers, who could more easily be displaced and rehired (casualization). At the same time, globalization altered international patterns of employment; information technology displaced traditional skills and required new ones; new emphases on multiskilling and teams weakened traditional demarcations around jobs, occupations, and professions; and the feminization of the workforce introduced employees who needed new, more flexible patterns of work.

The effect of this organizational restructuring was to increase involuntary turnover and intercompany movements and to destabilize the careers of many workers. Careers that seemed stable and progressive were tarnished by unexpected layoffs. Consider the following case studies, all of men who lost their jobs suddenly through restructuring in a period of great economic turbulence.

Reacting to Job Loss

Albert, an engineer, was laid off three times in a year. He talked his way into temporary work as a barman, got promoted to bar manager, then later was able to return to work as an engineer, keeping his bar manager work as a second (evening) job.

Brett, a stock dealer (see Chapter 6), lost his job, found temporary work plastering a house, and went on to develop a successful plastering business. He feels that, in any case, he was never cut out to be a company employee.

Cedric, a business manager, was laid off and decided to use his experience and networks to start his own business partnership with a friend. But the "friend" disappeared, taking the partnership's assets with him. Cedric and his wife next created another business selling computer consumables. He found that "running his own show" was much to his taste and that he was able to relax more. Overall, he is glad he was laid off.

Norman, an accountant, walked out during a recession because of his concerns that his company was unethical. Now unemployed for several years, he keeps hoping a job will turn up but makes little active effort to find one. He seems destined to spend the rest of his life unemployed.

Sam, a manager and an immigrant, worked very hard for a number of years to do a good job for his company and to become a member of the company "team." But when the company restructured, it offered him only a low-status job. He refused and walked out. Since then, Sam has been mainly unemployed, though he now has a part-time clerical job. He is very bitter, not just about the company that got rid of him but about business in general.

Source: Arthur et al. (1999).

Laid-off employees typically find new jobs eventually and may even experience greater satisfaction than they did in the old job, but it appears their commitment and trust in organizations is reduced by the experience (Feldman & Leana, 2000). In addition, restructuring tends to break the ties of loyalty that many employees feel toward their employers, leading to alienation not only by the "victims" of restructuring but also by those who remain in the restructured organization—the "survivors"—who of course find that even though they still have jobs their expectations of promotion are substantially reduced (Goffee & Scase, 1992; Heckscher, 1995). Career attitudes and behavior may change after a layoff (Brockner, 1988; Jiang & Klein, 2000). The new generation of employment relationships is characterized by psychological contracts that have ceased to be relational—based on the expectation of a long-term, mutually rewarding relationship between organization and individual—and have instead become transactional—based on short-term exchanges of work for monetary rewards (Rousseau, 1995).

Pressures on organizational careers come also from changes in industry structures. For example, the U.S. semiconductor industry in Silicon Valley developed a totally new model of organizing, based not on large monolithic organizations but on clusters of small, flexible project-based companies, in and out of which highly qualified young staff members developed careers based on constant new learning (Saxenian, 1996).

Today's more flexible structures present major challenges to the traditional management focus on the organization and consequently to business's assertion of the primacy of organizational careers. Career scholars in the business schools became increasingly interested in external labor markets and careers that took place between organizations rather than within organizations (Inkson & Arthur, 2002). Arthur and Rousseau's *The Boundaryless Career* (1996) specifically dealt with the management of careers that were not confined to a single employment setting. Peiperl and Baruch (1997) noted that organizations' consideration of careers must move back to a square zero and envisage how to respond to new forms of postcorporate careers. In 2002, Boston University academic Tim Hall followed up his 1976 *Careers in Organizations* with *Careers in and out of Organizations.*

Combining Organizational and Individual Career Management

There has been recent speculation about the relationship between organizational career management (OCM) and career self-management by the individual (CSM) (King, 2004), with one suggestion being that far from being in opposition to each other the two can be combined, in well-managed organizations, into a virtuous circle of complementary career management activities (Sturges, Guest, Conway, & Mackenzie Davey, 2002). There is evidence that organizational career management does indeed increase employees' commitment to continue their careers in that organization (Sturges, Conway, Guest, & Liefooghe, 2005).

Here, we can put another spin on the resource idea by suggesting that if indeed the employee's career is a resource available to the organization in reaching its organizational goals, then it is also true that the organization is a resource available to the employee in reaching his or her career goals. The efforts that organizations make to meet their goals through the development of their employees often provide massive opportunities for personal and career development by employees, even if their career is destined eventually to move outside that particular organization.

This creates a major paradox for managers: The more they facilitate the personal development of employees within their organization for the benefit of the organization, the more they may simultaneously be increasing the same employees' attractiveness on the external labor market (Ito & Brotheridge, 2005). The key to resolving this dilemma is for managers to retain open communication with each employee so that an employee's interest in making a career move to a new organization is not regarded as disloyalty but as a problem to be openly discussed in the hope of joint resolution (Parker & Inkson, 1999).

In outlining a shared responsibility for career management, Cascio (2003) summarizes as follows: "[Managers] assign employees the responsibility for managing their own careers, and then provide the support they need to do it" (p. 372).

Where does that support come from? Much of it takes the form of the organization's own HRM activities. Organizational performance appraisals, training programs, development opportunities, projects, transfers, promotions, formal mentorship, and coaching, primarily intended to increase employees' performance in the company, can all add value to employees' long-term career, whether inside or outside the organization. In larger, more sophisticated organizations, the quality of these experiences may be enhanced by the use of specialist human resource development staff or consultants (Desimone et al., 2003).

Career Management Interventions in Organizations

It should be clear from the previous discussion that employing organizations can make lots of career benefits, in the form of their human resource management and human resource development activities, available to their employees. These benefits are termed *interventions* because they are deliberate attempts by the organization to intervene in the individual's career. Smart organizations arrange their interventions to maximize their human resources in relation to their strategic plans; smart employees can take advantage of such interventions for their own career development. However, unthinkingly using organizationally sponsored development for one's own career can bring its problems, as the following case shows.

A Company Specialist

Claire, an information technology specialist, acquired early-career expertise working as a programmer and analyst using a software package called Florex. When she moved to a new city to be with her partner, she scanned the help-wanted section of the newspaper until she found an opportunity for a permanent job with a consulting company specializing in Florex applications. During the next 5 years, Claire was very happy in her position as an analyst and later technical manager for Florex applications. It was a pleasant company to work in, her skills were recognized, and her boss sent her to out-of-state training courses and Florex conferences several times to hone her skills.

After 3 years, it was suggested that she might like to take on new responsibilities, perhaps in sales or client liaison. But Claire regarded herself as a technical person and resisted these opportunities. Then she began to feel "taken for granted" in the company and was offered fewer development opportunities. At the end of her 4th year, she was told her work was satisfactory but was offered no salary increase. The same thing happened at the end of her 5th year. After hearing this, for the first time since joining her company she scanned the help-wanted ads and was concerned to notice that there appeared to be no vacancies in the city for someone with her background. It seemed that interest in Florex was on the wane. With alarm she realized that outside of Florex her marketable skills were slender.

The next day Claire told her boss she had been upset not to receive a salary increase. She said that if the decision were not changed, she would have to consider looking elsewhere. Her boss was unperturbed. "Where?" he said.

In this case, Claire has probably developed too much of a specialization in her line of work and too great a dependence on her current employer. What is good for the employer (i.e., keeping Claire on as a relatively low-cost programmer who will not move on because she has no options) is not good for Claire's long-term career. It is good for employees to look for areas of overlap of interests with the employer but wrong to assume that they are there and that the employer will always act to assist their development.

Nevertheless, a good employer can provide its staff with a wide range of valuable career development opportunities. It lies beyond the scope of this book to provide a detailed description and evaluation of every type of intervention; for further information see sources oriented more specifically to organizational outcomes, such as Arnold (1997), Baruch (1999, 2003), and Desimone et al. (2003).

However, a brief summary of the most popular types of career-related interventions is provided in the following sections. Each type of intervention is designed for the benefit of the organization but offers opportunities for the individual to take advantage of them for personal career benefit.

Selection and Training

Every organization has to conduct day-to-day staffing functions, such as advertising for and hiring employees, orienting new hires to the organization, and training them to do their jobs. Good practice in such activities is beneficial to the organization, not just in ensuring that the people who are hired are suitable but also in providing a positive image of the organization and building employees' commitment. Individuals' careers can also benefit.

For example, many organizations are realizing the value, at the recruitment stage, of realistic job previews (Wanous, 1992), in which the applicant, rather than being provided with a "glowing" picture of the wonderful company he or she has applied to join, is provided with a more balanced picture. This simultaneously "vaccinates" the person against overoptimistic expectations and enables better decision making as to whether to pursue the opportunity. The practice therefore assists both sides to ensure a good match. Another individual benefit of organizational personnel selection—even if the individual is not offered a job—is the experience it provides in gaining insight into employing companies and the opportunity to practice self-presentation in the stressful situation of the job interview. When I was a postgraduate student, I applied for various jobs I didn't want, just to improve my interview skills.

Training for the job is a means of providing employees with the knowledge and skills to do the job for which they are being employed. Training therefore directly increases the value of the individual to the organization. Whether the training increases the value of the individual in settings other than the job for which it was designed depends on the generalizability of the skills. For example, being trained as a sales representative to demonstrate new photocopier systems to potential clients may include a lot of technical knowledge that is only applicable to that job at that time. But the training may also develop general knowledge about office systems or skills of persuasion or self-confidence that are applicable to a range of situations. Smart employees can turn apparently job-specific training into much broader personal development.

Human Resource Development

Training is designed to enable employees to develop the skills to do their jobs. Development has a longer term and wider focus, preparing people for future jobs with different and usually greater responsibilities than those they currently have. Smart organizations realize that to enable employees to contribute to their fullest they must develop employees' potential ahead of time, so the employees arrive at their new challenges already equipped, at least in part, to deal with them.

The most obvious means of facilitating development is to add to employees' tasks work that will call for the development of new skills. Arnold (1997) called attention to the value of developmental work assignments—sometimes called stretch assignments because they are likely to develop the assignee by stretching his or her capacity—in enabling skills development while still getting something useful done for the organization. Examples might be rotation to a new job once the original job has been learned; completing a special short-term project, such as a feasibility study for a proposed new program; or assignment to an interdepartmental task force. All of these are likely to involve not only working on fresh problems but also working with new people who are quite likely to have different ideas. The opportunities for personal development and career enhancement should be obvious.

Such assignments are examples of on-the-job employee development. Large organizations sometimes sponsor off-the-job development as well. For example, in recent years, outdoor education in which employees build confidence and teamwork by rafting, hiking, or solving outdoor problems in groups has gained credibility as a staff development method (Hwang, 2003; Judge, 2005). More common are staff development courses with expert speakers in technical and managerial techniques, run either in-house or through management consultants. In other cases, organizations are sometimes willing to sponsor key employees to complete relevant tertiary educational programs, such as a master's degree, by providing time off from work and even reimbursement of fees.

Whether such beneficence pays off for the organization depends on the relevance of the development experiences to the organization's future needs and the retention of the developed staff members within the organization. With the increasing turbulence organizations face, future needs are harder to predict and retention less certain: This leads to organizations being increasingly reluctant to spend money on activities from which they may receive no return. For staff members, it may mean that increasingly they will have to look after their own development. Nevertheless, it should be evident that it may be good for staff members to learn to take advantage of relevant employee development opportunities in their organization and perhaps even to seek such opportunities actively.

Staffing Systems

Each organization has its own way of filling internal vacancies. Employees need to consider which career opportunities are likely to arise for them in their organization and how such opportunities are created and filled. Is the organization seeking to expand its workforce, and if so, what additional skills does it need? Does it have a philosophy of "making" its senior appointees (by developing them internally in the organization) or "buying" them (by hiring outsiders)? "Making" creates more career opportunities for current employees and strengthens their commitment but limits the addition of new ideas through recruitment (Ulrich & Lake, 1991). Clearly, the staffing strategy adopted by the company is a major determinant of individual opportunities.

In a nice use of metaphor, Sonnenfeld (1989) distinguished four career systems. A "baseball team" is open to external talent and employs networks of talent spotters; competition between members for top positions is fierce and encouraged. An "academy" is a stable institution that staffs itself by means of the development of its own highly committed members. A "club" looks after its members but may favor egalitarianism and seniority over merit as a criterion for development. A "fortress" is more interested in the organization's survival than in what happens to its members, and its commitment to them will be low. Can you see how understanding your employing organization's staffing strategy can help you to anticipate its interest in your career and enable you to make better career decisions?

At a more mundane level, the information shared with staff about business plans, the internal advertising of new positions (made much easier nowadays by company Web sites), and the quality of the automatic human resource information systems and informal networks of the organization in communicating opportunities are all important. Job postings may be used, where positions are made known to current employees (e.g., on its intranet) before being advertised outside the organization. In succession planning, human resource inventories identify potential successors if a position is vacated (Garman & Glawe, 2004; Rothwell, 1994). In the dual-career path system, special tracks for advancement are created for professional employees who want to advance but who also want to remain professional specialists rather than managers (Tucker, Moravec, & Ideus, 1992). Employees who want to get ahead monitor internal sources of information closely and pay attention to the intraorganizational career paths that appear to result in success.

Appraisal and Assessment

In Chapter 5, I emphasized that if individuals are to make good decisions about the kinds of jobs and occupations that best fit them, they need good information about themselves. But organizations, too, increasingly assess their staff members for performance improvement purposes and provide feedback to them regarding their attributes and performance. Employees can make good use of such information to assist their careers.

Individual performance appraisal (sometimes called performance evaluation) is nowadays commonplace in many organizations and often provides a major opportunity for the individual to assess him- or herself and also to receive feedback from others concerning current performance and future potential and goals (Murphy & Cleveland, 1991). Typically, a set of numerical ratings of performance by the person's superior, a formal document, and arrangements to set future goals—including, sometimes, career goals, based on past performance—are used.

A recent development is 360-degree feedback—evaluation not just by one's boss but by peers, subordinates, and others (Edwards & Ewen, 1996; Tyson & Ward, 2004; Van der Heijden & Nijhof, 2004). Unfortunately, appraisals are often inaccurate due to things like subjectivity and hidden agendas of appraisers, such as conflict avoidance. Individuals are often defensive about judgments made about them, particularly if there are financial rewards or promotions at stake. In addition, appraisal of performance on a specific job may not be a good guide to the person's wider career potential. Organizational improvements in appraisal technique, however, can certainly enhance the value of the practice for both the organization and the individual (Murphy & Cleveland, 1991).

Another assessment technique is the assessment center (Bray, 1985; Howard, 1997; Joiner, 2002), a process for evaluating individuals—current employees as well as job candidates—often by means of standardized tests, interviews, and work simulations that are judged by expert assessors across a range of skills and aptitudes relevant to potential in the organization and for the wider career. Assessment center techniques can be tailored to the needs of the organization, are often sophisticated and valuable in terms of ability to predict job performance, and again—provided results are shared with the individuals who participate—can provide valuable information related to participants' career goals.

Organizational Career Development

In a last category of organizational interventions in careers, some organizations provide direct career development assistance to employees (Baruch, 1999). For example, organizations may provide employees with career workbooks or computer-assisted career management programs (in big organizations sometimes consolidated into career resource centers), career workshops and preretirement workshops, courses for minorities in promoting their own careers, individual career counseling, and outplacement counseling (i.e., counseling for employees who are being laid off).

Why would organizations intervene in these ways? After all, some organizations are very sensitive about employee "loyalty" to a point where many employees are afraid of talking openly about their careers, including the possibility of leaving the company (Parker & Inkson, 1999). Career consciousness-raising of employees through workshops and other means may show them new possibilities and persuade them that their most sensible career option would be to leave the organization. Proponents of career interventions argue that such assistance builds employee commitment, performance, and acceptance of the organizational culture; identifies employees with high potential; and enables employees to be developed in line with business needs (Gutteridge, Liebowitz, & Shore, 1993)—all organizational rather than individual purposes. Another purpose, however, might be to assist participants to improve their career adaptability or resilience (Waterman, Waterman, & Collard, 1994)—an important attribute in changing times, whether the individual stays with the organization or leaves it. Sometimes it is in the interest of the organization to assist long-service employees who may have become overdependent on the organization to manage their careers, to become more independent and proactive.

Among the various techniques mentioned, those involving direct discussion of the individual's career—workshops and one-to-one counseling—are perhaps the most powerful. Much depends on the skills and objectives of the workshop leader or counselor, and the guidance may be given by anyone, from a rough-and-ready supervisor providing amateur career advice during a performance appraisal session to a formal company mentorship program, as described in Chapter 8, to an independent professional counselor hired by the company. Further information on career counseling is provided in Chapter 12. Here, it merely needs to be noted that career guidance by the organization runs the risk of being either limited in quality or biased, or both. Nevertheless, like all the types of interventions listed in this section, this intervention presents a good opportunity for any employee who wants to do some serious thinking and planning related to his or her career.

Psychological Contracts and Careers

A welcome development in our understanding of careers, particularly organizational careers, is an emphasis, particularly in British research, on the notion of the psychological contract as a means of understanding how careers work between employer and employee (Atkinson, Barrow, & Connors, 2003; Herriot & Pemberton, 1996; Sturges et al., 2005). In this context, "contract" is of course a metaphor—there needs to be no written contract, merely a shared understanding by the two parties of reciprocal wants and expectations (e.g., the employer's expectations of standards of work by the employee and the employee's expectation of security and loyalty from the employer). An organizational career can be conceptualized as a constantly renegotiated series of psychological contracts (Herriot & Pemberton, 1996): This view recognizes the rights of both parties to joint determination of the career and allows for processes of career change, even radical career change, without changes of organization.

Career Capitalism

If a career belongs to the individual who is living it, and is based on his or her knowledge resources, one way to understand it is through the metaphor of "career capital" (Inkson & Arthur, 2001). In career capitalism, it is assumed that people's career capital is knowledge capital gained through career and other experiences. According to DeFillippi and Arthur (1996), career capital includes "knowing-why" capital (the individual's motivation and values and the way in which these energize work behavior), "knowing-how" capital (skills, qualifications, expertise, and experience), and "knowing-whom" capital (contacts, networks, and reputation).

Consider, for example, John Patrick's success, outlined at the beginning of this chapter, in promoting the uptake of Internet applications within IBM. John's knowing-why was his fascination with, and passion for, the Internet and its commercial potential, producing a driving energy for change. His knowing-how was a combination of technical knowledge, managerial ability, and skills of communication and promotion, acquired mainly through his long and diverse experience in the company. His knowing-whom was his long-held familiarity with IBM and the people who worked there, including the key decision makers.

Particularly important is any knowledge capital that is in scarce present or future supply. Metaphorically, each of us is, actually or potentially, a knowledge capitalist, a trader and investor of accumulated learning and a joint venture partner of every economic institution within which we work. In the case of Claire the programmer, her knowing-how career capital (expertise in Florex software) declined in value, her knowing-why capital (motivation to be a programmer only) is too narrow, and her knowing-whom capital has become confined to one organization.

Knowing-why, knowing-how, and knowing-whom are complementary forms, or currencies, of career capital. Each job or project change in our careers typically requires us to invest at least one currency. For example, in the commitment we make to a new job or project (e.g., John Patrick's sudden passion for the Internet), we are typically making an investment in our employer from our current motivation, or knowing-why. When we offer an employer skills or experience transferred from an earlier job (e.g., John Patrick's all-around experience in IBM), we are drawing most on knowing-how. When we enhance our work through our network contacts (e.g., John Patrick's engagement of other IBM-ers in his "crusade"), we are drawing largely on knowing-whom. In each case, the fresh investment from one way of knowing has consequences for the other two.

As we continue in our careers, our stock of career capital changes. The organization's investment in us may pay off for us as well as the employer. Our work may provide new unforeseen opportunities, thus affecting our knowing-why. It may involve us in gaining new knowledge or becoming familiar with a new industry, thus increasing our stock of knowing-how. It may enhance our interactions and reputation among work associates, thus developing our knowing-whom. But capital accumulation is far from guaranteed: A dead-end job may reduce our capital or make it obsolete. To make our capital work for us, we have to work with our capital. Here is an example.

Building Capital From Diverse Sources

Marie qualified and practiced briefly as an intensive care nurse, but marriage and child care intervened. Realizing her job was not enough for her, she assisted her businessman husband with his property investment and share portfolios, gradually moving from secretarial assistance to researching and making investment decisions on his behalf. She also learned to do the catering for his business functions. Seeking to extend herself, she trained as a chef and managed a restaurant owned by her husband. Eventually, she bought her own restaurant: She purchased an old warehouse, designed and refurbished it by herself, and created a high-quality gourmet restaurant that soon had an outstanding reputation.

At this point, Marie's husband suddenly died. When his estate was examined, huge debts were revealed. Marie was forced to sell her successful restaurant and was left with almost nothing. Also, she found that the idea of the restaurant business now seemed trivial and unappealing. Pondering her strengths and weaknesses, she concluded that what she was best at, and liked best, was planning and organizing. As a nurse, she had made a major contribution to the design of a new intensive care facility; as a partner to her husband, she had successfully integrated information from a wide range of sources to plan new real estate developments; as a restaurateur, she had received her main satisfaction from workplace and menu planning. Her restaurant work had also shown her that she had a wide range of management skills, particularly the ability to communicate her plans to others in a way that inspired as well as informed them.

Marie set up shop as a management consultant. Her initial work was done for business friends of her late husband's, who were "helping her out" as much as trying to improve their businesses. But Marie's single-mindedness and the quality of her work soon led to repeat contracts and new invitations. High fees rolled in. Soon she was able to take advanced university courses in new planning techniques. For perhaps the first time she felt her career was truly underway.

Marie's career involved the gradual accumulation of capital from a range of experiences. Her knowing-why included the restlessness that impelled her to continually seek new ventures to plan and the sudden recognition of what it was that she was most interested in. Her knowing-how involved a range of skills developed through her work in three different industries—health, finance, and hospitality. When her husband died her knowing-whom resources were thin—his friends—but she quickly used them and her other capital to create a strong network of clients.

The principles of investing career capital, stated Inkson and Arthur (2001), are similar to those for financial capital—you spot a good investment opportunity, get into the market, and work with others to make investments succeed. Inkson and Arthur offered six principles:

- *Improvise your part.* The new capitalism takes place in a rapidly shifting labor market. You cannot predict the investment opportunities as an actor rehearses a script; you must rather improvise, like a street performer, seizing opportunities as they flash by and imposing yourself on the investment rather than allowing external forces to determine the outcome.
- *Enhance the script.* This is about adding new elements to the investment. You don't have to restrict yourself to the stock that is offered to you on the market. You can invent and invest in your own stock or invest in a new stock with others. Enhancing the script is about volunteering, adding to the investment by adding to your own job description.
- *Keep good company.* Good company is company that is good for one's career. It may or may not be available where you are working at present. It may be in your home. Your relationships—the company you keep—are an active part of your career capital. The world works better because of what you have done together. Your stock goes up.

- *Champion your industry.* Whatever industry you have chosen to invest in—health, education, information technology, manufacturing—you seek through your investment to add value for your industry's customers. From an economic standpoint, industries are more important than companies, and championing your industry is simply ethical investing.
- *Take on a mess.* Despite conventional advice to stay out of trouble, investing in a mess can be a very good thing indeed. It is an invitation to use your career capital to make a real difference, to help to transform the world. If you succeed, you will win knowing-whom respect. If you fail, you will gain major knowing-how learning.
- *Use your stuff!* The definition of *stuff*—rather like resource or capital—refers to both the material something is made of and the purpose for which it may be used. The point about your stuff is that it has different facets. The *right stuff* refers to your courage and commitment (knowing-why). You are also urged to *know your stuff* (knowing-how) in new situations and to *strut your stuff* to others (knowing-whom) to show what you can do. You also collect *new stuff* as you go about your business—new ambitions, new skills, new contacts. Use your stuff well, and you will be rewarded.

Conclusion

Careers embody the energy, the know-how, and the networks that individuals have developed over time. The use of these resources gives every career an economic or societal value that can be used both by the person whose career it is and by other people and institutions, particularly the organizations in which the person is employed. Negotiating how to use this resource for individual and wider benefit may be difficult, but in most cases win-win scenarios can be devised so that the person and the organization both benefit. What is critical is that the career resource should not be allowed to depreciate through lack of development—both individual and organization must constantly seek to invest in its development.

Key Points in This Chapter

- Careers have economic value. To organizations, employees are often seen as resources—as in human resource management—to be used with other resources to achieve organizational goals. The employee's potential is typically built up over a career, making the career also a resource.
- In the resource-based view of the organization, employees represent major sources of competitive advantage. Organizations often seek to protect this resource by retaining employees in organizational careers. Large organizations often offer attractive career paths and other rewards to encourage loyalty.
- Organizationally structured career paths may impede organizational flexibility, necessitating restructuring of the organization. Resultant layoffs damage both careers and loyalty.

- A good organization may be a major resource to employees' careers. Organizations frequently offer selection and training, human resource development, staffing systems, appraisal and assessment, and organizational career development, providing major potential benefits to members' careers.
- Career capitalism provides a model for individuals to develop their own career resources for their own benefit. Key elements are knowing-why (motivation), knowing-how (expertise), and knowing-whom (networks), all of which can be invested and grown by the individual.

Questions From This Chapter

General Questions

1. Do you consider yourself to be a resource? If you don't, why not? If so, in what sense? Who does the resource belong to?

2. Think of some organizations you know or have worked in. To what extent do you think the expertise of their employees built up over their careers is a source of competitive advantage or superior organizational performance?

3. Are you attracted to the idea of having an organizational career such as John Patrick's? What do you think are some of the advantages and disadvantages of this type of career?

4. Think of some organizations you know or have worked in. To what extent do they provide programs with potential career benefits for their staff, such as training, appraisal, and staff development? Would they be good organizations to work for, from a career point of view?

5. Make an assessment of your own career capital, covering knowing-why, knowing-how, and knowing-whom. Where did you obtain it, where are you currently investing it, and how can you grow it in the future?

Career Case Study Questions

1. Ask your career case person to identify the main benefits his or her career has had for the case person's employers. Have these benefits been apparent in organizational performance?

2. For which organization did your career case person work the longest? What incentives were there for loyalty to the organization? What were the benefits of the relationship in terms of the case person's career?

References

Allen, R. E. (Ed.). (1990). *Concise Oxford dictionary.* Oxford, UK: Clarendon Press.

Arnold, J. (1997). *Managing careers into the twenty-first century.* London: Paul Chapman.

Arthur, M. B., Inkson, K., & Pringle, J. K. (1999). *The new careers: Individual action and economic change.* Thousand Oaks, CA: Sage.

Arthur, M. B., & Kram, K. (1989). Reciprocity at work: The separate, yet inseparable possibilities for individual and organizational development. In M. B. Arthur, D. T. Hall, & B. S. Lawrence (Eds.), *Handbook of career theory* (pp. 292-312). Cambridge, UK: Cambridge University Press.

Arthur, M. B., & Rousseau, D. M. (Eds.). (1996). *The boundaryless career: A new employment principle for a new organizational era.* New York: Oxford University Press.

Atkinson, P. H., Barrow, C., & Connors, L. (2003). Models of police probationer career progression: Preconceptions of the psychological contract. *Human Resource Development International, 6*(1), 43-56.

Barney, J. (1991). Firm resources and sustained competitive advantage. *Journal of Management, 17*(1), 99-120.

Baruch, Y. (1999). Integrated career systems for the 2000s. *International Journal of Manpower, 20*(7), 432-457.

Baruch, Y. (2003). Career systems in transition: A normative model for career practices. *Personnel Review, 32*(2), 231-251.

Bird, A. (1996). Careers as repositories of knowledge: Considerations for boundaryless careers. In M. B. Arthur & D. M. Rousseau (Eds.), *The boundaryless career: A new employment principle for a new organizational era* (pp. 150-168). New York: Oxford University Press.

Boeing. (n.d.). *Employee benefits.* Retrieved June 15, 2005, from www.boeing.com/employment/benefits/index/html

Boxall, P., & Purcell, J. (2003). *Strategy and human resource management.* New York: Palgrave Macmillan.

Bray, D. W. (1985). Fifty years of assessment centers: A retrospective and prospective view. *Journal of Management Development, 4*(4), 4-12.

Brockner, J. (1988). The effects of work layoffs on survivors: Research, theory and practice. In L. L. Cummings & B. M. Staw (Eds.), *Research in organizational behavior* (pp. 213-255). Greenwich, CT: JAI Press.

Cascio, W. F. (1995). *Managing human resources: Productivity, quality of life, profits* (4th ed.). New York: McGraw-Hill.

Cascio, W. F. (1998). *Managing human resources: Productivity, quality of life, profits* (5th ed.). New York: McGraw-Hill.

Cascio, W. F. (2003). *Managing human resources: Productivity, quality of life, profits* (6th ed.). New York: McGraw-Hill.

Dany, F. (2003). "Free actors" and organizations: Critical remarks about the new career literature, based on French insights. *International Journal of Human Resource Management, 14*(5), 821-838.

Deal, T. E., & Kennedy, A. (1982). *Corporate cultures.* Reading, MA: Addison Wesley.

DeFillippi, R. J., & Arthur, M. B. (1996). Boundaryless contexts and careers: A competency-based perspective. In M. B. Arthur & D. M. Rousseau (Eds.), *The boundaryless career: A new employment principle for a new organizational era* (pp. 116-131). New York: Oxford University Press.

Denisi, A. S., & Griffin, R. (2005). *Human resource management* (2nd ed.). New York: Houghton Mifflin.

Desimone, R. L., Werner, J. M., & Harris, D. M. (2003). *Human resource development* (3rd ed.). Mason, OH: Thomson South-Western.

Dessler, G. (2004). *A framework for human resource management.* Upper Saddle River, NJ: Prentice Hall.

Duffus, L. R. (2004). The personal strategic plan: A tool for career planning and advancement. *International Journal of Management, 21*(2), 144-148.

Edwards, M. R., & Ewen, A. J. (1996). *360 degree feedback.* New York: American Management Association.

Feldman, D. C., & Leana, C. R. (2000). Whatever happened to laid-off executives? A study of re-employment challenges following downsizing. *Organizational Dynamics, 29*(1), 64-75.

Fernandez, R. M., & Castilla, P. M. (2000). Social capital at work: Networks and employment at a phone center. *American Journal of Sociology, 105*(5), 1288-1356.

Garman, A. N., & Glawe, J. (2004). Succession planning. *Consulting Psychology Journal: Practice and Research, 56*(2), 119-128.

Goffee, R., & Scase, R. (1992). Organizational change and the corporate career: The restructuring of managers' job aspirations. *Human Relations, 45,* 363-365.

Gutknecht, J. E., & Keys, J. B. (1993). Mergers, acquisitions and takeovers: Maintaining the morale of survivors and protecting employees. *Academy of Management Executive, 7*(3), 26-36.

Gutteridge, T. G., Leibowitz, Z. B., & Shore, J. E. (1993). *Organizational career development.* San Francisco: Jossey-Bass.

Hall, D. T. (1976). *Careers in organizations.* Pacific Palisades, CA: Goodyear.

Hall, D. T. (2002). *Careers in and out of organizations.* Thousand Oaks, CA: Sage.

Hall, D. T., & Associates. (Eds.). (1996). *The career is dead—Long live the career! A relational approach to careers.* San Francisco: Jossey-Bass.

Hamel, G. (2000). Waking up IBM. *Harvard Business Review, 78*(4), 137-146.

Hamel, G., & Prahalad, C. (1994). *Competing for the future.* Boston: Harvard Business School Press.

Heckscher, C. (1995). *White collar blues: Management loyalties in an age of corporate restructuring.* New York: Basic Books.

Herriot, P., & Pemberton, C. (1996). Contracting careers. *Human Relations, 49*(6), 757-790.

Howard, A. (1997). A reassessment of assessment centers: Challenges for the 21st century. *Journal of Social Behavior and Personality, 12*(5), 13-52.

Hwang, A. (2003). Adventure learning: Competitive (Kiasu) attitude and teamwork. *Journal of Management Development, 22*(7), 562-578.

Inkson, K. (1999). The death of the company career: Implications for management. *University of Auckland Business Review, 1*(1), 10-21.

Inkson, K., & Arthur, M. B. (2001). How to be a successful career capitalist. *Organizational Dynamics, 31*(3), 48-61.

Inkson, K., & Arthur, M. B. (2002). Career development: Extending the "organizational careers" framework. In S. G. Niles (Ed.), *Adult career development: Concepts, issues, and practices* (3rd ed., pp. 285-304). Columbus, OH: National Career Development Association.

Ito, J. K., & Brotheridge, C. M. (2005). Does supporting employees' career adaptability lead to commitment, turnover, or both? *Human Resource Management, 44*(1), 5-19.

Jiang, J. J., & Klein, G. (2000). Effects of downsizing policies on IS survivors' attitudes and career management. *Information and Management, 38*(1), 35-45.

Joiner, D. A. (2002). Assessment centers: What's new? *Public Personnel Management, 31*(2), 179-185.

Judge, W. (2005). Adventures in creating an outdoor leadership challenge course for an EMBA program. *Journal of Management Education, 29*(2), 284-300.

King, Z. (2004). Career self-management: Its nature, causes and consequences. *Journal of Vocational Behavior, 65*(1), 112-133.

Lengnick-Hall, M. L., & Lengnick-Hall, C. A. (2003). HR's role in building relationship networks. *Academy of Management Executive, 17*(4), 53-63.

Leonard, D. (1998). *Wellsprings of knowledge: Building and sustaining the sources of innovation.* Boston: Harvard Business School Press.

Mayfield, M., Mayfield, J., & Lance, S. (2003). Human resource information systems: A review and model development. *Advances in Competitiveness Research, 11*(1), 139-152.

Murphy, K. R., & Cleveland, J. N. (1991). *Performance appraisal: An organizational perspective.* Boston: Allyn & Bacon.

Nonaka, I., & Takeuchi, H. (1995). *The knowledge-creating company.* New York: Oxford University Press.

Osterman, P. (1987). Choice of employment systems in internal labor markets. *Industrial Relations, 26*(1), 46-67.

Ouchi, W. G. (1981). *Theory Z.* Reading, MA: Addison Wesley.

Parker, P., & Inkson, K. (1999). New forms of career: The challenge to human resource management. *Asia-Pacific Journal of Human Resources, 37*(1), 67-76.

Peiperl, M. A., & Baruch, Y. (1997). Back to square zero: The post-corporate career. *Organizational Dynamics, 25*(4), 7-22.

Porter, M. E. (1985). *Competitive advantage: Creating and sustaining superior performance.* New York: Free Press.

Rothwell, W. J. (1994). *Effective succession planning: Ensuring leadership continuity and building talent from within.* Saranac Lake, NY: AMACOM.

Rousseau, D. M. (1995). *Psychological contracts in organizations: Understanding written and unwritten agreements.* Thousand Oaks, CA: Sage.

Saxenian, A.-L. (1996). Beyond boundaries: Open labor markets and learning in Silicon Valley. In M. B. Arthur & D. M. Rousseau (Eds.), *The boundaryless career: A new employment principle for a new organizational era* (pp. 23-39). New York: Oxford University Press.

Schein, E. H. (1978). *Career dynamics: Matching individual and organizational needs.* Reading, MA: Addison Wesley.

Schein, E. H. (1985). *Organizational culture and leadership.* San Francisco: Jossey-Bass.

Sonnenfeld, J. A. (1989). Career system profiles and strategic staffing. In M. B. Arthur, D. T. Hall, & B. S. Lawrence (Eds.), *Handbook of career theory* (pp. 202-224). Cambridge, UK: Cambridge University Press.

Sturges, J., Conway, N., Guest, D., & Liefooghe, A. (2005). Managing the career deal: The psychological contract as a framework for understanding career management, organizational commitment and work behavior. *Journal of Organizational Behavior, 26*(7), 821-838.

Sturges, J., Guest, D., Conway, N., & Mackenzie Davey, K. (2002). A longitudinal study of the relationship between career management and organizational commitment among graduates in the first ten years at work. *Journal of Organizational Behavior, 23*(6), 731-749.

Tucker, R., Moravec, M., & Ideus, K. (1992). Designing the dual career-track system. *Training and Development, 46*(6), 55-58.

Tyson, S., & Ward, P. (2004). The use of 360 degree feedback technique in the evaluation of management development. *Management Learning, 35*(2), 205-223.

Ulrich, D., & Lake, D. (1991). Organizational capability: Creating competitive advantage. *Academy of Management Executive, 5*(1), 77-92.

Van der Heijden, B. I. J. M., & Nijhof, A. H. (2004). The value of subjectivity: Problems and prospects for 360-degree appraisal systems. *International Journal of Human Resource Management, 15*(3), 493-511.

Wanous, J. P. (1992). *Organizational entry: Recruitment, selection, orientation and socialization of newcomers* (2nd ed.). Reading, MA: Addison-Wesley.

Waterman, R. H., Waterman, J. A., & Collard, B. A. (1994). Toward a career resilient workforce. *Harvard Business Review, 72*(4), 87-95.

Weber, M. (1947). *The theory of social and economic organization.* New York: Free Press. (Original work published 1922)

Weick, K. E. (1996). Enactment and the boundaryless career: Organizing as we work. In M. B. Arthur & D. M. Rousseau (Eds.), *The boundaryless career: A new employment principle for a new organizational era* (pp. 40-57). New York: Oxford University Press.

Whitener, E. M. (2001). Do "high commitment" human resources practices affect employee commitment? A cross-level analysis using hierarchical linear modeling. *Journal of Management, 27*(5), 515-535.

CHAPTER 10

Careers as Stories

The Cocktail Waitress's Story

In the 1980s hit song "Don't You Want Me, Baby?" sung by the Human League, a man sings to his girlfriend about her career.

When he met her, 5 years previously, she was working as a waitress in a cocktail bar. He saw her potential to do better. He picked her out, shook her up, and turned her into something new. Now she was fabulously successful, the world at her feet. But don't forget, the man sings, that he was the one who made her, and if he wanted he could break her, too.

The woman replies by telling the same story back to him. The facts are the same, but the interpretation is different.

Yes, sings the woman, it is true that she once worked as a waitress in a cocktail bar. But even then she knew that she could do much better in her career and could do so either with or without the man's help. She has had a really good time with him over the 5 years and still loves him. But now she thinks it is time to leave him behind and live her life on her own.

One problem with careers (as with most social phenomena) is that, even when people agree on what happened, they seldom agree on what caused it.

In the previous case, the same career elicits two totally different stories. The man sees the woman's career as having been dramatically changed by his actions. His view suggests that powerful people can substantially influence the careers of others. When he says he turned the woman "into something new," we are reminded of George Bernard Shaw's play *Pygmalion* (1916), in which the powerful and knowledgeable mentor Professor Henry Higgins coaches working-class flower seller Eliza Doolittle into a great society lady. The story evokes myths and legends about sorcerers who can transform ordinary people.

Can other people turn our careers around in this way? Some of the material in Chapter 8 of this book (on careers as relationships) and in Chapter 9 (on careers as resources) suggest that sometimes people can. If so, the implied career strategy for those seeking success would be to play a "political" game, to seek influential and skillful mentors and advisors and to entrust one's career to superior knowledge and networks (Weatherly & Beach, 1994). The career model in this case dictates that it's whom you know, not what you know, that counts, and to get ahead, you must "oil the wheels."

In contrast, the woman in the Human League song apparently thinks that her career success was mainly a matter of her own talent, self-belief, and personal action. She clearly believes in self-motivation and self-management as a means of career advancement. Moreover, she thinks that she can continue in her success on her own—in fact, she has reached the stage where she feels that her relationship with her mentor may be counterproductive and best severed. In the story, as she tells us about herself, she reminds us of Madonna's career, which we reviewed in Chapter 4—the loner who succeeds on the basis of raw ability, determination, and perseverance, though Madonna also used networks of influential people. Legends of heroism involve similar individualism and proactive action. The career model might involve phrases such as "believe in yourself" and "you can pull yourself up by your own bootstraps."

Who is right about the cocktail waitress's career—the man or the woman? It could be either. It could be both. It could be neither—perhaps her success was a matter of pure luck. What we see in this illustration is a career story—or rather two different stories about the same career, each with its own hero or heroine, plot line, and dramatic sequence. With all our understanding of career dynamics, we are unable to say that one of the stories is right and the other one wrong.

Suppose, then, that there is no ultimate "truth" about any individual career—that careers are no more or less than the stories we tell about them and that every story has its own validity.

Storytelling

Consider this career story, told by Catherine to me some years ago.

Catherine's Story

Catherine completed her undergraduate degree with a specialization in accounting, and continued directly to MBA studies to broaden her credentials. She spent a year as a financial analyst and then moved on to a banking job. She earned her professional accountant's accreditation but realized early on that she wanted to "escape accounting." A positive experience doing part-time tutoring in marketing led her to explore the academic

(Continued)

(Continued)

job market. Soon she secured a lecturer position at an institution that was rapidly expanding its business programs. Here she learned the theory of marketing ("like being a student again"). Being "thrown in at the deep end," she developed skills of teaching and course organization, and built up her self-confidence. She also developed practical marketing expertise by working on her institution's own marketing of its academic programs. But after four years she was told, "you won't get tenure until you do some research." Feeling let down after years of hard work, Catherine started to think about her career choices. She decided that she was in danger of being "branded an academic" and that, although she loved teaching, "I'd be more credible if I had practical experience."

Through a consultant, Catherine secured a job with a major telecommunications company, and stayed four years. She moved through four jobs, learning market segmentation and analysis in the first, strategic marketing in the second, advertising and promotion in the third, and pricing and product management in the fourth. These moves involved three relocations: one against the wishes of her boss, because "you had to be in [head office] if you wanted to be involved in the

implementation of plans"; one because "I was beginning to get sucked more into the accounting side" instead of more "hands on, producing materials" experience; and once when her husband was relocated and she persuaded the company to relocate her as well.

Next, frustrated because she was not continuing to learn in her fourth company job, and feeling that "I was not going to be stuck in telecommunications," Catherine saw a newspaper advertisement for a job as marketing manager of a travel company. She got the job, and for the first time had the experience of managing staff and working across the breadth of the marketing function. "Market research, writing a marketing plan, training up the branches, doing promotions, window displays, everything to do with marketing I had a dabble in. Great experience!" After a year, however, frustrated by a new boss, who "doesn't have a computer on his desk and doesn't practise management and knows nothing about marketing," and pregnant with her first baby, Catherine left her job to take some time off and consider the further development of her career.

Source: From Arthur, Inkson, & Pringle (1999, pp. 22–23, reprinted with permission).

The case is a summary of the career story that Catherine told me late in 1995 in her home in Auckland, New Zealand, as my colleagues and I conducted interviews to collect the career stories for our book *The New Careers* (Arthur, Inkson, & Pringle, 1999). The story took 1.5 hours for Catherine to tell, and this version—reproduced exactly as it appeared in 1999—is only a summary of the key features.

I like Catherine's story because it has so many interesting career lessons for us to learn: how Catherine set out to lose her stereotype and follow her true interests, how she used her employment at a teaching institution as a personal resource for the learning of theory and practice, how she rotated specialist jobs in a single organization to build all-around expertise, and how she used constant early-career mobility to progress into management. But what about Catherine's loyalty, or lack of it, to her various employers? Catherine's story provides good role modeling and an interesting basis for discussions about careers. It also covers both the objective career—the moves that Catherine made and the jobs that she held—and the subjective career—what she thought and felt about it, as conveyed particularly by her direct quotes (Chapter 1).

Much as I liked Catherine's story, I enjoyed the process of being told it even more. Catherine's vocal expressions and body language added to the impression of a woman who was in charge of her life, striving to make sense of it in her mind and eager to figure out the next stage. She brought energy to the tale. I remember that when I initially mistook her comment "branded an academic" for "brain-dead academic," I felt slightly offended, being an academic myself. Because I was there and heard the whole story, in Catherine's words, it impressed me more than would, perhaps, the flat print version given here. I even went back 5 years later to find out how the story had turned out. Catherine was still at home with her children but was continuing to cultivate her career through a small home-based business and distance teaching in marketing: more learning for the future.

Storytelling is a fundamental human activity (Polkinghorne, 1988). Children who tell their families stories about that day's basketball game, shoppers recounting to friends the altercations between them and cashiers, job applicants explaining to interviewers their reasons for leaving previous jobs—all of these people are storytellers. Stand-up comedians and barroom bores tell funny stories. Short story writers, biographers, and novelists use the written word to become professional storytellers. And listening to or reading stories and then responding to them are key parts of the process.

When we talk about our careers, we tell stories about ourselves. For example, every time we leave a job, get a new job, or experience a career crisis, there is a story to tell, an account of what happened. Such incidents are, as it were, chapters in a book, and each book is the story of a life, and it is not finished until the person dies. Any career is essentially a story.

In my 15 years as a researcher of careers, I have asked many people to tell me their career stories. In some cases, my request was a formal part of a research investigation; in other cases, it was driven by sociability and curiosity: "I'm interested in careers—can you tell me about your career?" The responses are interesting. The most common one is, "Oh, you don't want to hear about my career—my career is kind of strange," or even, "Sorry, I don't have a career." This is because many people have a different definition of *career* than I have: They tend to believe that a career should follow a predictable, continuous, linear story line, as occupational and organizational careers do, and that their own work history is somehow too complicated and discontinuous to be a real career. The viewpoint of this book, in contrast, is that everyone has a career (see Chapter 1) but that nowadays, as shown elsewhere in the book, discontinuous careers are the norm and continuous careers are unusual.

In the end, most people I ask do tell me their career stories, and it seems to me that they invariably enjoy doing so. Something about careers is personal and intimate: Sharing one's career story with someone else is not threatening, as sharing information about, say, one's personal relationships, religion, politics, or finances might be. In addition, as we shall see, telling one's career story often helps to make sense of one's career (Cohen & Mallon, 2001). People say things like, "That's interesting—I'm beginning to understand myself better now."

In a variation of the exercise, I ask my students, as an assignment, to elicit a career story from an older person, usually one of their parents; to write it down; and to try to analyze it using theoretical frameworks such as those in this book. (This is essentially the exercise recommended in the introduction to this book and reinforced at the end of each chapter.) The stories the students write for me are frequently inspiring—people go through such difficulties in their careers and do such amazing things. I am constantly in awe. Many students have told me that listening to their father's or mother's career story was a great experience for them, too. Frequently, it was the first time they had heard the story. Frequently, it led them to a new understanding of their parents or of their parents' own childhood (e.g., "So that's why Dad was always so angry!"). For female students, it is frequently shocking (but enlightening) for them to hear the barriers of gender discrimination that their mothers faced when trying to pursue their early careers. In some cases, students report that understanding their parents' careers in this way helped draw them closer to their parents.

Career storytelling and the recording and analysis of the stories are also major methods in career research, and stories are a major source of understanding about how careers work. Many of the theories in this book are based on research studies in which researchers assembled empirical information about careers by recording the stories of research participants and clients. Of course, this is not universal: Some researchers endeavor to make sense of careers by other methods—for example, by administering tests and questionnaires assessing variables such as career interests, job characteristics, mentor behavior, career indecision, and career satisfaction and using statistical techniques to measure the relationships between them, and draw general conclusions about career dynamics. This kind of work has advantages of orderliness, generalizability, and efficiency but may miss out on the authenticity of stories.

In my view, career storytelling is usually good, both for the teller and for the listener. Storytelling is also increasingly recognized as a potentially valuable means of eliciting data to developing career theory (e.g., Young & Valach, 2000), offer informed criticism of conventional career thinking and practice (e.g., El-Sawad, 2005), and develop new paradigms of career guidance (e.g., Cochran, 1997; see also Chapter 12 of this book). But why are stories so important to us? What do they do for us? If we think about our careers as stories, how does that help us to understand them or find direction in them?

Stories

A story may be worth the telling, both for itself and for the meaning we attach to it. Consider the following stories.

Getting Into Engineering

How do people decide to become engineers? Here are summaries of four true stories told by four engineers about their choice.

Linda Katehi, living on the Greek island of Salamis in 1966 and 12 years old, had her imagination caught by the sight, on the television in a neighbor's house, of Neil Armstrong, the first man to walk on the moon. But the shots of mission control in Houston, its rows of lights and screens, gripped her even more than those of Armstrong. Although a math teacher helped her, her father told her that if she were an engineer, no one would hire her and no one would marry her. By 1984, she was doctorally qualified.

Wallace Fowler grew up in Greenville, Texas, crazy about airplanes. He knew the specifications of every plane and could tell which engine a B36 had by the sound it made. At that stage, he wanted to be a test pilot. However, health problems prevented that, and he obtained a math degree and became a computer programmer instead. To help him communicate some of his programming analysis to engineers, he took an engineering course. Eventually, he studied engineering at graduate school and later became a top aircraft and aerospace engineering professor.

Janie Foulke grew up on a farm in North Carolina and out of sheer necessity learned to fix things. When she was 9 years old, she received a chemistry set as a Christmas present. When it proved too messy for her bedroom, her father built her a laboratory in an outbuilding. The next year her present was a dissecting kit. Marriage and children interfered with her ambition to go to medical school, but in due course she took a graduate course in medical engineering—a first step to a career in research.

James Melsa's talent for math and science was noticed by his class teacher in Nebraska. The teacher was a science fiction fan and lent him sci-fi books, which caught the boy's imagination and convinced him that he belonged in the laboratory. Afraid that pure science might not bring him the saleable skills of electrical engineering, James enrolled for the latter. Then, in his first job after graduation, he found out that his neighbor was a professor of electrical engineering. James enrolled in his course and so impressed the professor that an academic job quickly followed.

Source: Grose (2005).

What can we conclude, from these four cases, about becoming an engineer? There are some common factors that several stories share: The engineers had built-in interests, childhood experiences, fortunate chances, and parental and teacher support. On the other hand, each story is unique, and each might inspire different people. In presenting the stories, Grose (2005), the storyteller who reconfigured the stories told to him by the engineers, did not try to draw lessons. He simply told the stories, in much greater detail than they are presented here, and allowed the narratives to speak for themselves.

In contrast, Valkevaara (2002), seeking to understand the careers of human resource development (HRD) professionals, found (from a detailed analysis of the career stories with contrasted patterns of objective career) that all revealed "a similar emphasis on the centrality of people, a personal style as a working tool, and understanding of learning as the cornerstones of professional expertise in the practice of HRD" (p. 183). Valkevaara therefore used stories to try to interpret general features common to HRD careers. Similarly, Broadbridge (2004) examined stories from male and female retail managers and noted that men were more likely than women to construct career success narratives involving self-promotion. Whether we consider stories individually or collectively, we tend to interpret meanings from them.

The growing interest in stories as a means of understanding is part of two theoretical movements labeled constructivism and social constructionism (Blustein, Kenna, Murphy, DeVoy, & DeWine, 2005; Cohen, Duberley, & Mallon, 2004; Young & Collin, 2004). With both theories, people's actions are based on their own personal view of the world, and they go through a personal process of constructing knowledge on the basis of their experiences. In constructivism, the emphasis is on the internal processes through which people learn, whereas in social constructionism the creation of individual reality is considered more of a social process, in which views are shaped by shared experiences, such as those presented in the mass media.

Social scientists have begun to take an increasing interest in the process of narrative, which can loosely be defined as storytelling. As people experience things, and tell stories about their experiences, they also construct their personal realities and views of the world. Although careers contain good stories and make good stories in their own right, the use of narrative is far from being confined to career studies. For example, organization theorists observe that we can gain a rich understanding of organizations by the stories that members tell about their experiences in the organizations (Boje, 1991), and indeed we can use stories to determine organizations' strategic changes (Dunford & Jones, 2000).

At the same time, there is strong interest in learning from existing narratives in the public domain—for example, books, short stories, plays, biographies, autobiographies, and television programs—by analyzing their discourse and looking for the underlying messages (Gabriel, 2000). As an example, Sparkes (2004) analyzed the autobiography of cyclist Lance Armstrong, who recovered from cancer to become a multiple Tour de France winner, in terms of a series of narratives including a cyborg narrative, a restitution narrative, and a quest narrative.

Narrative is "a written or spoken account of connected events in order of happening" (Allen, 1990, p. 788). The notions of *connectedness* and *order of happening* are important here because they provide the essential structuring on which stories depend for their functions in relation to career. "When people punctuate their own living into stories, they impose a formal coherence on what would otherwise be a flowing soup" (Weick, 1995, p. 128). Narrative involves *temporality* (how events are related in time) and *causality* (how events cause each other). But the time involved is subjective, rather than clock measured, and the causality is subjective and loose, rather than rational and precise (Gibson, 2004).

According to Polkinghorne (1988), we use narrative to give meaning to our experiences, to join incidents together in coherent wholes, and to understand past events and plan future ones. Narrative is, says Polkinghorne, "the primary scheme by means of which human life is made meaningful" (p. 11). One might object that the psychological functions of concept formation and thinking are what enable meaning to be formulated, but these can be conceptualized as part of the narrative process. Even if we do not verbalize our narratives to others, we rehearse them to ourselves and thereby make sense of our lives.

For example, in the story "Harry's First Day" in Chapter 3, Harry recounts a series of events that happened to him on the first day of his new job, all of them centered around the theme of "doing things wrong—not fitting in." In the process of observing the events and putting them together as a story, Harry thus provides himself with a coherent understanding of his way of behaving in his new workplace. By telling the story to himself, he reinforces this understanding in his mind. He may now begin to project the story ahead to the next day as a means of seeking solutions to his predicament. If he tells the story to others, he may also be able to engage their sympathy and support. Career stories are typically told across a wider time span than 1 day, but the processes that we go through in telling our career stories are similar: We perceive and strengthen patterns in our careers and provide ourselves with the basis to project the story usefully ahead.

Stories are not necessarily told overtly. Their most important functions may be discharged when we tell them internally to ourselves:

> Individuals mentally structure the story of their own work life using the social structure provided by society's grand narrative of careers. The narrative frames people's stories of work and its consequences as they think about and take stock of their work lives. In addition to providing a commonsense framework, the grand story of career synchronizes individuals to their culture by telling them in advance how their work lives should proceed and prompting them to stay on schedule. (Savickas, 2005, p. 49)

Thus, noted Savickas (2005), we implicitly compare our own career story with other great narratives of our time—the progress story of the American Dream and the new narratives of greater social justice, new flexible work organizations and globalization that ensure that "the grand narrative changes from stability to mobility" (p. 50). Savickas thus brought in personal story as a key element and societal story as a key context for his overarching theory of career construction (Chapters 3 and 4).

Functions of Career Stories

A career story is a personal moving perspective on our working life, including the objective facts and the subjective emotions, attitudes, and goals of our careers. We create stories retrospectively as a means of determining and explaining the meaning of day-to-day events.

Whereas some conceptions of career, particularly the "fit" approach (Chapter 5), rely on a relatively static conceptualization in terms of understanding where people are, a narrative approach enables us to get a sense of how people got to where they are and how they understand their situation. In this view, careers are "less about positions and professions and more about the fashioning of identity over time, through enacted narrative" (Gibson, 2004, p. 178). Thus, the narrative approach explicitly accords the subjective career primacy over the objective. According to an increasing number of theorists and researchers of careers and other social phenomena, the stories that people tell "can illuminate the ways in which individuals make sense of their careers as they unfold through time and space" (Cohen & Mallon, 2001, p. 48). Some go further, insisting that "our own existence cannot be separated from the account we give of ourselves . . . it is in telling our own stories that we give ourselves an identity" (Ricoeur, 1985, p. 214).

Identity

As indicated in Chapter 7, identity represents a person's sense of individuality and personality—who he or she is. Identity can be conceptualized as being embodied in the stories we tell about ourselves. In Chapter 7, I provided the example of Sara Ford, who identified herself as a mathematician rather than a software tester or organization member. According to narrative theory, Sara arrived at that conclusion by observing, narrating, and interpreting her own experiences. Identity construction "implies a telling of the self that synthesizes a number of the elements in a way that shows their coherence and unity" (Bujold, 2004, p. 473). Identity may be a personal myth (McAdams, 1995), but it is one that we constantly feed through the stories we create and tell about ourselves. Writing one's story is not a statement of the objective truth about oneself but an interpretation of the self based on multiple experiences (Peavy, 1998). And, if variation of identity is needed, we can use stories to reinvent ourselves.

A critique of today's flexible, dynamic society (Castells, 1996), with its contingent work, portfolio careers, improvisation, multiple roles, transactional contracts, and multiskilled workforces, is that it potentially fragments our sense of self (Sennett, 1998). In the multiplicity of our new identities, our core identity may be lost. "The emerging context may not be able to sustain the kinds of continuing and coherent identities that had been generated in the more stable conditions of the past" (Collin, 2000, p. 171). Young and Collin (2000) went so far as to suggest that we may be witnessing the demise or death of careers as the continuous entities we have hitherto assumed them to be and asked "whether career experiences . . . can [now] be expected to be increasingly discontinuous" (p. 9). In all of this confusion, perhaps the narrative process (i.e., storytelling) provides us with the opportunity to find coherence in the midst of complexity, and continuity in the midst of discontinuity.

Meaning

In the process of articulating a story, we develop our own meanings and interpretations of events. We reinforce these interpretations by listening to ourselves. The story also enables listeners, such as spouses, colleagues, employers, and counselors, to make their own interpretations and reach their own conclusions so that narrative construction is followed by narrative criticism (Cochran, 1990). Understanding the overall meaning of a career may thus enable a listener to grasp the issues relevant to a career decision by understanding the meanings of the story, of which that decision is part (Bujold, 2004; Cochran, 1991).

A story needs a theme, a plot, and a way of arranging the characters and events so that the relationships between them are seen. Ibarra and Lineback (2005) suggested that good stories have key characteristics: a protagonist, or main character, the listener cares about; a background situation requiring the protagonist to take action; trials and tribulations as obstacles appear in the protagonist's path; a turning point when things must change; and a resolution of triumphant success or tragic failure. These elements are all present in Brenda's career story.

A "Walking Out" Story

Brenda was a prison officer for 20 years. With limited education and training and having entered the job only because it was secure and better paying than the alternatives available at the time, Brenda had little early ambition. But as time went by and her skills developed, she began to see possibilities for eventual advancement to managerial ranks. The organization was bureaucratic, and there was a prescribed career path laid out in terms of different types of job experience and off-the-job study. Brenda began preparing herself for the job of prison superintendent. This involved many hours of study in addition to her full-time job. Also, because of her interest in her work, she took leave at one point to go to a university in another city, where she earned a degree in criminology. After many years of study, including a major assessment center evaluation (see Chapter 9) that lasted several days, she reached a point where she had only one more course to pass to be able to be considered for superintendent. But at that point, the prison service announced a major restructuring. Brenda was called to a one-to-one meeting with a consultant to explain the effects of the restructuring. Calmly, the consultant explained that Brenda's job was unaffected but that the new structure had abolished many superintendent jobs. In addition the training and development program that Brenda underwent had been deemed obsolete and scrapped; hence, if Brenda wanted to be qualified to become a superintendent, she would have to start again. Furious, Brenda glared at the consultant and then said, deliberately, "I'll tell you what you can do with your job!" Then, she walked out. At that point, she had absolutely no idea what she would do next. But she knew she would never go back. And she felt exultant.

Retrospective Sense Making

Because of the length of careers, much of the meaning we make about them is retrospective. According to Weick (1996), careers consist of "improvised work experiences which rise prospectively into fragments and fall retrospectively into patterns" (p. 40).

Stories help us to impose these patterns. In developing narratives of our lives, we have the benefit of hindsight. We know what we want in the present, and that guides us retrospectively in our search for a plausible story (Weick, 1995). Our subjective view of our career, say, 10 years ago, is no longer available to us, so we try to remember it: "I left university early because. . . ." But the events and feelings of 10 years ago have to fit into a story that is coherent over a long period. For example, one man I know, who is in his 50s, blames his career adversity on his father's decision to withdraw him from high school at age 15 years and put him into an apprenticeship. This plot line provides a high degree of coherence to his ongoing career narrative.

With the benefit of hindsight, and faced with the common social expectation that a career should have some sort of pattern or plan behind it, we can perhaps make more sense of our careers later than we could when we were experiencing them. For example, "most of us have had the experience of looking back through our chaotic lives and making sense of how all those funny things that have happened to us prepare us perfectly for whatever job it is that we have applied for" (Sims, 2002).

Creating the Future

The characteristics of narrative include its sequencing over time. By interpreting the past, we use narrative to make sense of the present and thereby see a way to the future. Career narratives don't end, or at least they don't end until our careers end. When we narrate our careers, we must constantly reconfigure the story to take account of new events. The story line from the past, however, typically provides a strong framework in which present events can be understood and may even give direction for the future. According to Sims (2002), "we would expect people to tell themselves and their careers as a story, and perhaps to create story lines which they then live out. [There are] things that people need to do in order for their stories to be satisfactory as narratives." Sims emphasizes the need, in job interviews, for us to be able to tell convincing stories about our futures in the employing organization.

Individual Behavior or Social Context?

Discourses about career, at least in Western society, tend to view career as an individualized project (career as action or agency; see Chapter 4). Individual ego involvement in the career story may occasionally lead to the career being presented as a personal project independent of external influences. On the other hand, most people are keenly aware of the role of external influences in the story and tell their stories in terms of interactions between themselves and their environments.

For example, many accounts of career include stories about cultural and organizational obstacles encountered and sometimes overcome in pursuit of career goals. People tell tales of how they initially failed because they were from "the wrong side of the tracks" or how they followed bad advice from teachers or how they were laid off by an inhumane organization or how the constant pressure to achieve resulted in stress and illness. These accounts typically do not simply explain a personal event; they also provide a commentary on the contexts in which the career was conducted. Authors such as Marshall (1995) and Cohen et al. (2004) used career stories told by women in "male" occupations, such as those in management and science, to create critical commentaries on the organizations involved. Like the Chicago School (Chapter 7), these writers asserted that through the analysis of career narratives we can "access the parts [of career] that other approaches cannot reach" (Cohen et al., 2004, p. 407) and thereby gain an appreciation of society that goes far beyond the careers of individuals.

Stories and Reality

What about the issue of truth? Does it matter that any event, or indeed any career, can yield many different stories to describe it? "The narrative is not a reproduction of events but a construction that the [story]teller thinks the other should know about" (Young, Valach, & Collin, 2002, p. 219). Narrative is essentially creative (Bujold, 2004). Consider how the events of a single career can result in quite different career stories.

One Career, Two Stories

Wendy: My career? Not much to tell, really. I was a high school dropout. I bummed around for a few years, waitressing work mainly. I had a job in a circus once. I was young, sowing my wild oats. And great experience. When you sleep rough for a few months, you really learn how to look after yourself. I always knew I'd get it right. I planned for it. When I was 20 years old, I started going to night school. Then I went back home for full-time study. By the time I was 25, I had my degree, a business qualification. My grades weren't great, but it's what you can do, what you can talk yourself into that counts. So, I got taken on as a trainee manager by Gracefield Manufacturing. I did a couple of projects for them, organizational development, marketing, lots of fun. I built connections. The company is OK but not very exciting. I've stuck it out for 5 years, but I'm looking around. I can do much, much better.

Wendy's mother: Wendy's career? You don't want to know! A nightmare. She was trouble in school, expelled for disruptive behavior at 15. We did our best for her, but she walked away from home at 16, never worked much. She got into bad company and was in trouble with the police. There were drugs, thefts, probably worse. We bailed her out all the time, but she still spent time in jail when she was about 19. In the end, the only way we could get her out of her way of life was to buy her the best psychotherapy we could get. It cost us tens of thousands, but it seemed to settle her a bit, and she met her boyfriend, Gary, who was a real stabilizing influence. Even so, she was pretty well unemployable until Jim Gracefield, a family friend, agreed to take her on, as a favor, in low-level accounts work and tea making. Gary more or less forced her to go to community college, and eventually she got some kind of diploma. And she's stayed out of trouble and stayed with Gary. But I don't think Jim Gracefield sees much future for her, so I only hope she can hold on to her job. We've looked after her so far, but we can't look after her forever.

One career, two stories. No doubt Jim Gracefield, Gary, Wendy's father, and Wendy's friends would tell different stories about Wendy's career. So what is the truth about the career? Is there a single truth? Are Wendy and her mother even telling the truth as they see it? Could the self-confident, ambitious young woman and the anxious, pessimistic mother both be right or both be wrong? Perhaps Wendy's career is no more than the tales people tell about it. And if that is true of Wendy's career, is it not true for all careers?

Stories are always interpretations, and the same events yield different stories that are given different interpretations by different storytellers. An example was the different accounts of 2004 U.S. presidential candidate John Kerry's military career in Vietnam. By the Kerry campaign's account, Kerry was a brave, medal-winning war hero; however, according to the Swift Boat Veterans, Kerry told false stories about his service to further his political career. In the absence of definitive evidence, which account does one believe? The answer may depend on one's political persuasions. Storytellers can choose and embellish their stories to suit their own purposes, and listeners can choose which story to believe.

This book is full of career stories, several per chapter. A few are summarized from publicly available sources, such as Web sites and biographies. But Internet writers and biographers have their own point of view. Most of the stories were based on interviews with the person concerned with little other checking, but people tend to put their own gloss on their own careers. In a few cases, I amalgamated different career stories to make the point or altered details to protect anonymity. All of these stories are therefore authentic, but not every last word in them is true. Every story in the book is included for the purpose of illustrating a career principle, such as inheritance, cycles, or the problems of a particular form of career. I massaged the stories to make the point as effectively as I could—I didn't change the stories, but I chose which parts of them to put in and to emphasize.

None of the stories, therefore, is a pure, objective, unembellished account of the career it represents. Perhaps no such thing as a "pure" career story exists. Is there a single absolutely true account of your career? You might like to think your resume is the plain unvarnished truth about you, but, if you're honest, isn't it really a sales promotion document? Certainly plenty of advice exists about how to tell this particular story: what employers want to see and how to say it (Bright & Earl, 2006). Academics who have professional expertise, for example, frequently have more than one resume available: an "academic" one denoting research and teaching to impress university people and a "professional" one containing claims of successful practice and consultancy assignments, which professional practitioners will value. Sims (2002) suggested that job candidates typically smooth out their career stories so that sudden discontinuities that might seem to denote unreliability or whim instead appear to listeners to be gradual character development and change.

According to Linde (1993), we typically keep several stories going at once. The value of stories is not that they convey absolute facts or truths about the world but that (1) they enable us to understand the world better and to learn from other people's understanding of it and (2) they enable us to find alternative explanations that suit our circumstances.

Public Stories

Although one person cannot experience directly what another experiences, the story enables "its sense, its meaning, to become public" (Ricoeur, 1985, p. 16). Once the story is told, it is out there for others to listen to and learn from. Relatives, friends, coworkers, and others tell their own stories and invite imitation.

Institutions such as employing organizations and professional associations present us with scripts (see Chapter 7) for our career stories to follow. Young and Valach (2004) are among the writers emphasizing the importance of social interaction in enabling us, or even inducing us, to develop narratives in sympathy with our social contexts. Sims (2002) noted that the prospective stories that we imagine into our futures and communicate to prospective employers are based on role models we have observed and dramas—often fictional—we have seen on television or film. Cultural images in the media and elsewhere impinge on consciousness. What do we learn about careers from these public stories?

In many career stories, the storyteller is also the hero, and the story takes an epic form. Great epics such as *The Odyssey* present what is considered to be an absolute, objective story in which storyteller and audience share a single view of the world. Osland (1995), in her account of the stories of expatriates living and working far from their home country, used the epic form of the hero's adventure (Campbell, 1968), in which career heroes travel from safe havens to unknown and dangerous places, pursue challenging goals, face great obstacles, receive help from strange sources, fight battles, and return home "the masters of two worlds instead of one" (Osland, 1995, p. 152). Similarly, ordinary people telling the stories of their careers may find meaning and reassurance by representing themselves as the heroes of their own career epics. Collin (2000) noted, however, that the epic form of story is underpinned by the idea of pattern and destiny and therefore tends to the view that a career should involve progression and destination (or, in the terms of the epic, destiny).

The related imagery of career is often competitive, with would-be heroes striving to become career winners. Hansen (2004) documented how the establishment of leading figures in medical research, such as Louis Pasteur, within the pantheon of early 20th-century comic-book heroes, "successfully conveyed both values and information while telling a good story" (p. 148). Mattuozzi (2002) showed how, even in the 1920s, the career of polar explorer Richard Byrd was significantly affected by the ballyhoo of the media and was "sold" as heroism, a commodity lapped up by a credulous public. Not every worker has such aspirations, and not every career fits such a pattern, but the imagery of the epic, the hero, and winning is attractive. Retrospective sensemaking doubtless enables many people in disorderly and mundane careers to project themselves into stories of heroism and destiny.

In contrast to the epics of the past, the modern novel focuses on the evolving realities of its characters and the tension between their inner consciousness and outward action. There is no single viewpoint shared by characters or by author and audience—each makes his or her own interpretation (Collin, 2000). According to Collin, "the traditional career, loosely interpreted as linear, upward, focused and masculine, [is] like the epic, whereas the increasingly open-ended career of today [is] like the novel" (p. 165). Collin also noted that there is an intermediate category, modern epic, in which the notion of final destiny is replaced by that of perpetual exploration and revitalization, that of linear time by the interweaving of times and places, and that of a single world-view by multiple reflections. That is, she says, "an even more effective analogy for the fragmented, diverse, open-ended career of today" (p. 165).

Stories may be contrasted with scripts—institutionally determined sequences of role behavior, such as an organization's view of loyalty or society's view of appropriate jobs for women (Barley, 1989; Gioia & Poole, 1984; Martin, 1982; see also Chapter 7). Scripts are a means whereby powerful institutions predetermine individuals' career stories by writing them in advance, in corporate hype or in reassurances to insecure employees. But such scripts may be untrustworthy. Arthur Miller's (1968) play *Death of a Salesman* catalogs the collapse of the career of the fictional (but all too real) Willy Loman as he is discarded "like an empty orange peel" once his productive years in the workforce are over: The scripts that Willy knows and built his life around, scripts of individual enterprise and collective loyalty, are exposed as cruel fictions. In keeping with the time-honored role of the rebel in fiction, many career stories are about people's refusal to allow themselves to be dominated by others' scripts.

Stories and Rhetoric

Stories and scripts both involve rhetoric—language designed to impress and persuade. Even apparently commonplace discourses—for example, "What about a career in banking?" or "This company could be your career"—are scripts and can be classed as rhetorical to the extent that they provide (occupational or organizational or boundaryless) models of what careers should look like. In the attempt to socialize workers to appropriate organizational behavior, organizations offer desirable images of career success (Derr, 1986), which influence career conceptualization and planning. For example, Sonnenfeld (2002) used the biographies of famous people to develop a recipe for creative resilience and the mastery of career adversity.

The mass media present images such as blockbuster films, professional sports events, and career tournaments such as *American Idol* and *Big Brother* in which the strong and talented dominate and the weaker are gradually eliminated. These presentations send the following message: "It's a tough world, but anyone with talent, self-belief, and persistence can succeed." Some individuals seek to emulate such scripts in the stories they create and those they tell. This rhetoric also provides validation for careers in which people display and practice their individualism in a mass society (Collin, 2000). But it is worth remembering that a rhetorical story is only one way to tell a story. Jack's case provides an example.

Jack and the Bean Counters

Jack Welch rose from humble origins to become the chief executive officer (CEO) of General Electric, a position he held from 1980 to 2000. He became legendary for his tough, informal, no-nonsense management style; his ability to reduce hard-bitten executives to tears in his relentless quest for performance; and his "invention" of the boundaryless organization (Ashkenas, Ulrich, Jick, & Kerr, 1995). In 2001, Welch published his autobiography, *Jack.*

Welch's career story, as told in his book, is a piece of unremitting rhetoric and was critiqued by two British academics, Kathryn Haynes and Patrick Reedy, in a 2002 article.

Welch's autobiography portrays his life as a self-directed journey toward a clear success goal. Welch tells stories of his working-class parents' beliefs in competition, goal setting, hard work, commitment, and ambition, and he also tells stories about obstacles overcome in his early career to get a foothold on the managerial ladder. He was physically unimposing and had health problems, but his willpower kept him going. He was tough, blunt, independent, and totally self-confident. He never thought outside the corporate frame and never doubted himself, changed his mind, or displayed weakness. He was "Jack the Giant Killer," defeating bureaucracy and poor performance, firing those who couldn't keep up. He was a workaholic obsessed with the corporate hierarchy, and, if judged by his own story, he had no personal life to speak of—his family was present in his story only to celebrate his success. He was, it seems, stupendously successful, but his story is linear, one-dimensional, and boring.

Haynes and Reedy (2002) compared Welch's story with the career narratives provided to them by two accountants (bean counters), both women, as a way of showing that career stories can be quite different in the way they frame individual identity. Unlike Jack, the accountants had no sense of destiny and no career plan; instead, they struggled and compromised as best they could among the competing tides and eddies of personal drift and indecision, boredom, performance standards, desire for approval, overwork, professional requirements, company practice, maternity, coping, and professional identity. They climbed onto the roller coaster of professional practice and found that it was propelling them faster than they wanted to go and was hard to control. They lacked Jack's (or Jack's rhetoric's) focus and looked for nonwork satisfactions. They felt different possible identities, whereas Jack remained "Jack."

The authors concluded that even conflicting and uncertain multiple identities may be preferable to the total simplicity of the "Jack" narrative. I prefer to believe that no one is as straightforward and consistent as Jack, and certainly no one's career is as straightforward and consistent as Jack's; in this instance, rhetoric may have been allowed to swamp reality. Most of us, I think, would empathize with the bean counters and find Jack an improbable vision. We need to beware the "false gold" of rhetorical oversimplification.

Source: Haynes & Reedy (2002).

In the 1980s, Gowler and Legge (1989) noted a rhetoric of managerial careers in bureaucratic organizations: Managerial careers were extolled, whereas nonmanagerial careers were represented as commodities. In the 1990s, Hirsch and Shanley

(1996) railed against "the rhetoric of boundaryless": the popularization of stories and discourse presenting the new dejobbed workplace as offering flexibility and autonomy to workers (Bridges, 1994), when in fact it contained the seeds of insecurity, job loss, and marginalization. The new career rhetorics are about autonomy, flexibility, and self-determination, but they are also about constructing career narratives alone, in terms of one's own standards, because shared standards no longer exist (Collin, 2000).

Facilitating Career Change

Career narratives are not only the embodiment of a new theory of careers but also important tools for professional career counselors to use in facilitating career change (e.g., Bujold, 2004; Cochran, 1997; Peavy, 1998).

It lies beyond the scope of this chapter to consider the use of narrative in career counseling—that will be covered by Mary McMahon in Chapter 12—but here we may note that even without a professional facilitator individuals may use narrative processes to transform or reinvent themselves, as the experiences of those who make a habit of keeping narrative diaries can testify.

Perhaps emplotment—that is, casting oneself as the main character in a productive career narrative, a technique recommended by Cochran (1997) in career counseling—can be practiced by the individual. Here, the narrative process consists not just of rehearsing the past and making sense of it in the present but also of developing the meaning of the past in terms of a vision for the future and projecting it as an alternative future narrative (Young et al., 2002). For example, we can play out alternative stories in our own minds about what we might do if we got a new job. Here, narrative becomes narrated fantasy, but the fantasy is likely to connect to the story up until the present and may reveal important new meanings. Narrative may also have special importance immediately after a change, as the individual seeks to establish meaning and an identity that make sense of the story line created by the change (McAdams, Josselson, & Leiblich, 2001, cited in Bujold, 2004).

Stories may be particularly important when we are undergoing major career transitions—for example, changing organization or occupation or losing a job. And, as Cohen and Mallon (2001) pointed out, explaining a major transition may require knowledge of the whole story, the story of the entire career; otherwise the experience may be like walking in on the last scene of a movie.

Ibarra and Lineback (2005) noted that although most people can tell stories of a sort about what led to a change, the storytellers who most readily engage the sympathy of listeners (e.g., prospective employers) are those whose stories follow the classic form outlined earlier and who use the storyteller's tricks of emphasizing drama, tension, and change. As an example, Ibarra and Lineback describe the story of an information technology professional whose growing discontent with her job and desire to make a fresh start were triggered into action by three specific incidents: first, a positive experience at a conference of people in the occupation she was thinking of moving to; second, involvement in a "political" restructuring at her place of work; and third, a remark by her husband about how unhappy she was looking. Sequenced into a coherent story and told with enthusiasm, these elements could certainly provide a convincing drama for listeners.

Ibarra and Lineback (2005) suggested impression management (Chapter 8) techniques for storytelling—ways for you to tell your own stories to emphasize coherence, continuity, and causality to engage the minds and hearts of listeners, particularly those such as interviewers whom you want to convince of the logical continuation of your story in their organization. For example, in the story, you should make your motivation central and consistent and show evidence for it. You should also find a good plot line. The coming-of-age plot line, where a number of past instances in your life coalesce into a fundamental change, is a good example. So is the story told by Marie in a case in Chapter 9. Ibarra and Lineback also recommend cultivating multiple stories, or different versions of the same story, to be tailored to the interests of different listeners to whom the story is told. This, they say, is not a matter of deception or untruth but a matter of presentation. They even recommend practicing storytelling to friends and advisers.

Conclusion

As defined in the dictionary, the idea of *story* provides a wide range of ways that narrative can take place: "an account of imaginary or past events; a narrative, tale or anecdote"; "the past course of life of a person etc."; "the narrative or plot in a novel or play etc."; "facts or experiences that deserve narration"; "a fib or lie" (Allen, 1990, p. 1203). Stories thus extend to imaginative interpretation, creative fiction, and deliberate untruths. This chapter showed that career stories can take all these forms and that the consequences of paying attention to stories—even if they are personal interpretations or pieces of rhetoric—rather than seeking an ultimate "truth" about a career may well be beneficial. Indeed, telling our stories, getting others to tell their stories, and seeking to extend career stories into the future may be the most enjoyable and rewarding activities of all.

Key Points in This Chapter

- Storytelling is a universal, fundamental, and often very productive human experience.
- Accounts of careers typically contain good stories and are good stories. Many stories are worthwhile both in themselves and as a basis for thinking about careers and analyzing them.
- Career stories enable us to establish our identity, find meaning in what we do, make retrospective sense of our experience, and reflect on the future. They are therefore of value both to the storyteller and to listeners such as counselors.
- Stories tell us about both personal and contextual aspects of careers. They provide commentaries on external institutions affecting careers as well as personal experience.

- Any career story is only one possible version of the career it describes; stories involve subjectivity, personal interpretation, and personal purpose. A story cannot be expected to be a single unembellished truth. Stories strongly represent the subjective career.
- Career stories sometimes become public. Literature and the mass media often communicate images or archetypes of careers. These can be informative or misleading. Stories and other discourse about careers can be used as rhetoric to promote particular types of career.
- Being able to tell a good story is a fundamental element of major career change.

Questions From This Chapter

General Questions

1. Reflect on a story—not necessarily a career story—that someone recently told you about themselves. What did you think of the story? What did you learn about the person from the story?

2. If you had to tell someone a story about your career so far, what story would you tell? Write it down. What can you learn from the story in terms of your identity and the meaning of your career or work experiences?

3. Tell, or write, the story from Question 2 in two different ways: first, emphasize your own motivation, attitudes, and behavior; then, emphasize things in the external world that were important in the story, such as other people and organizations.

4. In evaluating what we hear about people's careers, is it possible to establish the truth?

5. Read a newspaper or magazine story about a celebrity's past career. Also read some job advertisements for high-level jobs. Think about what you have read in terms of the language and discourse used. What impression is the writer trying to make? How much do you believe what you are being told?

6. Imagine you are being interviewed for a job and the interviewer says, "Tell me the story of why you decided to move on from where you are?" What story would you tell? How would you make it effective?

Career Case Study Questions

1. Ask your case person to relate the story about one positive and one negative personal career incident. Invite the case person not to simply identify the incident but to explain exactly what happened in detail. What function do you think the story has for the person?

2. How would you summarize the story that the case person told you, using the various exercises in this book, as it relates the case person's entire career? Does the story suggest any "plot lines" running through to the future?

References

Allen, D. (Ed.). (1990). *Concise Oxford English dictionary.* Oxford, UK: Oxford University Press.

Arthur, M. B., Inkson, K., & Pringle, J. K. (1999). *The new careers: Individual action and economic change.* Thousand Oaks, CA: Sage.

Ashkenas, R., Ulrich, D., Jick, T., & Kerr, S. (1995). *The boundaryless organization: Breaking the chains of organizational structure.* San Francisco: Jossey-Bass.

Barley, S. R. (1989). Careers, identities and institutions: The legacy of the Chicago school of sociology. In M. B. Arthur, D. T. Hall, & B. Lawrence (Eds.), *Handbook of career theory* (pp. 41-65). Cambridge, UK: Cambridge University Press.

Blustein, D. L., Kenna, A. C., Murphy, K. A., DeVoy, J. E., & DeWine, D. B. (2005). Qualitative research and career development: Exploring the center and margins of discourse about careers. *Journal of Career Assessment, 13*(4), 351-370.

Boje, D. M. (1991). The storytelling organization: A study of storytelling in an office supply firm. *Administrative Science Quarterly, 36,* 106-126.

Bridges, W. (1994). *JobShift: How to prosper in a workplace without jobs.* Reading, MA: Addison-Wesley.

Bright, J., & Earl, J. (2005). *Amazing resumes: What employers want to see—And how to say it.* Indianapolis, IN: JIST Works.

Broadbridge, A. (2004). It's not what you know, it's who you know. *Journal of Management Development, 23*(5/6), 551-562.

Bujold, C. (2004). Constructing career through narrative. *Journal of Vocational Behavior, 64,* 470-484.

Campbell, J. (1968). *The hero with a thousand faces.* New York: Bollingen Foundation.

Castells, M. (1996). *The information age: Economy, society and culture. Vol. 1: The rise of the network society.* Malden, MA: Blackwell.

Cochran, L. (1990). Narrative as a paradigm for career research. In R. A. Young & W. A. Borgen (Eds.), *Methodological approaches to the study of career* (pp. 71-86). New York: Praeger.

Cochran, L. (1991). *Life-shaping decisions.* New York: Peter Lang.

Cochran, L. (1997). *Career counseling: A narrative approach.* Thousand Oaks, CA: Sage.

Cohen, L., Duberley, J., & Mallon, M. (2004). Social constructionism in the study of career: Accessing the parts that other approaches cannot reach. *Journal of Vocational Behavior, 64*(3), 407-422.

Cohen, L., & Mallon, M. (2001). My brilliant career: Using stories as a methodological tool in careers research. *International Studies of Management and Organization, 31*(3), 48-68.

Collin, A. (2000). Epic and novel: The rhetoric of career. In A. Collin & R. A. Young (Eds.), *The future of career* (pp. 163-177). Cambridge, UK: Cambridge University Press.

Derr, C. B. (1986). *Managing the new careerists.* San Francisco: Jossey-Bass.

Dunford, R., & Jones, D. (2000). Narrative in strategic change. *Human Relations, 53*(9), 1207-1226.

El-Sawad, A. (2005). Becoming a "lifer": Unlocking career thought through metaphor. *Journal of Occupational and Organizational Psychology, 78*(1), 23-32.

Gabriel, Y. (2000). *Storytelling in organizations.* Oxford, UK: Oxford University Press.

Gibson, P. (2004). Where to from here? A narrative approach to career counseling. *Career Development International, 9*(2), 176-189.

Gioia, D. A., & Poole, P. P. (1984). Scripts in organizational behavior. *Academy of Management Review, 9*(3), 449-459.

Gowler, D., & Legge, K. (1989). Rhetoric and boundaryless careers: Managing the meaning of management success. In M. B. Arthur, D. T. Hall, & B. S. Lawrence (Eds.), *Handbook of career theory* (pp. 437-453). Cambridge, UK: Cambridge University Press.

Grose, T. K. (2005). The mechanics of a career. *ASEE Prism, 14*(7), 24-29.

Hansen, B. (2004). Medical history for the masses: How American comic books celebrated heroes of medicine in the 1940s. *Bulletin of the History of Medicine, 78*(1), 148-191.

Haynes, K., & Reedy, P. (2002, July). *"I did it my way": Stories of professional and managerial identity.* Paper presented in Sub-Theme 14, the Colloquium of the European Group for Organization Studies, Barcelona, Spain.

Hirsch, P. M., & Shanley, M. (1996). The rhetoric of boundaryless: Or how the newly empowered managerial class bought into its own marginalisation. In M. B. Arthur & D. M. Rousseau (Eds.), *The boundaryless career: A new employment principle for a new organizational era* (pp. 218-233). New York: Oxford University Press.

Ibarra, H., & Lineback, K. (2005, January). What's your story? *Harvard Business Review,* 63-71.

Linde, C. (1993). *Life stories: The creation of coherence.* New York: Oxford University Press.

Marshall, J. (1995). *Women managers moving on: Exploring career and life choices.* London: Routledge.

Martin, J. (1982). Stories and scripts in organizational settings. In A. Hastorf & A. Islen (Eds.), *Cognitive social psychology* (pp. 255-305). London: Routledge.

Mattuozzi, R. N. (2002). Richard Byrd, polar exploration and the media. *The Virginia Magazine of History and Biography, 110*(2), 209-236.

McAdams, D. P. (1995). What do we know about a person? *Journal of Personality, 63,* 365-396.

McAdams, D. P., Josselson, R., & Leiblich, A. (2001). Turns in the road: Introduction to the volume. In D. P. McAdams, R. Josselson, & A. Leiblich (Eds.), *Turns in the road: Narratives of lives in transition* (pp. xv-xxi). Washington, DC: American Psychological Association.

Miller, A. (1968). *Death of a salesman.* London: Heinemann Educational.

Osland, J. S. (1995). *The adventure of working abroad.* San Francisco: Jossey-Bass.

Peavy, R. V. (1998). *Sociodynamic counseling: A constructivist perspective.* Victoria, BC, Canada: Trafford.

Polkinghorne, D. E. (1988). *Narrative knowing and the human sciences.* Albany: State University of New York Press.

Ricoeur, P. (1985). *Interpretation theory: Discourse and the surplus of meaning.* Fort Worth, TX: Texas Christian University Press.

Savickas, M. L. (2005). The theory and practice of career construction. In S. D. Brown & R. W. Lent (Eds.), *Career development and counseling: Putting theory and research to work* (pp. 42-70). Hoboken, NJ: Wiley.

Sennett, R. (1998). *The corrosion of character: The personal consequences of work in the new capitalism.* New York: W. W. Norton.

Shaw, G. B. (1916). *Pygmalion.* New York: Brentano.

Sims, D. (2002, July). *Careers as prospective story telling: A narrative understanding.* Paper presented at Sub-Theme 14, the Colloquium of the European Group for Organization Studies, Barcelona, Spain [Electronic version].

Sonnenfeld, J. A. (2002). Creative resilience and the mastery of adversity. In M. A. Peiperl, M. B. Arthur, & N. Anand (Eds.), *Career creativity: Explorations in the remaking of work* (pp. 142-158). Oxford, UK: Oxford University Press.

Sparkes, A. C. (2004). Bodies, narratives, selves and autobiographies: The example of Lance Armstrong. *Journal of Sport and Social Issues, 28*(4), 397-428.

Valkevaara, T. (2002). Exploring the construction of professional expertise in HRD: Analysis of four HR developers' work histories and career stories. *Journal of European Industrial Training, 26*(2/4), 183-195.

Weatherly, K., & Beach, L. R. (1994). Making the right impression. *Contemporary Psychology*, *39*, 416-417.

Weick, K. E. (1995). *Sensemaking in organizations*. Thousand Oaks, CA: Sage.

Weick, K. E. (1996). Enactment and the boundaryless career: Organizing as we work. In M. B. Arthur & D. M. Rousseau (Eds.), *The boundaryless career: A new employment principle for a new organizational era* (pp. 40-57). New York: Oxford University Press.

Welch, J. (2001). *Jack*. London: Headline.

Young, R. A., & Collin, A. (2000). Introduction: Framing the future of career. In A. Collin & R. A. Young (Eds.), *The future of career* (pp. 1-17). Cambridge, UK: Cambridge University Press.

Young, R. A., & Collin, A. (2004). Introduction: Constructivism and social constructionism in the career field. *Journal of Vocational Behavior, 64*(3), 373-388.

Young, R. A., & Valach, L. (2000). Reconceptualising career theory and research. In A. Collin & R. A. Young (Eds.), *The future of career* (pp. 181-196). Cambridge, UK: Cambridge University Press.

Young, R. A., & Valach, L. (2004). The construction of career through goal-directed action. *Journal of Vocational Behavior, 64*(3), 499-514.

Young, R. A., Valach, A., & Collin, A. (2002). A contextualist explanation of career. In D. Brown & Associates (Eds.), *Career choice and development* (4th ed., pp. 206-252). San Francisco: Jossey-Bass.

CHAPTER 11

Careers in Practice

Four Career Problems

Steve, 16 years of age, has to decide which program to specialize in at school. He wants to focus on English and social studies, which he loves, but his parents want him to stick to math and science, which he is good at but dislikes. "You'll have better career prospects," says Steve's father. Is he right? What should Steve do?

Marquita, 28 years old, is a Black American from a poor background. She has three children whom she supports as best she can by taking odd jobs, mainly cleaning offices and factories. She has a friend who has a college degree and has decided she wants to better herself. She thinks she might like to be a teacher. But she has no college degree, no qualifications, and no relevant experience. Is her dream realistic? How can she find out? What can she do?

Stacey, 33 years of age, is a successful corporate manager and is married to Dave, a 35-year-old high school music teacher. They want to start a family. But they both love their work and don't want to give it up. Both are anxious to "get to the top." Stacey earns a higher salary than Dave, and they have developed a lifestyle that depends on her high income and bonuses. How can they meet both their family objectives and their work objectives?

Ramon, 48 years of age, is a mechanical engineer. For 25 years he worked as an engineer and later as a manager for the same company. Not long ago the company was taken over, and Ramon was laid off. He realizes that his fortunes were very much tied to his company and that his engineering know-how is out of date. He feels he is "on the scrap heap" and wonders how to make a fresh start.

I f these vignettes of people with career problems are vaguely familiar to you, it is because they were at the start of this book, in the introduction. In Chapter 1, I noted that sociological, psychological, and business approaches to careers each take a different perspective but that all are relevant: In these cases, Marquita struggles against her sociological background, Steve seeks to understand his own psychological makeup, and Ramon feels shortchanged by his business employer. Stacey and Dave try to balance their own development against their roles at home.

In this chapter, I seek to integrate, as best I can, all the different aspects of career—to show, as I started to do with the case of Aston in Chapter 1—that most careers can be viewed from a range of different viewpoints and that each viewpoint has something distinctive and valuable to say about careers. I also seek to say something about the practical application of career studies to the very real problems that people like Steve, Marquita, Stacey, Dave, and Ramon face. Can they use the material in this book to help themselves?

If you think about the various metaphors, you will note some obvious applications to the cases:

- Steve is under pressure to make a career decision that will likely lead him into an educational program and perhaps later into a job or occupation that is apparently a poor *fit* (Chapter 5) with his own interests. His challenge—a difficult one for a 16-year-old—is to explore the issue of fit further, to establish whether his or his parents' view of what is best for him is really the better one, to find out more about himself and the various possibilities into which he may have to fit, and, if necessary, to persuade his parents to allow him to make his own choice.
- Marquita is apparently held back by her *inheritance* (Chapter 2), probably including social class, ethnicity, and gender factors. Her challenge is to recognize the barriers that may have held her back and that she now has to overcome and to find new ways of thinking about her career—perhaps forms of the "action" metaphor (Chapter 4) or the "journey" metaphor (Chapter 6)— to assist her to change things.
- Stacey and Dave face an issue of *role* conflict (Chapter 7), both between each other's desired roles and between their work roles, leisure roles, and prospective roles as parents. Their challenge is to role innovate over time, to review and change their current roles and to take on new roles in synchrony so that together, in the long term, they can both get more of what they want.
- Ramon appears to have allowed his career *resources* (Chapter 9) to run down in the service of his employer. His challenge is either to find an acceptable niche where these resources can be used or to work to grow his resources and invest them in new opportunities so that they can be built up again to allow him more choice. Alternatively, Ramon can find a new line of work to which he is now suited.

The Complexity of Careers

The diagnoses and challenges presented for the career problems in the cases cited earlier are oversimplified, just as the presentation of the four original career problems were: "stories" to make a point. Each of the protagonists—Steve, Marquita, Stacey and Dave, and Ramon—most likely has other career issues, problems, past experiences, and opportunities that may be highly relevant but not presented in the cases.

The different viewpoints embodied in our nine career metaphors make it clear that although a single metaphor can be a good starting point to understand a career, careers are so complex that no career can be done justice by a single metaphor. Each of our nine metaphors has its own point to make about all careers:

- The "inheritance" metaphor reminds us that we each have a unique starting point in our careers, which we can understand and take account of but may be able to change only to a limited extent.
- The "cycle" metaphor reminds us that we cannot expect either ourselves or the world to stay constant and that there are natural rhythms in life that may override predetermined plans or immediate actions.
- The "action" metaphor reminds us that despite the changing world we are able to exercise a degree of agency in our careers, to express ourselves, and to make career decisions, as well as try to manage our own careers.
- The "fit" metaphor reminds us that finding a good fit between who we are and what we do is often the key to a happy and successful career and that by gathering and applying knowledge about ourselves and the world of work we can enhance the degree of fit.
- The "journey" metaphor reminds us that careers are whole-of-life experiences—they take us to new places, there are issues of destination involved, and there are myriad different routes we can take and types of travel we can employ.
- The "roles" metaphor reminds us that different stakeholders, including ourselves, have different views of how we should conduct our working and nonworking lives and that much career behavior involves determining and negotiating roles with others.
- The "relationships" metaphor reminds us that careers are conducted in social contexts, have meaning and effects in relation to other people and institutions, and are to a large extent expressions of the networks to which we belong.
- The "resource" metaphor reminds us that the ultimate societal purpose of most careers is economic, that careers can be viewed as resource components of business systems, and that we all should be conscious of the resource base of our individual careers and develop the resource where we can.
- The "story" metaphor reminds us that careers are largely subjective phenomena that help us to understand and express our identities and find meaning at work and that we can use the interpretive aspect of careers productively in developing helpful story lines for career development.

All these factors are likely to impinge, in complex interactions, on every career. Consider the more detailed career history of Bridget.

A Complex Career

Bridget was the eldest of five children in a small-town Australian family. Her father was an unskilled laborer and her mother had no qualifications. Bridget's father was killed in a road accident when she was 12 years old, and for the next 10 years it fell to Bridget as the eldest in the family to look after her brothers and sisters as best she could while her mother did casual jobs. The family was frequently on welfare and sometimes lived hand-to-mouth. Bridget's mother had a drinking problem, and Bridget often had to take responsibility for the care of her siblings. As a result, she decided early on that if she ever had children she would do whatever it took to avoid the horrors of poverty.

Fortunately, Bridget was also bright and was able to acquire high school credentials along the way. Her experience looking after her family also made her skilled and assiduous in the care of others. When she was 22 years old, she enrolled as a trainee nurse at a hospital in her state capital. Her best friend, Angela, had been accepted for the training and suggested to Bridget that they train together. Nursing seemed a secure occupation, and after the insecurities of Bridget's childhood she valued security. She did well on the academic side of her program but found some aspects of the practical side of nursing distasteful.

Early in their training, Bridget and Angela fell in with another fellow trainee, Laura, and the three became constant companions, both through the training program and in their first jobs in the hospital. Together the group decided that Australia was a constraining influence on their lives and that they should travel. Their qualifications provided them with the opportunity to work as nurses in many overseas countries. Because Laura was of Irish extraction and wanted to see her family in Ireland, the group decided to start their adventure in Dublin. After 18 months of working and saving, they obtained work in a Dublin hospital, made the journey together, and found an apartment to share.

The next 3 years were the happiest that Bridget had known. She felt financially secure, and by working lots of overtime she and her friends were able to earn enough money to travel extensively in Europe. Bridget found that she loved the history and romance of the places she visited, and during this period she focused primarily on enjoying her nonworking life, broadening her knowledge, and learning some of the language and customs of other countries. She was competent in her work but did not think much about her career.

After 3 years, the Dublin idyll ended when Laura married and went to live with her physician husband in London, and Angela returned to Australia to care for her cancer-stricken mother. Still hooked on travel and wanting to make a major change, Bridget took a short-term contract as a nurse in the United Arab Emirates and lived there for 9 months. It was less exotic than she had expected, but the job paid very well. She spent the money on a wonderful 3-month trip though India and the Far East.

What to do next? Back in Dublin, Bridget took stock of her situation. She was now 28 years old. She had had various boyfriends but had never felt like developing a long-term relationship. She felt more at home in Europe, and certainly in Dublin, than she ever had in her own country. And, she realized with some concern, she didn't actually like nursing very

(Continued)

(Continued)

much. She didn't care for the hospital smells, the constant closeness to disease and death, the shift work and irregular hours. Nursing had served as a necessary backdrop to her social and cultural life, but the thought of spending the rest of her career in health care environments was unattractive.

To buy time while she decided what to do, Bridget called her friend Laura in London and arranged to stay as the guest of Laura and her husband. To get an idea of alternative occupations she might pursue, she took casual jobs waiting tables, looking after children as a nanny, and working as a tour guide. None of the jobs seemed particularly interesting or well paid. Thinking that her interest in travel might provide new opportunities, she took a part-time qualification and secured a job in a travel agency, but in practice she found the work mundane and boring. What to do? Should she go to college? She couldn't afford to! And she was beginning to outstay her welcome with Laura.

Bridget's problem was solved when, on a short holiday in Greece, she met Clive, an Englishman, and they fell in love. Clive was an industrial engineer but had recently decided to go out on his own and had purchased a business in a town in the North of England—a shop selling heating and ventilation systems. Clive employed an assistant to look after the shop while he spent his time installing the systems in customers' homes. The business was not doing too well, and the assistant was leaving. Would Bridget like to become his partner in business as well as his partner in life? Yes! Within a few weeks Bridget moved to live with Clive in the town where his business was located and started to work in the shop. They married a few months later.

Bridget quickly established why the business was not successful. Clive was a competent engineer, but neither he nor his assistant was good at selling, and Clive disliked the administrative side of business. The finances were a complete mess, with lots of accounts unpaid. Quickly, Bridget took charge. Gleaning what she could about small businesses by reading library books and attending evening classes, she cleaned up and computerized the accounts. She ran two inexpensive promotion campaigns, which effectively doubled the size of the business. She persuaded the bank to increase Clive's loan and designed the refurbishment of the shop. She wrote a business plan. She worked long hours, but it was fun, watching her own creation thrive and grow. The following year, they opened a new outlet in another part of town, and then a third.

Bridget and Clive had always planned to have children, and at the age of 31 Bridget became pregnant for the first time. They hired a new manager for the business but resolved that Bridget would maintain general supervision as well as her family role. Bridget's first child, Bronwen, was born the following year, followed, another year later, by her second child, Jonathan. She withdrew largely from the business to devote time to her children in their formative years. Without Bridget's constant attention, the business stopped growing but continued to be prosperous. It seemed that Bridget's life was complete.

Bridget's world came crashing down when Clive announced that he had fallen in love with another woman and was leaving Bridget. She moved out of their house the same day and went to stay with friends. She was devastated. But worse was to follow. Clive contested custody of the children and refused to agree to a financial settlement. He was the legal owner of the business. He was able to persuade the courts that it was his engineering know-how and business contacts rather than Bridget's commitment that had been the key factors in building it. Bridget was awarded custody of Bronwen and Jonathan, but her financial settlement was minimal. Now 34 years old, Bridget was faced with the old nightmare of her own childhood—the thought that she might not be able to look after her children adequately. Her life, she reflected, had certainly had its ups and downs—a real roller coaster ride. How, she wondered, had she got into this mess?

It is evident that each of our nine metaphors has something to contribute to our understanding of Bridget's career.

From her childhood experiences, Bridget no doubt *inherited* some of her capabilities and outlooks—for example, her self-sufficiency, her skills in caring for others, and her fear of insecurity and of being an inadequate provider. Her expected career *cycle* may have been disrupted because she sought to establish her career in nursing early, without an exploration phase; her nursing career and shop manager career both ran through important learning cycles, and her career as a whole was overtaken by a family cycle. Bridget's own *actions* certainly affected her career, particularly in her determined work in her husband's business. As far as *fit* is concerned, nursing turned out to be a poor fit for Bridget—the consequence, perhaps, of making a convenient choice without thinking it through—but her successful experience in sales and administration may provide a useful indicator of where her talents and interests lie. Her career *journey* has no clear destination beyond family security, but she has already become adept at crossing boundaries—organizational, occupational, and national—in pursuit of what she wants. Although nursing most likely tied her to hospital-dictated *roles,* she subsequently gave herself the experience of alternative roles: She practiced role innovation in the shop, and her non-work roles as tourist and wife and mother certainly left their imprint on her career. Her major jobs and job moves were mediated by her *relationships*—particularly with Angela, Laura, and Clive. The career *resources* she developed include her "knowing-why" drive to look after her family and avoid mundane occupations, her "knowing-how" nursing qualification and small-business experience, and the "knowing-whom" network of friends who have always been there to support Bridget. All of these facets of Bridget's career combine in a *story* she tells herself about her life, epitomized in her "roller coaster ride" metaphor, but no doubt Clive, for example, would have a very different story to tell about her time in his shop.

Despite all this, we can perhaps be rather critical of Bridget for the lack of forethought and planning that has characterized much of her career behavior. She does not seem to have had particularly good reasons for selecting nursing as her initial choice—that it was her friend's choice and secure is not enough. She apparently failed to explore other options and to respond to early cues that nursing was not right for her. She paid insufficient attention to her career during her time in Dublin and seemed surprised to realize that she disliked it. When she left nursing, she did some on-the-job exploration, but again she did not carry out any systematic assessment of either her own qualities or the range of opportunities that might be available. Her development of new skills in her husband's business was commendable, but she failed to protect herself by seeking the legal stake in the business to which she was surely entitled. Treating her own career with the seriousness it deserved might perhaps have enabled her to avoid all these errors.

If Bridget's approach to her career so far represents poor career practice, what does good career practice look like? How can research information such as that contained in this book be used to help us manage our careers better than Bridget seems to have managed hers?

Career Stakeholders

An initial question about career practice is, who precisely are the practitioners? Most obviously, each person who has a career is his or her own career practitioner, with a life to build around employment, a series of career problems to solve and decisions to make, and possibly a long-term career plan. Although people such as family, friends, teachers, and managers can help (or sometimes hinder) individuals with their career, in the end the individuals must make the career decisions and remain responsible for the career. Many of the end-of-chapter questions in this book focus on your career because it is you who carry that responsibility. If this book does not suggest to you some principles you can use in your future career, then it has failed in one of its objectives. Understanding careers should therefore be a basis for career practice—skilled behavior in areas such as assembling information, understanding yourself, developing career strategies, setting career goals, and making career decisions.

But there are others in addition to career protagonists who may share some of the responsibility for their careers. In the cases at the beginning of this chapter, for example, key participants are Steve's parents, Marquita's friend, Stacey and Dave (who each share responsibility for the other's career), their respective managers, Ramon's former employer, and his career counselor.

Thus, we can identify different sets of career stakeholders—people who have a direct personal interest in career outcomes and are in a position to apply career theory to practice:

• *Relatives and friends.* As Chapter 8 indicated, careers are social. In addition to managing our own careers, each of us becomes involved occasionally in helping relatives, friends, colleagues, social contacts, and others with their careers. For example, we might comment, "If you don't like that job, why not give it up?" or "I think you'd make a great teacher!" We also support others when they have career difficulties and suggest job openings to them. Each of us is therefore a potential and often an actual career counselor—another responsibility for which understanding careers ought to prepare us. The role of parents in guiding or facilitating the initial career decisions and choices of their children is particularly important (Kracke, 2002; Young & Valach, 2004), and it may be that for some readers the key insights they gain from this book are not about their own careers but about their children's. As friends and relatives, we need to be as knowledgeable as we can.

- *Managers and supervisors.* An advertising campaign promoting the pharmacy profession portrays the pharmacist as "the health professional you see most frequently." In a parallel viewpoint, managers and supervisors are perhaps the career professionals that you see most frequently. That is, your manager or immediate supervisor—and, sometimes, human resource managers and other managers in your employing organization—deals with you daily and is normally responsible, within the organization at least, for ensuring your training, assessment, development, evaluation, and often your transfer and promotion (Chapter 9), not to mention your possible layoff or dismissal. So managers, too, have a responsibility to understand how careers work and to use that understanding judiciously in their management of staff. Some readers of this book will already be undertaking management education, and many others will in the course of their careers become managers and will be expected to discharge this responsibility. As managers we have obligations both to the organizations we work for and to our subordinates, and these obligations are not always easily compatible with each other (see the issues of role conflict in Chapter 7 and resource ownership in Chapter 9). One thing we may have to recognize as managers is that a person who continues to work in an organization despite being unhappy or not meeting his or her full potential is likely to suffer in the long term—as is the employing organization.

- *Career counselors.* If managers are like pharmacists in terms of being the career professionals whom career holders see most frequently, then career counselors are like general practitioners in terms of being the career professionals who offer the greatest expertise and objectivity. Although those who are preparing for their careers, such as high school and college students, often have good access to counselors, most people can only see a career counselor if they can pay for the service, and most are only willing to do this if they think they have a major career problem to solve. So career counselors may deal with relatively few career holders on a day-to-day basis, but counselors have the opportunity to provide major assistance when they do.

If you went to see a career counselor for assistance, you would expect the counselor to have an understanding of the careers field beyond the level of this book, an understanding of the current local structure of career opportunities, and training and experience in counseling processes. Many career counselors have an excellent background in the psychological variables underlying careers, such as those discussed in Chapter 5, and expertise in assessing these variables using properly validated instruments. Assessment enables counselors to provide precise feedback to clients about their personal makeup and the types of occupations they may be best suited to. (If you are interested in understanding some of the work of a career counselor in assessment, it might pay to reread Chapter 5 with the notions of assessment and guidance firmly in mind.) Other counselors have skills in helping clients develop their own thinking about career directions, particularly by having clients tell their career stories (Chapter 10) and assisting them to extend these stories toward a satisfactory conclusion by methods of narration and co-construction.

Because of the importance of career counseling, and because some readers of this book are reading it as part of their introductory education as career counselors, Chapter 12, written by practicing counselor Mary McMahon, was added. This chapter includes a number of case studies of counselor–client interactions.

Despite all this, the major potential stakeholders for career studies are, and will remain, ordinary people trying to find success and satisfaction in their careers. The emphasis in this book has been not so much on "doing" careers as on understanding them, and it lies beyond the scope or space available in this book to provide anything approaching worthwhile guidance on how to have a successful and happy career. In the remainder of this chapter, I attempt only to provide some worthwhile overarching principles and ideas as well as some pointers to the resources likely to be most beneficial in taking the process further.

Recipes for Success

There is no shortage of advice to those seeking career success. Since Dale Carnegie (1936) published *How to Win Friends and Influence People,* a practical guide to operationalizing the "relationships" metaphor, the self-help movement has offered innumerable guides to getting what you want in careers. You can "think and grow rich"—a visualization metaphor (Hill, 1960)—or try "winning through intimidation"—a competition metaphor (Ringer, 1973). Other writers give their recipes for success in the titles of their works: For example, in *Career Warfare: Ten Rules for Building a Personal Brand and Fighting to Keep It* (D'Allessandro, 2004), the author encourages you to apply a marketing metaphor and brand yourself to sell in a tough market. In *Dig Your Well Before You're Thirsty: The Only Networking Book You'll Ever Need* (Mackay, 1997), the author encourages you to cultivate and store social contacts before you need them. Lore (1998) calls you *The Pathfinder* and tells you *How to Choose or Change Your Career for a Lifetime of Satisfaction and Success,* and Sinetar (1987) urges you to have faith and if you *Do What You Love, the Money Will Follow:* good news, no doubt, for all starving artists. Sher (1994), in *I Could Do Anything, if I Knew What It Was,* offers you the route to "a richly rewarding career, based on your heart's desire" in which you can "recapture long lost goals, overcome the blocks that inhibit your success, decide what you want to be, and live your dreams forever" (back cover). Count the metaphors and clichés! Hundreds of similar books could be cited.

Such recipes no doubt work for some people, but there are a number of problems with them. They are simplistic, particularly in their assumptions that one size fits all and their conflation of career success and career satisfaction. They tend to encourage an individualistic success-at-all-costs or me-ahead-of-all-other-people philosophy that many would find objectionable. They focus on the attitudes and behavior of individuals but ignore the likely human limitations of ability and motivation and some of the obstacles discussed in this book, such as social structure, labor market realities, and variable human energy. They are often narrow in their conceptualization of human psychology, ignorant of the vast reservoir of research available on career development, and contradictory of each other's points of view.

Although it is sometimes worth reading carefully chosen material of this genre to boost action in respect of career, studying these texts is not a substitute for systematic career planning and action based on sound scholarly and personal research.

Career Management

Scholarly writers tend to take an approach that is more complicated (because, as this book has shown, people and their careers are complicated), more disciplined, and more rational than the recipes-for-success genre. For example Greenhaus, Callanan, and Godschalk (2000) provided a model of career management that has affinities with the elementary processes of business management learned by beginning business students:

- Businesses plan their activities in advance from logical consideration of their internal resources and external opportunities.
- Businesses break the plan down into steps and execute it as best they can.
- Businesses monitor the results, modify their actions to conform to the plan, or change the plan according to changed circumstances.

Individuals can manage their careers in a similar manner (Figure 11.1):

- As in business, the process is embedded in, and influenced by, a context of important contextual influences—information, opportunities, and support from educational, family, work, and societal institutions.
- Similar to organizations weighing their own resources and external opportunities and constraints (e.g., in SWOT analysis: strengths, weaknesses, opportunities, threats), there is an information-gathering phase in which individuals become aware of their own career resources and the opportunities available in the environment. In career exploration (Box A), individuals engage in information gathering about themselves and context, as advocated by Parsons (1909) and all his followers, a process repeatedly emphasized in this book. This leads to awareness of self and environment (Box B)— for example, interests, values, talents (self), opportunities, options, and obstacles (environment).
- Similar to business planning and goal setting, this awareness enables a plan to be expressed in terms of goals sought (Box C). For example, an individual might decide to earn a degree in engineering or (at a later stage in the process) to apply for jobs as a mechanical engineer in the auto industry or seek a job with a special project team within the present work setting or change to part-time work to spend more time looking after family members.
- The setting of goals enables individuals to develop and implement a strategy to achieve the goals (Boxes D and E). For example, the goal of promotion to a higher level in the organization might lead to strategies of improving performance on the current job, taking night classes, attracting the attention of key decision makers, and so on. The goal of becoming a veterinary surgeon

Figure 11.1 Model of Career Management

Source: Reprinted from: J Greenbaus et al. (2000). *Career Management, 3rd Edition* (p. 24). Dryden Press. Published by permission of Thomson Learning.

in private practice might lead to a series of strategies for enrolling in course-work, seeking family support, finding sources of business capital, and so on.

- As in business, implementation of a strategy will most likely lead to progress of some sort toward the goal, as well as feedback for the individual (Boxes F and G). For example, our hypothetical aspiring veterinary practitioner may find that she enjoys and is successful at completing her qualifications but is not able to gather the necessary capital to start a business. She may receive feedback that she has a special facility with horses. Such developments are bound to lead to a fresh appraisal of the career (Box H), leading to fresh exploration (Box A) and most likely to new awareness, revised goals, changed strategy, and so on. For example, the veterinary practitioner may postpone her plan to go into business and instead conduct background research on possible employed positions in the horse-breeding industry.

Greenhaus et al. (2000) describe the process in much greater detail. The process embodies the notion that careers can be rationally planned and that career plans, though they can be precisely executed, can also be modified in light of experience. The process is cyclic, symmetrical, and logical.

This approach conceptualizes career management as a "problem-solving, decision-making process" (Greenhaus et al., 2000, p. 25). If individuals have problems to solve and decisions to make, this should be done in the most rational manner possible, based on maximum relevant information. The image of career that one develops on this basis is of a constantly reiterated series of decisions such that each decision changes the situation that produced it and creates a new problem to be solved by a new decision. The material in this book on inheritance, cycle, journey, roles, and so forth thus becomes additional information that can be drawn on as individuals proceed through life making this series of decisions.

Career Decision Making

Career practitioners have applied the notion of career decision making to the notion of choice from among career options. The model of occupational choice implicit in the work adjustment theory of Dawis and Lofquist (1994; see Chapter 5, especially Figure 5.2) is an example of the process of matching people and occupations likely to be involved.

Applied models have been developed, particularly regarding students and other young people making critical early-career decisions, such as which subjects to major in and which occupation to pursue. For example, Reardon, Lenz, Sampson, and Peterson (2006) provided a textbook of career planning that is also a manual for students to help them make their initial career choices. Their career choice system is based on a career information processing (CIP) model, previously published by Peterson, Sampson, and Reardon (1991), that represents the way in which people think, and weigh information, about their careers. By following the CIP model, the authors state that students can "formulate personal goals and action plans designed to proactively enhance [their] careers" and "develop personal, employment related skills and information" (Reardon et al., 2006, p. ix).

The choice process according to Reardon et al. (2006) is sustained by a pyramid of information-processing domains, which are shown in Figure 11.2. At the lowest level, we see the familiar domains of background knowledge—knowledge of self and knowledge of the world of work, though in this (student) context the latter is defined as occupational knowledge, signaling that the model is mainly concerned with choosing an occupation, usually the student's first occupation. The next level up is a decision-making-skills domain, likened by the authors to a computer program that individuals use to process information to make career decisions. At the apex of the pyramid is a domain of metacognitions—controlling and ordering the decision making taking place at lower levels. These metacognitions provide an overall framework of priorities within which the decision making can take place.

As shown in Figure 11.2, the skills in the decision-making level are labeled "CASVE," an acronym for a repeated cycle of communication, analysis, synthesis,

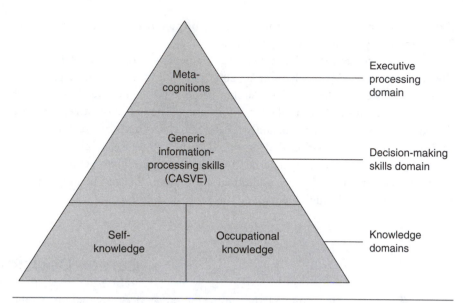

Figure 11.2   Pyramid of Information-Processing Domains in Career Decision Making

Source: From *Career Development and Services, A Cognitive Approach* (1st ed.) by Peterson/ Sampson Jr./Reardon © 1991. Reprinted with the permission of Wadsworth, a division of Thomson Learning: www.thomsonrights.com. Fax 800 730-2215.

valuing, and execution, which Reardon et al. (2006) believe are involved in career decision making (see Figure 11.3). The CASVE elements are as follows:

- *Communication* involves communication to the individual that there is a problem to be solved, usually identified by a gap between the person's current and desired situation or the knowledge that a choice needs to be made.
- *Analysis* involves asking questions about the problem and gathering information about both the personal and contextual aspects of the problem, comparing and reflecting on this information, and thinking about the process of decision making.
- *Synthesis* involves processing information to identify alternative solutions to the problem: the "what can I do?" stage. At this point, potential solutions may be noted or discarded. The problem may be simplified by reducing the number of options available.
- In *valuing,* the prospective options are considered in terms of the person's values and the effects of the chosen option on the person and others whom the person considers important, such as family members. Then, the remaining options are ranked in order, and the person chooses the best option and commits to implementing it.
- *Execution* involves "forming means-end relationships and determining a logical series of steps to reach a goal" (Reardon et al., 2006, p. 62)—similar to "strategy" in the Greenhaus et al. model (Figure 11.1)—thereby providing

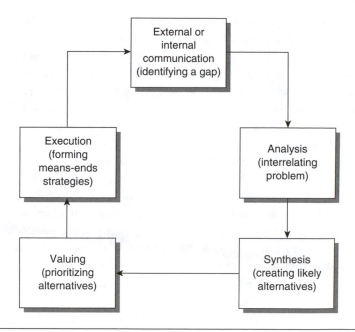

Figure 11.3   CASVE Cycle of Information-Processing Skills

Source: From *Career Development and Services, A Cognitive Approach* (1st ed.) by Peterson/Sampson Jr./Reardon © 1991. Reprinted with the permission of Wadsworth, a division of Thomson Learning: www.thomsonrights.com. Fax 800 730-2215.

energy and direction for the choice. Included in this step is *trying out—* trying to gain relevant experiences.

Accessing Career Information

A career planning system, however, is only as good as the information to which the various steps apply. Chapter 5 presented various means of assembling information about one's own interests, abilities, and values. In this area, some authors provide resources in the form of career workbooks, through which individuals can simultaneously gather general information, reflect on some of the key factors affecting careers and career decision making, and interact with the book by completing questionnaires to assemble personally tailored information.

For example, Sears and Gordon (2002) provide a book of more than 160 pages for the career aspirant to work through. The book provides many questionnaires—and, in some cases, rudimentary measures—on factors such as the person's socioeconomic background, personality, interests, skills, preferred occupations, motivation, attitudes about college major, and decision-making style. Provision is made for identifying alternatives and writing action plans, as well as improving performance by identifying stressors and unethical behaviors, selling oneself, writing a resume, and finding jobs. This approach attempts to program a complex phenomenon and tends to be less problematic than "real life," but the approach will help some people.

A key element, at least in the important decision-making area of occupational choice, is information about the various occupational options available—the kinds of career maps introduced in Chapter 6. In this area, individuals obtain relevant information about such matters as the nature of the work and the required personal characteristics and qualifications. This information may come from professional and trade bodies, employing organizations, government information sources, friends and relatives who work in the occupation, and specialist careers counselors. For example, as shown in Chapter 5, a Holland RIASEC profile can be found for the most common occupations and can be compared with individuals' own profiles.

One problem with career planning is that careers last a long time—40 years or more in many cases. Information about the world of work is subject, in changing times, to its own dramatic changes. Decisions made now, such as which occupation to enter in 2008, may have consequences for the individual up to 2048 and beyond. The occupation you seek to enter now may not even exist in 40 years' time, and if it does, the way of doing it may change beyond recognition: just ask today's older workers how their occupations have been changed by new technology. Career decision making based on the assumption that the external conditions will remain static—or cannot be predicted and therefore cannot be taken into account—is flawed.

For example, in the United States, statistical information is available from the U.S. Department of Labor (2004) detailing hundreds of different popular occupations: it lists the 2002 employment numbers in each one, the projected employment change between 2002 and 2012, and information on employment prospects. "Hot" occupations—with more than 140,000 employees in 2002 and expected to increase more than 25% in the period—are shown in Table 11.1. Note the predominance of the service industries, particularly information, health, education, and personal services.

Occupations expected to decline over the period include data entry and information processing operators (projected to decrease 18% in the period); farmers, ranchers, and agricultural managers (17%); textile, apparel, and furnishings workers (14%); communications equipment operators (11%); petroleum engineers (10%); media announcers (10%); procurement clerks (7%); order clerks (6%); aerospace engineers (5%); bookbinders (5%); rail and transportation workers (5%); stock clerks and order fillers (4%); postal service workers (4%); and assemblers and fabricators (4%). Note the preponderance of routine, clerical, agricultural, and manual occupations in this list.

But there are information sources that go beyond raw numbers such as these. You may, for example, be interested not just in the occupations but in the industries that are growing fastest. You may want to find out about the relative average earnings in some of the occupations you are considering. You may want to discover the personal interests that are congruent with these occupations. You may want to find the *Fifty Best Jobs for Your* (Holland RIASEC) *Personality* (Farr & Shatkin, 2005) or the *200 Best Jobs for College Graduates* (Farr & Ludden, 2003). Reardon et al. (2006) provided a wealth of such information, including the complexity levels (Gottfredson & Holland, 1996) and Holland RIASEC codes for many occupations. In terms of the Holland system, the categories that appear to characterize growth occupations are S (for social) and E (for enterprising), whereas R (for realistic) and C (for conventional) appear to be on the decline: The momentum in employment for the moment seems inexorably away from the manual and the routine and toward the interpersonal (personal services) and the conceptual.

Table 11.1   Big Occupations Expected to Increase Employment, 2002–2012

Occupation	Employment 2002	Projected % change, 2002–2012
Medical assistants	364,600	+59%
Social and human service assistants	305,200	+49%
Computer software engineers	675,200	+45%
Dental hygienists	148,000	+43%
Computer systems analysts, database administrators, and computer scientists	979,200	+42%
Dental assistants	266,000	+42%
Personal and home care aides	607,600	+40%
Teachers—postsecondary	1,581,200	+38%
Computer and information system managers	284,400	+36%
Teachers—adult literacy and remedial and self-enrichment education	280,400	+34%
Computer support specialists and systems administrators	758,300	+33%
Emergency medical technicians and paramedics	179,100	+33%
Public relations specialists	158,100	+33%
Security guards and gaming surveillance officers	1,004,400	+32%
Nursing, psychiatric, and home help aides	2,014,300	+31%
Management analysts	577,400	+30%
Recreation and fitness workers	484,800	+30%
Teachers—special education	432,900	+30%
Pharmacists	230,200	+30%
Medical and health service managers	243,600	+29%
Paralegals and legal assistants	199,600	+29%
Pharmacy technicians	210,800	+29%
Registered nurses	2,284,500	+27%
Social workers	476,600	+27%
Advertising, marketing, promotions, public relations, and sales managers	700,100	+26%
Human resources, training, and labor relations managers and specialists	676,700	+25%
Financial analysts and personal financial advisors	298,300	+25%
Market and survey researchers	154,700	+25%

Source: U.S. Department of Labor (2004).

Job Hunting

At the most operational end of the planning spectrum comes the important career-related activity known as job hunting. At the time of this writing, unemployment is relatively low in developed countries, though at least minimal educational qualifications and interpersonal skills are required for most jobs. So getting a job may not be too difficult. But what kind of job? Even flipping burgers may have some career value if it inculcates career-relevant skills such as punctuality, reliability, concern for quality, collaboration with coworkers, and customer service. But many people will set higher standards for the jobs they want. And however ambitious your objectives or suitable your preferred occupation in terms of "fit," you will not get to first base if you are unable to land the job that will set you on your chosen path. It is worth putting considerable time and energy into this periodic career task and learning the specific skills and drills that have been shown to lead to success.

Reardon et al. (2006) recommended a job "campaign"—another military metaphor that underscores the significance of the task. In such a campaign, it is assumed you have already determined objectives, such as the occupation and type of position you are interested in. The formal steps in the process include assembling information about available jobs, specifying employers, preparing letters of application and resumes, contacting employers "cold" or with formal applications, undertaking job interviews, and making choices from job offers.

It lies beyond the scope of this book to provide a complete guide to the art of job hunting, but a few indicative points may be made (Bolles, 2004; Bright & Earl, 2005; Reardon et al., 2006; Wegemann, Chapman, & Johnson, 1985):

- The starting point for the job-hunting process is the matching, decision-making, and career strategy processes already described. Job hunting is not about finding any job: It is about finding a job that fits you and your career.
- Job hunting, if done in a properly committed way, is itself a full-time job requiring a high level of commitment (a few hours a week will be insufficient).
- Job hunting leads to many negative experiences, and most people require social support to maintain their momentum.
- Because most jobs are never advertised, informal networking is a key activity (Chapter 8).
- The number of interviews gained and job offers secured tends to be proportional to the time spent seeking interviews.
- The Internet is a potent tool for sourcing job opportunities. Books are available to assist you in using the Internet for this purpose (e.g., Kehm, 2002; Wood, 2002).
- Informational interviews can be arranged with employers and others expert in the relevant field. These interviews are not about directly seeking jobs but about gathering relevant information about opportunities in a particular occupation or organization.

- There are good and bad ways of contacting employers, writing letters of application, and presenting your resume. Likewise, there are ways of presenting yourself in an interview that will increase your chances of securing a job. It is worth learning relevant job-hunting skills.
- Finding and accepting a job involves additional issues, such as agreeing on salary, conditions of work, learning opportunities, and so on. It is worth thinking through these issues in advance and being able and willing to negotiate what you want.

Understanding the Future

However, career development goes far beyond being able to choose an appropriate occupation, so the information that a good career planner needs in today's world goes far beyond assessments of occupations. Elsewhere in this book, I noted some of the effects of external political, economic, and organizational factors on careers in the recent past—for example, the replacement of relational with transactional contracts, the decline in organizational careers, the decline of manufacturing employment, and the growth of contingent work. In their preparation of students for career choice and development, Reardon et al. (2006) provided chapters on topics such as careering in a changing world, working in the new global economy, and new ways to work. But if you wish to plan your career, you need information not just about the present, not just about current conditions and trends, but about the future. Indeed, to some extent you need to be a futurologist.

Various commentators have observed how economic, technological, and societal changes continue to affect the world of work, with likely consequences on employment and jobs and therefore on careers. The following are among the factors that seem important:

- The "new deal at work"—the move to transactional rather than relational contracts (Chapter 8)—and the consequent loss to employees of critical means of career development, such as security and training (Cappelli, 1999)
- Possible effects of the new dynamism and fragmentation of modern organizations and forms of work in removing the stable base of working life and thereby "corroding" human character and relationships (Sennet, 1998)
- The decline of jobs in the sense of neat 40-hour-a-week packages designed to fit in with employees' other needs and roles and the disappearance through mechanization, automation, and new information technology of many common forms of work, such as clerical and manual work (Rifkin, 1995)
- The rise of the Internet and the consequent rapid movement of capital, the rise of "informational capitalism," and the consequences in terms of employment outcomes (Castells, 1996)
- The increasing divergence between the best-off and most marginalized sections of society (Hutton, 1995)
- The rise of new work and occupations in the creative industries (Peiperl, Arthur, & Anand, 2002)

Such commentaries are well worth considering by those seeking to plan their careers. Would you be comfortable with a life of short-term contracts rather than long-term job security? How would you feel about taking responsibility—including financial responsibility—for your own training and development? If your favorite occupation is in decline, do you still want to take your chances in it? Would you enjoy being a semiautonomous worker in a wide, nonhierarchical network rather than a clear organization structure? How do you feel about a life in a multinational organization where the only way you can achieve your career goals is to travel and work in foreign cultures?

When you ask yourself questions like these, you begin to realize that career choice is a lot more complex than finding an occupation with a good fit to your personal interests. The personal characteristics you may need may be things like adaptability (to cope with sudden changes in your circumstances), geographical mobility (to be able to move to where the jobs are), tolerance of ambiguity (to enable you to handle relatively unstructured, nonhierarchical situations), and self-direction (to enable you to assume full responsibility for your own career). If you lack such characteristics, it does not mean you cannot have a successful and happy career, but you may have to work harder to find the kinds of more structured, secure opportunities and conditions that you may seek.

Career Strategies

As indicated earlier, a *career strategy* can be defined as "a plan of activities designed to attain the career goal" (Greenhaus et al., 2000, p. 25). The word *strategy* has military origins and is much used nowadays in business, as signifying that an organization intends to be in charge of its own future and will devise a grand master plan, perhaps looking 5 or more years ahead. Within such a strategy, shorter term tactical plans and day-to-day operational plans may be fitted. Against such standards, any career planning approach that focuses only on deciding on the next occupation (the focus of some of the approaches we have been considering and perhaps a tactical activity), or getting the next job (as in job hunting—an operational activity), may look a little short term and narrow.

Moreover, choosing an occupation and seeking a job are activities that occupy the transitions between education and work or between different jobs (see the material on role transitions in Chapter 7). But careers are continuous and proceed during the periods when we are in employment (and out of employment) as well as during the period when we are between employment roles. If you want to plan your career, you must plan your activities in jobs (and in periods of voluntary nonemployment) as well as between jobs. For example, what should be your criteria for deciding whether to undertake further part-time study? What kind of relationship should you try to develop with your boss? Should you take opportunities to seek new assignments in your work? More broadly, should you aim to average no more than 2 years in any new job you take (to cultivate diversity of experience) or stay for at least 5 years (to demonstrate loyalty and build expertise)?

If you look at some of the more successful careers detailed in this book, you will find that the protagonists exercised consistent career strategies, not in the sense of having specific goals and means to get there but in the sense of ways of enacting their careers:

- Madonna (Chapter 4) campaigned on her own behalf in terms of self-publicity and networking until she got what she wanted.
- Brett the plasterer (Chapter 4) conducted experiments almost compulsively and was willing to try anything until he found what he wanted (even though at the beginning he didn't know what it was).
- Christopher Reeve (Chapter 7) cultivated many roles in his early career and became so versatile that when a tragic accident cut his main career short, he had plenty of experience (career capital; see Chapter 9) to fall back on.
- John Patrick, the IBM executive (Chapter 9), moved rapidly around his chosen organization throughout his career and so acquired unusual breadth and knowledge of the company.
- Catherine the marketing manager (Chapter 10) made learning the main focus of most of her work activity.

Effective career self-development is therefore more than a set of short-term decisions; it is a personal way of thinking and acting in relation to one's objectives. But clearly there is a wide variety of career strategies. For example, consider these keys to a successful management career (Robbins, 1994):

- Select your first job judiciously.
- Do good work.
- Present the right image (to your organization).
- Learn the power structure.
- Gain control of resources.
- Stay visible (to those in power).
- Get a promotion or transfer early.
- Find a mentor (higher in the organization).
- Support your boss.
- Stay mobile (within the organization).
- Think laterally—if you aren't getting ahead, consider leaving.

It seems to me there is some value in such a strategy—for a relatively small number of individuals, namely those who seek organizational careers, whose career goal is to achieve high status and power within that organization and who aren't averse to the kind of impression management and self-centered networking described, but also implicitly criticized, in Chapter 8. Few people I meet nowadays have this mentality.

In contrast, consider this list, which I developed for undergraduate college students contemplating their forthcoming careers, who have not yet formulated precise career goals but want to be well equipped to pursue them when they do (Inkson, 2000):

- Be open to discontinuity.
- Conduct self-designed apprenticeships.
- Develop self-reliance through travel.

- Conduct experiments.
- Treat employers as temporary partners, not permanent bosses.
- Learn, learn, learn.
- Build networks and reputation.
- Consider self-employment.
- Leverage your experience.
- Keep your options open.

This list is specifically attuned to the dynamic context of contemporary careers and emphasizes adaptability, learning, and employability. In today's world, for example, the occurrence of discontinuity—for example, in the sudden loss of, or radical change to, an apparently secure job—is to be expected. Self-designed apprenticeships (described in Chapter 4), experiments (changes or extensions of role designed to provide career-relevant information as shown by the question "Could I handle more work?"; see the information on role innovation in Chapter 7), and periods of self-employment (Chapter 6) are exercises in career learning. As far as travel is concerned, there is nothing like living and working in a foreign country, preferably one where people speak a different language, to develop interpersonal and cross-cultural skills and self-confidence (international journeys; see Chapter 6). Leveraging experience means using what you know to create fresh opportunities, while ensuring that these opportunities add to what you know (building career capital; see Chapter 9). The partner concept of boss prevents you from surrendering career needs to ensure your employer's business needs (Chapter 9), and the benefits of wide networking are indicated in Chapter 8. The use of the term *options* reminds us that in today's world employability is more important than employment.

Like the earlier list, this one will not suit everyone. People who are in mid- or late career or have substantial family commitments, or who have a clear and stable career direction that they feel able to pursue in their own way, may find the list lacks direction and appears too energy consuming. The point is not for everyone to have *this* strategy but for everyone to have *a* strategy that is based on a good understanding of today's world of employment and of personal characteristics.

Conclusion

Every career can be viewed through the lenses of the nine metaphors on which this book is based and involves issues on which these metaphors focus. We can use the metaphors to provide us with the information and awareness we need on an ongoing basis to conduct our careers successfully. Effective action on careers involves different levels, which can be labeled "strategic," "tactical," and "operational." Thus, determining broad career objectives or a way of going about your career might be considered strategic; choosing an occupation tactical, and job hunting operational. The three levels form a related hierarchy. Managing one's career on an ongoing basis and making specific career decisions can be structured in a systematic way to optimize logic and rationality.

Overall, looking after one's career is an important activity that can affect one's quality of life substantially in the long term. I hope this chapter, and indeed this whole book, has provided some illumination to enable you to understand careers in general and your own career in particular and to live your career as a happy and productive part of your life.

Key Points in This Chapter

- Careers are complex. Each career involves elements of inheritance, cycle, action, fit, journey, roles, relationships, resource, and story. These different interpretations can assist us not just to understand our careers but also to act practically to improve them.
- The stakeholders in a person's career include not just the person but also his or her relatives, friends, managers, and others. Career counselors may also be involved. These groups can influence careers. Nevertheless, individuals have to take responsibility for their own careers.
- Aids to career action range from simplistic recipes for success to sophisticated, individualized career guidance.
- Models of career management and career decision making are available that seek to put career planning and action on a rational basis that maximizes the use of valid information.
- Information about the world of work, particularly about occupations, is available from a variety of sources. Means of gathering and applying information about oneself are also available, sometimes in the form of programmed workbooks.
- Career management and decision making should ideally sit within a wider career strategy.
- Job hunting is at the operational end of career management and involves specific learnable principles and skills.

Questions From This Chapter

General Questions

1. Reread the four minicases at the beginning of the chapter. What further information would you need to begin to determine solutions to the problems? What potential solutions do you see?

2. Write some notes on the application of each of the nine metaphors to your own career or life as you see it at present.

3. Identify other stakeholders or potential stakeholders in your career. Do you feel they help or hinder you at present in determining and enacting your career? How could they best help you?

4. How applicable do you think the Greenhaus career management model and the CIP career decision-making model are to your career decision making? What are their main advantages and disadvantages?

5. Outline in your own words some career strategies you think you could follow. Write some principles that might work for you.

6. Find some resources on job hunting. What could you do to improve your skills as a potential job hunter?

Career Case Study Questions

1. Ask your career case person to identify the key three or four external or internal factors influencing the case person's career. Which metaphors (if any) do the case person's answers appear to represent?

2. Ask your career case person to (1) explain his or her decision-making process, particularly as it applies to choosing occupations and jobs; (2) identify any career strategy used; (3) describe his or her job-hunting methods; and (4) offer any advice about job hunting.

References

Bolles, R. (2004). *The 2005 what color is your parachute?* Berkeley, CA: Tenspeed Press.

Bright, J., & Earl, J. (2005). *Amazing resumes: What employers want to see—And how to say it.* Indianapolis, IN: JIST Works.

Cappelli, P. (1999). *The new deal at work.* Boston: Harvard Business School Press.

Carnegie, D. (1936). *How to win friends and influence people.* New York: Simon & Schuster.

Castells, M. (1996). *The rise of the network society.* Cambridge, MA: Blackwell.

D'Allessandro, D. F. (2004). *Career warfare: Ten rules for building a personal brand and fighting to keep it.* New York: McGraw-Hill.

Dawis, R. V., & Lofquist, L. H. (1984). *A psychological theory of work adjustment.* Minneapolis, MN: University of Minneapolis Press.

Farr, M., & Ludden, L. L. (2003). *200 best jobs for college graduates* (2nd ed.). Indianapolis, IN: JIST Publishing.

Farr, M., & Shatkin, L. (2005). *Fifty best jobs for your personality.* Indianapolis, IN: JIST Publishing.

Gottfredson, G. D., & Holland, J. L. (1996). *Dictionary of Holland occupational codes.* Odessa, FL: Psychological Assessment Resources.

Greenhaus, J. P., Callanan, G. A., & Godschalk, V. M. (2000). *Career management* (3rd ed.). Orlando, FL: Dryden Press.

Hill, N. (1960). *Think and grow rich.* New York: Random House.

Hutton, W. (1995). *The state we're in.* London: Cape.

Inkson, K. (2000). Rewriting career development principles for the new millennium. In R. Wiesener & B. Millett (Eds.), *Management and organisational behaviour: Contemporary challenges and future directions* (pp. 11-24). New York: Wiley.

Kehm, R. (2002). *Internet job search almanac* (6th ed.). Avon, MA: Adams Media Corporation.

Kracke, B. (2002). The role of personality, parents and peers in adolescents' career exploration. *Journal of Adolescence, 25*(1), 19-30.

Lore, N. (1998). *The pathfinder: How to choose or change your career for a lifetime of satisfaction and success.* New York: Fireside.

Mackay, H. (1997). *Dig your well before you're thirsty: The only networking book you'll ever need.* New York: Doubleday.

Parsons, F. (1909). *Choosing a vocation.* Boston: Houghton Mifflin.

Peiperl, M. A., Arthur, M. B., & Anand, N. (Eds.). (2002). *Career creativity: Explorations in the re-making of work.* New York: Oxford University Press.

Peterson, G. W., Sampson, J. P., Jr., & Reardon, R. C. (1991). *Career development and services: A cognitive approach.* Pacific Grove, CA: Brooks/Cole.

Reardon, R. C., Lenz, J. G., Sampson, J. P., & Peterson, G. W. (2006). *Career planning and development: A comprehensive approach* (2nd ed.). Mason, OH: Thomson Custom Solutions.

Rifkin, J. (1995). *The end of work: The decline of the global labor force and the dawn of the post-market era.* New York: Putnam.

Ringer, R. J. (1973). *Winning through intimidation.* New York: Ballantine.

Robbins, S. P. (1994). *Management* (4th ed.). Upper Saddle River, NJ: Prentice Hall.

Sears, S. J., & Gordon, V. N. (2002). *Building your career: A guide to your future.* Upper Saddle River, NJ: Prentice Hall.

Sennet, R. (1998). *The corrosion of character: The personal consequences of the new capitalism.* New York: Norton.

Sher, B. (1994). *I could do anything, if I knew what it was.* New York: Dell.

Sinetar, M. (1987). *Do what you love, the money will follow.* New York: Dell.

U.S. Department of Labor. (2004). *Occupational outlook quarterly.* Washington, DC: Author.

Wegemann, R., Chapman, R., & Johnson, M. (1985). *Looking for work in the new economy.* Salt Lake City, UT: Olympus.

Wood, L. (2002). *Your 24/7 online job search guide.* New York: Wiley.

Young, R. A., & Valach, L. (2004). The construction of career through goal-directed action. *Journal of Vocational Behavior, 64*(3), 499-514.

CHAPTER 12

Career Counseling and Metaphor

Mary McMahon

Tell Me What to Do[1]

Marcus almost marched into my office and repeatedly called me ma'am. I felt he would salute me if he had half a chance. His request of me was quite simple—"tell me what to do." Marcus told a story about his life in the military, how it was his passion and all he had ever wanted to do. He explained how a recurring injury had resulted in his having to leave the job that he loved. The military had essentially told him he must go, and he was absolutely lost. In the military, he had a technical job related to communications and computers that he loved. He had completed training in courses that the military provided, had traveled overseas with his work, and had lived in many locations throughout Australia in accommodations provided by the military. The military life suited him.

Both his father and grandfather had been in the military and had encouraged him to follow in their footsteps, and Marcus never wanted to do anything else. He joined the school cadets as soon as he could and always enjoyed it. His family always lived where his father was posted by the military. While Marcus was at school, he never had to make decisions about which subjects to study because he always chose recommended classes that would assist him in gaining entry into the military. Even when he was applying for the military, he knew which service to apply for—that which his father and grandfather had belonged to.

As Marcus told his story, it became apparent that he had no decision-making experience. He had always been told what to do within his family and within the military, and he wanted me to continue in that vein. He had been told by the military to

---

Note: 1. The case studies presented in this chapter represent composites of many clients I have met during my years of career counseling. No particular client is represented here and no real names have been used.

> make an appointment with a career counselor who would be able to tell him what he could do. He wanted me to be an expert, or at least a parent or commanding officer, who could tell him what to do. Indeed, Marcus believed I could and would tell him what to do.

Some readers of this book are on their way to becoming career counselors. Others will inevitably find themselves, in due course, considering whether to seek guidance from a career counselor concerning their own careers. Like careers, career counseling can be understood through metaphors. What metaphor best represents your picture of career counseling? A doctor seeking to treat a patient's symptoms? An expert providing information on opportunities? A psychologist testing and measuring a person's psychological potential and dysfunctions? An employment agent providing job openings? A listener providing an audience for stories and a sounding board for frustrations? A coach offering encouragement and support? All of these metaphors and more may be acted out in counseling, often with positive outcomes for the client in terms of self-knowledge and clear direction. In addition, as I later show, counselors frequently use metaphor—clients' metaphors and their own—as part of the counseling process. In this chapter, I add insight on what career counseling entails, both for clients and for counselors.

"Tell me what to do" is a metaphor through which Marcus lived his life. However, as this case study shows, it also illustrates a commonly held expectation of career counseling. Such expectations may be traced to the origins of career counseling when, over a century ago, as indicated in Chapter 1 and Chapter 5, Frank Parsons (1909) advanced a "three-step 'formula'" that became the "first conceptual framework for career decision making" and the "first conceptual guide for career counselors" (Brown, 2002, p. 4). The following list shows Parsons's three key elements of career selection:

- First, a clear understanding of yourself, aptitudes, abilities, interests, resources, limitations, and other qualities;
- Second, a knowledge of the requirements and conditions of success, advantages and disadvantages, compensation, opportunities, and prospects in different lines of work;
- Third, true reasoning on the relations of these two groups of facts. (p. 5)

Parsons (1909) is best known for these three much-cited concepts, and the matching process they suggest has dominated career practice to the present day because it spawned what has come to be known as the trait-and-factor approach (see Chapter 5) and its more recent derivative, the person-environment-fit approach to career theory and practice. Interestingly, the metaphor "test and tell" has frequently been applied to trait-and-factor counseling. Key questions in career counseling are, "Who handles the understanding of self and work environment? Who does the true reasoning?" Marcus expects the counselor to do all the work and tell him what to do. Many counselors work instead from a client-centered model in which the counselor may provide information but expects the client to do the reasoning and independently work out "what to do."

Contrast Marcus's expectations of career counseling with those of Jamie in the following case study.

Let Me Tell My Story

Jamie came to counseling carrying a wad of paper under his arm. He sat down and put the wad on the coffee table for the counselor to see. The wad was a battery of career assessments that Jamie had completed at another career service. He asked, "What do these mean? I don't understand them. What do I do with them?" Jamie explained how he had previously made an appointment with another career counseling service. When he arrived there, he found that he and three other clients had all arrived at the same time. They were all seated at desks and completed the same battery of tests. Each was then given a time to come back for their results. When Jamie went back, the counselor told him what his results were and which occupations he might be suited to. Jamie began to ask questions and was told that if he wanted counseling he would have to make another appointment. By then Jamie felt let down by the service: He believed that his needs had not been met and that the counselors didn't really want to listen to him. He decided he would go to another career counselor and take his assessment battery with him.

As this case study illustrates, Jamie didn't want to be told what to do. He wanted to make sense of and understand his situation and really feel that he had been heard. Jamie particularly wanted an opportunity to speak with a counselor—to tell his story and be listened to. But Jamie's counselor adopted a similar frame of reference to Marcus in the previous case and cast himself in the role of expert: "I'll tell you what to do." Small wonder that Jamie felt dissatisfied. In any counseling situation, it is desirable that clients, not the counselor, take responsibility for resolving their issues. In so doing, clients become more committed to the solution, and, moreover, they will learn problem solving for the future.

This oversimplified view of career counseling as a test-and-tell process, as illustrated by Marcus's expectations and Jamie's counselor, was never what Parsons (1909) intended for career counseling work or how he conducted his own work. Rather, he advocated an active role for clients in which they actively engaged in information gathering from a variety of sources and self-assessment. In addition, he encouraged his clients to involve influential people from their social systems and to reflect on contextual influences, such as family, health, lifestyle, mobility, and resources, such as financial factors. Further, Parsons (1909) recommended that a client should "come to wise decisions himself" (p. 4) because no one may decide what occupation another person should choose.

Thus Parsons's approach is better reflected in the case study of Lucy and that of Ellen, which is given later in this chapter.

Test and Guide

Lucy was in her mid- to late 20s when she came to career counseling, frustrated that she didn't know what to do with her life and conscious of her family's disapproval about her not knowing and thus changing jobs so often. Since leaving school, Lucy had worked in many jobs, ranging from retail assistant to waitress to laborer for a landscape gardener to administration assistant to bus driver. Lucy had also spent some time traveling and working overseas.

The career counselor engaged Lucy in a discussion about her favorite jobs and those she disliked the most. Further, Lucy was encouraged to recall what she liked about particular positions and what she disliked. With the counselor's assistance, Lucy began to see some patterns emerge regarding which tasks she enjoyed doing. To encourage Lucy to go further in developing her self-understanding, the counselor gave her a Self-Directed Search to complete at home and an Occupations Finder (Holland, 1994a, 1994b; see also Chapter 5).

When Lucy returned for her second appointment with the career counselor, she had completed the Self-Directed Search and used the Occupations Finder. Together, Lucy and the counselor discussed Lucy's results and how she used the Occupations Finder. Lucy had also discussed her results with her parents, who were able to recall activities Lucy enjoyed as a child, at home and at school. Lucy told the career counselor that she was beginning to understand herself better and had listed some jobs that she thought "could be possibilities." In addition, the Occupations Finder reminded her of two jobs she had seen former colleagues doing that she thought looked interesting. Lucy was feeling more positive and was ready to find out more about these jobs. The career counselor gave her sources for information, including Web sites. Lucy also decided to contact her former colleagues to find out more about their work.

The client expectations and counseling scenarios depicted in the previous case studies are indicative of some of the diversity of practice that now exists within career counseling. Contributing to such diversity are the changed and changing world of work and recent thinking about career development and career counseling. World of work changes have been described metaphorically by Knowdell (1996), who suggested that career decision making is now a process rather than a once-in-a-lifetime event. He made the following claim:

In 1950, at the midpoint of the 20th century, planning, acquiring, and maintaining a career was very much like boarding and riding a train. When you wanted to use a train to go somewhere, you purchased a ticket for your destination and boarded the train at the gate with your destination printed on it. The train moved steadily along the fixed and stable tracks until it reached your destination. No detours. No changes in the route. Just sit back and relax. The engineer, conductor and crew would take you to your destination. (p. 183)

Note the "journey" metaphor (Chapter 6) employed in this analysis. Knowdell (1996) suggested that by the 1960s and 1970s the "train" metaphor had become obsolete and that a more appropriate metaphor had come into use—that of a "bus":

> When you boarded your bus for work each day, you didn't get on a vehicle that operated on fixed and stable tracks. With the bus you were on a vehicle that could change its route when the road conditions and traffic patterns changed. You were now on a vehicle that could change its ultimate destination. You could even transfer or change buses in mid-route if you desired. Career decision making in the 1970s became much more flexible, allowing the occupation to change with the technology and economy and permitting the individual to make mid-career changes and transfers. But, like the train, we still relied on the bus company to set the schedule and route as they could be heard to say "leave the driving to us." (pp. 183–184)

However, Knowdell (1996) claimed that even the "bus" metaphor is obsolete and that a more appropriate metaphor for career planning and decision making in the 21st century may be that of an "all-terrain vehicle" (ATV):

> The ATV is fast and flexible. It doesn't require fixed tracks. It doesn't require transit schedules or even paved roads. Routes can be changed or modified every year, month, week, day, hour or even minute. And the ATV has one other distinguishing difference from the train and bus. When you ride the train or bus, someone else is in the driver's seat. But in the all terrain vehicle, the individual needs to take control of the situation and control his/her own course. In career planning, the individual needs to take the controls and "drive" his/her own unique career toward success. (p. 184)

In this new world of work, Jarvis (2003) claimed that individuals will have "a succession of jobs in a number of industry sectors during their working lives"(p. 1). Corresponding with these changes, individuals are viewed as responsible for managing their own careers, and in so doing it has been suggested that they may access career services several times in a lifetime. Unlike the counselors at the beginning of the 20th century, when the predominant issue dealt with in career counseling was the occupational choice of the dominant client group, school leavers, the career counselors of the 21st century face a diverse range of clients and an equally diverse range of counseling issues, such as occupational choice, lifelong learning, work–life balance, workplace harassment, international work experience, career transition, unemployment, dual-career management, stress, and financial management. In this context, there have been calls for the provision of career guidance services for people across the life span (e.g., Watts & Sultana, 2004).

Just as the world of work is very different from when career counseling began, so too are conceptualizations about career, career development, and career counseling. These differences may be attributed to the different philosophical positions or worldviews on which theory and practice have been based—logical positivism and constructivism. Brown (2002) summarizes the differences. Theory and practice that subscribe to the logical-positivist worldview assume that individual behavior is observable, measurable, and linear; that individuals can be studied separately from their environments; and, consequently, that the contexts within which individuals live and work are of less importance than individuals' actions. By contrast, theory and practice that subscribe to the constructivist worldview assume that there is an interconnectedness between individuals and their environments and that behavior needs to be understood in context. Related to this is the importance of the subjective knowledge of individuals and recognition that behavior cannot be explained by laws or principles or by the inference of cause and effect. Thus, constructivism is holistic and recognizes that individuals are active agents constructing their own lives.

In practice, counseling approaches based on the logical-positivist worldview maintained an expert model, relied heavily on assessment and diagnosis, and generally followed a linear sequence through steps such as analysis, synthesis, diagnosis, prognosis, counseling, and follow-up (e.g., Williamson, 1939, 1965). As previously mentioned, such approaches became known as test-and-tell approaches (Chapter 5). The three previous case studies reflect a key issue centered on the nature of tell: "tell me what to do" versus "help me to understand myself." By contrast, constructivism encourages individuals to be active and expert participants in the counseling process through the telling of their story or narrative (Chapter 10). In so doing, and in collaboration with the career counselor, meaning and understanding are enhanced. Together individuals and career counselors co-construct possible future scenarios. The test-and-tell approach has dominated career practice since its inception. However, it is important not to assume an either-or position on the two worldviews and their associated practices. Rather, their differences are to be valued, and the contributions of both approaches to career counseling have been recognized. It is likely that career counselors will incorporate elements of both worldviews into their practice (McMahon & Patton, 2002). Indeed, as Lucy's case illustrates, both philosophical positions can coexist harmoniously in career counseling, and their complementarities may enrich the process.

The irreversibly changed world of work and the influence of constructivism in conceptualizations about career development and career counseling have resulted in challenges for career psychology and career counseling to reinvigorate and redefine themselves (e.g., Savickas, 1993, 2002). Thus, career counseling is a profession and process in evolution. In particular, the gap between personal and career counseling is becoming narrower (e.g., Manuele-Adkins, 1992; Subich, 1993) as life, learning, and work issues are being increasingly viewed as inseparable and as counselors broaden their range of approaches. Metaphorically, a shift is occurring in career counseling, from scores to stories or from test-and-tell to narration and co-construction. Different practices of counseling may emphasize one metaphor more than another, or they may combine metaphors. Counselors offer different benefits to different clients. As the previous case studies illustrate, metaphor provides a tool through which career counselors may conceptualize and define their work.

Also, as the previous examples illustrate, metaphor is a tool through which people understand and live their lives. Lakoff and Johnson (1980) suggested that metaphor is a part of everyday life that is reflected in language, thought, and action (see Chapter 1). The shift to a narrative metaphor for career counseling brings with it greater opportunity for clients to tell their stories. Inherent to story telling is the use of metaphor. Consider Simon and Carl, who we meet later in this chapter. They describe "drowning in a tide" and being in a "tug-of-war." Such metaphors paint vivid pictures of career situations and opportunities through which meaning may be elaborated. However, to date, the use of metaphor as a tool in career counseling has not been explored in depth.

It seems that metaphor may be an underused resource in career counseling in terms of both conceptualizations about the profession and as a tool in career counseling. This chapter explores possible uses of metaphor in career counseling. First, it explores the possibilities offered by metaphor to assist in conceptualizing career counseling. For example, metaphors about the nature of career counseling and the role of career counselors is proposed and discussed. Second, this chapter discusses the use of metaphor as a tool within the counseling process for elaborating meaning and story. Examples of client metaphors are presented and their use in the counseling process to elaborate story and meaning illustrated. Suggestions are provided for elevating the use of metaphor in career counseling from the status of throwaway line to that of constructive meaning-making tool.

Metaphors of Career Counseling

At a theoretical level, Patton and McMahon (1999) used a theatrical metaphor to describe the shift in career counseling from approaches informed by the logical-positivist worldview to those informed by the constructivist worldview. It is this theoretical shift that makes an examination of the use of metaphor in career counseling more possible. Patton and McMahon explained that behind the scenes of career counseling is the vocational guidance movement, which was unified theoretically and practically by the work of Parsons (1909) as discussed earlier. The trait-and-factor approach evolved out of the work of Parsons and has retained its place at center stage in career counseling (Patton & McMahon, 1999). Essentially, this approach to counseling is a linear, expert-driven model predicated by assessment, whereby factors such as the client's personality, interests, abilities, or values are matched with occupations. This has promulgated the "counselor as expert" metaphor reflected in the case studies of Marcus, who believed that the career counselor could tell him what to do, and Jamie, whose career counselor took an expert role and operated according to a matching or test-and-tell approach. Lucy's career counselor, however, was also an expert in terms of professional knowledge and responsibility for the counseling process but did not assume an expert role in providing answers for Lucy.

Just as a scene change has occurred in the world of work, so too a scene change is evolving in career counseling through the influence of constructivism (Patton & McMahon, 1999). With an emphasis on holism, individual agency, meaning, and story, Patton and McMahon describe constructivism as "waiting in the wings"—a "trend that may make career counseling more relevant and responsive to the times"

(p. 230). The importance of story and meaning making in the context of people's lives is fundamental to the constructivist worldview. Metaphor is intrinsic to story telling and therefore sits comfortably with the constructivist worldview.

At a practical level, metaphors have also been used to describe the extension of career counseling from its logical-positivist origins to embrace its constructivist possibilities. For example, Savickas (1993) described a move away from trying to fit individuals into a mainstream culture toward affirming diversity and enabling individuals to plan their lives. This is reflective of Law's (2003) claim that to date in career counseling there have been "too many lists, not enough stories" (p. 25) and Savickas's (1993) suggestion that career counseling moves to "stories rather than scores" (p. 213). Similarly, Peavy (1995) observed that career counselors should take more of a self-as-narrative view of clients, rather than a self-as-trait view. Thus, the move from the logical-positivist psychometric self to the constructivist narrated self (Peavy, 1998) has implications for the role of career counselors who are being called on to act more as "biographers who interpret lives in progress rather than as actuaries who count interests and abilities" by listening for clients' life themes and stories (Savickas, 1992, p. 338). Whereas some of these metaphors suggest an either-or position, recent career counseling texts (e.g., Amundson, Harris-Bowlsbey, & Niles, 2005) are more reflective of a both-and position that values the contribution and complementarity of the two approaches.

Peavy (2004) suggested that the language and vocabulary of counseling that was developed in the positivist era may be becoming obsolete. In his SocioDynamic approach, Peavy uses the metaphor of "help-seeker," rather than "client," and "bricoleur" to describe career counselors' capacity to apply creative solutions to problems. Peavy (1998) explained that a *bricoleur* is a jack-of-all-trades, "a professional do-it-yourself person, one who takes the cultural knowledge at hand and uses these life-relevant materials to solve concrete problems which people encounter in everyday living" (p. 25). As a metaphor, "bricoleur" implies a degree of flexibility and an ability to be responsive to changing situations. It implies having a repertoire of skills and not being wedded to a particular approach or model. Payne (2000) suggested that "the metaphors through which we organize our work have a powerful influence on both what we perceive and what we do" (p. 1). Thus, career counselors who organize their work through the "test-and-tell" or "expert" metaphor may provide their clients with critical information but may have less scope for flexibility than those who organize their work through the metaphors of "narrative" and "bricoleur."

The use of metaphor to conceptualize the role of career counselors is not new. Carson and Hinkelman (1999) noted that metaphors have been used since the time of Parsons (1909). For example, Parsons frequently used the metaphor of "building," related to building a career, and he extended his metaphor to include career counselors as "architects": "No-one would think of building a dwelling or a business block without carefully selecting an appropriate and advantageous site and drawing out a well-considered plan with the help of an architect or expert builder" (p. 101). Consider what we may learn about career counseling by conceptualizing counselors as architects. Architects engage in planning and are detailed, creative, able to work in a team, and aware of context, such as foundations and building materials. The objectivity of architecture in planning, measurement, and detail is consistent with the logical-positivist worldview, and the subjectivity of the elements of design and creativity and the element of context are consistent with the constructivist worldview.

As the work of Parsons (1909) thus indicates, career counselors may display examples of practice from both worldviews. Whereas the test-and-tell metaphor predominated for most of the past century and continues to do so, and whereas psychometric assessments remain useful tools in the career counseling process, career counselors may now draw on a greater range of metaphors through which to organize their work. For example, McMahon and Patton (2002) suggested that career counselors may operate on a continuum of practice that reflects both the "test-and-tell" metaphor and the "narrative" metaphor. Consider the following case study, which incorporates elements of both worldviews.

Testing and Telling a Story

Ellen came to counseling with her parents. She was 18 years old, in her final year of school, and had no idea what she wanted to do when she left school. She was becoming worried and so were her parents. The counselor suggested that Ellen may already know useful information and that more information could be gathered if Ellen undertook some career assessment. The counselor explained that the information provided by Ellen, her parents, and the tests could be used to build a career story about her that would help her develop ideas about what she might do when she left school. Ellen and her parents agreed that Ellen would meet with the counselor for two more sessions, during which Ellen would complete some career assessment tests. The counselor explained that during these sessions they would compile a folder of information related to Ellen's career story, which would be hers to take home. This information might help her plan her next step after school and possibly even help her beyond this step. They also agreed that in one final session, Ellen, her parents,

and the career counselor would discuss possible futures for Ellen.

During the remainder of their first meeting, Ellen talked about the subjects she was studying at school, and the career counselor helped her identify what she liked and disliked about those subjects. As they spoke about each subject, the career counselor made some notes that she put into a folder with Ellen's name on it. Also during this first meeting, Ellen's parents explained what they believed were Ellen's strengths and the qualities they admired in Ellen that they thought would be helpful to her in the future.

In the second session, the counselor suggested, on the basis of what they had discussed in their last interview, that a clear understanding of Ellen's aptitudes may be helpful. In particular, she suggested that Ellen complete the Differential Aptitude Tests for Verbal Reasoning and Abstract Reasoning. Each of these tests contained 30 multiple-choice items, with the Verbal Reasoning taking 20 minutes to complete and the Abstract Reasoning Test taking

15 minutes to complete. In their third interview, Ellen completed the 16PF (Cattell, Cattell, & Cattell, 1993) to find out more about which occupations might suit her personality. After each test, the counselor and Ellen spent time discussing the results and comparing them to information they had gathered in the previous sessions. They began to identify apparent themes in Ellen's life that were reflected in the school subjects she performed well in and liked and in her after-school activities. Ellen began to understand more about herself and what she liked and disliked and why. Her previous decisions and her interests began to mean more to her, and she began to see how this knowledge might help her in future decisions.

Between sessions, Ellen took her story folder home and was encouraged by the counselor to add to it by visiting career Web sites, such as Australia's national online career information system and myfuture.edu.au, and by completing short online assessment instruments. Ellen completed these tasks enthusiastically. Ellen was also encouraged to talk with her parents about the counseling sessions.

Ellen and her parents attended the final appointment with the career counselor. Ellen's parents reported that Ellen seemed less worried and that she had told them a lot about the information she was collecting in her folder. They were feeling more confident that Ellen would be able to plan a way forward; they had seen her completing tasks on the computer and following up on occupations identified by various tests that she had completed with the career counselor and on the Internet. Ellen explained that things were making more sense to her now and that she understood herself better. Together, Ellen, her parents, and the counselor discussed Ellen's possible future. Ellen was able to describe a number of occupations that she had researched. In addition, she was able to explain why she thought the occupations suited her and what she would like about them. She was able to make sense of occupational information as it related to her and was able to construct possible stories of herself in these occupations. In addition, by knowing where to find information, Ellen was now actively engaged in the construction of her future.

Ellen's case study demonstrates how career counselors can structure their work by applying the traditional "test-and-tell" metaphor and the more recent "narrative" metaphor in a complementary process that is meaningful for clients. In Ellen's case, assessment instruments derived from the logical-positivist worldview were incorporated into a constructivist process in which Ellen was actively involved in understanding and applying the results in the context of her life. Ellen was recognized as a capable expert in the construction of her life.

In addition to the "test-and-tell" and "narrative" metaphors, other metaphors, such as "coach," "advocate," "nurturer," and "believer," may be observed in the way career counselors structure their work. Consider the career counselor in the following case study, who structured career counseling around the metaphor of "coach."

The Coach

Hayley was beside herself with anxiety when she made an appointment with the school career counselor. It was her final semester of school, and she explained that she had "just stopped." She just stared at her school books at night neither writing nor reading. Nothing like this had happened to her before. At first she thought it was just a phase, but the longer it lasted, the more convinced Hayley was that she had a problem, and she became worried that she would not do well in her final exams. She explained that she was involved in a school orchestra and had a part-time job, both of which she enjoyed very much. It wasn't that she didn't have time at home to do her schoolwork, Hayley explained. It was just that she couldn't get started. She felt that she was falling behind, and now she simply didn't know where to start, even if she could.

With her career counselor, Hayley drew up an extensive list of all that she had to do. She then rated the items on the list in terms of their urgency. Eventually, Hayley identified the assignment that was at the top of her list. With her career counselor, she broke the assignment down into tiny steps. She agreed to a tiny step she believed she could complete that night. The next day, Hayley went back to the counselor with a short paragraph of notes she had made. Hayley explained that she had stared at her books for quite a while but finally did what she had agreed to do. She felt that she had made a start but had a long way to go. The career counselor affirmed her achievement and explored with her what it meant to her to have started and no longer be stopped. Again, they agreed on another step.

This process continued daily for a few days—Hayley checking in briefly with the career counselor, agreeing on a goal, and then reporting back. She began to feel more positive and finally one day reported that she had done more than she had previously agreed. She began visiting the career counselor less frequently, always reporting on her achievements and always leaving with an achievable goal. As time went by, the counselor had a significantly reduced role to play in Hayley's goal setting as Hayley assumed more responsibility for herself. However, the career counselor always affirmed Hayley's achievements and the strategies she developed that would lead her to achieving her goal. Hayley went on to successfully complete her final exams and to undertake university study.

By conceptualizing the intervention with Hayley through the metaphor of "coach," the counselor was guided by her agenda and focused on results by taking action to close the gap between where the client was and where the client wanted to be (Bench, 2001). In essence, through the "coaching" metaphor, the counselor helped Hayley turn her vision into a plan (Hudson, 1999) by focusing on concrete goals that were achievable. Stevens (1998) claimed that the "coaching" metaphor requires career counselors to have an understanding of the "self-reliant career development process" (p. 2), an understanding that was clearly evident in the case of Hayley. However, affirmation of client self-reliance is important, and Stevens suggested that career counselors using the "coach" metaphor may also assume the role of companion, through which they monitor clients' well-being; support, motivate, and praise their clients; and celebrate significant achievements with them.

Whereas the metaphor of "coach" has become increasingly common, the metaphor of "advocate" is not as common. In the following case study Tom, the career counselor, recognizes a social justice issue in his workplace and assumes the metaphor of "advocate" for his work.

The Advocate

Tom was a career counselor who worked for an employee assistance service that visited several organizations. In one of these organizations, a manufacturing company, some team leader positions were available, and Tom was asked to provide a workshop for staff on applying for jobs and addressing key selection criteria. At the workshop, he discovered that many of the staff spoke English only as a second language. After the workshop, one participant asked him for help. Although he could speak English with reasonable proficiency, his written English was weak, and he felt that he and many of his colleagues would be disadvantaged in the selection process. At least one of his colleagues had decided not to apply.

Although Tom could offer individual assistance, he believed that it was an issue that the company needed to address more holistically. Tom recounted his observations to the human resources manager and suggested that good applicants may be disadvantaged in the selection process because of their limited fluency in written English and the requirement for a written application. The manager appreciated Tom's concern. Together they resolved that a computer would be made available to all staff during the lunch hour and before and after work to assist staff members with their applications. They also decided to extend the deadline for application. In addition, one of the manager's assistants would be available to proofread applications and provide assistance on English expression. Staff members were informed that they would not be disadvantaged by a lack of fluency in English.

As the previous case study illustrates, Tom conceptualized the issue presented by his client in the broader context of organizational policy and procedures and their implications for the population of workers with a non-English-speaking background. Tom successfully lobbied on behalf of his clients to improve their access to promotional positions, and in so doing he assisted other workers as well. Such a view of the issue is reflective of constructivist approaches to career counseling that take a holistic view of clients and their careers and, in so doing, are able to examine the links between culture and social justice. Stead (2004) noted that culture may sometimes create boundaries and limit resources to people inside and outside the culture. In addition, culture may constrain occupational choice (Arthur, 2006). Arthur and McMahon (2005) encouraged career counselors to locate clients' issues in a broader context and to adopt advocacy roles in work settings or in the broader community to assist clients to address inequities.

With the increased influence of the constructivist worldview on career counseling, new metaphors are emerging. For example, Parker (2002) suggested the metaphor of "nurturer" and McMahon (2004) discussed the importance of believing in the active agency of clients—the "believer" metaphor. Both metaphors illustrate the constructivist belief in the importance of the counselor–client relationship, a belief that is not emphasized in the "test-and-tell" metaphor. "The development of a quality therapeutic relationship with such characteristics as acceptance, understanding, trust, and caring" (Granvold, 1996, p. 350) is one of the main objectives of constructivist career counselors. Consider the metaphor of "nurturer" in the case of Kathryn.

The Nurturer

For some time, Kathryn had saved her money for a visit to a career counseling service. She was separated from an abusive partner and worked menial jobs to support two teenage children. She had worked, among other things, as a cleaner, which she hated, and as an assistant in a facility for older adults, which she loved. All were low-paying jobs. She thought, "I can do more than this," and she thought that if she completed further study, more satisfying and better paying employment opportunities would be available to her. Without a support network and struggling to make ends meet from day to day, Kathryn invested in a career counseling session. Although her daily struggles had caused her to lose sight of her life's achievements, she held on to the hope that she could do something "better."

The counselor listened to Kathryn and invited her to tell forgotten and discounted stories about occupations she had held many years before—occupations in which Kathryn had high levels of responsibility—and about the distance education she undertook to earn basic qualifications. Together they began to co-construct a story of competence and achievement that would assist Kathryn in her application for study. In addition, the counselor provided Kathryn with the information she needed to prepare her application. After one interview, which was all that Kathryn could afford, the counselor invited her to continue the counseling process through follow-up phone calls, which was part of the usual practice of the counseling service. Kathryn spoke with the counselor several times by phone. The counselor also offered to provide feedback on Kathryn's application during her lunchtime and between Kathryn's shifts, a process that occurred a couple of times. In this way, Kathryn didn't have to pay more money and the counselor could help her prepare her application for study.

The counselor became a support network for Kathryn. It was easy for Kathryn's circumstances to overwhelm her and for her not to believe in herself. Always affirming Kathryn's competencies and what she had achieved, the career counselor played an important role for Kathryn. After Kathryn began study, she phoned the counselor from time to time if she needed help, and her calls were always within the boundaries of the counselor's work role. In time, as Kathryn built a more extensive support network and began to succeed in her studies, her phone calls dropped off. Apart from the co-construction with Kathryn of a story of competence and achievement that contributed to the construction of a preferred story, the career counselor's main role was to support and nurture Kathryn.

The career counselor built a relationship with Kathryn, which led Kathryn to believe that she really mattered. A mattering climate was created (Schlossberg, Lynch, & Chickering, 1989) in which Kathryn felt valued, cared about, and appreciated. Amundson (1998) suggested that Rogers's (1951) necessary conditions for counseling—genuineness, unconditional positive regard, and empathic understanding—are essential for such a climate. In addition, the previous case study is reflective of a suggestion by Amundson (2003) that career counselors examine the conventions of career counseling to open up possibilities for clients by demonstrating flexibility in their approach.

All of the case studies presented here also clearly demonstrate another key element of career counseling from a constructivist worldview, that of active agency, the belief in clients to "act for themselves and speak on their own behalf" (Monk, Winslade, Crocket, & Epston, 1997, p. 301). Consider the young woman in the following case study whose letter highlights the importance of affirming and respecting the agency of the client.

The Believer

I received a letter from a young woman who had been my client 5.5 years before. Her letter began "I'm not sure if you remember me." I didn't, and I had to go back in our archived files to find out what she had come to see me about. When I saw her previously, she had just completed high school and was devastated that her school results weren't good enough to do what she wanted to do. She wanted to study business, and she was passionate about working in a competitive industry that had high personnel turnover and low success rates. Her parents were concerned that she would fail and wanted her to consider other options. However, the clarity of her vision in terms of her talents and demonstrated interests and the passion in her voice were compelling. Together we explored possible pathways that could enable her to achieve her dream. In her brief letter, she told me how she had completed her degree, had established her own company, and had won an award. The final line of her letter reminded me of the importance of our role: "Thank you for believing in me back then."

As the previous case study indicates, affirming the young woman's abilities and vision and co-constructing a plan to achieve her planned vision were important to her. At one level, fostering agency involves identifying and affirming clients' strengths, knowledge, attitudes, and skills that will be helpful in creating their preferred futures. At another level, fostering agency involves affirming, supporting, encouraging, and creating optimism around clients' capacity to create their preferred future. Mattering relationships nurture clients and enhance their capacity to believe in themselves, their agency, and their capacity to construct a preferred future.

In this regard, Peavy (1998) suggested the following three main tasks of counselors, including career counselors:

1. to enter into sensible and trustworthy communication with the other,

2. to develop a mutual understanding of the particular difficulty which the other faces, and

3. to plan and construct activity projects which are designed to:
   a) increase self-responsibility and personal control,
   b) increase the other's meaningful participation in social life, and
   c) help the other choose and move toward preferred futures. (p. 50)

Clearly, these tasks were reflected in the previous case studies. No matter which metaphor informed the work of the career counselors in the studies, the ultimate goal was for the clients to move toward their preferred futures. Further, the metaphors through which they structured their work were largely responses to the uniqueness of their clients and their life, learning, and work issues. Michael White (2004) reminded us of the uniqueness of the clients we meet and also of the uniqueness of the journey we travel with each of them in the following reflection about his first meetings with people who consult him:

> I experience feelings of anticipation, degrees of apprehension, and a sense of heightened expectations. This is the anticipation of other journeys to be had— not just any old journeys, but ones that will like those before it, take me to destinations that I could not have predicted, by routes not previously mapped. This is an apprehension that relates to the responsibility that I have, as a therapist for the travelling circumstances, and for the journey's outcome. (p. 45)

Although each of the previous case studies recognized clients as active agents in the construction of their careers, as Michael White suggested, the counselors were responsible for the nature of the journey they traveled with their clients.

Using Metaphor in Career Counseling

With Michael White's (2004) thoughts in mind about counselor responsibilities for the counseling process and outcomes, we move to consider the use of metaphor within the counseling process. Metaphor has been used as a tool in career counseling since the days of Parsons (1909), when he encouraged clients to go "sailing with chart and compass" and "competing in a race without handicaps" (p. 5). These counselor-generated metaphors were used in an advisory capacity by Parsons to emphasize the importance of planning, identifying strengths, and minimizing weaknesses (Carson & Hinkelman, 1999).

Metaphors are also client generated. They permeate our everyday language and are frequently present in the stories clients tell. To date, career counseling, with its logical-positivist origins and prevailing "test-and-tell" metaphor, has placed little emphasis on the use of language and story and even less on the use of metaphor as a technique. The emergence of the constructivist perspective has located the use of language, narrative, and stories more centrally in the counseling process as a means to understand the personal and social realities of clients (Lyddon, Clay, & Sparks, 2001). Consequently, greater attention has been focused on the use of metaphorical language and its role in human knowing and meaning making. However, using metaphor as a technique in career counseling is not well understood, and it is not unreasonable to ask, "How do we use metaphor in career counseling and why would we want to?"

Why Use Metaphor?

In a study on the intentional use of metaphor, Martin, Cummings, and Hallberg (1992) found that if metaphors were developed collaboratively and repetitively, then clients tended to recall them two thirds of the time, and when they did, they found the session more helpful than when they recalled other therapeutic events. These researchers also found the following functions of metaphor:

- enhancing emotional awareness and understanding;
- bridging between concepts;
- enhancing the relationship with therapist; and
- clarifying goals. (p. 145)

Even though this study was very small and was conducted in the field of psychotherapy, its findings are interesting because they reflect the purposes and potential benefits of using practitioner-elaborated metaphor (e.g., Carson & Hinkelman, 1999; Fox, 1989; Perry, 2004). For example, Carson and Hinkelman (1999) suggested that the purposes of using metaphor include developing rapport by constructing meaning, helping clients understand the nature of change in career development over the life span, and helping clients get unstuck from previous ways of thinking about a career or shift how they view their career (p. 15).

These purposes are reflected in the following potential benefits of working with metaphors, which were proposed by Fox (1989):

- Metaphors are nonthreatening.
- They promote multiple responses.
- They evoke more than intellectual responses.
- Metaphors operate on many levels.
- They highlight the moment.
- Metaphors are indirectly revealing.
- They make interactions memorable.
- Metaphors are gripping and engaging.
- They supply variety and uniqueness.

Importantly, client-generated metaphors may provide insight into clients' cultural influences through the symbols and values that are present in their metaphors (Carson & Hinkelman, 1999; Kopp, 1995). Essentially, metaphor may be useful in career counseling in three important ways—specifically, building relationships, guiding communication, and facilitating change. Each way is briefly elaborated in the following sections.

Building Relationships

There is widespread agreement that one of the main purposes and advantages of using metaphor is its contribution to client–counselor relationships (e.g., Combs & Freedman, 1990; Fox, 1989; Lyddon et al., 2001; Perry, 2004; Wickman, Daniels, White, & Fesmire, 1999). Combs and Freedman (1990) explain "when we use a person's metaphors, rapport is enhanced. A person can't help but feel more at home. It's like walking into a person's home and finding your favorite music playing" (p. 19). When career counselors are attuned to client metaphors, the relationship between client and counselor is strengthened. Metaphor may help career counselors empathize with clients (Wickman et al., 1999). These authors explain that since the days of Rogers (1957), "speaking a client's language has long been understood as a means to join with clients, gain their trust, and bring about the necessary and sufficient conditions for change" (p. 393). Although rapport and empathy have always been important elements of counseling relationships, they have not traditionally been emphasized in career counseling because of its trait-and-factor traditions, in which expert-driven approaches were not predicated on an effective working relationship. However, with the influence of constructivism in career counseling, greater emphasis is now being placed on relationships.

Guiding Communication

Client-generated metaphors can provide a common language for the career counseling process and become tools for insight and change (Carson & Hinkelman, 1999). Metaphors may assist clients to articulate their experience and to express feelings, and they may also provide a means to organize information and experience and convey it succinctly and vividly by "packing a great deal of meaning into a very small space" (Sims, 2003, p. 531).

Listening for metaphoric images is an important communication skill because information about how clients see their problems and their abilities to overcome the problems is embedded within the images (Amundson, 1998). In addition, clients' confidence in counselors' capacity to understand them is enhanced, an important consideration in effective communication. Metaphors may be used in any setting, may assist in breaking the ice with difficult or resistant clients, and can also accommodate learning styles, such as visual and auditory styles (Carson & Hinkelman, 1999).

Facilitating Change

Metaphor is also an intervention technique that may bring about change (Wickman et al., 1999). Sims (2003) suggested that metaphor presents a convenient and easily followed path through which clients and counselors may create shared meaning and collaborate in the development of fruitful outcomes. The path is designated by clients' words and expressions, and their metaphors, which are valued and become a focus for shared exploration of their imagery and implications (Sims, 2003). In this way, a culture of counseling is created (Babits, 2001), whereby there is space between fantasy and reality where reflection, meaning making, and creativity may occur. In this way, metaphor may promote a connection between past and present and the discovery of connecting patterns and themes in clients' lives (Fox, 1989), a feature of career counseling that has gained increased importance since the influence of constructivist approaches. For example, in the case of Marcus earlier in this chapter, the metaphor that recurred throughout the stories he told was "tell me what to do."

A caution in the use of metaphor: If the metaphors don't fit the client, then they will not be effective. Zindel (2001) suggested that "catching metaphors is like lassoing a hummingbird . . . you can destroy the very thing you are trying to catch" (p. 11). Counselors should respect the individuality of client metaphors and refrain from overevaluating or judging them—for example, as acceptable or not acceptable (Carson & Hinkelman, 1999). Further cautions relate to explaining, analyzing, or interpreting metaphor (Fox, 1989), with Warme (1996) suggesting that explanation limits the possibility of further reflection. Similarly, Sims (2003) suggested that there is a tendency for practitioners to redescribe what clients say, a process that essentially leads them away from clients' actual descriptions toward the counselor's own conceptual and explanatory schemas or preferred metaphors. By contrast, describing metaphors invites further exploration and description. As Sinai's (1997) following description of her client metaphors illustrates, metaphors are multilayered and may be developed from thin descriptions into rich and thick descriptions:

> I realized his stories were just like his paintings. They were full of multiple images and layers that intermingled, revealed integrated parts, emphasized what he was trying to hide, and hid what he did not even know. In a sense I did not have to create the metaphors, they were already there. . . . I matched my language to his, using his words and reflecting his own images. (p. 276)

In working with metaphor, Fox (1989) made the following suggestion:

> As with a poem, breaking apart a metaphor by analyzing or interpreting it deprives it of power. Interpretation is inadequate. A more productive approach is to work with it affirmatively—encourage it, nurture it, draw it out, propel it, transformation rather than translation is the key. Extending, enlarging the metaphor, shaping and dramatizing it leads to alterations in clients' views of reality. (p. 235)

In this regard, the use of client-generated metaphors has been found to be better received and better recalled than counselor-generated metaphors (Sims, 2003).

Strategies for Using Metaphor

A number of authors (e.g., Carson & Hinkelman, 1999; Perry, 2004; Sims, 2003) have suggested models and strategies for using metaphor in career counseling that reflect Fox's (1989) previous suggestions. For example, Carson and Hinkelman suggested that counselors ask clients for elaboration of a metaphor to clarify meaning or understanding or for an additional metaphor to better assess the situation. In so doing, counselors may use language parallel to that being used by the client (Wickman et al., 1999). These most basic of strategies are reflected in the case studies presented later in this chapter. In addition to working with metaphor through dialogue, several authors suggested using strategies such as drawing and collage (e.g., Amundson, 1988, 1997; Vahamottonen, Keskinen, & Parrila, 1994). Amundson (1988) suggested that visually representing metaphors through drawing or collage extends their usefulness by making them more concrete than is possible in a verbal interaction. Such processes may appeal to clients who are visual learners.

The first and perhaps most important step in using metaphor is in hearing and recognizing them in the client's story as it is being told. However, listening for and recognizing client metaphors is not always easy because "people's everyday language contains metaphoric expressions so pervasive, common, and seemingly mundane that they go largely unnoticed" (Wickman et al., 1999, p. 392). This sentiment is expressed in the previous comment by Sinai (1997) about her counseling work with an artist. In addition to listening for and recognizing client metaphor, Sinai provided a further clue into working with client metaphor—specifically, using the language of metaphor in responses to the client.

As Sinai (1997) indicated, matching the language of the metaphor and using the client's words are important first steps once a metaphor is recognized. Zindel (2001) metaphorically suggested that the first step in the intentional use of metaphor in career counseling is "catching" the metaphor:

> How to catch a metaphor. Listen. Use imagination. Creativity. Be in the moment. Tolerate chaos together. Allow for paradox. Ambiguity. Give us a need to know. Speak from unconscious to unconscious. Have the capacity for illusion. Suspend elements of reality. Be playful. Know each other's language and share it. And listen to the rumblings. (p. 11)

Consider the following examples of client-generated metaphors and how the counselor caught them.

1. *Client:* I feel like a rudderless boat, just drifting around all over the place.

   Counselor: Rudderless and drifting around. I'm curious about the places you've drifted to and how you feel about all that drifting.

2. *Client:* I've hit a brick wall. I can't go any further in my company without a degree, but I figure if I have to study, I may as well do something I'm interested in. But that's not what they want me to study, so it wouldn't get me a promotion anyway.

   Counselor: Some images and questions have come into my mind about you hitting the brick wall. I'm wondering if you saw it coming or if you had no idea it was there, and I'm trying to imagine what speed you hit it at. Can you help me to understand more about hitting the brick wall from your point of view?

3. *Client:* It's like I've won the lottery.

   Counselor: What opportunities does winning the lottery provide for you and what problems does it present?

Once caught, a metaphor may be used as a tool in career counseling, and a number of models have been suggested for working with metaphor. Acknowledging the metaphor, using the metaphorical language, and collaborating with the client to expand the metaphor are common elements of most models of working with client-generated metaphors. The models range from Babits's (2001) two-stage model to Sims's (2003) six-stage model. Babits's two stages are creating the metaphor by being attuned to the client's language or inviting the client to describe his or her situation and then elaborating the metaphor. These two stages are clearly evident in the models proposed by Perry (2004) and Sims (2003). For example, Perry (2004) offers the following crucial stages for working effectively with client-generated metaphor:

- Identifying the client's use of metaphorical language
- Exploring the metaphor collaboratively with the client
- Encouraging the client to transform the metaphor in some way
- Affirming application of the changed metaphor within the context of the client's world. (p. 56)

In this way, client and counselor collaborate in a creative process of meaning making related to the client's goals. Similarly, Sims's (2003) model suggests the following stages:

- Hearing a metaphor
- Validating a metaphor
- Expanding a metaphor
- Playing with possibilities
- Marking and selecting
- Connecting with the future

The steps of hearing and validating a metaphor are illustrated in the examples presented earlier of catching a metaphor and establishing the metaphor as the focus for communication between counselor and client. Expanding a metaphor invites the client to explore various aspects of the metaphor and to share the emotions of the metaphor. In this way, a rich and thick story is developed. Counselors may also tentatively offer their own associations with the metaphor that they believe could be helpful. Playing with possibilities invites the client to expand his or her associations with the metaphor so that possible new meanings and new ways of being and doing are generated. Marking and selecting involve selection from the rich descriptions generated, those that the client believes may be helpful. Connecting with the future is closely related to the active agency of the client who identifies tasks he or she may work on to achieve his or her preferred future. The case study of Simon depicts the elements of these models.

Drowning in the Tide

Hearing a Metaphor

Simon was in a bad way. He was the owner of a business that required long work hours. He had sole responsibility for his two young children. By the time he attended to them in the morning, spent the day at work, and spent some time with his children in the evening, there was no time left for anything else. He had fallen hopelessly behind with the books of the business and couldn't keep up with all of the household cleaning, washing, and ironing. He was very proud of his company, which was doing very well, but he could see that if he didn't do something soon even the company would be in trouble. "I'm just drowning in the tide," he said.

Validating a Metaphor, Expanding a Metaphor

Counselor: Drowning in the tide gives me a pretty strong picture of what things are like for you at the moment. I'm wondering if you're completely under water or whether your head is above the water sometimes?

Simon: I just don't know what to do or where to start, and I'm getting desperate. I have only one technician working for me, and we have a big contract, so I work long hours in the field with the technician to get the contract done. I'm good at that sort of work, but I don't want to do it all the time. And because I spend so much time in the field, I haven't done any paperwork in ages, and I'm completely drowning in it. It's getting serious because some of it is overdue, and if I don't get it done soon, it could cause me problems legally. But I hate paperwork, I'm not good at it, and anyway I just don't have time. When I began this company, I had a vision of where it was going, and that's what I like to

do—plan. That's how I started. I was working for someone else and saw an opening and started my own company, and it's worked really well until now. I never seem to get my head above the technical work to make any plans, and when I do I realize what a mess things are in and what I'd rather be doing.

Playing With Possibilities/ Transforming a Metaphor

Counselor: I'm curious to know what it is that you glimpse when your head is above water.

Simon: I'd be spending at least a day a week looking over things, like from above. The paperwork would be under control. I'd have some time to myself where I can do things I want to do. I'd be happy to be in the field sometimes, but not all the time. (hearing a new metaphor)

Marking and Selection

Counselor: What do you mean when you say "like from above"? (elaborating the new metaphor)
Simon: It's like I'd be at a big desk up here (arm reached above his head) looking down at everything and able to see things and plan.

Connecting With the Future

Our career counseling sessions became Simon's time when his head was above water and all that was drowning him, when he had some time for himself, and when he could look down from above and regain sight of and strengthen his vision of what he wanted. We didn't actually make any plans about what he would do between sessions or a timetable of actions he could take. Simon had good sight from above. Simon visited for five sessions over a 10-week period. Each time, the metaphor built, and each time Simon made some progress. He hired a bookkeeper. Once he took his children to the beach for an afternoon. By then he was treading water. He hired another technician.

Eventually, he wasn't drowning anymore: He was swimming along. Prior to the sixth appointment, Simon phoned to cancel his appointment. He was to spend the day sailing with friends, his first day off in ages. He felt the tide had turned, and he thought he would be OK from now on.

As the previous case study illustrates, a respectful empathic exploration of a metaphor will, in general, reflect the stages of the models outlined earlier. However, it is not the intention that these stages be followed prescriptively. Essentially, working with metaphor requires hearing the metaphor, using the language of the metaphor, elaborating the metaphor, and extending the metaphor to incorporate images or actions that contribute to the client's design of his or her possible future. This may not necessarily happen in a step-by-step or stage-by-stage process. These essentials are also reflected in the case study of Carl, in which the counselor invites him to draw his metaphor.

A Tug-of-War

Hearing the Metaphor

Carl: I'm not sure about being here, but I had to talk to someone. I'm a designer, and I've been with the same company for years. They like me, and I like them, and I'm really happy in my job. But now they've offered me this manager's job. I know nothing about management, but my family thinks I should take the job. It's like I'm in a tug-of-war with them. They want me to do it, and I don't want to. Normally, everything in my family is fine, but I really can't talk about this anymore with them because we aren't getting anywhere.

Validating the Metaphor and Using It as a Counseling Tool

Counselor: I'm wondering if you could help me understand a little more about this tug-of-war by drawing it on paper.

Carl gladly accepted the invitation because he felt uncomfortable talking with a stranger. He placed himself at one end of a rope, and at the other end he placed his family, including his wife, children, and parents.

Using the Language of the Metaphor to Invite Further Elaboration

Counselor: What does it feel like at the end of the rope so far from the people you care most about?

Carl: I'm beginning to feel really isolated from them. We've never had something like this before that we can't talk about. I also don't want to disappoint them, especially my parents, who are already disappointed in me. My parents never wanted me to do design; they wanted me to do something better. But I'm pleased I've done design because I've

(Continued)

(Continued)

always enjoyed it and think I made a good choice. Now that this manager's job has come up, they want me to do it and so does my wife. They're really keen for me to accept the position, but it doesn't feel right for me—so we're at opposite ends of the rope. I know the new job would pay more and have more responsibility and it sounds better, but it'll take me away from the work I like, and I think I'll find it very stressful because I know nothing about management. My family just doesn't understand that I didn't say yes straight away. Sometimes I think I should take it just so my family can get back to the way it was, but I don't want them to pull me into something that I am not ready for and don't want.

Counselor: It sounds a bit like you're holding two ropes, the rope of the manager's job and the rope of the designer's job, but your family has let go of the designer rope.

Carl: Yes, it's about like that.

He drew another rope in his other hand.

Counselor: What does it feel like holding two ropes, the rope of designer and the rope of manager?

Carl: Not as daunting because I'm holding on to something I enjoy and am good at, but I also have an opportunity to try something new. I get confidence from designing.

Counselor: Where is your employer in this tug-of-war?

He placed his employer close to him with his hands on Carl's hands, each of which was holding a rope.

Carl: My employer wants me to stay with the company no matter what. So I'll still have a job with them. It's just that the company is growing, and I'm very experienced, and I've been with them for a long time, and they offered me this new job. But really, they're still working it all out, the new positions and everything.

Creating Images and Actions That May Contribute to a Preferred Future

Counselor: So the employer needs you and needs both jobs to be done. If you were designing the new company structure, what would it look like?

Carl: Well, they'll be hiring a few new designers. They don't have any background in the company, and some won't have much experience, and I think they need someone to show them the ropes and make sure that they fit into the company.

Counselor: So am I right in thinking that somewhere between the designer rope and the manager rope, you're seeing another rope?

Carl: Yes—I think I am.

Counselor: How would this new rope factor into the tug-of-war?

Carl: Well, I think it would take the pressure off. I think my family would support me. I think my boss would like the idea because he really wants to get the company right. I think it would make sense to my boss. He really doesn't know what to do with me because I've worked with them for so long and have so much experience. I might even learn a bit about management. But I'd still be designing.

Taking Steps Toward the Construction of a New Future

Counselor: Where to next with this tug-of-war?

Carl: I think I'll talk to my boss about it. We have a good relationship, so it would be easy to do.

Carl asked if he could take his drawing with him. It would help him to talk with his family.

As is evident in this and the previous case studies, the relationship between career and personal counseling has narrowed as life, learning, and work are increasingly viewed as interrelated and inseparable. In keeping with the constructivist worldview, the issues presented by all of the clients in the case studies cannot be viewed independently of their contexts. All of the clients were experts on their situations and were able to take an active role in constructing alternative futures for themselves. Both Simon and Carl introduced a metaphor into the counseling dialogue that was "caught" by the career counselor. The metaphors provided a language for exploring the career concern and for constructing possible future scenarios. In addition, they facilitated the development of empathy and an environment in which the client felt understood.

Carson and Hinkelman (1999) suggested that, in general, students are not prepared to use metaphor in their career counseling work. This corresponds with concerns about a decline in interest in career counseling by students in counselor education programs (Heppner, O'Brien, Hinkelman, & Humphrey, 1994). This decline may be attributed to the lack of creativity evident in career counselor training programs, which are still largely steeped in the traditions of the "test-and-tell" metaphor. However, as suggested in this chapter, the traditional metaphor may be used as a complement to the narrative metaphor in a creative process that personalizes career counseling for clients and also involves them as active agents. In addition, metaphor itself offers creative possibilities for conceptualizing and structuring career counseling, and it may also be an effective tool in the career counseling process.

Conclusion

This chapter examined the possibilities offered by metaphor in relation to career counseling. First, through the metaphors of "test-and-tell," "narrative," "story telling and testing," "coach," "advocate," "nurturer," and "believer," the chapter illustrated how career counseling may be conceptualized and structured through the use of metaphor. Second, the chapter discussed the purposes of using metaphor as a tool in career counseling. Examples were provided of career counselors using metaphors as tools in their work with clients. It is hoped that this chapter will spark more widespread interest in the use of metaphor in career counseling and that its status may be elevated from throwaway line to that of constructive meaning-making tool.

Key Points in This Chapter

- Career counseling clients have different expectations of the counselor (e.g., "tell me what to do" vs. "let me tell my story").
- Theory and practice in counseling have been dominated by a logical-positivist test-and-tell approach emphasizing understanding of self and occupations through assessment and seeking congruence between the two ("fit" metaphor). Theory and practice are now adopting more of a

constructivist narrative approach emphasizing co-construction of the client's biography and future ("story" metaphor).

- Other roles often taken on by career counselors as a basis to structure their work are those of coach, advocate, nurturer, and believer.
- Career metaphors are increasingly used by counselors. These metaphors may be generated by either the counselor or the client.
- In counseling, metaphors serve many of the same purposes as the metaphors in this book (e.g., enhancing awareness, generating new ways of seeing things). Metaphors also assist client–counselor relationships and facilitate change.
- Counselors using metaphor must be able to notice and respect client metaphors and use them constructively to enable clients to resolve career issues.

Questions From This Chapter

General Questions

1. Why do you think some people consult professional career counselors and some do not, even when they have critical career decisions to make?

2. In the first two cases in this chapter, what are the advantages and disadvantages to the client of taking (a) Marcus's approach and (b) Jamie's approach? As a client, which approach do you think you would be more likely to adopt? Can you see a way of compromising between them?

3. In your current career situation, can you see ways where having a counselor who was a coach, an advocate, a nurturer, and a believer could assist you? If these metaphors are not relevant to you now, under what circumstances might they be?

4. Think about the various counselor–client interactions reported in the cases in this chapter. What do they teach you about counseling that you didn't know before? Is there anything that surprised you? What actions of the counselors would you like to adopt or prefer not to adopt?

5. Imagine that you are a career counselor and different clients use the metaphors "stuck in a bog," "bouncing like a Ping-Pong ball," and "building a castle" to describe their current career situation. (Invent a few more of your own if you wish.) What might you consider saying to the clients to facilitate the development of the metaphors?

Career Case Study Questions

1. Ask your case person to recount any experiences he or she has had that involved career counseling or professional guidance or advice. Include school, careers, teachers, and the like. Evaluate the experiences in the light of this chapter. What did you learn?

2. Ask your career case person for a metaphor summarizing his or her current career situation. Think of ways that the metaphor might be used in counseling.

References

Amundson, N. E. (1988). The use of metaphor and drawings in case conceptualisation. *Journal of Counseling and Development, 66,* 391-393.

Amundson, N. (1997). Myths, metaphors, and moxie: The 3Ms of career counseling. *Journal of Employment Counseling, 34,* 76-84.

Amundson, N. E. (1998). *Active engagement: Enhancing the career counselling process.* Richmond, Canada: Ergon Communications.

Amundson, N. E. (2003). *Active engagement: Enhancing the career counselling process* (2nd ed.). Richmond, Canada: Ergon Communications.

Amundson, N. E., Harris-Bowlsbey, J., & Niles, S. G. (2005). *Essential elements of career counseling.* Upper Saddle River, NJ: Pearson.

Arthur, N. (2006). Infusing culture in constructivist approaches to career counseling. In M. McMahon & W. Patton (Eds.), *Career counseling: Constructivist approaches* (pp. 57-68). Boston: Allyn & Bacon.

Arthur, N., & McMahon, M. (2005). Multicultural career counseling: Theoretical applications of the Systems Theory Framework. *The Career Development Quarterly, 53,* 208-222.

Babits, M. (2001). Using therapeutic metaphor to provide a holding environment: The inner edge of possibility. *Clinical Social Work Journal, 29,* 21-33.

Bench, M. (2001). Career coaching: The new methodology for maximizing personal fulfillment and human capital. In G. R. Walz, R. Knowdell, & C. Kirkman (Eds.), *Staying innovative and change focused in the new economy: A collection of special papers generated for the 2001 International Career Development Conference.* Washington, DC: Office of Educational Research and Improvement. (ERIC Document Reproduction Service No. ED458482)

Brown, D. (2002). Introduction to theories of career development and choice: Origins, evolution and current efforts. In D. Brown & Associates (Eds.), *Career choice and development* (4th ed., pp. 3-23). San Francisco: Jossey-Bass.

Carson, A. D., & Hinkelman, J. M. (1999, August). *Metaphors for vocation and career.* Paper presented at the Annual Conference of the American Psychological Association, Boston.

Cattell, R. B., Cattell, A. K., & Cattell, H. E. P. (1993). *16PF* (5th ed.). Champaign, IL: Institute for Personality and Ability Testing.

Combs, G., & Freedman, J. (1990). *Symbol, story and ceremony: Using metaphor in individual and family therapy.* New York: Norton.

Fox, R. (1989). What is meta for? *Clinical Social Work Journal, 17,* 233-244.

Granvold, D. K. (1996). Constructivist psychotherapy. *Families in Society, 77*(6), 345-359.

Heppner, M. J., O'Brien, K. M., Hinkelman, J. M., & Humphrey, C. F. (1994). Shifting the paradigm: The use of creativity in career counseling. *Journal of Career Development, 21*(2), 77-86.

Holland, J. L. (1994a). *The occupations finder.* Odessa, FL: Psychological Assessment Resources.

Holland, J. L. (1994b). *Self-directed search.* Odessa, FL: Psychological Assessment Resources.

Hudson, F. (1999). Career coaching. *Career Planning and Adult Development Journal, 15,* 69-80.

Jarvis, P. (2003). *Career management paradigm shift: Prosperity for citizens, windfall for governments.* Retrieved February 3, 2006, from http://lifework.ca/ACAREERMANAGE-MENTPARADIGMSHIFT1202.doc

Knowdell, R. (1996). Perspectives shaping career planning in the future. In R. Feller & G. Walz (Eds.), *Career transitions in turbulent times: Exploring work, learning and careers* (pp. 183-192). Greensboro, NC: Educational Resources Information Center, Counseling and Student Services Clearinghouse.

Kopp, R. (1995). *Metaphor therapy: Using client-generated metaphors in psychotherapy.* New York: Brunner/Mazel.

Lakoff, G., & Johnson, M. (1980). *Metaphors we live by.* Chicago: University of Chicago Press.

Law, B. (2003). Guidance: Too many lists, not enough stories. In A. Edwards (Ed.), *Challenging biographies: Re-locating the theory and practice of careers work* (pp. 25-47). Southborough, England: Canterbury Christ Church University College.

Lyddon, W. J., Clay, A. L., & Sparks, C. L. (2001). Metaphor and change in counseling. *Journal of Counseling and Development, 79,* 269-274.

Manuele-Adkins, C. (1992). Career counseling is personal counseling. *Career Development Quarterly, 40,* 313-323.

Martin, J., Cummings, A. L., & Hallberg, E. T. (1992). Therapists' intentional use of metaphor: Memorability, clinical impact, and possible epistemic/motivational functions. *Journal of Consulting and Clinical Psychology, 60,* 143-145.

McMahon, M. (2004, April). *An inn on the journey to tomorrow.* Paper presented at the 10th annual Consultation for Career Development, Edmonton, Alberta, Canada.

McMahon, M., & Patton, W. (2002). Using qualitative assessment in career counselling. *International Journal of Educational and Vocational Guidance, 2*(1), 51-66.

Monk, G., Winslade, J., Crocket, K., & Epston, D. (1997). *Narrative therapy in practice: The archaeology of hope.* San Francisco: Jossey-Bass.

Parker, P. (2002). Working with the intelligent career model. *Journal of Employment Counseling, 39,* 83-96.

Parsons, F. (1909). *Choosing a vocation.* Boston: Houghton Mifflin.

Patton, W., & McMahon, M. (1999). *Career development and systems theory: A new relationship.* Pacific Grove, CA: Brooks/Cole.

Payne, M. (2000). *Narrative therapy: An introduction for counselors.* Thousand Oaks, CA: Sage.

Peavy, R. V. (1995). *Constructivist career counseling.* Retrieved February 27, 2006, from http://www.ericdigests.org/1997-3/counseling.html

Peavy, R. V. (1998). *SocioDynamic counseling: A constructivist perspective.* Victoria, Canada: Trafford.

Peavy, R. V. (2004). *SocioDynamic counseling: A practical approach to meaning making.* Chagrin Falls, OH: Taos Institute.

Perry, C. (2004). Reflecting on narrative: Metaphorically speaking. *Psychotherapy in Australia, 11*(1), 54-59.

Rogers, C. (1951). *Client-centered therapy.* Boston: Houghton Mifflin.

Rogers, C. (1957). The necessary and sufficient conditions for therapeutic personality change. *Journal of Consulting Psychology, 21,* 95-103.

Savickas, M. L. (1992). New directions in career assessment. In D. H. Montross & C. J. Shinkman (Eds.), *Career development: Theory and practice* (pp. 336-355). Springfield, IL: Charles C Thomas.

Savickas, M. L. (1993). Career counseling in the postmodern era. *Journal of Cognitive Psychotherapy: An International Quarterly, 7,* 205-215.

Savickas, M. L. (2002). Reinvigorating the study of careers. *Journal of Vocational Behavior, 61,* 381-385.

Schlossberg, N. K., Lynch, A. Q., & Chickering, A. W. (1989). *Improving higher education environments for adults.* San Francisco: Jossey-Bass.

Sims, P. A. (2003). Working with metaphor. *American Journal of Psychotherapy, 57,* 528-536.

Sinai, J. (1997). The use of metaphor by an artless first-time psychotherapist. *American Journal of Psychotherapy, 51,* 273-288.

Stead, B. G. (2004). Culture and career psychology: A social constructionist perspective. *Journal of Vocational Behavior, 64,* 389-406.

Stevens, P. (1998). *Gaining commitment to change through career coaching.* Sydney, Australia: Centre for Worklife Counseling. (ERIC Document Reproduction Service No. ED437534)

Subich, L. M. (1993). How personal is career? [Special section]. *The Career Development Quarterly, 42,* 129-131.

Vahamottonen, T. T. E., Keskinen, P. A., & Parrila, R. K. (1994). A conceptual framework for developing an activity-based approach to career counseling. *International Journal for the Advancement of Counseling, 17,* 19-34.

Warme, G. (1996). *The psychotherapist.* Northvale, NJ: Aronson.

Watts, A. G., & Sultana, R. G. (2004). Career guidance policies in 37 countries: Contrasts and common themes. *International Journal for Educational and Vocational Guidance, 4,* 105-122.

White, M. (2004). *Narrative practice and exotic lives: Resurrecting diversity in everyday life.* Adelaide, Australia: Dulwich Centre Publications.

Wickman, S. A., Daniels, M. H., White, L. J., & Fesmire, S. A. (1999). A "primer" in conceptual metaphor for counselors. *Journal of Counseling and Development, 77,* 389-394.

Williamson, E. (1939). *How to counsel students: A manual of techniques for clinical counselors.* New York: McGraw-Hill.

Williamson, E. (1965). *Vocational counseling: Some historical, philosophical, and theoretical perspectives.* New York: McGraw-Hill.

Zindel, B. (2001). The metaphor goddess in three quarter time: A relational use of story and metaphor. *Clinical Social Work Journal, 29,* 9-20.

Author Index

Subject Index

About the Author and Contributor

Kerr Inkson is Professor of Management at the University of Otago, visiting Professor of Management at Victoria University of Wellington, and honorary Research Fellow at Massey University, all in New Zealand. Since commencing his academic work in the 1960s, he has had a distinguished career in management studies and organizational behavior and has worked at a number of business schools in New Zealand, the United Kingdom, and the United States. Since the early 1990s, his research has focused on careers, and he published *The New Careers* (coauthored by Michael B. Arthur and Judith K. Pringle) with Sage in 1999. He is author of 11 other books and more than 100 refereed journal articles and book chapters, many of them on career themes. His Web site is www.commerce.otago.ac.nz/mgmt/staff/kinkson.htm.

Mary McMahon is a lecturer in the School of Education at the University of Queensland, Australia. She publishes extensively in the field of career development, and her coauthored and coedited books are prescribed texts in many postgraduate courses in Australia and elsewhere.